Essential Chinese Voca

Essential Chinese Vocabulary: Rules and Scenarios is an indispensable guide for beginner to intermediate students of Chinese who wish to use essential Chinese words and phrases accurately.

The book provides the crucial context and explanations of grammar structures and language rules related to important Chinese words and phrases, too often glossed over in primary textbooks. Students are given the tools necessary to refine their use of these words and phrases in order to communicate effectively in Chinese.

Key features:

- In-depth explanations of commonly used words and phrases contextualized with a range of authentic examples providing learners with a comprehensive understanding of the vocabulary-use and allowing them to express themselves accurately and appropriately.
- Bridges the gap between grammar and vocabulary by presenting the frequently neglected rules that govern the use of words and phrases.
- Clear and systematic comparisons between the uses of ostensibly similar words, highlighting the nuances of the Chinese language.
- Examples provided in simplified Chinese characters, pinyin and English.
- Identifies common mistakes made by learners and ways to avoid them.
- Extensive cross-references.

Essential Chinese Vocabulary: Rules and Scenarios is a unique reference and useful complement to basic and intermediate Chinese language textbooks.

Wen-Hua Teng is Senior Lecturer in the Department of Asian Studies at the University of Texas at Austin.

Essential Chinese Vocabulary
Rules and Scenarios

Wen-Hua Teng

Routledge
Taylor & Francis Group

LONDON AND NEW YORK

First published 2016
by Routledge
2 Park Square, Milton Park, Abingdon, Oxon OX14 4RN

and by Routledge
711 Third Avenue, New York, NY 10017

Routledge is an imprint of the Taylor & Francis Group, an informa business

British Library Cataloguing-in-Publication Data
A catalogue record for this book is available from the British Library

Library of Congress Cataloging-in-Publication Data
Names: Teng, Wen-Hua.
Title: Essential Chinese vocabulary : rules and scenarios / Wen-Hua Teng.
Description: Milton Park, Abingdon, Oxon ; New York, NY : Routledge, [2016]
Identifiers: LCCN 2015035515 | ISBN 9780415745390 (hardback : alk. paper) |
ISBN 9780415745406 (pbk. : alk. paper) | ISBN 9781315797908 (ebook)
Subjects: LCSH: Chinese language–Vocabulary. | Chinese language–Terms and phrases. |
Chinese language–Grammar.
Classification: LCC PL1271 .T47 2016 | DDC 495.183/421–dc23
LC record available at http://lccn.loc.gov/2015035515

ISBN: 978-0-415-74539-0 (hbk)
ISBN: 978-0-415-74540-6 (pbk)
ISBN: 978-1-315-79790-8 (ebk)

Typeset in Times New Roman
by Graphicraft Limited, Hong Kong

Printed and bound in the United States of America by Publishers Graphics,
LLC on sustainably sourced paper.

Contents

Introduction for *Essential Chinese Vocabulary: Rules and Scenarios*

Since I taught my first Chinese class to English speakers nearly 30 years ago, the landscape of teaching and learning Chinese as a foreign language has undergone a tremendous transformation. Such a transformation is manifested by the increasing number of students, modern and innovative teaching methodologies, as well as the almost daily emergence of new materials, both printed and digital.

As Chinese as a foreign language is rapidly gaining popularity worldwide, both the quantity and quality of resources, such as textbooks and reference supplements, have reached an all-time high. Today's teachers and students enjoy a wide selection of materials that can aid them in teaching and learning, a luxury that was not available to my students or me three decades ago.

However, amid all the growth and improvements, one area has stayed static; that is, the instruction or acquisition of vocabulary has remained surprisingly traditional and one-dimensional. A student's task, when it comes to learning new vocabulary, rarely goes beyond memorizing characters, pronunciation and definitions. While it is often easy to define (and memorize) a word, it is not nearly as easy to capture the versatility of any vocabulary word in its entirety. This may be a reason that accounts for the lack of attention paid to the instruction of Chinese vocabulary, and is also what motivated me to bring this important pedagogical issue to light via this book.

Vocabulary is fluid; the meaning or function of a word is rarely confined by its definition, but is in relation to the context in which it appears. I encourage readers to peruse the entry for 意思 (*yìsi*) in this book to see a case in point.

Perhaps many readers are familiar with the Chinese phrase 见树不见林 (*jiàn shù bú jiàn lín*), literally 'seeing the trees (but) not seeing the forest'. And this phrase seems to depict the current state of vocabulary teaching and learning quite accurately. One goal I hope to achieve in this book is to show learners of Chinese how to develop a broader perspective in order to perceive the whole picture of language use (the 'forest'), instead of clinging to individual isolated items (the 'trees') of the language.

And this is why readers of this book will encounter these recurrent words throughout the entire book: connotation, implication, interpretation and context. While definitions of the vocabulary words I have chosen to include in this book are still provided, what I wish to emphasize is the actual use of these words in realistic situations, a task that goes much beyond knowing their definitions. Therefore, there is an abundance of examples; each is built upon a scenario. These scenarios, some simple and some elaborate, aim to create a sense of reality which helps add dimensions (or even some fun) to students' vocabulary learning process.

While linguistic terminology is not a prevalent feature in this book, I hasten to point out that the use of vocabulary is governed by language rules. Perhaps a simple word, 多 (*duō*), can illustrate this point. I discuss five major usages of 多, each of which involves a different sentence pattern (language rules), and each is supported by a number of scenarios. Although much space in this book is devoted to examples and scenarios, I do not intend to downplay the importance of rules and patterns; instead, I aim to achieve a balance between rules and actual use of these vocabulary words. 'Rules and scenarios' being part of the title of this book makes this abundantly clear.

Clearly stated rules can help learners avoid making mistakes. Thirty years of teaching Chinese to English speakers has not only taught me to predict what mistakes learners would make, but also helped me develop an understanding of the sources of common mistakes. While making mistakes might be a valuable part of the learning process, knowing how to avoid common mistakes is one way to make the process that much smoother.

In this book, I share with readers the insight I have gained from observing my students' efforts to make progress, and straightforwardly point out common mistakes they have made. It is my hope that readers of this book can benefit from the mistakes made by their fellow learners even though some of them may have belonged to a different generation.

This book is a collection of about 200 vocabulary words, the majority of which are presented in alphabetical order of their pinyin; others are presented as 'related expressions' to certain words. Each entry starts with a general statement of the word, followed by a list of descriptions of the rules or patterns. The highlight of each entry is the examples or scenarios that show the word and its rules 'in action'. Simplified Chinese characters are used; pinyin and English translations are provided. There is also an index that helps readers quickly locate words or expressions and navigate the book easily.

Granted, 200 words are a mere drop in the sea of Chinese vocabulary; but each of these words receives an in-depth treatment. My decision as to which words to include in this book may be subjective, but not random. These are words that regularly appear in standard Chinese curriculum or textbooks from beginning to pre-advanced levels, and their proper and accurate uses are often confusing to learners if no clear explanations are provided. Keen readers might notice the absence of two important words, 就 (*jiù*) and 才 (*cái*). This omission is intentional because detailed discussions on these two words can be found in my first book, *YUFA: A Practical Guide to Mandarin Chinese Grammar* (Routledge Concise Grammars).

In my 30 years as a Chinese language teacher to American college students, I have found nothing more rewarding than seeing the sparkle in a student's eyes when the student reaches an *aha* moment because something that has been confusing suddenly makes sense. I sincerely hope that readers will have such a moment many times over when reading this book.

Finally, I would like to express my gratitude to Samantha Vale Noya, my commissioning editor, who is the major contributing factor to the birth of this book. Her support and confidence during the writing process affirm the value of this book.

班 *bān*

The word 'class' (related to school activities) in English can refer to either the subject matter (content) of a class or the people (students) in a class. 课 (*kè*) is the word referring to the subject matter, and 班 refers to the people.

→ See 课 (*kè*) for related information.

a. 班 means **a group of people** taking the same class (课). Therefore, a **pronoun showing plural** (你们, 我们, 他们) is usually used to refer to someone's class.

(Scenario: Two students are taking the same course, but they are in different classes.)

王同学:	张明说，**他们班**有二十个同学；**你们班**有几个？
Wáng tóngxué:	*Zhāng Míng shuō, tāmen bān yǒu èrshí ge tóngxué; nǐmen bān yǒu jǐ ge?*
李同学:	有十五个。
Lǐ tóngxué:	*Yǒu shíwǔ ge.*
王:	什么？只有十五个？**我们班**有三十个，我要转到**你们班**去。
Wáng:	*Shénme? Zhǐ yǒu shíwǔ ge? Wǒmen bān yǒu sānshí ge, wǒ yào zhuǎn dào nǐmen bān qù.*
Student Wang:	Zhang Ming said that there are 20 students in **his class**. How many are there in **your class**?
Student Li:	There are 15.
Wang:	What? Only 15? There are 30 in **my class**. I am going to switch to **your class**.

b. The measure word for 班 is **个** (*ge*), but it is **optional**.

王老师:	这学期我教**两(个)班**；**这两班**的学生都很努力。
Wáng lǎoshī:	*Zhè xuéqī wǒ jiāo liǎng (ge) bān; zhè liǎng bān de xuéshēng dōu hěn nǔlì.*
Teacher Wang:	This semester I am teaching **two classes** (two groups of students). All of the students in **these two classes** are hardworking.

c. The expression for the **whole class** is often **班上** (*bān shàng*) or **全班** (*quán bān*). When the word 班 is not preceded by another word (such as 我们班 and 这班), 全 in 全班 or 上 in 班上 becomes necessary. This means 班 is not used as a stand-alone word.

这次考试实在太难了，**全班**都不及格。虽然李明是**班**上成绩最好的
学生，可是他也考得很差。

Zhè cì kǎoshì shízài tài nán le, quán bān dōu bù jígé. Suīrán Lǐ Míng shì
bān shàng chéngjī zuì hǎo de xuéshēng, kěshì tā yě kǎo de hěn chà.

This test was truly too difficult; **the entire class** (everyone in the class)
failed. Although Li Ming is the best student **in the class**, he also did poorly.

d.   While 课 (referring to the subject matter) can be preceded by the title of the
class, 班 cannot.

我这学期选了一门**数学课**(Do not say 数学班)，**班**上只有一个女生，
这个女生也是**全班**成绩最好的学生。

Wǒ zhè xuéqī xuǎn le yī mén shùxué kè, bān shàng zhǐ yǒu yī ge nǚshēng,
zhè ge nǚshēng yě shì quán bān chéngjī zuì hǎo de xuéshēng.

I am taking (I signed up for) a **mathematics class** this semester; there is
only one female student **in the class**; this female student is also the best
student **in the entire class**.

这学期有八十多个学生报名上**中文课**，所以我们把这些学生分成**五(个)**
班。

Zhè xuéqī yǒu bāshí duō ge xuéshēng bàoming shàng Zhōngwén kè, suǒyǐ
wǒmen bǎ zhèxiē xuéshēng fēn chéng wǔ (ge) bān.

There are over 80 students who are enrolled in the **Chinese class** this semester;
so we have divided these students into **five classes** (five groups of students).

Related expressions

上班 *shàng bān* and 下班 *xià bān*

班 in 上班 or 下班 has a different meaning from those appearing in the above
discussions. 上班 and 下班 refer to 'going to work' and 'getting off work'
respectively. This is because 班 also has the definition of 'work shift'.

In terms of usage, 上班/下班 is similar to 上课/下课 (*shàng kè/xià kè*: going to
a class/getting off a class). 上班 is an action that **can last** (for a duration of time),
whereas 下班 is an **instantaneous verb**. The action of 'getting off work' cannot last.

→ See 上课 (*shàng kè*) and 下课 (*xià kè*) for related information.

今天我好忙！上午先去办公室上了四小时**班**；**下班**以后，又到学校去上
了三小时**课**，五点才**下课**。

Jīntiān wǒ hǎo máng! Shàngwǔ xiān qù bàngōngshì shàng le sì xiǎoshí bān;
xià bān yǐhòu, yòu dào xuéxiào qù shàng le sān xiǎoshí kè, wǔdiǎn cái xià kè.

I was so busy today. First, I went to my office to **work for four hours**;
after **getting off work**, I went to school to **attend classes for three hours**.
I did not **get off my classes** until 5:00.

必须 *bìxū*

必须 means 'must' or 'to have to', suggesting duty/obligation or necessity/ requirement. 必须 and 得 (*děi*) share similarities in meaning and usage, but 得 is typically used in casual, conversational speech.

→ See 得 (*děi*) for related information.

a. Indicating **duty/obligation** or **necessity/requirement.**

> A: 经理说，明天的会议，每个人都**必须**参加，而且也都**必须**发言。(duty/obligation)
> *Jīnglǐ shuō, míngtiān de huìyì, měi ge rén dōu bìxū cānjiā, érqiě yě dōu bìxū fāyán.*
> B: 我们发言的时候，**必须**特别小心，因为经理会请秘书录音。(necessity)
> *Wǒmen fāyán de shíhòu, bìxū tèbié xiǎoxīn, yīnwèi jīnglǐ huì qǐng mìshū lùyīn.*
> A: The manager says that everybody **must** attend tomorrow's meeting; also, everybody **must** speak at the meeting.
> B: When we speak at the meeting, we **must** be particularly careful, because the manager will ask the secretary to record what we say.

> 在中国，想上大学的人，都**必须**先通过考试。(requirement)
> *Zài Zhōngguó, xiǎng shàng dàxué de rén, dōu bìxū xiān tōngguò kǎoshì.*
> In China, those who want to go to college **must** first pass the exam.

> 这张桌子太重了，两个人搬不了，**必须**四个人来搬。(necessity)
> *Zhè zhāng zhuōzi tài zhòng le, liǎng ge rén bān bù liǎo, bìxū sì ge rén lái bān.*
> This table is too heavy; two people cannot move it. It **requires** four people to move it.

b. 必须 has **two negative forms**: **不必** (*búbì*) and **不用** (*búyòng*). Both mean **'no need to'**, **'it's not necessary'**, etc. 不必须 is not a legitimate expression.
  Although both 不必 and 不用 are frequently used in conversational speech, 不用 seems a more casual word than 不必. In addition, when used to give a short answer, 不必 may sound somewhat blunt, whereas 不用 is milder in tone. Sometimes, 不用了 is used to help make the speaker sound more polite, especially when turning down an offer of help.

> A: 经理，我知道今天的会议很重要，每个人都**必须**参加，可是我今天真的很不舒服。
> *Jīnglǐ, wǒ zhīdào jīntiān de huìyì hěn zhòngyào, měi ge rén dōu bìxū cānjiā, kěshì wǒ jīntiān zhēnde hěn bù shūfú.*
> B: 没关系，既然你不舒服，就**不必**(or **不用**)来了，在家休息吧！
> *Méi guānxì, jìrán nǐ bù shūfú, jiù búbì (or búyòng) lái le, zài jiā xiūxi ba!*

A: Manager, I know today's meeting is important and everybody **must** attend it, but I really don't feel well today.

B: It's OK. Since you don't feel well, you **don't have to** come. Why don't you rest at home!

A: 你的箱子重不重？要不要我来帮你一下？
Nǐ de xiāngzi zhòng bú zhòng? Yào bú yào wǒ lái bāng nǐ yīxià?

B: **不用(了)**，我自己提得动，谢谢。(不必 is less appropriate because it may sound blunt.)
Búyòng (le), wǒ zìjǐ tí de dòng, xièxie.

A: Is your suitcase heavy? Do you want me to help you?

B: It's **not necessary**. I can carry it myself. Thank you.

c. Although 必须 is often translated as 'must', it cannot be used to **make an assumption** as 'must' is sometimes used for this function in English. To make an assumption, use **一定** (*yīdìng*).

→ See 一定 (*yīdìng*) for related information.

(Scenario: A workplace situation.)

A: 昨天我们说的话，经理怎么会知道？**一定**是小李告诉他的。(assumption)
Zuótiān wǒmen shuō de huà, jīnglǐ zěnme huì zhīdào? Yīdìng shì Xiǎo Lǐ gàosù tā de.

B: 对！以后我们在办公室诉苦的时候，**必须**特别小心。(necessity)
Duì! Yǐhòu wǒmen zài bàngōngshì sùkǔ de shíhòu, bìxū tèbié xiǎoxīn.

A: How did the manager learn about what we said yesterday? It **must have been** Little Li that told him about it.

B: That's right! From now on, when we complain in the office, we **must** be especially careful (about what we say).

Related expression

需要 *xūyào*

需要 means 'to need'; it shares similarities with 必须 in that both can be used to express **necessity or requirement**. What frequently confuses learners is the proper use of the characters 需 and 须 since they have the exact same pronunciation.

Despite their similarities, 需要 and 必须 have the following differences in usage:

a. 必须 cannot be used in an **affirmative-negative question**, but 需要 can; in other words, 必须不必须 is not a legitimate expression, whereas 需(要)不需要 is correct. In addition, 不需要 has the same meaning as 不必／不用.

A: 今天的聚会比较正式，大家都**必须**穿西装外套，不能只穿衬衫。
　　Jīntiān de jùhuì bǐjiào zhèngshì, dàjiā dōu bìxū chuān xīzhuāng wàitào,
　　bù néng zhǐ chuān chènshān.

B: **需(要)不需要**打领带？
　　Xū(yào) bù xūyào dǎ lǐngdài?

A: **不需要**(or **不必/不用**)打领带。
　　Bù xūyào (or búbì/búyòng) dǎ lǐngdài.

A: Today's get-together is quite formal. Everybody **must** wear a suit jacket.
　　You can't only wear a shirt (without a jacket).

B: Do we **need to** wear a tie?

A: There is **no need to** wear a tie.

b. 需要 can be **followed by a noun**; 必须 cannot. Furthermore, a **degree adverb**, such as 很 and 非常, can be used with 需要, but such a word cannot be used with 必须.

(Scenario: A secretary asks a new hire what kind of office equipment he needs.)

经理:　　王先生，我很高兴你接受这份工作；我们公司**非常需要**你的**专长**。

Jīnglǐ:　　*Wáng xiānsheng, wǒ hěn gāoxìng nǐ jiēshòu zhè fèn gōngzuò; wǒmen gōngsī fēicháng xūyào nǐ de zhuāncháng.*

秘书:　　您的办公室**需要**什么？请告诉我。

Mìshū:　　*Nín de bàngōngshì xūyào shénme? Qǐng gàosù wǒ.*

王:　　我**需要**一个平板电脑跟一台印表机。

Wáng:　　*Wǒ xūyào yī ge píngbǎn diànnǎo gēn yī tái yìnbiǎo jī.*

秘书:　　没问题！您**需(要)不需要**影印机？

Mìshū:　　*Méi wèntí! Nín xū(yào) bù xūyào yǐngyìn jī?*

王:　　影印机**不需要** (or a short answer: **不用了**)。

Wáng:　　*Yǐngyìn jī bù xūyào.*

Manager:　　Mr Wang, I am pleased that you have accepted (the offer of) this position. Our company **really needs** your expertise.

Secretary:　　What do you **need** in your office? Please let me know.

Wang:　　I **need** a tablet and a printer.

Secretary:　　No problem! Do you **need** a copier?

Wang:　　A copier is **not necessary**.

c. 需要 can be used **as a noun**. 必须 cannot.

阳光、水、肥料是植物生长的基本**需要**。
Yángguāng, shuǐ, féiliào shì zhíwù shēngzhǎng de jīběn xūyào.
Sunlight, water and fertilizer are the basic **needs** for the growth of plants.

别的 *biéde*

The distinction between 别的 and 另外 (*lìngwài*) is often a source of confusion for learners. Many tend to overuse 别的 and underuse 另外. Although these two words share similarities, they are used in different contexts. It is important to know the differences between the two and the proper uses for each of them.

→ See 另外 (*lìngwài*) for more information.

不必 *bú bì*

→ See 必须 (*bìxū*) for more information.

不但...而且(也)... *búdàn... érqiě (yě)*...

不但...而且... is frequently used as a pair to indicate 'not only...but also...'. As a pair, 而且 is actually optional as long as 也 is used in the 而且 clause. What's important from a grammatical point of view is whether or not the 不但 and 而且 clauses share **the same subject or topic**.

a.　When the two clauses share **the same subject or topic**, the subject/topic should appear **before 不但**, and should **not be repeated** in the 而且 clause. A similar sentence in English can have a more flexible word order; therefore, this grammar rule merits special attention.

我的数学老师**不但**对学生很凶，**而且**教得**(也)**不好，所以大家都不喜欢他。
(我的数学老师 is the subject of the sentence; it must appear before 不但.)
Wǒde shùxué lǎoshī búdàn duì xuéshēng hěn xiōng, érqiě jiāo de (yě) bù hǎo, suǒyǐ dàjiā dōu bù xǐhuān tā.
Not only is my mathematics teacher rude and unfriendly to students, **but** he is **also** a bad teacher (literally: he teaches badly), so no one likes him.

这个地区**不但**环境清幽，**而且**交通**(也)**很方便，所以房价特别高。
(这个地区 is the topic of the sentence. 交通方便 means the location is convenient; and it is easy to get around town.)
Zhè ge dìqū búdàn huánjìng qīngyōu, érqiě jiāotōng (yě) hěn fāngbiàn, suǒyǐ fángjià tèbié gāo.
Not only are the surroundings of this area quiet and secluded, **but** the transportation (of this area) is **also** convenient; so the housing prices here are especially high.

b.　When 不但 and 而且 clauses **do not share the same subjects**, 也 in the 而且 clause **becomes necessary**; i.e. it is no longer an optional word. In addition, each of the subjects appears **after** 不但 and 而且.

A: 听说《西游记》是一本很有名的中国小说。
   Tīngshuō 'Xī yóu jì' shì yī běn hěn yǒumíng de Zhōngguó xiǎoshuō.

B: 是啊！**不但**很多中国人看过这本小说，**而且**不少外国人**也**看过翻译的版本呢！(不但 and 而且 each appears before the subject of its clause, and 也 **is not optional**.)
   Shì a! Búdàn hěnduō Zhōngguó rén kàn guo zhè běn xiǎoshuō, érqiě bùshǎo wàiguó rén yě kàn guo fānyì de bǎnběn ne!

A: I heard that *Journey to the West* is a very famous Chinese novel.

B: Yes! **Not only** have many Chinese read this novel, **but also** many foreigners have read its translation.

c. 不但 can be replaced by **不只** (*bùzhǐ*) or **不仅** (*bùjǐn*)/**不仅仅** (*bù jǐnjǐn*). 不只 is more casual and is often used in speaking, whereas 不仅 or 不仅仅 is more formal and is often used in writing. In addition, 不仅 or 不仅仅 is frequently followed by the verb 是.

   唐诗**不仅(仅)是**中国古典文学的精髓，**而且(也)是**中国传统文化的代表。
   Táng shī bù jǐn(jǐn) shì Zhōngguó gǔdiǎn wénxué de jīngsuí, érqiě (yě) shì Zhōngguó chuántǒng wénhuà de dàibiǎo.
   Tang poetry **is not only** the essence of Chinese classical literature, **but is also** the epitome of Chinese traditional culture.

d. Because the 而且 clause usually makes a point that further intensifies the 不但 clause, **连 . . . 也/都** (*lián . . . yě/dōu*), which means '**even**', can be used in the 而且 clause.

   小张穷得**不但**没有钱交房租，**而且连**吃饭的钱**都**没有。
   Xiǎo Zhāng qióng de búdàn méiyǒu qián jiāo fángzū, érqiě lián chīfàn de qián dōu méiyǒu.
   Little Zhang is so poor that **not only** does he not have money to pay his rent, **but also** he does not **even** have money for food.

   → See 连 . . . 也/都 (*lián . . . yě/dōu*) for more information.

e. When 不但 and 而且 share **the same subject** and **the same verb**, or the two verbal phrases are of similar meanings, **还** (*hái*) can be used in place of 也, although 也 is perfectly acceptable. Also, when 还 is used, both sentences must be **positive**.

   张先生**不但是**享誉国际的钢琴家，而且**还是**一位很有才华的画家。(same verb 是)
   Zhāng xiānsheng búdàn shì xiǎng yù guójì de gāngqínjiā, érqiě hái shì yī wèi hěn yǒu cáihuá de huàjiā.
   Mr Zhang **is not only** an internationally well-known pianist **but also** a talented painter.

10 不但...反而(还)... búdàn ... fǎn'ér (hái) ...

李老师**不但**精通英文、法文，**而且还**会说西班牙文。(精通 and 会说 are similar.)
Lǐ lǎoshī búdàn jīngtōng Yīngwén, Fǎwén, érqiě hái huì shuō Xībānyáwén.
Teacher Li is **not only** highly proficient in English and French, **but he can also** speak Spanish.

不但...反而(还)... *búdàn ... fǎn'ér (hái)* ...

Unlike the 不但...而且... structure, the 不但...反而... structure, with rare exceptions, should have **only one subject**. This means that **the subject appears before** 不但 and cannot be repeated in the 反而 clause.

a. What follows 不但 must be a **negative** sentence (with 不, 没有, etc.) and what follows 反而 must be **positive** in structure. The connotation is that not only what was expected or supposed to have happened did not happen, but **the opposite** happened.

虽然大家都知道李文生能进那所有名的大学是因为他爸爸捐了很多钱给学校，可是文生**不但不**觉得不好意思，**反而(还)**洋洋得意。
Suīrán dàjiā dōu zhīdào Lǐ Wénshēng néng jìn nà suǒ yǒumíng de dàxué shì yīnwèi tā bàba juān le hěnduō qián gěi xuéxiào, kěshì Wénshēng búdàn bù juéde bù hǎo yìsi, fǎn'ér (hái) yángyáng déyì.
Although everyone knows that the reason Li Wensheng could get into that famous university is because his father donated a lot of money to the school, **not only** does Wensheng **not** feel embarrassed about it, he, **on the contrary**, is very proud.

王小中得了绘画比赛第一名，可是他爸爸**不但没有**赞美他，**反而(还)**说学画画是浪费时间，所以现在小中**不但不**兴奋，**反而**很难过。
Wáng Xiǎozhōng dé le huìhuà bǐsài dì yī míng, kěshì tā bàba búdàn méiyǒu zànměi tā, fǎn'ér (hái) shuō xué huà huà shì làngfèi shíjiān, suǒyǐ xiànzài Xiǎozhōng búdàn bù xīngfèn, fǎn'ér hěn nánguò.
Wang Xiaozhong had won first place in the art contest, but **not only did** his father **not** praise him, **but** he said that learning to paint was a waste of time. So right now **not only** is Xiaozhong **not** happy, **but** he is feeling sad.

b. 反而 can be used as a **stand-alone word** without the presence of 不但. In this case, what should have been in the 不但 clause is self-explanatory and clear in the context. Thus, it would be redundant to actually mention it.

In a situation like this, 反而 must be understood based on the context, one's common knowledge or the shared knowledge between the interlocutors; it has **no direct counterpart or translation** in English. What must be kept in mind is the **subject** must **appear before** 反而.

In the following scenario, what was omitted in the 不但 part is 老师**不但没有**骂他 (**not only** did the teacher **not** scold him). For the teacher to scold a student under such circumstances is something that is normally expected.

A: 高大明考得这么差，老师怎么**反而(还)**称赞他？
Gāo Dàmíng kǎo de zhème chà, lǎoshī zěnme fǎn'ér (hái) chēngzài tā?
B: 因为他上次考得更差，这次他进步了很多。
Yīnwèi tā shàng cì kǎo de gèng chà, zhè cì tā jìnbù le hěn duō.
A: Gao Daming did so poorly on the test; how come the teacher would praise him (instead of scolding him, which would have been the normal thing for the teacher to do)?
B: Because he had done even worse last time; he improved a lot this time.

c. Although 还 in the 反而 clause is optional, when 还 is used, 反而 becomes optional.

小李知道他这学期的数学一定会不及格，所以虽然明天有数学考试，可是他今天晚上**不但不**在家准备考试，**还**跟朋友一起去看电影。
Xiǎo Lǐ zhīdào tā zhè xuéqī de shùxué yīdìng huì bù jígé, suǒyǐ suīrán míngtiān yǒu shùxué kǎoshì, kěshì tā jīntiān wǎnshàng búdàn bú zài jiā zhǔnbèi kǎoshì, hái gēn péngyǒu yīqǐ qù kàn diànyǐng.
Little Li knows that he will definitely fail his mathematics class this semester; therefore, although there is a mathematics test tomorrow, **not only** is he **not** studying for the test at home this evening, he (**on the contrary**) is going to a movie with his friends.

不得不 *bù dé bù*

→ See 得 (*dé/děi*) for detailed information.

不管 *bùguǎn*

不管 has two major definitions and uses. One is a **conjunction** that means '**no matter**' or '**regardless**'; the other is a **verb**. Although each would appear in a different pattern, it is important to pay attention to the context 不管 appears in.

a. When defined as 'no matter' or 'regardless', 不管 is generally considered interchangeable with **无论** (*wúlùn*). In terms of actual use, 不管 tends to be used in **more casual speech** than 无论.

→ See 无论 (*wúlùn*) for more information.

What follows 不管 is **a question**, and **都 must be used** in the main sentence. The implication is that the conditions may vary, but the outcome remains the same.

The pattern is '不管 + **question** + 都 **verb**'. If the sentence has only one subject, the subject should appear only once and it can be used in either the dependent clause with 不管 or the main sentence with 都.

Sometimes, 都 can be replaced with 也, especially when **the main sentence is a negative sentence**. Occasionally, 总 (*zǒng*) is used to replace 都.

(i)   The question can be represented by an **interrogative pronoun**, which is similar to a wh- question word in English.

王大中决定了要做一件事以后，**不管多**难，他**都**一定要做到。比方说，他去年决定辞职去开餐馆，**不管谁**劝他，他**都**(or **也**)不听。
*Wáng Dàzhōng juédìng le yào zuò yī jiàn shì yǐhòu, **bùguǎn duō nán**, tā dōu yīdìng yào zuò dào. Bǐfāngshuō, tā qùnián juédìng cízhí qù kāi cānguǎn, **bùguǎn shéi quàn tā**, tā dōu (or yě) bù tīng.*
Once Wang Dazhong has decided to do something, **no matter how** hard it is, he will definitely achieve it. For example, he decided to quit his job and open a restaurant last year; **no matter who** tried to dissuade him, he would not listen.

(Scenario: A young man is starting his own business. His parents are very supportive.)

爸爸: 别忘了，你**不管**有**什么**问题，**都**可以来找我商量。(你 can appear either before 不管 or 都, but it should not be used twice.)

Bàba: *Bié wàng le, nǐ **bùguǎn yǒu shénme wèntí**, dōu kěyǐ lái zhǎo wǒ shāngliáng.*

妈妈: 还有，**不管**我们在**哪里**，**不管几点**，你**都**可以随时打电话来。

Māma: *Háiyǒu, **bùguǎn wǒmen zài nǎlǐ**, **bùguǎn jǐdiǎn**, nǐ dōu kěyǐ suíshí dǎ diànhuà lái.*

Father: Don't forget that, **no matter what** problems you have, you can come and discuss them with me.

Mother: Also, you can call us **no matter where** we are and **no matter what time** it is.

A: 王先生想到国外的分公司工作，我们应该派他去哪个国家？
Wáng xiānsheng xiǎng dào guówài de fēn gōngsī gōngzuò, wǒmen yīnggāi pài tā qù nǎ ge guójiā?

B: **不管哪**个国家他**都**不能去，因为他一句外语都不会说。
Bùguǎn nǎ ge guójiā tā dōu bù néng qù, yīnwèi tā yī jù wàiyǔ dōu bú huì shuō.

A: Mr Wang wants to go to one of the branches overseas to work. Which country should we send him to?

B: He cannot go to any foreign country (= he cannot go **no matter which country** it is), because he does not speak any foreign language.

(ii) The question can be **an alternative question with 还是** (*háishì*) or an **affirmative-negative** (yes-no) question. 也 is normally not used in the main sentence even when the sentence is negative; 都 is the proper word to use here.

(Scenario: A woman has just found out that she is pregnant, and she knows that her husband's parents really want a grandson.)

妻子:	要是生女孩怎么办？
Qīzi:	*Yàoshì shēng nǚhái zěnme bàn?*
丈夫:	你放心，**不管**是男孩**还是**女孩，我**都**会非常爱这个孩子.
Zhàngfū:	*Nǐ fàngxīn, bùguǎn shì nánhái háishì nǚhái, wǒ dōu huì fēicháng ài zhè ge háizi.*
Wife:	What (are we going to do) if we have a girl?
Husband:	Don't worry! **Regardless of whether** it is a boy **or** a girl, I will love this child very much.

(Scenario: Li is interested in joining the new company his friend Gao is about to start.)

高:	可是刚开始的时候，要是赚不了钱，你可能会没有薪水。
Gāo:	*Kěshì gāng kāishǐ de shíhòu, yàoshì zhuàn bù liǎo qián, nǐ kěnéng huì méiyǒu xīnshuǐ.*
李:	**不管有没有**薪水，我**都**愿意做这份工作。
Lǐ:	*Bùguǎn yǒu méiyǒu xīnshuǐ, wǒ dōu yuànyì zuò zhè fèn gōngzuò.*
Gao:	But at the beginning, if we cannot make any money, you probably will not have a salary.
Li:	**It does not matter whether** there is a salary **or not**, I am willing to do the job.

(iii) Learners who are English speakers often mistranslate the English expression '**no matter what**'. In Chinese, the proper way to say 'no matter what' is not to use the interrogative pronoun '什么' but to use '**怎么样**'.

(Scenario: A young man is in financial trouble again. This time his father refuses to help him. His mother attempts to make him change his mind.)

妈妈:	**不管怎么样**，他**总** (or 都) 是你的儿子！要是你不帮他，谁会帮他呢？
Māma:	*Bùguǎn zěnme yàng, tā zǒng (or dōu) shì nǐ de érzi! Yàoshì nǐ bù bāng tā, shéi huì bāng tā ne?*
爸爸:	这次**不管**你说**什么**，我**都** (or 也) 不会再帮他了。
Bàba:	*Zhè cì bùguǎn nǐ shuō shénme, wǒ dōu (or yě) bú huì zài bāng tā le.*
Mother:	**No matter what**, he is your son. If you won't help him, who will?
Father:	This time, **no matter what** you say, I will not help him anymore.

(iv) Both **不管** and **无论** are actually **optional** words. As long as the main sentence has the word **都** (or **也**), the meaning of the sentence is clear. Such a pattern is used in very casual, conversational speech.

(v) In **very casual, conversational speech**, 不 is omitted, but the word 他 is added. The expression, thus, becomes **管他**. (无论 does not have this option.)

王大中打算明年参加马拉松，所以**管他**(= 不管)是晴天**还是**下雨天，他**都**会去练习跑步。

Wáng Dàzhōng dǎsuàn míngnián cānjiā mǎlāsōng, suǒyǐ guǎn tā shì qíng tiān háishì xiàyǔ tiān, tā dōu huì qù liànxí pǎo bù.

Wang Dazhong plans to participate in a marathon next year, so **regardless of whether** it is a sunny day **or** a rainy day, he will go and practice running.

When addressing a **specific person**, the expression is **管你**.

(Scenario: A man calls his girlfriend because he wants to cancel their date. His girlfriend insists that he should come.)

男: 我今天好累，下了班想回家休息。
Nán: *Wǒ jīntiān hǎo lèi, xià le bān xiǎng huí jiā xiūxi.*
女: **管你**累不累，你**都**得来，我还约了别的朋友，我不能让她们笑我。
Nǚ: *Guǎn nǐ lèi bú lèi, nǐ dōu děi lái; wǒ hái yuē le biéde péngyǒu, wǒ bù néng ràng tāmen xiào wǒ.*
Man: I am so tired today. I want to go home to get some rest after work.
Woman: **It doesn't matter whether** you are tired **or** not, you have to come. I have asked other people to join us. I cannot allow them to laugh at me.

(Scenario: A man is trying to park in front of the building of a big company.)

A: 喂！这里不能停车。
       Wèi, zhèlǐ bù néng tíng chē.
B: 我是主管的儿子，我开的是我爸爸的车，我为什么不能在这里停？
       Wǒ shì zhǔguǎn de érzi, wǒ kāi de shì wǒ bàba de chē, wǒ wèi shénme bù néng zài zhèlǐ tíng?
A: **管你**是**谁**，**都**不可以在这里停车。
       Guǎn nǐ shì shéi, dōu bù kěyǐ zài zhèlǐ tíng chē.
A: Hey! There is no parking here.
B: I am the executive's son, and the car I am driving belongs to my father. Why can't I park here?
A: **No matter who** you are, you cannot park here.

b.   Although **不管 as a verb** is considered the negative form of 管, it is frequently used as a stand-alone word that means '**to not care**', '**to ignore**', '**to pay no attention**', etc.

妈妈:	王大中人品不好，又没有工作，我不准你跟他结婚。
Māma:	*Wáng Dàzhōng rénpǐn bù hǎo, yòu méiyǒu gōngzuò, wǒ bù zhǔn nǐ gēn tā jiéhūn.*
女儿:	我**不管**！我爱他，所以我一定要跟他结婚。
Nǚ'ér:	*Wǒ bù guǎn! Wǒ ài tā, suǒyǐ wǒ yídìng yào gēn tā jiéhūn.*
妈妈:	好！你不听我的话，我**不管**你了；婚礼的费用，我也**不管**。
Māma:	*Hǎo! Nǐ bù tīng wǒ de huà, wǒ bù guǎn nǐ le; hūnlǐ de fèiyòng, wǒ yě bù guǎn.*
爸爸:	**不管**她要跟**谁**结婚，她**都**还是咱们的女儿。女儿要结婚，我们怎么能**不管**？
Bàba:	*Bùguǎn tā yào gēn shéi jiéhūn, tā dōu háishì zánmen de nǚ'ér. Nǚ'ér yào jiéhūn, wǒmen zěnme néng bù guǎn?*
Mother:	Wang Dazhong's moral character is bad, and he does not have a job. I will not allow you to marry him.
Daughter:	I **don't care**! I love him, so I definitely will marry him.
Mother:	Fine! You won't listen to me; **you are on your own** now. Also, I will **not be responsible for** (I will **ignore**) the expenses for your wedding.
Father:	**Regardless of whom** she wants to marry, she is still our daughter. Now that our daughter is getting married, how can we **ignore** it? (How can we **pay no attention to** the event?)

不好意思 *bù hǎo yìsi*

不好意思 is a common expression with rich connotations but without direct translations. Therefore, it can only be accurately interpreted based on the **actual situation** in which it appears. In addition, '**不好意思 + verb**' and '**不好意思地 + verb**' imply two opposite situations. It is important to **observe the context** when interpreting a sentence with 不好意思.

→ See 意思 (*yìsi*) for detailed information.

不见得 *bú jiànde* and 不一定 *bù yídìng*

Both **不见得** and **不一定** can be interpreted as '**not necessarily**' (not to be confused with 'not necessary', which is 不必: *búbì* or 不用: *búyòng*). Although they are generally considered interchangeable, in certain contexts 不见得 may not be proper and only 不一定 can be used. This suggests that 不一定 is slightly broader in use than 不见得.

When a certain point has been **established** by one of the speakers or is **pre-existent** in the context, either 不一定 or 不见得 can be used. Without such a context, it is not proper to use 不见得. Therefore, 不见得 is usually used to **dispute a pre-existent assumption**. Phrases that are used to indicate one's opinion, such as 我看, 我觉得 and 我认为, are frequently used with 不见得. Without a **pre-existent assumption** in the context, 不见得 is not proper.

不见得 is often used in casual conversations. **未必** (*wèibì*) has the same meaning and use as 不见得 and can be used in both spoken and written communications.

A: 下星期的舞会，收到邀请函的人，哪些回覆了？
   Xià xīngqī de wǔhuì, shōudào yāoqǐng hán de rén, nǎxiē huífù le?
B: 李先生说他**不一定**(不见得 is not proper)能来，张先生、王小姐都说他们一定会来。周先生还没有回覆。
   Lǐ xiānsheng shuō tā bù yídìng néng lái, Zhāng xiānsheng, Wáng xiǎojiě dōu shuō tāmen yídìng huì lái. Zhōu xiānsheng hái méiyǒu huífù.
A: 周先生这么喜欢跳舞，他应该会来。
   Zhōu xiānsheng zhème xǐhuān tiàowǔ, tā yīnggāi huì lái.
B: **我觉得**他**不见得**(不一定 is acceptable)会来，因为他最近特别忙。
   Wǒ juéde tā bú jiànde huì lái, yīnwèi tā zuìjìn tèbié máng.
A: Which of those who were invited to the dance next week have replied?
B: Mr Li says that he **may not** be able to come. Both Mr Zhang and Miss Wang say that they definitely will come. Mr Zhou has not replied.
A: Mr Zhou likes to dance so much. He should (probably will) come.
B: **I think it is not necessarily true that** he will come, because he has been particularly busy lately.

A: 王先生那么有钱，他的生活无忧无虑，我真羡慕他。
   Wáng xiānsheng nàme yǒuqián, tā de shēnghuó wú yōu wú lǜ, wǒ zhēn xiànmù tā.
B: 财富**不见得**买得到快乐，健康才是幸福。王先生身体不好，**我看**他**不见得**是个无忧无虑的人。
   Cáifù bú jiànde mǎi de dào kuàilè, jiànkāng cái shì xìngfú. Wáng xiānsheng shēntǐ bù hǎo, wǒ kàn tā bú jiànde shì ge wú yōu wú lǜ de rén.
A: Mr Wang is so rich. His life is worry-free. I really envy him.
B: Wealth **cannot necessarily** buy happiness. Only health is happiness. Mr Wang is in poor health. **In my opinion**, he is **not necessarily** a worry-free person.

→ See 一定 (*yídìng*) for related information.

不仅/不仅仅 *bùjǐn/bù jǐnjǐn*

→ See 不但 . . . 而且 . . . (*búdàn . . . érqiě . . .*) for more information.

不论 *búlùn*

→ See 无论 (*wúlùn*) for related information.

不然 *bùrán*

不然 means '**otherwise**' or '**if not**', and is considered interchangeable with 否则 (*fŏuzé*), 要不 (*yào bù*) and 要不然 (*yào bùrán*). In very casual speech, 不然 can sometimes be used to **offer an alternative solution**, but 否则 does not have this use. Therefore, when 不然 is used for this function, it cannot be replaced with 否则, and should not be translated as 'otherwise'; also, the expression often ends with 吧 or sometimes 好了.

> (Scenario: A couple is at a furniture store trying to decide which sofa set they should purchase.)
>
> 丈夫:　　这套白色的虽然很漂亮，可是容易脏；这套黄色的也不错，可是太贵。
>
> *Zhàngfū:*　*Zhè tào báisè de suīrán hěn piàoliàng, kěshì róngyì zāng; zhè tào huángsè de yě búcuò, kěshì tài guì.*
>
> 妻子:　　**不然**我们买这套绿色的**吧**！又便宜又漂亮。
>
> *Qīzi:*　*Bùrán wǒmen mǎi zhè tào lǜsè de ba! Yòu piányí yòu piàoliàng.*
>
> Husband:　Although this white set is pretty, it will be easily stained. This yellow set is not bad, either, but it is too expensive.
>
> Wife:　　(Since those don't work,) let's buy the green set. It is both inexpensive and pretty.

→ See 否则 (*fŏuzé*) and 要不 (*yào bù*) for more information.

不如 *bùrú*

There are three important patterns for the uses of 不如, each of which indicates or implies **a comparison**.

a.　不如 is used in a comparison to indicate '**worse**' or '**inferior**'. Thus, '**A 不如 B**' means '**A is inferior to B**' or '**A is not as good as B**'. It is used when the feature being compared is clearly indicated in the **context**.

> 王大中和李明都从小就开始学钢琴；论天赋才华，王大中**不如**李明，但是他肯勤练苦学，所以论成就，李明**不如**王大中。
>
> *Wáng Dàzhōng hé Lǐ Míng dōu cóngxiǎo jiù kāishǐ xué gāngqín; lùn tiānfù cáihuá, Wáng Dàzhōng bùrú Lǐ Míng, dànshì tā kěn qín liàn kǔ xué, suŏyǐ lùn chéngjiù, Lǐ Míng bùrú Wáng Dàzhōng.*
>
> Wang Dazhong and Li Ming both began learning piano from childhood. When it comes to gift and talent, Wang Dazhong is **inferior to** Li Ming; but he has been willing to practice diligently and study hard; therefore, when it comes to achievement, Li Ming is **inferior to** Wang Dazhong.

> 爷爷年纪大了，体力、精神都**不如**从前了。
>
> *Yéye niánjì dà le, tǐlì, jīngshén dōu bùrú cóngqián le.*
>
> My grandfather is old; his energy and spirit are **not as good as** they used to be.

李先生有博士学位，在大学教书；他儿子不喜欢读书，但至少也有大学文凭；而他的孙子上高中的时候就辍学了。大家都说李家一代**不如**一代。

Lǐ xiānsheng yǒu bóshì xuéwèi, zài dàxué jiāoshū; tā érzǐ bù xǐhuān dúshū, dàn zhìshǎo yě yǒu dàxué wénpíng; ér tā de sūnzi shàng gāozhōng de shíhòu jiù chuòxué le. Dàjiā dōu shuō Lǐ jiā yī dài bùrú yī dài.

Mr Li has a doctoral degree and he teaches in a college; his son did not like to study but he at least had a college diploma. His grandson dropped out of high school. Everybody says that one generation is **worse than** the other in the Li family.

b. When the feature being compared is mentioned as an adjective, the pattern is '**A 不如 B +(那么) adjective**'. If the **status of B is indicated or pre-exists** in the context, 那么 can be used. It should be noted that, since 不如 implies inferiority, the feature being compared normally indicates a **positive quality**.

虽然张家**不如**李家**有钱**，可是小李**不如**小张**大方**，所以小李的朋友也**不如**小张**多**。(有钱, 大方 and 多 are positive qualities.)

Suīrán Zhāng jiā bùrú Lǐ jiā yǒuqián, kěshì Xiǎo Lǐ bùrú Xiǎo Zhāng dàfāng, suǒyǐ Xiǎo Lǐ de péngyǒu yě bùrú Xiǎo Zhāng duō.

Although the Zhang family is **not as wealthy as** the Li family, Little Li is **not as generous as** Little Zhang; therefore, Little Li **does not have as many** friends as Little Zhang, either.

A: 为什么**张文**考试总是考得**不如**李中**好**？
   Wèi shénme Zhāng Wén kǎoshì zǒngshì kǎo de bùrú Lǐ Zhōng hǎo?
B: 因为他**不如**李中**聪明**，也**不如**李中**努力**，所以他的成绩当然**不如**李中**那么好**。(Since 张文's superior school performance is mentioned, 那么好 can be used.)
   Yīnwèi tā bùrú Lǐ Zhōng cōngmíng, yě bùrú Lǐ Zhōng nǔlì, suǒyǐ tā de chéngjī dāngrán bùrú Lǐ Zhōng nàme hǎo.
A: Why is it that Zhang Wen **never** does **as well as** Li Zhong on any tests?
B: Because he is **not as smart as** Li Zhong, and he is also **not as hardworking as** Li Zhong; so of course his school performance is **not as good as** Li Zhong's.

When the feature being compared is considered a **negative quality**, using 比 to make the comparison is more appropriate than using 不如.

A: 長江餐馆的菜**不如**成都饭馆的**好吃**，可是成都的生意却**比**長江**差**，真奇怪！
   Chángjiāng cānguǎn de cài bùrú Chéngdū fànguǎn de hǎochī, kěshì Chéngdū de shēngyì què bǐ Chángjiāng chà, zhēn qíguài!
B: 那是因为成都的服务**不如**長江的**亲切**。
   Nà shì yīnwèi Chéngdū de fúwù bùrú Chángjiāng de qīnqiè.
C: 而且成都的价格也**不如**長江的**公道**。
   Érqiě Chéngdū de jiàgé yě bùrú Chángjiāng de gōngdào.

A: Changjiang Restaurant's food is **not as delicious as** Chengdu Restaurant's, but Chengdu's business is **worse than** Changjiang's. This is really strange!

B: That is because Chengdu's service is **not as cordial as** Changjiang's.

C: Furthermore, Chengdu's prices are **not as fair as** Changjiang's.

A: 这个房子**不如**那个**新**，花园也**不如**那个**好看**，为什么**比**那个**贵**？
Zhè ge fángzi bùrú nà ge xīn, huāyuán yě bùrú nà ge hǎokàn, wèi shénme bǐ nà ge guì?

B: 因为那个房子**比**这个**小**，地点也**不如**这个**好**，所以**比**这个**便宜**。(It is not proper to say 这个房子不如那个小 since 小 is considered a negative quality here.)
Yīnwèi nà ge fángzi bǐ zhè ge xiǎo, dìdiǎn yě bùrú zhè ge hǎo, suǒyǐ bǐ zhè ge piányí.

A: This house is **not as new as** that one; the garden is also **not as pretty as** the garden of that one; why is it **more expensive than** that one?

B: Because that house is **smaller than** this one; the location is also **not as good as** the location for this one. So it is **cheaper than** this one.

c. There are **two variations** for the '**A 不如 B + adjective**' pattern.

(i) Using 没有

不如 can be replaced with **没有**. However, the feature being compared (i.e. the adjective) in the '**A 没有 B (那么) + adjective**' pattern can be a word indicating a **negative quality**.

这次考试，王大中考得非常差；李明虽然考得也不好，但是**没有**王大中**那么差**。(To say 李明考得不如王大中那么差 is improper since 差 is considered an adjective of **negative quality**.)
Zhè cì kǎoshì, Wáng Dàzhōng kǎo de fēicháng chà; Lǐ Míng suīrán kǎo de yě bù hǎo, dànshì méiyǒu Wáng Dàzhōng nàme chà.
Wang Dazhong did extremely poorly on this test. Although Li Ming did not do well either, he still **did not do as poorly as** Wang Dazhong did.

A: 王明比较胖还是李中比较胖？
Wáng Míng bǐjiào pàng háishì Lǐ Zhōng bǐjiào pàng?

B: 王明**没有**李中那么**胖**，但是他身体**不如**(= **没有**)李中**好**，因为他**没有**(= **不如**)李中注重营养。
Wáng Míng méiyǒu Lǐ Zhōng nàme pàng, dànshì tā de shēntǐ bùrú (= méiyǒu) Lǐ Zhōng hǎo, yīnwèi tā méiyǒu (= bùrú) Lǐ Zhōng zhùzhòng yíngyǎng.

A: Does Wang Ming weigh more or does Li Zhong weigh more? (Literally: Is Wang Ming fatter or is Li Zhong fatter?)

B: Wang Ming does **not** weigh **as much as** Li Zhong, but his health is **not as good as** Li Zhong's because he is **not as mindful as** Li Zhong about nutrition.

(ii) Using 不像 ... 那么

While **那么** is optional in the 'A 不如/没有 B (那么) + adjective' pattern, it is **required when 不像 is used** to replace 不如 or 没有.

Adjectives of both positive and negative qualities can be used in the '**A 不像 B 那么 + adjective**' pattern, and the **status of B** must **have been indicated** or be **pre-existent** in the context.

In the following scenario, it is implied that the younger son is smart but lazy. However, when it comes to academic performance, it does not clearly indicate whether the older son is outstanding; it only indicates that his performance is better than his younger brother's. These implications are suggested by **the presence or absence of 那么**.

王家有两个儿子。哥哥虽然**不像**(= **不如** or **没有**)弟弟**那么**聪明，**但是也不像**(= **没有**)弟弟**那么**懒(懒 is a negative quality)，所以弟弟的成绩总是**没有**(= **不如**)哥哥好。

Wáng jiā yǒu liǎng ge érzi. Gēge suīrán búxiàng (= bùrú or méiyǒu) dìdi nàme cōngming, kěshǐ yě búxiàng (= méiyǒu) dìdi nàme lǎn, suǒyǐ dìdi de chéngjī zǒngshì méiyǒu (= bùrú) gēge hǎo.

The Wang family has two sons. Although the older son is **not as smart as** his younger brother, he is also **not as lazy as** his younger brother; therefore, the younger brother's school performance is **never as good as** his old brother's.

d. 不如 can be used to indicate **the better choice between two given options**. In this pattern, 不如 is followed by a verb or a sentence; also, the **two options must be pre-existent** in the context.

When the two options are explicitly mentioned in the interaction, the pattern is '**与其** (*yǔqí*) **A, 不如 B**'. B is the **preferred choice** of the two. Therefore, 不如 as a stand-alone expression (without 与其) is frequently translated as '**might as well**'. An **optional 还** can precede 不如, and sometimes 吧 is used at the end of the sentence. It should be noted that 还 in 还 不如 should not be interpreted as 'still'.

→ See 与其 (*yǔqí*) ... 不如 ... (*bùrú*) for related information.

A: 这件事请助理去办吧！
   Zhè jiàn shì qǐng zhùlǐ qù bàn ba!
B: 你大概还不知道吧！这个助理是老板的侄子，只拿薪水不做事。算了！**(还)不如**我自己去办**吧**！
   Nǐ dàgài hái bù zhīdào ba! Zhè ge zhùlǐ shì lǎobǎn de zhízi, zhǐ ná xīnshuǐ bú zuò shì. Suàn le! (Hái) bùrú wǒ zìjǐ qù bàn ba!
A: Why don't you ask the assistant to handle this business!
B: You probably didn't know that this assistant is the owner's nephew; he only gets paid but does not do anything. Never mind! I **might as well** go do it myself!

A: 你在这里等一下，我去把车开过来，我们开车去。
Nǐ zài zhèlǐ děng yīxià, wǒ qù bǎ chē kāi guòlái, wǒmen kāi chē qù.

B: 开车去还得找停车位，而且今天天气这么好，我们**(还)不如**走路去，怎么样？
Kāichē qù hái děi zhǎo tíngchē wèi; érqiě jīntiān tiānqì zhème hǎo, wǒmen (hái) bùrú zǒulù qù, zěnme yàng?

A: You wait here for a moment. I will go bring the car here, and we will drive there.

B: If we drive there, we will have to look for a parking space. Besides, today's weather is so nice; we **might as well** walk there. What do you think?

不是... (而)是... *bú shì... (ér) shì...*

The expression '**不是 A(而)是 B**' is easy to understand when it appears in a text in Chinese due to its obvious surface meaning. However, difficulty often arises when the task is to produce a sentence that requires the use of the 不是... (而)是... structure.

Basically, learners should keep in mind that 是 cannot be perceived as having any independent meaning, but is simply part of the structure.

In addition, there are **two variations** to this expression: one is that the positive part can appear first ('**是 B 而不是 A**'); the other is that **而 is optional**. In casual, conversational speech, 而 is often omitted.

The focus of this section will be **common mistakes** that learners should avoid. '不是 A 而是 B' and '是 A 而不是 B' will be used alternately.

a. When the main verb of the sentences is 是, it is integrated with 不是... 而是. This means that 是 will not be used twice.

(Scenario: A man is annoyed with his girlfriend because she nags about his bad habits. In their exchange, 而 most likely will be omitted since it is a casual conversation.)

男: 好了！别再说了！别忘了，你**不是**我妈妈，**(而)是**我女朋友。
Nán: Hǎo le! Bié zài shuō le! Bié wàng le, nǐ bú shì wǒ māma, (ér) shì wǒ nǚ péngyǒu.

女: 好！算了！反正你也只**是**我男朋友，**(而)不是**我儿子。
Nǚ: Hǎo! Suàn le! Fǎnzhèng nǐ yě zhǐ shì wǒ nán péngyǒu, (ér) bú shì wǒ érzi.

Man: Enough! Say no more. Don't forget that you **are not** my mother **but** my girlfriend.

Woman: Fine! Forget it! Anyway, you **are** only my boyfriend, **not** my son.

A **common mistake** made by learners is using 可是 or 但是 instead of 而是, since the English translation of such a sentence is often 'not A *but* B'.

我跟王太太聊了半个多小时才发现她**不是**王大中的太太，**而是**他妈妈。(Do not say 可是他妈妈。)

Wǒ gēn Wáng tàitai liáo le bàn ge duō xiǎoshí cái fāxiàn tā bú shì Wáng Dàzhōng de tàitai, ér shì tā māma.

I had chatted with Mrs Wang for over half an hour before I realized that she **was not** Wang Dazhong's wife **but** (was) his mother.

昨天王家请客，菜好吃极了！我跟王太太说，她的菜做得真好。可是她告诉我，那些菜**不是**她做的，**而是**王先生做的。(Do not say 但是是王先生做的。)

Zuótiān Wáng jiā qǐng kè, cài hǎochī jí le! Wǒ gēn Wáng tàitai shuō, tā de cài zuò de zhēn hǎo. Kěshì tā gàosù wǒ, nà xiē cài bú shì tā zuò de, ér shì Wáng xiānsheng zuò de.

Yesterday the Wangs had a dinner party. All the food was extremely delicious. I told Mrs Wang that she was such a good cook, but she told me that those dishes **were not** made by her **but** were made by Mr Wang.

b. 不是 A 而是 B is typically used **in context** to **refute a pre-existent idea** (by using 不是) and to **provide the fact** (by using 而是). This means **what appears after 不是 is pre-existent in the context.**

> A: 王中今天为什么又被老师骂了？他考试又不及格吗？ (This provides the context.)
> *Wáng Zhōng jīntiān wèi shénme yòu bèi lǎoshī mà le? Tā kǎoshì yòu bù jígé ma?*
> B: 老师骂他**不是**因为他考试不及格，**而是**因为他跟同学打架。
> *Lǎoshī mà tā bú shì yīnwèi tā kǎoshì bù jígé, ér shì yīnwèi tā gēn tóngxué dǎjià.*
> A: Why was Wang Zhong scolded by the teacher again today? Did he fail the test again?
> B: The teacher scolded him **not** because he failed the test **but** because he fought with a classmate.

c. There are two **common mistakes** that learners should avoid.

(i) Do not neglect **the need for** 是. A common mistake is to use two independent sentences (one positive and one negative) without taking into consideration the context.

> A: 你喜不喜欢王小英？
> *Nǐ xǐ bù xǐhuān Wáng Xiǎoyīng?*
> B: 我不太喜欢她。
> *Wǒ bú tài xǐhuān tā.*
> A: 可是我常常看到你去她家找她。(This provides the context.)
> *Kěshì wǒ chángcháng kàndào nǐ qù tā jiā zhǎo tā.*

B: 我**不是**去找她，**是**去找她妹妹，因为我喜欢她妹妹。(Do not say
  我不去找她，去找她妹妹。)
  *Wǒ bú shì qù zhǎo tā, shì qù zhǎo tā mèimei, yīnwèi wǒ xǐhuān tā
  mèimei.*

A: Do you like Wang Xiaoying?

B: I don't like her very much.

A: But I often see you **going** to her house to **visit her**.

B: I do **not go** there to **visit her**; (rather,) I **go** to **visit her younger
  sister** because I like her younger sister.

(Scenario: Xiaoying's mother points out her inappropriate behavior,
and Xiaoying is annoyed.)

小英: 你为什么总**批评**我？ (This provides the context.)

Xiǎoyīng: *Nǐ wèi shénme zǒng pīpíng wǒ?*

妈妈: 我**不是**批评你，**(而)是**关心你。(Do not say 我没有在批
  评你，我关心你。)

Māma: *Wǒ bú shì pīpíng nǐ, (ér) shì guānxīn nǐ.*

Xiaoying: Why do you always **criticize** me?

Mother: I am **not criticizing** you; I am showing my concern for
  you.

(ii) Because what follows 不是 is already existent in the context and is
  thus understood, it is **often omitted**. Learners who fail to take into
  consideration the omitted 不是 . . . part often neglect to use 是 in the
  positive part.
    It should be noted that **when 不是 . . . is omitted, 而 is no longer
  used**.

(Scenario: Upon learning that her daughter has been admitted to a world-
renowned university in the U.S., the mother cries.)

女儿: 妈妈，你别难过；我到了美国，一定会常常给你打电
  话。

Nǚ'ér: *Māma, nǐ bié nánguò; wǒ dào le Měiguó, yīdìng huì
  chángcháng gěi nǐ dǎ diànhuà.*

妈妈: 这么好的消息，我怎么会难过？我**是**高兴。(Do not simply
  say 我高兴。)

Māma: *Zhème hǎo de xiāoxí, wǒ zěnme huì nánguò? Wǒ shì
  gāoxìng.*

Daughter: Mother, don't be sad. After I go to the U.S., I will definitely
  call you often.

Mother: This is such good news; how could I be sad? (I cry because)
  I am happy (**不是**难过 '**not because** I am sad' is understood
  and omitted).

A: 小李真大方，常常请朋友吃饭、看电影。(This provides the context.)
Xiǎo Lǐ zhēn dàfāng, chángcháng qǐng péngyǒu chī fàn, kàn diànyǐng.

B: 他**是**喜欢炫耀财富，（**不是**大方）。
Tā shì xǐhuān xuànyào cáifù, (bú shì dàfāng).

A: Little Li is really generous; he often treats his friends to meals and movies.

B: (It's because) he likes to show off his wealth (not that he is generous).

不是...就是... *bú shì...jiù shì...*

Learners often misinterpret the '不是 A 就是 B' expression and confuse it with '不是 A 而是 B'. Actually, the 不是 part in these two expressions, although ostensibly identical, has two opposite underlying meanings.

不是 in the '不是 A 就是 B' expression means '**if not**', implying that it is **possible for what follows 不是 to be true**. On the other hand, in the '不是 A 而是 B' expression, what follows 不是 is **not the fact**.

→ See 不是...而是... (*bú shì...ér shì...*) for related information.

'不是 A 就是 B' can be interpreted as 'if it is not A, then it is B' or 'when it is not A, it is B'. In addition, '**either A or B**' is an acceptable interpretation. This suggests that '不是 A 就是 B' can be used in **two slightly different situations**.

Verbs, nouns and adjectives can follow 不是 and 就是. When there is **only one subject**, it should appear only once and **before 不是**.

a. There are two possibilities, and only one of them is the actual fact.

(Scenario: Li had agreed to meet with two of his classmates at 8:00, but has still not shown up at 8:30.)

A: 八点半了，小李怎么还没来？
Bā diǎn bàn le, Xiǎo Lǐ zěnme hái méi lái?

B: 他**不是**睡过头**就是**忘了，我们给他打个电话吧！
Tā bú shì shuì guò tóu jiù shì wàng le. Wǒmen gěi tā dǎ ge diànhuà ba!

A: It's already 8:30. How come Little Li is not here yet?

B: He has **either** overslept **or** forgotten about this meeting. Let's call him!

A: 我的英文老师李老师教得很好。
Wǒ de Yīngwén lǎoshī Lǐ lǎoshī jiāo de hěn hǎo.

B: 是吗？李老师是男的还是女的？
Shì ma? Lǐ lǎoshī shì nán de háishì nǚ de?

A: 很难说，我也不知道。
Hěn hán shuō, wǒ yě bù zhīdào.

B: 一个人**不是**男的**就是**女的；你怎么会不知道？
Yī ge rén bú shì nán de jiù shì nǚ de; nǐ zěnme huì bù zhīdào?

A: 现在这个问题似乎不那么单纯了。
Xiànzài zhè ge wèntí sìhū bú nàme dānchún le.

A:　My English teacher, Teacher Li, is a good teacher. (Literally: Teacher Li teaches well.)

B:　Is that so? Is Teacher Li a man or a woman?

A:　It's hard to say. I don't know, either.

B:　A person is **either** a man **or** a woman; how can you not know?

A:　Nowadays this issue does not seem to be so simple anymore.

(Scenario: At a party.)

A:　那个人好奇怪，跟我说了很多莫名其妙的话。

　　Nà ge rén hǎo qíguài, gēn wǒ shuō le hěn duō mò míng qí miào de huà.

B:　别理他；他**不是**疯了**就是**醉了。

　　Bié lǐ tā; tā bú shì fēng le jiù shì zuì le.

A:　That man is so strange. He said a lot of ridiculous things to me.

B:　Ignore him. He is **either** crazy **or** drunk.

The two possibilities can be two sentences.

(Scenario: Two chess players are taking a game very seriously and compare it to war.)

今天这场比赛，**不是**你死**就是**我亡。

Jīntiān zhè chǎng bǐsài, bú shì nǐ sǐ jiù shì wǒ wáng.

In today's game, **either** you die **or** I perish. (Only one will survive.)

b.　It is used to support a more general statement by **providing examples**; therefore, **both possibilities are valid** but may not refer to the same people, the same time, etc. It is, thus, similar to the expression '**有的 A, 有的 B**'.

去逛夜市的时候，要特别小心，因为夜市里坏人很多，**不是**扒手**就是**骗子。不熟悉这个情况的游客，常常**不是**被偷**就是**被骗，所以一定要注意。

Qù guàng yèshì de shíhòu, yào tèbié xiǎoxīn, yīnwèi yèshì lǐ huài rén hěn duō, bú shì páshǒu jiù shì piànzi. Bù shóuxī zhè ge qíngxíng de yóukè, chángcháng bú shì bèi tōu jiù shì bèi piàn, suǒyǐ yīdìng yào zhùyì.

(**不是**扒手**就是**骗子 means 有的是扒手, 有的是骗子; **不是**被偷**就是**被骗 means 有的时候被偷, 有的时候被骗 or 有的人被偷, 有的人被骗.)

When one goes to visit the night market, one must be particularly careful, because there are lots of bad people at the night markets; they are **either** pickpockets **or** scammers. Tourists who are not familiar with the situation often **either** have their pockets picked **or** are scammed. So one must be careful (must pay attention).

A:　你们去过王小兰家没有？她家客厅里的装饰品，**不是**名画，**就是**古董；实在很惊人！

　　Nǐmen qù guo Wáng Xiǎolán jiā méiyǒu? Tā jiā kètīng lǐ de zhuāngshì pǐn, bú shì mínghuà, jiù shì gǔdǒng; shízài hěn jīngrén!

B: 我还看过她的衣橱呢！里面**不是**名牌的皮包、皮鞋，**就是**高级的服
饰。

Wǒ hái kàn guo tā de yīchú ne! Lǐmiàn bú shì míngpái de píbāo, píxié, jiù shì gāojí de fúshì.

C: 我真没想到王小兰家这么有钱，因为她出门的时候，**不是**坐公车，
就是走路。她为什么要省这个钱？

Wǒ zhēn méi xiǎngdào Wáng Xiǎolán jiā zhème yǒu qián, yīnwèi tā chū mén de shíhòu, bú shì zuò gōngchē, jiù shì zǒu lù. Tá wèi shénme yào shěng zhè ge qián?

A: 她**不是**要省钱，**而是**要多运动。

Tā bú shì yào shěng qián, ér shì yào duō yùndòng.

A: Have you been to Wang Xiaolan's house? The decorations in her living room are **either** famous paintings **or** antiques. It is truly amazing.

B: I have even seen her closet. Inside her closet, it's **either** brand-name handbags and shoes **or** high-end clothing.

C: I really would not have thought that Wang Xiaolan's family is so wealthy, because when she goes out, she **either** takes public transport **or** walks. Why would she want to save money?

A: She does **not** want to save money, **but** wants to exercise more. (She does this **not** because she wants to save money **but** because she wants to exercise.)

不用 *bú yòng*

→ See 必须 (*bìxū*) for more information.

不只 *bùzhǐ*

→ See 不但 . . . 而且 . . . (*búdàn . . . érqiě . . .*) for more information.

不住 *búzhù*

→ See 住 (*zhù*) for more information.

除非 *chúfēi*

Although 除非 is often simply translated as '**unless**', it must be kept in mind that in certain contexts, 除非 actually means '***not . . . unless***'. This section explains how to use 除非 in five different patterns.

a. **除非 A, 才 B**: This pattern can be used to set up a **pre-condition (A)** for a **desired result (B)**.

When the context clearly indicates what B (the desired result) entails, the sentence with 才 can be omitted. It should be noted that in this case, 除非 must be interpreted as '***not* unless**'.

A: 你可不可以告诉我李小姐的电话号码？
   Nǐ kě bù kěyǐ gàosù wǒ Lǐ xiǎojiě de diànhuà hàomǎ?
B: **除非**你请我吃饭 (我**才**会告诉你)。
   Chúfēi nǐ qǐng wǒ chīfàn (wǒ cái huì gàosù nǐ).
A: Can you tell me Miss Li's telephone number?
B: **Not unless** you treat me to a meal. (I will **not** tell you **unless** you treat me to a meal.)

b.　**除非 A, 否则 B**: 否则 (*fǒuzé*) literally means 'otherwise'. When 除非 and 否则 are used together as a pair, what follows 否则 (B) is the **undesired** consequence when the pre-condition (A) is not met.

   Since the word 'otherwise' is not used with 'unless' in English, learners who are English speakers must consciously remind themselves that the word **否则 is not optional** if this pattern is used.

   It should be noted that **否则 appears before the subject** of the clause. In addition, 不然 (*bùrán*) or 要不然 (*yào bùrán*) can be used in place of 否则.

(Scenario: A son discusses his academic plan with his mother.)
儿子:　　我大学毕业以后，想出国留学，你想爸爸会同意吗？
Érzi:　　*Wǒ dàxué bìyè yǐhòu, xiǎng chū guó liúxué, nǐ xiǎng bàba huì tóngyì ma?*
妈妈:　　出国留学学费太贵；**除非**你申请到最好的学校，**否则**你爸爸一定不会同意的。
Māma:　　*Chū guó liúxué xuéfèi tài guì; chúfēi nǐ shēnqǐng dào zuì hǎo de xuéxiào, fǒuzé nǐ bàba yīdìng bú huì tóngyì de.*
Son:　　After I graduate from college, I want to go abroad to study. Do you think father will agree (to let me go)?
Mother:　Tuition for studying abroad is too expensive. Your father definitely will not agree **unless** you can get into the best school.

c.　It is not unusual to combine the above two patterns (**除非...才...否则...**). Special attention should be paid to the **location** (word order) of the **subject** in each clause.

儿子:　　我想搬出去住，可以吗？
Érzi:　　*Wǒ xiǎng bān chūqù zhù, kěyǐ ma?*
妈妈:　　**除非**你去找一个工作，自己付房租，我和爸爸**才**会同意，**否则**你得在家里住到大学毕业。
Māma:　　*Chúfēi nǐ qù zhǎo yī ge gōngzuò, zìjǐ fù fángzū, wǒ hé bàba cái huì tóngyì, fǒuzé nǐ děi zài jiā lǐ zhù dào dàxué bìyè.*
Son:　　I want to move out to live (by myself). Can I (be allowed)?
Mother:　Your father and I will **not** agree **unless** you go get a job and pay your own rent; **otherwise**, you will have to live at home until you graduate from college.

d. 除非 can appear **after the main sentence** as an **afterthought** to indicate the only situation in which something will not happen. In this case, 否则 is not used.

> 妻子: 客人六点半就会到，你六点以前回不回得来？
>
> *Qīzi:*   *Kèrén liùdiǎn bàn jiù huì dào, nǐ liù diǎn yǐqián huí bù huí de lái?*
>
> 丈夫: 一定回得来，**除非**路上堵车。(= **除非**路上堵车，**否则**我一定回得来。)
>
> *Zhàngfū:* *Yídìng huí de lái, chúfēi lùshàng dǔchē. (= Chúfēi lùshàng dǔchē, fǒuzé wǒ yídìng huí de lái.)*
>
> Wife: Our guests will be here at 6:30. Will you be able to come back before 6:00?
>
> Husband: I definitely can come back, **unless** there is a traffic jam.

e. **(如果)要 A, 除非 B**: In this pattern, A indicates the desired outcome, while B indicates the only way to achieve it. There is **no direct or literal translation for 除非** in this pattern. A widespread Chinese saying '若要人不知，除非己莫为' (*ruò yào rén bù zhī, chúfēi jǐ mò wéi*: literally, 'if you do not want other people to know about something, you can only achieve it by not doing it') is a good example for this pattern.

> 你得罪了王先生，**(如果)要**他原谅你，**除非**你亲自去向他道歉；光请花店送花到他家是没有用的。
>
> *Nǐ dézuì le Wáng xiānsheng, (rúguǒ) yào tā yuánliàng nǐ, chúfēi nǐ qīnzì qù xiàng tā dàoqiàn; guāng qǐng huādiàn sòng huā dào tā jiā shì méiyǒu yòng de.*
>
> You have offended Mr Wang. **If you want** him to forgive you, **the only way** (for him to forgive you) is for you to go and apologize to him personally. Simply asking the florist to deliver flowers to his house is of no use.

除了 *chúle*

除了 often appears with the **optional word 以外**. **除了 . . . (以外)** has two mutually exclusive meanings; one shows '**inclusion**' ('in addition to', 'besides', etc.); the other shows '**exclusion**' ('except'). It is the **context** as well as the structure of the **main sentence** that helps clarify the meaning of 除了 . . . (以外).

It should be noted that 除了 . . . (以外) should appear **before the main sentence**, although its counterpart in English can appear either before or after the main sentence. Also, the optional word 以外 can be **而外** (*érwài*) or simply **外**. In this section, 以外 is used.

a. To show 'inclusion', the **main sentence** should have **也** or **还**. Usually, what follows 除了 is the **known information**; the main sentence is used to give **additional** information.

(i) The subject can appear either before 除了 or in the main sentence, but it should not be used twice.

> A: 糟糕，外国客户来了！可是王先生今天病了，没有来上班。
> *Zāogāo! Wàiguó kèhù lái le! Kěshì Wáng xiānsheng jīntiān bìng le, méiyǒu lái shàng bān.*
>
> B: 别着急！**除了**王先生**以外**，我们**还**有两个会说英文的职员。
> *Bié zháojí! Chúle Wáng xiānsheng yǐwài, wǒmen hái yǒu liǎng ge huì shuō Yīngwén de zhíyuán.* (The sentence can also be 我们除了 王先生以外，还有两个会说英文的职员. But do not say 我们还 有两个会说英文的职员，除了王先生以外.)
>
> A: Oh, no! Our foreign clients are here! But Mr Wang is sick today; he did not come to work.
>
> B: Don't worry! **Besides** Mr Wang, we have two other (two more) employees who can speak English.

> A: 听说公司要派你去北京出差，真令人羡慕！（你）**除了**工作以 外，**还**(or 也)可以度假。
> *Tīngshuō gōngsī yào pài nǐ qù Běijīng chūchāi, zhēn lìng rén xiànmù! (Nǐ) chúle gōngzuò yǐwài, hái (or yě) kěyǐ dùjià.*
>
> B: 哪里有时间度假？只有两个星期，**除了**要去拜访十几个客户**以 外**，（我）**还**得去参观好几个工厂。
> *Nǎlǐ yǒu shíjiān dùjià? Zhǐ yǒu liǎng ge xīngqī, chúle yào qù bàifǎng shí jǐ ge kèhù yǐwài, (wǒ) hái děi qù cānguān hǎo jǐ ge gōngchǎng.*
>
> A: I heard that our company is going to send you to Beijing for a business trip. This really makes me envious. **Apart from** working, you can take a vacation.
>
> B: Where would I find the time for a vacation? There will only be two weeks. **In addition to** visiting more than ten clients, I **also** have to tour quite a few factories.

(ii) **Only** 也 can be used (and 还 cannot) when the 除了 ... 以外 part and the main sentence refer to **different subjects** but the same kind of verb.

> A: 大家都知道李先生反对这个议案，可是**除了**他**以外**，**还**有谁反 对？
> *Dàjiā dōu zhīdào Lǐ xiānsheng fǎnduì zhè ge yì'àn, kěshì chúle tā yǐwài, hái yǒu shéi fǎnduì?*
>
> B: **除了**李先生（反对）**以外**，张先生和王先生**也**反对，所以这个议 案最后没有通过。(Do not say 张先生和王先生还反对 since 李, 张 and 王 are different subjects.)
> *Chúle Lǐ xiānsheng (fǎnduì) yǐwài, Zhāng xiānsheng hé Wáng xiānsheng yě fǎnduì, suǒyǐ zhè ge yì'àn zuìhòu méiyǒu tōngguò.*
>
> A: Everybody knew that Mr Li was against this proposal. But who else, **besides him**, opposed it?
>
> B: **Besides** Mr Li, Mr Zhang and Mr Wang were **also** against it, so in the end this proposal was not approved.

In the following example, 也 (not 还) must be used in spite of the fact that the sentence only refers to one person (张大中). This is because 小提琴 (violin) must appear before 也, thus making 小提琴 and 钢琴 (piano) **two different subjects** from a grammatical perspective.

张大中很有音乐才华，他**除了**钢琴弹得很不错**以外**，小提琴**也**拉得很好。(It is improper to say 他除了钢琴弹得很不错以外，小提琴还拉得很好。)
Zhāng Dàzhōng hěn yǒu yīnyuè cáihuá, tā chúle gāngqín tán de hěn bú cuò yǐwài, xiǎo tíqín yě lā de hěn hǎo.
Zhang Dazhong is talented in music. **Besides** playing piano well, he **also** plays violin well.

b. To show 'exclusion', the **main sentence** should have words such as '**every**', '**all**' and '**others**', and 都 is necessary. If the main sentence has the word '**none**', then 都 is not used. What follows 除了 is the **exception**.

A: 这次考试实在太难了，所以**除了**高文生**以外**，**大家都**不及格。(exclusion)
   Zhè cì kǎoshì shízài tài nán le, suǒyǐ chúle Gāo Wénshēng yǐwài, dàjiā dōu bù jígé.
B: 你太夸张了！据我所知，**除了**高文生**以外**，李明、王中**也**考得不错。(inclusion)
   Nǐ tài kuāzhāng le! Jù wǒ suǒ zhī, chúle Gáo Wénshēng yǐwài, Lǐ Míng, Wáng Zhōng yě kǎo de bú cuò.
A: This exam was truly too hard, so **everybody** failed **except** Gao Wensheng.
B: You exaggerated it too much! From what I know, **in addition to** Gao Wensheng, Li Ming and Wang Zhong **also** did quite well.

A: 这学期的最后一天，我们的英文老师带了很多小礼物来送给学生。**除了**张美兰**以外**，**每个人都**得到一套漂亮的书签或者一个相框。(exclusion)
   Zhè xuéqī de zuìhòu yī tiān, wǒmen de Yīngwén lǎoshī dài le hěn duō xiǎo lǐwù lái sòng gěi xuéshēng. Chúle Zhāng Měilán yǐwài, měi ge rén dōu dédào yī tào piàoliàng de shūqiān huòzhě yī ge xiàngkuāng.
B: 张美兰没有得到礼物吗？
   Zhāng Měilán méiyǒu dédào lǐwù ma?
A: 有！她英文期末考了满分，所以**除了**书签、相框**以外**，她**还**得到了一本英文小说。(inclusion)
   Yǒu! Tā Yīngwén qīmò kǎo kǎo le mǎn fēn, suǒyǐ chúle shūqiān, xiàngkuāng yǐwài, tā hái dédào le yī běn Yīngwén xiǎoshuō.
B: 你们老师真大方！我们班的王大中英文也考了满分，所以我们老师也送了他一个礼物；可是**除**了他**以外**，**其他人**(can be 别人 or 我们)**都**没有得到礼物。(exclusion)
   Nǐmen lǎoshī zhēn dàfāng! Wǒmen bān de Wáng Dàzhōng Yīngwén yě kǎo le mǎn fēn, suǒyǐ wǒmen lǎoshī yě sòng le tā yī ge lǐwù; kěshì chúle tā yǐwài, qítā rén dōu méiyǒu dédào lǐwù.

A: On the last day of the semester, our English teacher brought many small gifts for the students. **With the exception of** Zhang Meilan, **everybody** received a set of pretty bookmarks or a picture frame.

B: Did Zhang Meilan not receive anything?

A: She did. She got a perfect score on the final exam; therefore, **in addition to** the bookmarks and the picture frame, she **also** received an English novel.

B: Your teacher was really generous! Wang Dazhong in my class also got a perfect score on the English test, so our teacher also gave him a gift. But **except** for him, **no one else** received any gifts.

(Scenario: A man has just shared some confidential information with a coworker.)

A: 这件事，**除了**你**以外，没有人**(can also be **没有别人**)知道，请你保持秘密。

   Zhè jiàn shì, chúle nǐ yǐwài, méiyǒu rén zhīdào, qǐng nǐ bǎochí mìmì.

B: 你放心！在公司里，**除了**你**以外**，我**没有别的**朋友，我去跟谁说？

   Nǐ fàngxīn! Zài gōngsī lǐ, chúle nǐ yǐwài, wǒ méiyǒu biéde péngyǒu, wǒ qù gēn shéi shuō?

A: **Nobody except** you knows about this matter. Please keep it a secret.

B: Don't worry. In the company, I have **no (other)** friends **except** you. Whom would I tell it to?

除了 . . . 就是 . . . *chúle . . . jiù shì . . .*

'除了 A 就是 B' is similar to '**不是 A 就是 B**' (either A or B) when it is used to show **two possibilities**, both of which are valid. It should be noted that 以外 **is not used** in this pattern.

→ See 不是 . . . 就是 . . . (*bú shì . . . jiù shì . . .*) for related information.

我哥哥上大学的时候，每天**不是**看电视，**就是**跟朋友出去玩，他很少学习，所以我以为大学生的日子很轻松；可是我自己上了大学以后，每天**除了**上课**就是**做实验，我累死了。

Wǒ gēge shàng dàxué de shíhòu, měi tiān bú shì kàn diànshì, jiù shì gēn péngyǒu chūqù wán, tā hěn shǎo xuéxí, suǒyǐ wǒ yǐwéi dà xuéshēng de rìzi hěn qīngsōng; kěshì wǒ zìjǐ shàng le dàxué yǐhòu, měi tiān chúle shàng kè jiù shì zuò shíyàn, wǒ lèi sǐ le.

When my older brother was in college, every day he **either** watched TV **or** went out with friends to have fun; he rarely studied; so I mistakenly thought that college life was easy. But since I myself started college, I have been **either** attending classes **or** doing experiments every day; I am so extremely tired (literally: tired to death).

A: 你去过南山夜市没有？想不想一起去逛逛？
  Nǐ qù guò Nán Shān yèshì méiyǒu? Xiǎng bù xiǎng yīqǐ qù guàng guàng?
B: 去过了，没意思；**除了**小吃，**就是**廉价的日用品；我不想去。
  Qù guo le, méi yìsi, chúle xiǎochī, jiù shi lián jià de rìyòng pǐn; wǒ bù xiǎng qù.
A: 可是我听说，**除了**小吃、日用品**以外**，**还**有各种好玩的游戏，我要去玩游戏。(inclusion)
  Kěshì wǒ tīngshuō, chúle xiǎochī, rìyòng pǐn yǐwài, hái yǒu gè zhǒng hǎowán de yóuxì, wǒ yào qù wán yóuxì.
A: Have you been to the South Hill night market? Would you like to go with me to have a look around?
B: I have been there, and it was boring. There were **either** snacks **or** cheap everyday items. I don't want to go.
A: But I heard that, **in addition to** snacks and everyday items, there are all kinds of fun games. I want to go play those games.

从来 *cónglái*

从来 implies 'all the time' but is nearly always followed by a **negative word**, such as 不 or 没有. Although 从来不 and 从来没有 are generally translated as 'never', they can have different implications depending on the **time frame** of the sentence. Because the Chinese language does not have tenses, the accurate interpretation of a sentence with 从来 can only be achieved by paying attention to the time frame of the situation. In addition, whether to use 不 or 没有 after 从来 depends on the context.

a. 从来不 refers to a **habitual** or **constant** situation **regardless of the time frame**.

  (i) It often implies one's **conscious choice or effort** to make the situation constant.

  我**从来不**吃没有洗过的水果，也**从来不**喝汽水。
  Wǒ cónglái bù chī méiyǒu xǐ guo de shuǐguǒ, yě cónglái bù hē qìshuǐ.
  I **never** eat fruit that has not been washed, and I **never** drink soda.

  A: 小李说的话，我**从来不**相信。
    Xiǎo Lǐ shuō de huà, wǒ cónglái bù xiāngxìn.
  B: 为什么呢？小李这个人**从来不**说谎。
    Wèi shénme ne? Xiǎo Lǐ zhè ge rén cónglái bù shuō huǎng.
  A: I **never** believe anything Little Li says.
  B: Why? Little Li **never** lies.

  If a person's conscious effort is **not** strongly indicated in the situation, **向来** (*xiànglái*) or **一向** (*yīxiàng*) might be a better choice of word than 从来.

我虽然很喜欢流行音乐，可是我**从来不**去听流行音乐会，因为我**一向(向来)不**喜欢去人多的地方。(不去 suggests a conscious effort, whereas 不喜欢 does not.)

Wǒ suīrán hěn xǐhuān liúxíng yīnyuè, kěshì wǒ cónglái bú qù tīng liúxíng yīnyuè huì, yīnwèi wǒ yīxiàng (xiànglái) bù xǐhuān qù rén duō de dìfāng.

Although I like pop music very much, I **never** go to pop music concerts, because I **never** like to go to places with many people.

→ See 向来 (*xiànglái*) and 一向 (*yīxiàng*) for more information.

(ii) The habitual or constant situation can refer to a **past time frame**. Learners should not confuse 从来不 in the past time frame with the expression 从来没有 . . . 过 (see below).

我认识小李以前，**从来不知道**世界上有会说十种语言的人。

Wǒ rènshì Xiǎo Lǐ yǐqián, cónglái bù zhīdào shìjiè shàng yǒu huì shuō shí zhǒng yǔyán de rén.

Before I met Xiao Li, I **had never known** that there were people in this world that could speak ten languages.

我小时候，我妈妈对我很严格；她**从来不**给我**买**太贵的玩具，也**从来不让**我去朋友家过夜。

Wǒ xiǎo shíhòu, wǒ māma duì wǒ hěn yángé; tā cónglái bù gěi wǒ mǎi tài guì de wánjù, yě cónglái bú ràng wǒ qù péngyǒu jiā guò yè.

When I was little, my mother was very strict. She **never bought** me (she **would never** buy me) toys that were too expensive, and she **never allowed** me (she **would never** allow me) to spend the night at a friend's house.

b. **从来没有 . . . 过**: 过 in this expression is not optional. It indicates that a certain situation (or experience) **never occurred once**. Therefore, it is similar to 没有 . . . 过 in meaning, but is stronger in tone.

English speakers often associate this structure with the present perfect tense. However, the following examples show that the **time frame** (either clearly indicated in the sentence or implied in the context) is an important factor in deciding the proper tense corresponding to a 从来没有 . . . 过 expression.

(i) 从来没有 + verb + 过 shows that one **does not have a certain experience (even once)** during a **specific time frame**. Whether or not one is experiencing it for the first time when the sentence is uttered is decided by the context. If one is experiencing something **for the first time** when the sentence is uttered, an **optional** 以前 can be used.

The following scenarios illustrate the fact that 从来没有 + verb + 过 can be translated into English by using **different tenses**. It is important to observe the **context** and **time frame** of the sentence in order to arrive at an accurate interpretation.

(Scenario: Two people are discussing going out to eat sushi **the next day**.)

A: 明天我请你去吃寿司，怎么样？

 Míngtiān wǒ qǐng nǐ qù chī shòusī, zěnme yàng?

B: 我**从来没有**吃**过**生鱼, 所以我不知道我会不会喜欢吃寿司。

 Wǒ cónglái méiyǒu chī guo shēng yú, suǒyǐ wǒ bù zhīdào wǒ huì bú huì xǐhuān chī shòusī.

A: 我**从来没有**碰**过**一个不喜欢吃寿司的人，所以我想你也一定会喜欢吃。

 Wǒ cónglái méiyǒu pèng guo yī ge bù xǐhuān chī shòusī de rén, suǒyǐ wǒ xiǎng nǐ yě yīdìng huì xǐhuān chī.

A: I will take you out to eat sushi tomorrow, how about it?

B: I **have never had** raw fish, so I don't know whether I will like sushi or not.

A: I **have never met** anyone who does not like sushi, so I think you will definitely like it, too.

(Scenario: Two people **are presently eating** sushi at a Japanese restaurant. Note that the optional word 以前 can be used in this scenario.)

A: 这是你**第一次**吃寿司，对不对？

 Zhè shì nǐ dì yī cì chī shòusī, duì bú buì?

B: 对，我**(以前)从来没有**吃**过**生鱼。

 Duì, wǒ (yǐqián) cónglái méiyǒu chī guo shēng yú.

A: This is your **first time** having sushi, isn't that right?

B: That is correct! I **have never had** raw fish **before**.

(Scenario: A girl is asking a friend about her fondness for sushi.)

A: 我常常看到你吃寿司，你很喜欢吃寿司，对不对？

 Wǒ chángcháng kàndào nǐ chī shòusī, nǐ hěn xǐhuān chī shòusī, duì bú duì?

B: 对，因为我男朋友是日本人。可是其实我认识他以前，**从来没有**吃**过**寿司。

 Duì, yīnwèi wǒ nán péngyǒu shì Rìběn rén. Kěshì qíshí wǒ rènshì tā yǐqián, cónglái méiyǒu chī guo shòusī.

A: I often see you having sushi. You like sushi very much, isn't that right?

B: That is correct. (I like sushi) because my boyfriend is Japanese. But actually before I met him, I **had never had** sushi.

(Scenario: Wang lived in Japan for two years and has just returned home. A friend asks him about eating sushi in Japan.)

朋友:　你在日本吃到的寿司一定很新鲜、地道吧？

Péngyǒu:　*Nǐ zài Rìběn chī dào de shòusī yīdìng hěn xīnxiān, dìdào ba?*

王:　你可能不相信，可是我在日本的时候，**从来没有**吃**过**寿司。

Wáng:　*Nǐ kěnéng bù xiāngxìn, kěshì wǒ zài Rìběn de shíhòu, cónglái méiyǒu chī guo shòusī.*

朋友:　是吗？为什么？

Péngyǒu:　*Shì ma? Wèi shénme?*

王:　因为我不喜欢吃寿司。

Wáng:　*Yīnwèi wǒ bù xǐhuān chī shòusī.*

朋友:　真的吗？我**从来没有**碰**过**一个不喜欢吃寿司的人，你是**第一个**。

Péngyǒu:　*Zhēn de ma? Wǒ cónglái méiyǒu pèng guo yī ge bù xǐhuān chī shòusī de rén, nǐ shì dì yī ge.*

Friend:　The sushi you had in Japan must have been very fresh and authentic.

Wang:　You probably won't believe it, but when I was in Japan, I **never had** sushi.

Friend:　Is that so? Why (not)?

Wang:　Because I don't like sushi.

Friend:　Really? I **have never met** anyone who doesn't like sushi. You are **the first one** (that I have met who does not like sushi).

(ii) Conscious choice/effort in **past time frame** (从来不) vs. **past occurrence/experiences** (从来没有 . . . 过): both can be past tense in English. It is important to observe the **subtle difference** in order to accurately interpret the speaker's attitude.

小李上高中的时候，上学**从来不**迟到；可是自从进了大学以后，他的学习态度放松了，上课**从来没有**准时**过**。(从来不迟到 indicates conscious effort; 从来没有准时过 indicates occurrence.)

Xiǎo Lǐ shàng gāozhōng de shíhòu, shàngxué cónglái bù chí dào; kěshì zìcóng jìn le dàxué yǐhòu, tā de xuéxí tàidù fàngsōng le, shàngkè cónglái méiyǒu zhǔnshì guo.

When Little Li was in high school, he **was never** late for class. But ever since he entered college, his learning attitude has become relaxed, and he **has never been** on time for class.

我以前住的地方离学校很近，所以我**从来没有**迟到**过**。(past occurrence)

Wǒ yǐqián zhù de dìfāng lí xuéxiào hěn jìn, suǒyǐ wǒ cónglái méiyǒu chídào guo.

Where I used to live was very close to school, so I **was never** late for class.

A: 我小时候，我爸妈**从来不**给我买任何贵的东西，因为他们怕我养成浪费的习惯。(This indicates conscious choice in a past time frame.)

Wǒ xiǎo shíhòu, wǒ bàmā cónglái bù gěi wǒ mǎi rènhé guì de dōngxi, yīnwèi tāmen pà wǒ yǎngchéng làngfèi de xíguàn.

B: 我小时候，我爸妈也**从来没有**给我买**过**任何贵的东西，因为我家很穷。(This indicates past occurrence.)

Wǒ xiǎo shíhòu, wǒ bàmā yě cónglái méiyǒu gěi wǒ mǎi guo rènhé guì de dōngxi, yīnwèi wǒ jiā hěn qióng.

A: When I was little, my parents **never bought** me (**would never buy me**) anything expensive, because they were afraid that I would develop the habit of being wasteful.

B: When I was little, my parents also **never bought** me anything expensive, because my family was poor (had no money).

(iii)   An adjective can be used in the '从来没有 ... 过' pattern.

王先生进了现在这家公司以后，工作压力重大，他也不注重饮食，所以血压有时候太高，有时候太低，**从来没有**正常**过**。

Wáng xiānsheng jìn le xiànzài zhè jiā gōngsī yǐhòu, gōngzuò yālì zhòng dà, tā yě bú zhùzhòng yǐnshí, suǒyǐ xuěyā yǒu shíhòu tài gāo, yǒu shíhòu tài dī, cónglái méiyǒu zhèngcháng guo.

Ever since Mr Wang entered his current company, he has had major pressures from his work, and he also has not paid attention to his diet, so his blood pressure is sometimes too high, and sometimes too low; it (his blood pressure) **has never been** normal.

c.   '**从来没有** + 这么 (**or** 那么) + **adjective** + 过' is a specific pattern indicating that the situation (the adjective) **has never existed** before and is happening for **the first time**.

我儿子考上了最好的大学，我觉得自己**从来没有这么**高兴**过**。

Wǒ érzi kǎo shàng le zuì hǎo de dàxué, wǒ juéde zìjǐ cónglái méiyǒu zhème gāoxìng guo.

My son has tested into the best college; I feel like I **have never been this** happy **before.**

今年的天气很不正常；已经十二月了，大家都还穿短袖的衣服，这里的冬天**从来没有这么**暖和**过**。

Jīnnián de tiānqì hěn bú zhèngcháng; yǐjīng shí'èr yuè le, dàjiā dōu hái chuān duǎnxiù de yīfú, zhèlǐ de dōngtiān cónglái méiyǒu zhème nuǎnhuó guo.

The weather this year is not normal. It is already December; everyone is still wearing short-sleeved clothes. The winter here **has never been this** warm **before.**

Without 这么, the pattern '**从来没有** + **adjective** + **过**' conveys a **completely different** meaning. The following two examples with two opposite adjectives 好 (*hǎo*: good) and 坏 (*huài*: bad) actually convey similar meanings.

自从王中的女朋友跟他分手以后，王中的心情就**从来没有**好**过**。
Zìcóng Wáng Zhōng de nǚ péngyòu gēn tā fēnshǒu yǐhòu, Wáng Zhōng de xīnqíng jiù cónglái méiyǒu hǎo guo.
Ever since Wang Zhong's girlfriend broke up with him, Wang Zhong's mood **has never been** good.

王中的女朋友跟他分手了，王中的心情可以说**从来没有这么**坏**过**。
Wáng Zhōng de nǚ péngyǒu gēn tā fēnshǒu le, Wáng Zhōng de xīnqíng kěyǐ shuō cónglái méiyǒu zhème huài guo.
Wang Zhong's girlfriend has broken up with him; it can be said that Wang Zhong's mood **has never been this** bad (**before**).

Related expression

再也不 . . . 了 *zài yě bù . . . le* and 再也没有 . . . 过了 *zài yě méiyǒu . . . guo le*

Both 再也不 . . . 了 and 再也没有 . . . 过了 are expressions that indicate '**never**'. However, they are used in **different contexts** and have **different connotations** from 从来不/从来没有. Learners should observe the context before choosing the proper expression for 'never'.

→ See 再也不 . . . 了 (*zài yě bù . . . le*) and 再也没有 . . . 过了 (*zài yě méiyǒu . . . guo le*) for more information.

到底 *dàodǐ*

到底 is an **adverb** and is typically used to **emphasize one's point**. This section discusses its two major functions.

a.   到底 is used in a **question** to **emphasize** the inquiry in order to give the question **a stronger tone**. It usually shows the speaker's **impatience** or **strong puzzlement**.
    A **common mistake** made by learners who are English speakers is to use 就是 where 到底 is the correct word. This is because the closest counterpart in English for 到底 used in a question is '**exactly**'.

(i)   到底 normally appears before the predicate of the sentence. Since its function is to strengthen the inquiry, **the question** or puzzlement must have **already been mentioned or be pre-existent in the context**.
    It should be noted that 到底 **cannot** be used in a question with 吗.

(Scenario: A woman is not happy that a visitor will not identify himself.)

A: 你是谁？(到底 cannot be used because this is the first time the question has been asked.)
   Nǐ shì shéi?

B: 你可能还不认识我，不过，我认识你女儿。
   Nǐ kěnéng hái bú rènshì wǒ, búguò, wǒ rènshì nǐ nǚ'ér.

A: 你**到底**是**谁**？快说！
   Nǐ dàodǐ shì shéi? Kuài shuō!

A: Who are you?

B: You probably don't know me yet, but I know your daughter.

A: **Who exactly** are you? Tell me now!

A: 奇怪！为什么有两个价钱标签？你去问一下店员，这本书**到底多少**钱？(到底 can be used because the puzzlement already exists.)
   Qíguài! Wèi shénme yǒu liǎng ge jiàqián biāoqiān? Nǐ qù wèn yīxià diànyuán, zhè běn shū dàodǐ duōshǎo qián?

B: 你想买吗？
   Nǐ xiǎng mǎi ma?

A: 我也不知道，很难决定。
   Wǒ yě bù zhīdào, hěn nán juédìng.

B: 你**到底想不想**买？(Do not say 你到底想买吗？) 如果根本不想买，那我就不用去问了。
   Nǐ dàodǐ xiǎng bù xiǎng mǎi? Rúguǒ gēnběn bù xiǎng mǎi, nà wǒ jiù búyòng qù wèn le.

A: Strange! Why are there two price labels? Go ask the clerk **exactly how much** this book is.

B: Do you want to buy it?

A: I don't know, either. It's hard to decide.

B: (**Exactly**) do you want to buy it **or not**? If you don't want to buy it at all, then I don't have to go ask.

(Scenario: Two tourists need to find out how to go to the train station, but they have received conflicting information from two local people.)
你看，那里有一个警察。我们再去问一下，去火车站**到底怎么**走？
Nǐ kàn, nàlǐ yǒu yī ge jǐngchá. Wǒmen zài qù wèn yīxià, qù huǒchēzhàn dàodǐ zěnme zǒu?
Look, there is a policeman over there. Let's go ask again **exactly how** to go to the train station.

老师: 你昨天为什么没有来上课？
Lǎoshī: *Nǐ zuótiān wèi shénme méiyǒu lái shàng kè?*
学生: 说来话长，我不知道从哪里开始。
Xuéshēng: *Shuō lái huà cháng, wǒ bù zhīdào cóng nǎlǐ kāishǐ.*
老师: 快说，**到底为什么**？(The full sentence is 你**到底为什么**没有来上课？)
Lǎoshī: *Kuài shuō, dàodǐ wèi shénme?*

Teacher:	Why did you not come to class yesterday?
Student:	It's a long story. I don't know where to start.
Teacher:	Tell me now. **Exactly why** did you not come?

(ii) 到底 can be put directly at the beginning of a sentence if the subject is the question word e.g. 哪 (*nǎ*: which), 哪里 (*nǎlĭ*: where), 谁 (*shéi*: who).

(Scenario: Two tourists need to find a convenience store. They have been walking around but have not been able to find one.)
奇怪！**到底哪里**才有便利商店？（Do not say 哪里到底才有便利商店？）
Qíguài! Dàodĭ nǎlĭ cái yǒu biànlì shāngdiàn?
Strange! **Where in the world** is there (can we find) a convenience store?

A:	你的车在哪里？
	Nĭ de chē zài nǎlĭ?
B:	在那棵树下，那辆红的。
	Zài nà kē shù xià, nà liàng hóng de.
A:	那棵树下的两辆车都是红的；**到底哪**辆是你的？（Do not say 哪辆到底是你的？）
	Nà kē shù xià de liǎng liàng chē dōu shì hóng de, dàodĭ nǎ liàng shì nĭ de?
A:	Where is your car?
B:	Under that tree. The red one.
A:	Both cars under that tree are red. **Exactly which** one is yours?

b. When 到底 is not used in a question, it is often translated as '**after all**' or '**in the end**'; and it has three major functions.
   In the following examples, 到底 is used both in questions and in statements. It is important to observe **the structures and contexts** of sentences with 到底 in order to arrive at an accurate interpretation.

(i) '**到底是** + noun' is used to emphasize the **special traits** of the noun. The implication is that, despite other considerations, such traits are what led to an action or a phenomenon. The translation is often '**after all**', while the undertone of '**after all is said and done**' or '**no matter what**' is subtly implied.

(Scenario: A young man frequently gets himself in financial trouble. His father has vowed not to help him out anymore. Now he is in trouble again; his mother is pleading his case.)

爸爸:	我已经说过，我不会再帮他了。
Bàba:	*Wǒ yǐjīng shuō guo, wǒ bú huì zài bāng tā le.*
妈妈:	你**到底是**他的爸爸；要是你不帮他，还会有谁帮他呢？
Māma:	*Nĭ dàodĭ shì tā bàba; yàoshì nĭ bù bāng tā, hái huì yǒu shéi bāng tā ne?*

爸爸: 我**到底**要帮他**几**次他才学得会教训呢？

Bàba: *Wǒ dàodǐ yào bāng tā jǐ cì tā cái xué de huì jiàoxùn ne?*

妈妈: 他**到底**还**是**个小孩子，再给他一次机会吧，他慢慢地就会懂事了。

Māma: *Tā dàodǐ hái shì ge xiǎo háizi, zài gěi tā yī cì jīhuì ba! Tā màn màn de jiù huì dǒngshì le.*

Father: I have already said that I will not help him again.

Mother: You are his father **after all**. If you don't help him, who else will?

Father: **Exactly how many** times do I have to help him before he finally learns his lesson?

Mother: He is still a child **after all**. Give him another chance. He will gradually (slowly) become mature.

(ii) 到底 can appear **before a verb or an adjective** to emphasize one's point. Similar to the use of 到底是, the point being emphasized is the special trait(s) that explains a phenomenon.

(Scenario: The business partner of the aforementioned young man eagerly waits to find out whether or not the father will help them out.)

A: 快告诉我，你爸爸**到底**愿不愿意帮我们？

Kuài gàosù wǒ, nǐ bàba dàodǐ yuàn bú yuànyì bāng wǒmen?

B: 他跟我妈妈说，愿意再帮一次。

Tā gēn wǒ māma shuō, yuànyì zài bāng yī cì.

A: 太好了！血**到底**浓于水。

Tài hǎo le! Xuě dàodǐ nóng yú shuǐ.

A: Hurry and tell me! **Is** your father willing to help us?

B: He has told my mother that he is willing to help one more time.

A: Great! Blood is thicker than water **after all**.

A: 王先生得了一个怪病，看了好几个医生，没有一个医生知道他**到底**得了**什么**病。所以他上星期去看了你介绍的那个中医，没想到只吃了两天的药就好了。

Wáng xiānsheng dé le yī ge guài bìng, kàn le hǎo jǐ ge yīshēng, méiyǒu yī ge yīshēng zhīdào tā dàodǐ dé le shénme bìng. Suǒyǐ tā shàng ge xīngqī qù kàn le nǐ jièshào de nà ge Zhōngyī, méi xiǎngdào zhǐ chī le liǎng tiān de yào jiù hǎo le.

B: 李大夫**到底**有经验，什么怪病他都见过，也都治得好。

Lǐ dàifu dàodǐ yǒu jīngyàn, shénme guài bìng tā dōu jiàn guo, yě dōu zhì de hǎo.

A: Mr Wang had got some weird disease. He had seen quite a few doctors, but not one doctor knew **exactly what** he had. So last week he went to see the Chinese herbal medicine doctor you had recommended; who would have thought he would be cured after taking his medicine for only two days.

B: Dr Li is, **after all**, very experienced. He has seen all kinds of weird diseases and he can cure anything.

It should be noted that it is acceptable, albeit less common, to put 到底 at the **beginning of the sentence** without altering the meaning or emphasis.

(iii) 到底 can be used to describe **the result after a long wait, much effort or many obstacles**. The implication is that there may have been some uncertainty as to whether or not the result would happen or what the result might be.

A: 张文向王小兰求婚，小兰考虑了很久，**到底**还是拒绝他了。
Zhāng Wén xiàng Wáng Xiǎolán qiúhūn, Xiǎolán kǎolǜ le hěn jiǔ, dàodǐ háishì jùjué tā le.

B: 什么？张文人品好，又有好工作，他**到底**有**什么**让王小兰不满意的地方？
Shénme? Zhāng Wén rénpǐn hǎo, yòu yǒu hǎo gōngzuò, tā dàodǐ yǒu shénme ràng Wáng Xiǎolán bù mǎnyì de dìfāng?

A: 别忘了，张文**到底**比王小兰大了快二十岁。
Bié wàng le, Zhāng Wén dàodǐ bǐ Wáng Xiǎolán dà le kuài èrshí suì.

A: Zhang Wen had proposed to Wang Xiaolan; Xiaolan thought about it for a long time; **in the end**, she still rejected him.

B: What? Zhang Wen has a good moral character and a good job. **Exactly what** is it about him that makes Wang Xiaolan not happy (not satisfied with him)?

A: Don't forget that Zhang Wen is, **after all**, almost 20 years older than Wang Xiaolan.

(Scenario: A man has agreed to meet his friends at the train station so that the three of them can ride the train together to another town. He is the one that has the tickets for all of them and he is terribly late.)

A: 哎呀！你**到底**来了！我们都急得要命，以为你不来了！
Àiya! Nǐ dàodǐ lái le! Wǒmen dōu jí de yàomìng, yǐwéi nǐ bù lái le.

B: 是呀！你**到底**是被**什么**事耽误了？
Shì ya! Nǐ dàodǐ shì bèi shénme shì dānwù le?

A: Aiya (a Chinese exclamation)! You are here **finally (after all)**. We were both anxious to death. We thought you were not coming.

B: Yeah! **What in the world** caused you to be delayed?

Related expression

究竟 *jiūjìng*

究竟 is similar to 到底 in meaning and usage. An important difference between them is that **究竟 is a more formal word** than 到底; as such, 究竟 is used more often in written communication and less often in casual, conversational speech.

得 *dé/děi*

得 has various grammatical functions (verb, structural particle and modal verb) and three different pronunciations (*de*, *dé* and *děi*). Its proper pronunciation in a sentence depends on how it is used. This section discusses its major uses as a verb and a modal verb. Its use as a structural particle, pronounced *de* (i.e. complement of state, complement of potential), is not part of the discussion below.

a. When it is used as a verb, the pronunciation is *dé*; its definitions include 'to obtain', 'to acquire', etc. but there does not seem to be a direct English translation for it. It is also used to say someone has got sick or developed an illness.

张文真有才华，这学期他参加了演讲比赛跟舞蹈比赛，都**得**了第一名。
Zhāng Wén zhēn yǒu cáihuá; zhè xuéqī tā cānjiā le yǎnjiǎng bǐsài gēn wǔdǎo bǐsài, dōu dé le dì yī míng.
Zhang Wen is really talented. This semester, he participated in a speech contest and a dance competition; and he took home (he **got**/he **received**) the first prizes for both.

王先生不注重饮食，也不常运动，前几天去检查身体，医生说他**得**了糖尿**病**。
Wáng xiānsheng bú zhùzhòng yǐnshí, yě bù cháng yùndòng; qián jǐ tiān qù jiǎnchá shēntǐ, yīshēng shuō tā dé le táng niào bìng.
Mr Wang does not pay attention to his diet and he exercises infrequently. He went to have a physical check-up a few days ago, and the doctor told him that he is diabetic (he has **developed** diabetes).

The expression is sometimes 得到 (*dédào*). The implication is 'to acquire or attain something through work or effort'. 到 is the complement of result in the expression.

李明的爸爸对他的期望很高；李明用功学习，目的只是要**得到**他爸爸的赞美。
Lǐ Míng de bàba duì tā de qīwàng hěn gāo; Lǐ Míng yònggōng xuéxí, mùdì zhǐ shì yào dédào tā bàba de zànměi.
Li Ming's father has high expectations of him. Li Ming studies hard, and his purpose is only **to receive (to obtain)** praise from his father.

b. When 得 is pronounced as *děi*, it is a modal verb, meaning 'must', or 'to have to', indicating **duty/obligation** or **necessity**. It is used in casual, conversational speech. (A modal verb is typically followed by a regular verb.)

A: 晚上想不想一起去看电影？
   Wǎnshàng xiǎng bù xiǎng yīqǐ qù kàn diànyǐng?
B: 明天有一个考试，今天晚上我**得**在家准备考试。
   Míngtiān yǒu yī ge kǎoshì, jīntiān wǎnshàng wǒ děi zài jiā zhǔnbèi kǎoshì.
A: 是什么考试？
   Shì shénme kǎoshì?
B: 生词考试。上次我没有准备，所以不及格。这次我**得**考及格，否则老师会非常不高兴。
   Shēngcí kǎoshì. Shàng cì wǒ méiyǒu zhǔnbèi, suǒyǐ bù jígé. Zhè cì wǒ děi kǎo jígé, fǒuzé lǎoshī huì fēicháng bù gāoxìng.
A: Do you feel like going to a movie together this evening?
B: I have a test tomorrow; I **have to** study for the test at home this evening.
A: What test is it?
B: It is a vocabulary test. I did not study last time and so I failed the test. This time I **have to** pass it; otherwise, the teacher will be extremely unhappy.

It should be noted that 得 **cannot** be used in an **affirmative-negative** question. This means that 得不得 is incorrect. Use 吗 or 要不要 for a yes-no question. (One of the several definitions of 要 is 'must'.) Furthermore, 得 **cannot** be used to give a **short answer**.

A: 明天的会，新来的员工**得**参加**吗**？ (Do not say 得不得参加.)
   Míngtiān de huì, xīnlái de yuángōng děi cānjiā ma?
B: 大家都**得**参加。(Do not simply say 得.)
   Dàjiā dōu děi cānjiā.
A: 那新来的员工**要不要**发言？ (Do not say 得不得发言.)
   Nà xīnlái de yuángōng yào bú yào fāyán?
B: 参加的人都**得**发言。
   Cānjiā de rén dōu děi fāyán.
A: Do new employees **have to** attend the meeting tomorrow?
B: Everybody **has to** attend.
A: Then do new employees **have to** speak at the meeting?
B: All attendees **must** speak.

The **negative form** is not 不得, but 不必 (*búbì*) or 不用 (*búyòng*), which mean 'no need to', 'to not have to', 'it is not necessary to', etc.

A: 明天的午餐会，你去不去？
   Míngtiān de wǔcān huì, nǐ qù bú qù?
B: 一个人**得**交十块钱，所以我不想去。
   Yī ge rén děi jiāo shí kuài qián, suǒyǐ wǒ bù xiǎng qù.

A: 我们是新来的员工，所以我们**不必**(or **不用**)交钱。
   Wǒmen shì xīnlái de yuángōng, suǒyǐ wǒmen búbì (or *búyòng*) *jiāo qián.*
A: Are you going to tomorrow's lunch get-together?
B: Each person **must** pay ten *kuai*, so I don't want to go.
A: We are new employees, so we **don't have to** pay.

→ See 必须 (*bìxū*) for related information.

c. When 得 is pronounced *dé*, it means '**can**'. It has two connotations: in a positive sentence, it implies '**possibility**'; in a negative sentence, it implies '**no permission**'. It is not used in conversational speech and is normally used **in writing** to make announcements about **regulations**.
   The negative form is 不得; it is the same as 不可以, meaning 'to not be allowed', 'to be prohibited', etc.

无停车证者**不得**在此停车；违者最高**得**罚五十元。(元 is the written form for 块.)
Wú tíngchē zhèng zhě bù dé zài cǐ tíngchē; wéi zhě zuì gāo dé fá wǔshí yuán.
= 没有停车证的人**不可以**在这里停车；违反规定的人最高**可能会**被罚五十元。
= *Méiyǒu tíngchē zhèng de rén bù kěyǐ zài zhèlǐ tíngchē; wéifǎn guīdìng de rén zuì gāo kěnéng huì bèi fá wǔshí yuán.*
Those who do not have parking permits **are not allowed to** park here. Violators **may be** fined up to (as high as) 50 *yuan*.

Related expression

不得不 *bù dé bù*

不得不 and 只好 (*zhǐhǎo*) are similar in meaning and implication. Both imply 'being forced by the circumstances to do something' or 'having no choice but to do something'. 得 in this expression cannot be pronounced *děi*.

张明想到瀑布下面去照相，可是前面有一个栏杆，还有一个牌子，写着"游客**不得**跨越"，所以他**不得不**(= 只好)停住，不再往前走了。
Zhāng Míng xiǎng dào pùbù xiàmiàn qù zhàoxiàng; kěshì qiánmiàn yǒu yī ge lángān, hái yǒu yī ge páizi, xiě zhe 'Yóukè bù dé kuà yuè', suǒyǐ tā bù dé bù (= zhǐhǎo) tíng zhù, bú zài wàng qián zǒu le.
Zhang Ming wanted to go to the bottom of the waterfalls to take pictures. But ahead of him there was a fence and also a sign that said 'Visitors **are not allowed to** cross the fence'; so he **had to** (he **was forced to**; he **had no choice but to**) stop moving forward.

Because the surface structures of sentences with 得 as a modal verb are similar, learners must pay special attention to the context in order to avoid misinterpretation.

Although 得 (*děi*) and 不得不 can both be translated as 'have to', they have **different connotations** and are used in different contexts.

> A: 你看那个牌子，写着"住宅区**不得**超速"，可是这里又不是住宅区。
>
> *Nǐ kàn nà ge páizi, xiě zhe 'zhùzhài qū bù dé chāosù', kěshì zhèlǐ yòu bú shì zhùzhái qū.*
>
> B: 过了马路就是住宅区了。所以你过了红绿灯以后，就**得**开慢一点。
>
> *Guò le mǎlù jiù shì zhùzhái qū le. Suǒyǐ nǐ guò le hóng lǜ dēng yǐhòu, jiù děi kāi màn yīdiǎn.*
>
> A: 你放心，我知道。这个城市交通警察很多；不管有多紧急的事，也**不得不**照规定慢慢开。
>
> *Nǐ fàngxīn, wǒ zhīdào. Zhè ge chéngshì jiāotōng jǐngchá hěn duō; bùguǎn yǒu duō jǐnjí de shì, yě bù dé bú zhào guīdìng màn màn kāi.*
>
> A: Look at that sign, 'Speeding **is prohibited** in residential areas'. But this is not a residential area.
>
> B: It will be the residential area once you cross the main road. So after you cross the traffic lights, you **have to** drive a little slower.
>
> A: Don't worry, I know. There are many traffic policemen in this city. No matter how urgent your business is, you **have to** drive slowly according to regulations.

. . . 的话 *dehuà*

. . . 的话 is not a stand-alone word or expression; it can be considered a **suffix** because it always follows another word, phrase or sentence. In addition, it is **optional**; that is, the absence of it does not affect the meaning of the sentence or phrase. It is typically used in casual, conversational speech.

Words (and expressions including these words) such as 否则 (*fǒuzé*), 不然 (*bùrán*) and 要是 . . . (*yàoshì*) can be used with 的话. Note that 的话 cannot immediately follow 要是. Also, when . . . 的话 is used, 要是 becomes optional.

→ See 否则 (*fǒuzé*), 不然 (*bùrán*) and 要是 (*yàoshì*) for more information.

In very casual speech, . . . 的话 is sometimes used to **bring up a conversational topic that has** already **been mentioned** in the interaction.

> A: 你知不知道王家的两个孩子上哪个大学？
>
> *Nǐ zhī bù zhīdào Wáng jiā de liǎng ge háizi shàng nǎ ge dàxué?*
>
> B: 他们的儿子上北京大学；女儿**的话**，我就不知道了。
>
> *Tāmen de érzi shàng Běijīng Dàxué; nǚ'ér dehuà, wǒ jiù bù zhīdào le.*
>
> A: Do you know which universities the Wang family's two children attend?
>
> B: Their son goes to Beijing University. **As to** their daughter, I don't know (which university she goes to).

地方 *dìfāng*

The basic definition of 地方 is 'place', which usually refers to a **physical or geographical location**. However, the discussion below will be on the use of 地方 that conveys a **less concrete** meaning.

a. It can be used to refer to **parts of one's body**. This is particularly true when it is used to describe one's illness such as **aches and pains**; it can also be used to describe one's **physical features**.

(Scenario: A physician wants to find out what is bothering a patient.)
医生: **什么地方**不舒服啊？
Yīshēng: Shénme dìfāng bù shūfú a?
病人: 胃不舒服，背也常常会痛。
Bìngrén: Wèi bù shūfú, bèi yě chángcháng huì tòng.
医生 (pressing **different parts** of the patient's back):   **这个地方**痛不痛？
            这个地方呢？
Yīshēng: Zhè ge dìfāng tòng bú tòng? Zhè gè dìfāng ne?
Doctor: What's bothering you? (Literally: **What parts** of you are ill?)
Patient: My stomach is not feeling right; also my back often aches.
Doctor: Does it hurt **here**? How about **here**?

A: 你觉得王小姐漂亮不漂亮？
     Nǐ juéde Wáng xiǎojiě piàoliàng bú piàoliàng?
B: 很不错，她只有**一个地方**不漂亮。
     Hěn búcuò, tā zhǐ yǒu yī ge dìfāng bú piàoliàng?
A: 是吗？什么**地方**？
     Shì ma? Shénme dìfāng?
B: 她的嘴太大了。
     Tā de zuǐ tài dà le.
A: 什么？我觉得她的嘴是她最漂亮的**地方**。
     Shénme? Wǒ juéde tā de zuǐ shì tā zuì piàoliàng de dìfāng.
A: Do you think Miss Wang is pretty?
B: Not bad; there is only **one part (physical feature)** of her that is not pretty.
A: Is that so? **What part** (Which feature)?
B: Her mouth is too large.
A: What? I think her mouth is her prettiest **part (feature)**.

b. It means 'a **point**' or 'points' in one's **opinion, argument**, etc.

A: 您的观点，有几个**地方**，我不同意。
     Nín de guāndiǎn, yǒu jǐ ge dìfāng, wǒ bù tóngyì.
B: 是吗？哪些**地方**？欢迎你提出来跟我讨论。
     Shì ma? Nǎxiē dìfāng? Huānyíng nǐ tí chū lái gēn wǒ tǎolùn.

A:　There are several **points in your opinion** that I do not agree with.

B:　Is that so? Which **points**? You are welcome to bring them forward and have a discussion with me.

c.　It is used in a **more abstract** sense, and can be defined as '**feature**', '**trait**' or '**characteristic**'.

李小姐长得不漂亮，而且很胖，可是追她的人很多，我相信她的个性一定有吸引人的**地方**。

Lǐ xiǎojiě zhǎng de bú piàoliàng, érqiě hěn pàng, kěshì zhuī tā de rén hěn duō, wǒ xiāngxìn tā de gèxìng yīdìng yǒu xīyǐn rén de dìfāng.

Miss Li is not pretty; furthermore, she is overweight. But she has many male admirers. I believe that there must be **something** appealing in her personality (literally: her personality must have some appealing **characteristics**).

A:　大家都不喜欢小李，你为什么愿意跟他做朋友？

Dàjiā dōu bù xǐhuān Xiǎo Lǐ, nǐ wèi shénme yuànyì gēn tā zuò péngyǒu?

B:　小李脾气坏，这是他让人讨厌的**地方**，可是他其实也有很让人喜欢的**地方**；比方说，他很有幽默感。

Xiǎo Lǐ píqì huài, zhè shì tā ràng rén tǎoyàn de dìfāng, kěshì tā qíshí yě yǒu hěn ràng rén xǐhuān de dìfāng; bǐfāngshuō, tā hěn yǒu yōumò gǎn.

A:　Nobody likes Little Li. Why are you willing to be friends with him?

B:　Little Li is ill-tempered; this is where he is annoying (literally: this is his annoying **characteristic**). But actually there is also something likeable about him (literally: he has some likeable **traits**); for example, he has a good sense of humor.

d.　Because 地方 can indicate 'physical location' as well as 'abstract feature', it is important to **observe the context and the structure of the sentence** in order to arrive at an accurate interpretation. Occasionally, a sentence can be ambiguous in meaning and can be interpreted either way.

(Scenario: A man has just moved to a small town and is chatting with one of his new neighbors.)

A:　你为什么从大都市搬到这个**地方**来？我们这个小镇有让你特别喜欢的**地方**吗？(**地方** in 让你特别喜欢的**地方** can be interpreted as either '**feature**' or '**location**'.)

Nǐ wèi shénme cóng dà dūshì bān dào zhè ge dìfāng lái? Wǒmen zhè ge xiǎo zhèn yǒu ràng nǐ tèbié xǐhuān de dìfāng ma?

B:　这个小镇是我住过最美的**地方**，这附近也有不少我很喜欢的**地方**，尤其是镇外的瀑布区。

Zhè ge xiǎo zhèn shì wǒ zhù guo zuì měi de dìfāng, zhè fùjìn yě yǒu bùshǎo wǒ hěn xǐhuān de dìfāng, yóuqí shì zhèn wài de pùbù qū.

A: Why did you move here from the big city? Are there any **features** of our town that are specifically appealing to you? (or: Are there any **places** in our town that you particularly like?)

B: This town is the most beautiful **place** I have ever lived; also, there are many **places (areas)** nearby that I like very much, especially the water-falls outside of the town.

顿号 *dùnhào*

顿号 is a unique punctuation mark in Chinese; it has no counterpart in English. The term '**enumerating comma**' or '**series comma**' is used to refer to it. The reason it is being included in this book is because it **functions as a word**, meaning '**和/跟/与**' (*hé/gēn/yǔ*: and) or sometimes '**或者**' (*huòzhě*: or).

a. An enumerating comma is basically used to connect **two pronouns, two nouns** or **two adjectives**; therefore, it can be translated as '**and**' or sometimes '**or**', depending on the context. It should be noted that once an enumerating comma is used, the actual word ('and' or 'or') it refers to must not be used so as to avoid redundancy.

白老师、黄老师都是我的中文老师；他们都是负责、认真的好老师。
Bái lǎoshī, Huáng lǎoshī dōu shì wǒ de Zhōngwén lǎoshī; tāmen dōu shì fùzé, rènzhēn de hǎo lǎoshī.
Both Teacher Bai **and** Teacher Huang are my Chinese teachers. They are both good teachers who are responsible **and** conscientious.

这学期我忙死了，每星期都有三、四个考试。以前我一星期跟我女朋友见四、五次面，可是这学期我们一星期最多见一、两次。
Zhè xuéqī wǒ máng sǐ le, měi xīngqī dōu yǒu sān, sì ge kǎoshì. Yǐqián wǒ yī xīngqī gēn wǒ nǚ péngyǒu jiàn sì, wǔ cì miàn, kěshì zhè xuéqī wǒmen yī xīngqī zuìduō jiàn yī, liǎng cì.
I have been extremely busy ('busy to death') this semester; I have three **or** four tests each week. I used to meet with my girlfriend four **or** five times a week, but this semester, we meet at most once **or** twice a week.

b. When there are **three or more** items, an enumerating comma can be used between each of the items or the last two items can be linked with the actual word 和 or 或者. It must be kept in mind that an enumerating comma and the actual word cannot be used together.

去年暑假，我去了北京、上海、香港这三个地方。(和 can replace the enumerating comma between 上海 and 香港.)
Qùnián shǔjià, wǒ qù le Běijīng, Shànghǎi, Xiānggǎng zhè sān ge dìfāng.
I went to places such as Beijing, Shanghai **and** Hong Kong last summer.

c. Two **verb**s that indicate two **activities** can also be connected with an enumerating comma.

我平常忙得要命，所以周末只想在家看电视、玩电子游戏，别的事我都不想做。
Wǒ píngcháng máng de yàomìng, suǒyǐ zhōumò zhǐ xiǎng zài jiā kàn diànshì, wán diànzǐ yóuxì, biéde shì wǒ dōu bù xiǎng zuò.
On weekdays, I am extremely busy ('busy to death'); therefore, on the weekend, I only want to watch TV **and/or** play video games at home. I don't feel like doing anything else.

(Scenario: Zhang and Li are talking about a party Wang hosted two days ago.)

张: 听说老王前天在家请客，他请了几个人？
Zhāng: *Tīngshuō Lǎo Wáng qiántiān zài jiā qǐng kè, tā qǐng le jǐ ge rén?*
李: 请了六、七个。
Lǐ: *Qǐng le liù, qī ge.*
张: 是吗？他请了哪些人？
Zhāng: *Shì ma? Tā qǐng le nǎxiē rén?*
李: 他请了我、我女朋友、小谢、小高**跟**几个他的老同学。(Note: 跟 in this sentence should not be an enumerating comma since 几个他的老同学 and the previous words linked by enumerating commas are not the same kinds of expressions.)
Lǐ: *Tā qǐng le wǒ, wǒ nǚ péngyǒu, Xiǎo Xiè, Xiǎo Gāo gēn jǐ ge tā de lǎo tóngxué.*
张: 好玩吗？有什么菜？
Zhāng: *Hǎowán ma? Yǒu shénme cài?*
李: 老王做了红烧牛肉、鱼香茄子、麻婆豆腐**和**另外两、三道菜。吃了晚饭，我们聊天、下棋、听音乐。大家都玩得很高兴。
(和 in this sentence should not be an enumerating comma. See note above.)
Lǐ: *Lǎo Wáng zuò le hóngshāo niúròu, yúxiāng qiézi, mápó dòufu hé lìngwài liǎng, sān dào cài. Chī le wǎnfàn, wǒmen liáotiān, xiàqí, tīng yīnyuè. Dàjiē dōu wán de hěn gāoxìng.*
Zhang: I heard that Old Wang had a dinner party at his house the day before yesterday. How many people did he invite?
Li: He invited six **or** seven people.
Zhang: Is that so? Whom did he invite?
Li: He invited me, my girlfriend, Little Xie, Little Gao and a few of his old classmates.
Zhang: Was it fun? What dishes were there (What dishes did he serve)?
Li: Old Wang made beef stew, eggplant with garlic sauce, mapo doufu **and** two **or** three other dishes. After dinner, we chatted, played chess **and** listened to music. Everybody had a good time.

d. Two or more words that are **used so often together** to the point that they are **considered one word** should not have an enumerating comma between them. For example, 爸妈 and 姐妹 are 'parents' and 'sisters' respectively. To use an enumerating comma in these words is improper.

老师:	你有几个**兄弟姐妹**？(No enumerating commas are used in 兄弟姐妹.)
Lǎoshī:	*Nǐ yǒu jǐ ge xiōngdìjiěmeì?*
学生:	我有一个姐姐、两个妹妹；没有哥哥、弟弟。(哥弟 is not a legitimate word. To use 'brothers' in one word, it must be 兄弟: *xiōngdì*.)
Xuéshēng:	*Wǒ yǒu yī ge jiějie, liǎng ge mèimei; méiyǒu gēge, dìdi.*
老师:	你家还有哪些人？
Lǎoshī:	*Nǐ jiā hái yǒu nǎ xiē rén?*
学生:	我**爸妈**已经离婚了，我们的**祖父母**跟我们住在一起。(No enumerating comma is used between 爸 and 妈 or between 父 and 母.)
Xuéshēng:	*Wǒ bàmā yǐjīng líhūn le, wǒmen de zǔfùmǔ gēn wǒmen zhù zài yīqǐ.*
Teacher:	How many **siblings** do you have?
Student:	I have one older sister **and** two younger sisters; I don't have any brothers (older brothers **or** younger brothers.)
Teacher:	What other family members do you have?
Student:	My **parents** are divorced; our **grandparents** live with us.

多 *duō*

多 is a word that has many different meanings and uses. It is very important for learners to know how to use the correct sentence patterns involving 多 in different contexts. This section discusses five major usages of 多: as an **interrogative pronoun**, an **adjective**, an **adverb**, a **complement** and an **approximate number**.

a. **多 (interrogative pronoun) + adjective**

(i) 多 is an **interrogative pronoun** meaning '**how**' when it appears **before an adjective**.

A: 这是你女儿吗？她**多大**了？
   Zhè shì nǐ nǚ'ér ma? Tā duō dà le?
B: 她是我姐姐的女儿，今年两岁了。
   Tā shì wǒ jiějie de nǚ'ér, jīnnián liǎng suì le.
A: Is this your daughter? **How old** is she?
B: She's my older sister's daughter; she is two years old this year.

A: 你家**多大**?
   Nǐ jiā duō dà?
B: 非常小，只有一个卧室、一个洗澡间。
   Fēicháng xiǎo, zhǐ yǒu yī ge wòshì, yī ge xǐzǎojiān.
A: **How big** is your house?
B: Extremely small. There is only one bedroom and one bathroom.

(ii) When 多 is used this way (asking a descriptive question), an **optional verb 有** can appear before 多.

A: 这是一栋很老的房子。
   Zhè shì yī dòng hěn lǎo de fángzi.
B: 是吗?**(有)多老**?
   Shì ma? (Yǒu) duō lǎo?
A: **(有)**两百年了。
   (Yǒu) liǎng bǎi nián le.
A: This is a very old house.
B: Is that so? **How old**?
A: 200 years old.

(iii) Because **怎么** (*zěnme*) is an **interrogative pronoun** that also means '**how**', it is important to distinguish between these two question words and use each accurately. A **verb follows 怎么**, whereas an **adjective follows 多**.

(Scenario: Wang and Li have been waiting for the bus for a long time. Just when Wang is getting impatient, Li notices that the bus is coming.)
王:　　 等了这么久了！到底还要等**多久**? (久 is an adjective.)
Wáng: Děng le zhème jiǔ le! Dàodǐ hái yào děng duō jiǔ?
李:　　 再等三十秒钟车就来了！
Lǐ: Zài děng sānshí miǎo zhōng chē jiù lái le.
王:　　 是吗? 你**怎么知道**? (知道 is a verb.)
Wáng: Shì ma? Nǐ zěnme zhīdào?
李:　　 你看！那不是我们要坐的车吗?
Lǐ: Nǐ kàn! Nà bú shì wǒmen yào zuò de chē ma?
Wang: We have been waiting for so long already! Exactly **how long** do we still have to wait?
Li: We will wait another 30 seconds and the bus will be here.
Wang: Is that so? **How** do you **know**?
Li: Look! Isn't that the bus we want to ride?

(iv) '多 + adjective' can be used to make an **exclamatory statement**; **有 (before 多)** and a modal particle (at the end of the sentence) **啊** are often used; also, 多 in this pattern can be **多么** (*duōme*). This pattern is **(有)多(么) + adjective(啊)**!
   This expression tends to be used in **writing**.

妈妈过世以后我才知道自己**有多么**爱她**啊**！
Māma guòshì yǐhòu wǒ cái zhīdào zìjǐ yǒu duōme ài tā a!
Only after my mother had passed away did I realize **how much** I loved her!

When used in **conversational speech**, this expression is a **strong exclamation**.

这个孩子**多么**聪明**啊**！才三岁就认识两百个字了！
Zhè ge háizi duōme cōngmíng a! Cái sān suì jiù rènshì liǎng bǎi ge zì le!
How smart this child is! He is only three years old and he already recognizes 200 characters!

b. **多 as an adjective**

(i) 多 as an adjective is rarely used as a stand-alone word except when a yes-no question **多不多?** or **多吗?** is asked and when the **short answer** **多** is given to this question. Otherwise, 很多 is used.

It should be noted that 很多 simply means 'many' or 'much'; 很 does not literally mean 'very'. **很 is not optional** unless another degree adverb, such as 非常 (*fēicháng*: extremely) or 十分 (*shífēn*: extremely), is used to replace 很.

In addition, a **measure word** or 的 is not necessary when 很多 is followed by a noun, although either is **acceptable** (but **not both** at the same time) in casual, conversational speech.

昨天是王先生的生日，他请了**很多人**来他家吃晚饭。(In conversational speech, 很多**的**人 or 很多**个**人 is considered acceptable.)
Zuótiān shì Wáng xiānsheng de shēngrì, tā qǐng le hěnduō rén lái tā jiā chī wǎnfàn.
Yesterday was Mr Wang's birthday; he invited **many people** to his house for dinner.

这位作家很有名，我看过**很多(篇)**他写的文章。(篇 is the measure word for 文章.)
Zhè wèi zuòjiā hěn yǒumíng, wǒ kàn guo hěnduō (piān) tā xiě de wénzhāng.
This writer is famous; I have read **many articles** he has written.

昨天小张喝了**很多(瓶)**啤酒，所以张太太很不高兴。
Zuótiān Xiǎo Zhāng hē le hěnduō (píng) píjiǔ, suǒyǐ Zhāng tàitai hěn bù gāoxìng.
Yesterday Little Zhang drank **a lot of (bottles of)** beer, so Mrs Zhang was not happy.

(ii) When the noun after 很多 is clear in context, it is often omitted, and 很多 in this case functions as a **pronoun**.

(Scenario: Li had a meal at Mr Wang's house. Zhang asks him about the food.)

张: 王先生做的菜都很辣，你吃得惯吗？

Zhāng: *Wáng xiānsheng zuò de cài dōu hěn là, nǐ chī de guàn ma?*

李: 我最喜欢吃**辣的**，所以我吃了**很多**。(辣 and 很多 are both adjectives; when 菜 is omitted, 的 is necessary after 辣; but it should not be used after 很多. Do not say 很多的。)

Lǐ: *Wǒ zuì xǐhuān chī là de, suǒyǐ wǒ chī le hěn duō.*

Zhang: Dishes Mr Wang makes are all spicy-hot. Could you get used to it?

Li: My favorite food is **spicy food**, so I ate **a lot**.

(iii) 多 can be used as a **predicate**. When an English sentence has the verb 'to have' or 'there is/are', (很)多 can be used as the predicate of the sentence. The pattern is '**Subject + 很多/不多**'. Note that the word **有 is not used**.

小李有很多朋友。*Xiǎo Lǐ yǒu hěn duō péngyǒu.* (很多 before 朋友 is **a modifier**.)

= 小李的朋友很多。*Xiǎo Lǐ de péngyǒu hěn duō.* (很多 after 朋友 is **the predicate**.)

Little Li **has many** friends. (= Little Li's friends **are numerous**.)

This pattern is particularly useful when it is used in a **negative** statement with **不多**.

小李进大学以后，虽然认识了**很多**同龄的人，可是他的好朋友**不多**。

Xiǎo Lǐ jìn dàxué yǐhòu, suīrán rènshì le hěnduō tónglíng de rén, kěshì tā de hǎo péngyǒu bù duō.

Although Little Li has met **many** people of his age ever since he entered college, he does **not have many** good friends.

A: 昨天来开会的人**多不多**？

Zuótiān lái kāi huì de rén duō bù duō?

B: 来开会的人**不太多**，可是会后来聚餐的人**很多**。

Lái kāi huì de rén bú tài duō, kěshì huì hòu lái jùcān de rén hěn duō.

A: Were there **many people** who came to the meeting yesterday?

B: There were **not too many** people who came to the meeting, but there were **many people** who came to the dinner after the meeting.

When **a degree adverb** other than 很 is used, it is best to use 多 as a predicate.

(Scenario: Wang visits Li's house for the first time and is amazed at how many books Li has.)

王:　　哇！你的**书真多**！(你有真多书 would sound odd.)

Wáng: Wà! Nǐ de shū zhēn duō!

李:　　是啊！有时候我觉得我的**书太多了**！我没有时间看。

Lǐ: Shì a! Yǒu shíhòu wǒ juéde wǒ de shū tài duō le! Wǒ méiyǒu shíjiān kàn.

Wang:　Wow! You have **so many** books!

Li:　　Yeah! Sometimes I feel that I have **too many** books! I don't have time to read them.

c.　**多 + verb**

(i)　When 多 is placed **before a verb**, it is used as an **adverb** to indicate doing it (the action) **more** or **more often**. Learners who are English speakers often make mistakes when using this pattern because the word 'more' appears after the verb in English.

王先生身体不好，医生说他得**多休息**；李先生常常心情不好，他应该**多出去**走走。

Wáng xiānsheng shēntǐ bù hǎo, yīshēng shuō tā děi duō xiūxi; Lǐ xiānsheng chángcháng xīnqíng bù hǎo, tā yīnggāi duō chūqù zǒu zǒu.

Mr Wang is in poor health; the doctor says that he has to **rest more**. Mr Li is often in a bad mood (slightly depressed); he should **go out for walks more often**.

(ii)　When the action is '**verb + noun**', it is particularly important to use this pattern accurately since, in English, the word 'more' is placed before the noun.

我病了，医生叫我**多喝**水、**多睡**觉。(Do not say 喝多水 or 睡多觉.)

Wǒ bìng le, yīshēng jiào wǒ duō hē shuǐ, duō shuìjiào.

I am sick. The doctor told me to **drink more water** and to **sleep more**.

多吃蔬菜、水果对身体很有好处。(Do not say 吃多蔬菜.)

Duō chī shūcài, shuǐguǒ duì shēntǐ hěn yǒu hǎochù.

Eating more vegetables and fruit is very good for one's health.

少 can be used in the exact same manner to indicate 'less' or 'less often'.

要减肥的人应该**少吃**、**多运动**。

Yào jiǎnféi de rén yīnggāi shǎo chī, duō yùndòng.

Those who want to lose weight should **eat less** and **exercise more**.

(iii) （一）点 is often used in this pattern. It should immediately **follow the verb**.

你太瘦了！你应该**多吃一点**。
Nǐ tài shòu le! Nǐ yīnggāi duō chī yīdiǎn.
You are too thin! You should **eat a little bit more**.

你的身体不好，**少喝（一）点**酒吧！
Nǐ de shēntǐ bù hǎo, shǎo hē (yī)diǎn jiǔ bā!
Your health is poor. **Drink a little less** alcohol! (Don't drink so much!)

→ See 少 (*shǎo*) for related information.

d. **多 used as a complement (verb + 多)**

(i) 多 can be used as a **complement of result (verb + 多)**. This means that 多 (but not 很多) immediately follows the verb. Because this structure implies 'excessively/too much', 了 is often used.

今天中午老李请我吃饭，我可能**吃多了**，所以现在肚子很不舒服。
Jīntiān zhōngwǔ Lǎo Lǐ qǐng wǒ chī fàn, wǒ kěnéng chī duō le, suǒyǐ xiànzài dùzi hěn bù shūfú.
Today Old Li treated me to lunch. Maybe I **ate too much**, so now my stomach is upset.

A: 小李结婚才半年，现在竟然要跟他太太离婚了。
   Xiǎo Lǐ jiéhūn cái bàn nián, xiànzài jìngrán yào gēn tā tàitai líhūn le.
B: 这种事情我**看多了**，觉得一点也不稀奇。
   Zhè zhǒng shìqíng wǒ kàn duō le, juéde yīdiǎn yě bù xīqí.
A: Little Li has only been married for half a year; now (to my surprise) he is going to divorce his wife.
B: I have **seen too much** of this type of thing; I feel that it's not unusual at all.

(ii) 多 can be used as a **complement of quantity**, which appears **after a comparison** is made (or implied) to indicate **the difference** between the two things being compared. Since **at least two characters are needed**, the expression must be **很多, 得多** or **多了**. Sometimes 得多 了 can be used. But simply using 多 would not be correct.

A: 王中家大还是张文家大？
   Wáng Zhōng jiā dà háishì Zhāng Wén jiā dà?
B: 王中家（比张文家）大**得多（了）**。
   Wáng Zhōng jiā (bǐ Zhāng Wén jiā) dà de duō (le).

A: Is Wang Zhong's house bigger or is Zhang Wen's house bigger?
B: Wang Zhong's house is **much bigger** (than Zhang Wen's).

When the feature being compared is 多, it is possible to have **two 多 side by side**.

王老师有一百个学生，李老师只有十五个；王老师的学生比李老师**多多了**。(多多了 can also be 多得多 or 多很多.)
Wáng lǎoshī yǒu yī bǎi ge xuéshēng, Lǐ lǎoshī zhǐ yǒu shíwǔ ge; Wáng lǎoshī de xuéshēng bǐ Lǐ lǎoshī duō duō le.
Teacher Wang has 100 students; Teacher Li has only 15. Teacher Wang has **many more** students than Teacher Li.

e. **多 used as an approximate number**

When 多 is used as an approximate number, its meaning depends entirely on **the word it follows**. Basically, it only follows a **measure word**, 十 (*shí*: ten), 百 (*bǎi*: hundred), 千 (*qiān*: thousand) or 万 (*wàn*: ten thousand).

When 多 follows one of these words, it indicates a number **smaller than** the word it follows.

(i) When 多 **follows a measure word**, it indicates a fraction of one, meaning 'less than one'. For example, 三个多月 means **between three and four** months ('three months + **less than one** month').

Some words, such as 年 (*nián*: year) and 天 (*tiān*: day), do not have measure words; 多 can follow these words to mean 'less than one'. For example, **两年多** means **between two and three** years ('two years + **less than one** year'). **五天多** means **between five and six** days ('five days + **less than one** day').

我男朋友告诉我，他要去北京**三个多**月；可是他已经去了**半年多**了，还没有回来。
Wǒ nán péngyǒu gàosù wǒ, tā yào qù Běijīng sān ge duō yuè; kěshì tā yǐjīng qù le bàn nián duō le, hái méiyǒu huílái.
My boyfriend had told me that he was going to Beijing for **over three (3–4) months**; but he has been gone for **more than half (0.5–1) a year** already, and he has not come back yet.

(ii) When 多 **follows** 十, it indicates a number **smaller than ten (1–9)**, and it is **interchangeable with** 几 (*jǐ*). This is because 几 means 'a few' (2–9).

→ See 几 (*jǐ*) for related information.

王先生请了**三十多**个朋友来吃饭，可是他家只有**二十多**把椅子，所以他得去借**十多**把。(The three 多 in this sentence can all be changed to 几.)

Wáng xiānshēng qǐng le sānshí duō ge péngyǒu lái chī fàn, kěshì tā jiā zhǐ yǒu èrshí duō bǎ yǐzi, suǒyǐ tā děi qù jiè shí duō bǎ.

Mr Wang has invited more than 30 (**30–40**) friends to come for dinner, but his house only has 20 or so (**20–30**) chairs, so he will have to borrow more than ten (**10–20**) chairs.

When the noun is a word that does not have a measure word (such as 年 and 天), learners are frequently confused about the implication of 多.

For example, **十多天** (= 十几天) means **10–20** days ('ten days + **fewer than ten** days'); whereas **十天多** means **10–11** days ('ten days + **less than one** day').

(Scenario: This conversation among the four people takes place in **September 2017**.)

A: 你们在中国住了多久了?
   Nǐmen zài Zhōngguó zhù le duō jiǔ le?

B: 我是一九九〇年来中国的，我在中国住了**二十多**年了。(多 can be 几.)
   Wǒ shì yī jiǔ jiǔ líng nián lái Zhōngguó de, wǒ zài Zhōngguó zhù le èrshí duō nián le.

C: **十多**年了，我是二〇〇三年来的。(多 can be 几.)
   Shí duō nián le, wǒ shì èr líng líng sān nián lái de.

D: 我来了**十年多**了，我是二〇〇七年三月来的。(多 cannot be 几.)
   Wǒ lái le shí nián duō le, wǒ shì èr líng líng qī nián sān yuè lái de.

A: How long have you been living in China?

B: I came to China in 1990; I have been living in China for **over 20 (20–30)** years.

C: **More than ten (10–20) years**; I came in 2003.

D: I have been here for **a little over ten (10–11)** years. I came in March 2007.

Based on the above explanations, it can be concluded that 多 (or 几) cannot be used to indicate a number that is between two and four or between 50 and 70. It is possible to indicate a number between two and three (三个多) or a number between 50 and 60 (五十多 or 五十几).

(iii) When 多 **follows** 百 (*bǎi*: hundred), 千 (*qiān*: thousand) or 万 (*wàn*: ten thousand), it means **less than** 100 (百), 1,000 (千) or 10,000 (万) respectively.

It should be noted that 100,000 in Chinese is 十万; one million is 一百万; and ten million is 一千万.

A: 王先生和李小姐做的工作差不多，可是王先生一个月赚**一万多块钱**，李小姐每个月只赚**九千多块**。

Wáng xiānsheng hé Lǐ xiǎojiě zuò de gōngzuò chàbùduō, kěshì Wáng xiānsheng yī ge yuè zhuàn yī wàn duō kuài qián, Lǐ xiǎojiě měi ge yuè zhǐ zhuàn jiǔ qiān duō kuài.

B: 是啊！真不公平！王先生年薪**十多万**(= **十几万**)，李小姐年薪才**十万多**。

Shì a! Zhēn bù gōngpíng! Wáng xiānsheng nián xīn shí duō wàn (= shí jǐ wàn), Lǐ xiǎojiě nián xīn cái shí wàn duō.

A: Mr Wang and Miss Li do similar work, but Mr Wang makes **over 10,000 (10,000–20,000)** *kuai* a month; Miss Li only makes **over 9,000 (9,000–10,000)** *kuai* a month.

B: Yeah! It's really unfair! Mr Wang's annual salary is **over 100,000 (100,000–200,000)** *kuai*; Miss Li's annual salary is only **a little over 100,000 (100,000–110,000)** *kuai*.

(Scenario: Both Wang and Li are winners in lotteries. Note that when the amount is considered extremely large, the monetary unit is nearly always omitted.)

A: 王先生现在是百万富翁了，因为他上星期中了**三百多万**。

Wáng xiānsheng xiànzài shì bǎiwàn fùwēng le, yīnwèi tā shàng xīngqī zhòng le sān bǎi duō wàn.

B: 李先生更幸运，他上个月中了**两千多万**。

Lǐ xiānsheng gèng xìngyùn, tā shàng ge yuè zhòng le liǎng qiān duō wàn.

A: Mr Wang is a millionaire now because he won **over three (3–4) million** last week!

B: Mr Li is even luckier; he won **more than 20 (20–30) million** last month.

多少 *duōshǎo*

多少 can be used as an **interrogative pronoun** or an **adverb**.

a. There are two interpretations for 多少 as an **interrogative pronoun**: '**how much**' and '**how many**'. The following discussion focuses on the use of a **measure word** in a question with 多少.

(i) As 'how much', 多少 is followed by an **uncountable noun**; **no measure word** is involved.

(Scenario: Little Li has successfully organized a meeting. Two of his friends ask him about the preparation work.)

A: 小李，这次你主办的大会，非常成功；你花了**多少时间**准备？

Xiǎo Lǐ, zhè cì nǐ zhǔbàn de dà huì, fēicháng chénggōng; nǐ huā le duōshǎo shíjiān zhǔnbèi?

B:　更重要的是，主办单位一共花了**多少钱**？
　　*Gèng zhòngyào de shì, zhǔbàn dānwèi yīgòng huā le **duōshǎo qián**?*

A:　Little Li, the meeting you were in charge of organizing this time was very successful. **How much time** did you spend getting it ready?

B:　What's even more important is: **how much money** did the sponsoring organization spend?

(ii) When 多少 is used to mean '**how many**', **flexibility** is allowed as to whether or not a measure word is used.

(Scenario: A girl asks her mother for money so that she can go buy a new skirt.)

妈妈：　你自己去衣橱里看看，你已经有**多少(条)**裙子了？为什么还要买新的？

Māma:　*Nǐ zìjǐ qù yīchú lǐ kàn kàn, nǐ yǐjīng yǒu **duōshǎo (tiáo)** qúnzi le? Wèi shénme hái yào mǎi xīn de?*

Mother:　You go take a look at your own closet to see **how many skirts** you already have. Why do you want to buy more new skirts?

In general, the measure word is **optional** if the expected answer is **a large number**. And when the noun following 多少 refers to people, the measure word is, more often than not, omitted.

昨天的会员大会来了**多少人**？(多少个人 is less appropriate if a large number is expected to be the answer.)
*Zuótiān de huìyuán dà huì lái le **duōshǎo rén**?*
How many people came to the general meeting for members yesterday?

这个学校有**多少**外国**学生**？(多少个外国学生 is less appropriate.)
*Zhè ge xuéxiào yǒu **duōshǎo** wàiguó **xuésheng**?*
How many foreign **students** are there in this school?

我们只要看看一年内盖了**多少(株)**大楼，开了**多少(家)**餐馆，就可以知道这个城市发展得有多快。
*Wǒmen zhǐyào kàn kàn yī nián nèi gài le **duōshǎo (dòng)** dà lóu, kāi le **duōshǎo (jiā)** cānguǎn, jiù kěyǐ zhīdào zhè ge chéngshì fāzhǎn de yǒu duō kuài.*
As long as we take a look at **how many buildings** were built and **how many new restaurants** opened within one year, we will know how fast this city has developed.

(iii) If the speaker has a strong reason to expect the answer to be **a number around ten or smaller** than ten, then '几+ **measure word**' is normally used. Although 多少 is acceptable from a grammatical perspective, it is usually not considered the best choice of word.

→ See 几 (*jǐ*) for more information.

一个星期有**几天**? 一年有**多少(个)**星期? (天 does not have a measure word.)
Yī ge xīngqī yǒu jǐ tiān? Yī nián yǒu duōshǎo (ge) xīngqī?
How many days are there in a week? **How many weeks** are there in a year?

b. 多少 can be used as an **adverb** that means '**more or less**'. The implication is that it may not be huge or significant, but it still means something. Therefore, 一点 (*yīdiǎn*), 一些 (*yīxiē*) or a similar word that means 'a little bit' often follows the verb. This expression can also be **多多少少**.

(Scenario: Mr Li's best friend has asked him for a loan; but Mrs Li says that they don't have the money to lend to him. 多少 has two different uses in their interaction.)

李先生:	他是我最好的朋友，我们**多少**应该借他**一点**。
Lǐ xiānsheng:	*Tā shì wǒ zuì hǎo de péngyǒu, wǒmen duōshǎo yīnggāi jiè tā yīdiǎn.*
李太太:	那你觉得我们应该借他**多少**?
Lǐ tàitai:	*Nà nǐ juéde wǒmen yīnggāi jiè tā duōshǎo?*
Mr Li:	He is my best friend. We should **more or less** lend him **some**.
Mrs Li:	Then **how much** do you think we should lend him?

昨天小李取消了跟他女朋友的约会，虽然他女朋友了解那是因为他得加班，可是小李知道她**多多少少**还是会**有点**不高兴，所以就请花店送了一打玫瑰花给她。
Zuótiān Xiǎo Lǐ qǔxiāo le gēn tā nǔ péngyǒu de yuēhuì, suīrán tā nǔ péngyǒu liǎojiě nà shì yīnwèi tā děi jiābān, kěshì Xiǎo Lǐ zhīdào tā duō duō shǎo shǎo háishì huì yǒudiǎn bù gāoxìng, suǒyǐ jiù qǐng huādiàn sòng le yī dǎ méiguī huā gěi tā.
Yesterday Little Li cancelled his date with his girlfriend. Although his girlfriend understood that it was because he had to work overtime, Little Li knew that she would **more or less** feel **somewhat** unhappy, so he asked a florist to deliver a dozen roses to her.

而且 *érqiě*

In addition to being part of the 不但...而且... structure, 而且 can function as a stand-alone word. It is often translated as 'besides', 'moreover', 'furthermore', etc., and is used to **further add a point** to the point already made.

→ See 不但...而且... (*búdàn...érqiě...*) for more information.

a. The **subject** of the 而且 sentence can be **omitted** if it is clear in the context.

> A: 你为什么买这个牌子的手机？
>   *Nǐ wèi shénme mǎi zhè ge páizi de shǒujī?*
> B: 因为我的朋友都说这个牌子不错，**而且**最近在打折，所以我就买了。
>   *Yīnwèi wǒde péngyǒu dōu shuō zhè ge páizi búcuò, érqiě zuìjìn zài dǎzhé, suǒyǐ wǒ jiù mǎi le.*
> A: Why did you buy this brand of cell phone?
> B: Because all of my friends said that this brand was good; and **besides**, there was a sale recently, so I bought one.

b. If it is necessary to bring up the subject of the 而且 sentence, the **subject** should appear **after 而且**.

> A: 听说王先生跟王太太都是有名的慈善家。
>   *Tīngshuō Wáng xiānsheng gēn Wáng tàitai dōu shì yǒumíng de císhànjiā.*
> B: 没错！**而且他们**俩还是很有才华的艺术家。
>   *Méicuò! Érqiě tāmen liǎ hái shì hěn yǒu cáihuá de yìshùjiā.*
> A: I heard that both Mr and Mrs Wang are well-known philanthropists.
> B: That's correct! **Moreover**, both of them are talented artists.

c. If the point being made after 而且 is a long sentence, **a comma** is often used after 而且.

> A: 我的工作单位谣言、八卦总是不断，我受不了了，我要辞职、换工作。
>   *Wǒ de gōngzuò dānwèi yáoyán, bāguà zǒngshì bú duàn, wǒ shòu bù liǎo le, wǒ yào cízhí, huàn gōngzuò.*
> B: 为了这种事辞职太不值得。**而且**，只要有人的地方就有谣言、八卦，就算你到了别的地方也一样。
>   *Wèile zhè zhǒng shì cízhí tài bù zhíde. Érqiě, zhǐyào yǒu rén de dìfāng jiù yǒu yáoyán, bāguà, jiùsuàn nǐ dào le biéde de dìfāng yě yīyàng.*
> A: At my work place, there are never-ending rumors and gossip; I can't stand it anymore. I want to quit and change my job.
> B: Quitting your job for this type of thing is not worth it. **Besides**, as long as there are people, there will be rumors and gossip. Even if you went to work somewhere else, it would be the same.

反而 *fǎn'ér*

Whether 反而 is used as a stand-alone word or as part of the 不但 … 反而 … structure, 不但 and 反而 are always **a pair in meaning**; that is, the **不但** clause may not be explicitly said, but it must be **self-explanatory** or **pre-existent in the context** before 反而 can be used. The discussion in this section focuses on **the use of the subject** in a 反而 sentence.

→ See 不但 . . . 反而 . . . (*búdàn . . . fǎn'ér . . .*) for more information.

a. 反而 does not have a direct translation in English. It always implies that what actually happens is **opposite to** what is supposed (or expected) to have happened. The same subject is not repeated in the 反而 clause.

王先生发财以前，天天无忧无虑；现在他有钱了，**反而**变得非常不快乐。

Wáng xiānsheng fācái yǐqián, tiāntiān wú yōu wú lǜ; xiànzài tā yǒu qián le, fǎn'ér biànde fēicháng bú kuàilè.

Before Mr Wang made his fortune, he was always carefree and without a worry. Now he is rich, he (instead of being happier or even more carefree) has become very unhappy.

b. If it is necessary to have a **subject** in the 反而 sentence, the subject must **appear before 反而**. This is **different** from the use of 而且 as a stand-alone word. (The subject in a 而且 sentence appears after 而且.)

→ See 而且 (*érqiě*) for related information.

李先生和李太太为了买房子辛苦地工作了好几年，现在他们终于买了房子，可是**李先生反而**不爱待在家里，下了班常常跟朋友去喝酒，半夜才回家。

Lǐ xiānsheng hé Lǐ tàitai wèile mǎi fángzi xīnkǔ de gōngzuò le hǎojǐ nián, xiànzài tāmen zhōngyú mǎi le fángzi, kěshì Lǐ xiānsheng fǎn'ér bú ài dāi zài jiā lǐ, xià le bān chángcháng gēn péngyǒu qù hē jiǔ, bànyè cái huíjiā.

Mr and Mrs Li worked extremely hard for several years in order to buy a house. Now they have finally bought their own house, but Mr Li (instead of staying home and enjoying the house) does not like to be home anymore. He often goes out to drink with his friends after getting off work, and does not return home until very late at night.

花了这么大一笔医药费，**病情反而**越来越重，这是怎么回事？

Huā le zhème dà yī bǐ yīyào fèi, bìngqíng fǎn'ér yuè lái yuè zhòng, zhè shì zěnme huí shì?

After he has spent such a huge amount of money on his medical bill, his condition (instead of getting better) is getting worse and worse. What's going on here?

c. The expression can be **反而是**. It is used when the opposite-to-expectation situation has a different **subject** from the expected situation. The subject appears after 反而是, not before.

王老先生八十多岁了，他自己的儿子从来不管他的饮食生活，**反而是**他的侄子在照顾他。

Wáng lǎo xiānsheng bāshí duō suì le; tā zìjǐ de érzi cónglái bù guǎn tā de yǐnshí shēnghuó, fǎn'ér shì tā de zhízi zài zhàogù tā.

Old Mr Wang is in his eighties; his own son never pays any attention to his meals or daily life; instead (or unexpectedly), it is his nephew that is taking care of him.

否则 *fǒuzé*

否则 means 'otherwise' or 'if not' and is considered interchangeable with 要不 (*yàobù*), 要不然 (*yào bùrán*) or 不然 (*bùrán*). It can be used as a stand-alone word and can also be used with 除非 (*chúfēi*: unless) to form a conjunction pair. The discussion in this section focuses on the use of 否则 **as a stand-alone word**.

→ See 除非 (*chúfēi*) for more information.

a. 否则 is used to describe the outcome or consequence **if a condition is not met** or **if a certain situation is not true**.

我们现在就得出门，**否则**会赶不上八点的火车。

Wǒmen xiànzài jiù děi chū mén, fǒuzé huì gǎn bú shàng bādiǎn de huǒchē.

We have to leave the house now; **otherwise**, we will not be able to catch the 8:00 train.

刚开始学中文的时候，一定要把发音学好，**否则**以后别人听不懂你说的话。

Gāng kāishǐ xué Zhōngwén de shíhou, yīdìng yào bǎ fāyīn xué hǎo; fǒuzé yǐhòu biérén tīng bù dǒng nǐ shuō de huà.

When you first start to study Chinese, you must master the pronunciation; **otherwise**, other people will not be able to understand what you say later on.

b. The expression can be **否则的话**, which makes the speech sound less formal. A **comma** is used after 否则的话.

王大中跟李美兰一定分手了；**否则的话**，昨天的舞会他为什么请了另外一个女孩跟他一起去呢？

Wáng Dàzhōng gēn Lǐ Měilán yīdìng fēnshǒu le; fǒuzé de huà, zuótiān de wǔhuì tā wèi shénme qǐng le lìngwài yī ge nǚhái gēn tā yīqǐ qù ne?

Wang Dazhong must have broken up with Li Meilan; **otherwise**, why did he invite another girl to go with him to the dance yesterday?

刚 *gāng* and 刚才 *gāngcái*

Although 刚 and 刚才 share similarities in meaning, **刚才** is **limited in its connotation**. It is defined as '**just now**', and it strictly means 'shortly before the time the utterance is made'. As a rule of thumb, if a time period of, say, a couple hours has elapsed, one likely will not use 刚才 as the time word.

The distinction between 刚 and 刚才 is often a source of confusion for learners due to their similarities. In this section, comparisons between them as well as the independent uses of 刚, a more versatile word than 刚才, are presented.

刚 is an **adverb**, whereas **刚才** is a **time word**; therefore, 刚 appears before the verb (or verbal phrase) in a sentence. A sentence with 刚 can still have a time word.

a.   Since **刚才** is a **time word**, a sentence with 刚才 cannot have another time word, such as 'five minutes ago'. As a time word, 刚才 should appear **at the beginning of the sentence** or **after the subject** of the sentence.

小英: 为什么笑得这么高兴？有什么好事？
Xiǎoyīng: *Wèi shénme xiào de zhème gāoxìng? Yǒu shénme hǎo shì?*
小文: **刚才**小张给我发了一个短信，约我周末去看电影。(小张 and
         刚才 can be switched.)
Xiǎowén: *Gāngcái Xiǎo Zhāng gěi wǒ fā le yī ge duǎnxìn, yuē wǒ zhōumò*
         qù kàn diànyǐng.
Xiaoying: Why are you smiling so happily? Something wonderful happened?
Xiaowen: Little Zhang texted me **just now (a moment ago)**, and he asked me to go to a movie with him this weekend.

b.   刚 can be used to indicate 'just now' as well. In this case, it means the same as 刚才. For example, the above sentence **刚才**小张给我发了一个短信 can be 小张**刚**给我发了一个短信. However, 刚 is **broader in its connotation**. Its usage goes beyond the definition of 'just now'.

A sentence with 刚 is often **followed by another sentence** to imply that one event had **only just** taken place and another event immediately followed. The **first event has 刚**; the **second event** should have **就**. 就 can be interpreted as either 'already' or 'immediately' depending on the context.

唉！上个月**刚**给我儿子买了一双新鞋，这个月**就**穿不下了。
Ài! Shàng ge yuè gāng gěi wǒ érzi mǎi le yī shuāng xīn xié, zhè ge yuè jiù
chuān bú xià le.
Oh! I **only just** bought a pair of new shoes for my son last month, and they **already** don't fit (are too small) this month.

昨天我**刚**到家，**就**开始下雨了。
Zuótiān wǒ gāng dào jiā, jiù kāishǐ xiàyǔ le.
Yesterday I had **just** got home and it (**immediately**) began to rain.

c. If a 刚 sentence is not followed by another sentence, it usually implies that there is some kind of **impact or effect**. The impact (of the 刚 sentence) is not explicitly said because it is **understood in the context**.

A: 你喜欢吃饺子，对不对？今天我包了很多，要不要一起来吃一点？
   Nǐ xǐhuān chī jiǎozi, duì bú duì? Jīntiān wǒ bāo le hěn duō, yào bú yào lái yīqǐ chī yīdiǎn?
B: 你自己吃吧！我**刚**喝了两碗汤。(Implied: 现在不想吃东西。)
   Nǐ zìjǐ chī ba! Wǒ gāng hē le liǎng wǎn tāng. (Implied: Xiànzài bù xiǎng chī dōngxi.)
A: You like dumplings, right? I made a lot today. Do you want to have some with me?
B: Go ahead and have some without me! I **just** had two bowls of soup. (And so I don't feel like eating anything now.)

It can be concluded from the above that:

(i) a 刚才 sentence **can be** converted to a 刚 sentence, although the connotations may not be exactly the same, and

(ii) a 刚 sentence **may or may not be** converted into a 刚才 sentence since 刚才 strictly means 'a few moments ago'.

d. 刚 in the 刚 sentence can be replaced with 才 (*cái*).

客人: 时候不早了，我该回家了！
Kèrén: *Shíhòu bù zǎo le, wǒ gāi huí jiā le!*
主人: 怎么**刚**来**就**要走？(= 怎么**才**来**就**要走？)
Zhǔrén: *Zěnme gāng lái jiù yào zǒu? (= Zěnme cái lái jiù yào zǒu?)*
Guest: It's getting late. I should go home.
Host: You **only just** arrived; how come you are leaving **already**?

e. 刚 and 刚刚 can be considered interchangeable.

A: 张明好像很寂寞，我们给他介绍个女朋友，怎么样？
   Zhāng Míng hǎoxiàng hěn jìmò, wǒmen gěi tā jièshào ge nǚ péngyǒu, zěnme yàng?
B: 他本来有一个女朋友，他们**刚(刚)**分手，我想他现在还不想再交女朋友。
   Tā běnlái yǒu yī gè nǚ péngyǒu, tāmen gāng (gāng) fēnshǒu, wǒ xiǎng tā xiànzài hái bù xiǎng zài jiāo nǚ péngyǒu.
A: Zhang Ming seems lonely. How about if we set him up with a girlfriend?
B: He had a girlfriend before; they **just** (not too long ago) broke up. I don't think he wants to date yet.

f. It is possible to have 才 immediately after 刚刚, resulting in the phrase
    刚刚才, which should not be confused with 刚才.

    才 in 刚刚才 does not have a specific meaning. It serves the function of
    making the 刚刚 sentence **stronger in tone**; therefore, a 刚刚才 sentence
    is frequently followed by another sentence to emphasize the effect of the
    action that has just (刚刚才) taken place.

    (Scenario: A boy is eating a snack shortly after lunch time.)
    妈妈:　你不是**刚刚才**吃过午饭吗？怎么肚子又饿了呢？(刚刚才 can be
    　　　　replaced by 刚, 刚刚 or 才.)
    Māma:　Nǐ bú shì gānggāng cái chī guò wǔfàn ma? Zěnme dùzi yòu è le ne?
    儿子:　**刚才**吃饭的时候，我只喝了一碗汤。
    Érzi:　Gāngcái chī fàn de shíhòu, wǒ zhǐ hē le yī wǎn tāng.
    Mother:　Didn't you **just** eat lunch? How come you are hungry again?
    Son:　　When we ate lunch **just now**, I only had a bowl of soup.

g. 才 can appear before 刚 or 刚刚, resulting in 才刚(刚). It is similar in
    meaning to 刚刚才.

    (Scenario: A father has just got home from work; his young son is eager to
    play with him.)
    儿子:　爸爸，我们去后院玩接球，好不好？
    Érzi:　Bàba, wǒmen qù hòuyuàn wán jiē qiú, hǎo bù hǎo?
    妈妈:　爸爸**才刚**回家，先让他休息休息。
    Māma:　Bàba cái gāng huí jiā, xiān ràng tā xiūxi xiūxi.
    Son:　　Father, let's go to the backyard to play catch, OK?
    Mother:　Your father **only just** got home. Let him rest a little bit first.

h. The modal particle 了, which appears at the end of a sentence, is normally
    not used when the sentence has 刚 or 才刚.

    (Scenario: A man has just recovered from an illness and is eager to go out
    to do some physical activities. Note that the expression 'to have recovered'
    (好了) does not include the 了 when 才刚 is used.)
    丈夫:　我的病好了，这个周末一起去野外健行吧！
    Zhàngfū:　Wǒ de bìng hǎo le. Zhè ge zhōumò yīqǐ qù yěwài jiànxíng ba!
    妻子:　病**才刚**好Ø，还是在家休息休息吧！
    Qīzi:　Bìng cái gāng hǎo, háishì zài jiā xiūxi xiūxi ba!
    Husband:　I am well now (I have recovered from my illness). Let's go
    　　　　hiking this weekend.
    Wife:　　You have **only just** recovered. You had better rest at home.

i. The modal particle 了 can, however, appear in a sentence with **刚才** to
    indicate '**already**' (已经: *yǐjīng*).

A: 我们去问老师，明天可以不可以不考试，好不好？

Wǒmen qù wèn lǎoshī, míngtiān kěyǐ bù kěyǐ bù kǎoshì, hǎo bù hǎo?

B: 老师**刚才已经**说了，明天不考试，你没有听见吗？

Lǎoshī gāngcái yǐjīng shuō le, míngtiān bù kǎoshì, nǐ méiyǒu tīngjiàn ma?

A: Let's go ask the teacher if we can skip the test tomorrow, OK?

B: **A moment ago (just now),** the teacher **already** said there would not be a test tomorrow. Did you not hear it?

告诉 *gàosù*

告诉 means 'to tell'. But this English definition can be misleading since 告诉 is not always used the way 'to tell' is used in English.

a. 'To tell' in '**A tells B to do** something' is **not 告诉 but 叫** (*jiào*). What follows 告诉 is the **information** one receives, not an instruction or command to do something. From this perspective, 告诉 can also be defined as 'to inform'.

昨天我去检查身体；医生**告诉我**，我的血压很高，他**叫我**别再喝酒了。

Zuótiān wǒ qù jiǎnchá shēntǐ; yīshēng gàosù wǒ, wǒ de xuěyā hěn gāo, tā jiào wǒ bié zài hē jiǔ le.

Yesterday I went to have a physical check-up. The doctor **told (informed) me that** my blood pressure was high. He **told me not to** drink alcohol anymore.

→ See 叫 (*jiào*) for related information.

b. Certain expressions in English use the word 'to tell', but their Chinese counterparts do not use 告诉. For instance, 'to **tell lies**' is 说谎 (*shuō huǎng*); 'to **tell a story**' is 说故事 (*shuō gùshì*); 'to be able to tell (a certain sign)' as in 'I **can tell** he is not happy' is 看得出来.

It is important to not always directly translate the word 'to tell' as 告诉 without considering the actual expressions.

够 *gòu*

The accurate use of 够 is often elusive to learners, especially those who are English speakers. This is perhaps because, although 夠 is often simply translated as 'enough', its actual usages are quite different from the way the word '**enough**' is used in English.

够 can be used as an **adjective**, an **adverb** or a **verb**. Therefore, to simply think of 够 as 'enough' does not provide a complete picture as to how it is actually used.

a. As an **adjective** to describe a noun, 够 should be used as a **predicate**, not as a modifier (which appears before the noun). This means 够 appears **after the noun (subject of the sentence)**. English speakers should pay special attention to this because the word 'enough' typically appears before a noun in English.

  Also, the word **有 is not used** when 够 describes a noun; whereas 'to have enough + noun' is a common expression in English.

今天我去逛街，看到一件我喜欢的大衣，可是因为我带的**钱不够**，所以不能买。

Jīntiān wǒ qù guàng jiē, kàndào yī jiàn wǒ xǐhuān de dàyī, kěshì yīnwèi wǒ dài de qián bú gòu, suǒyǐ bù néng mǎi.

Today I went shopping, and I saw a coat that I liked; but because I did not bring **enough money** (literally: the money I brought was not enough), I could not buy it.

来听演讲的人太多了，**椅子不够**，你们快去搬几把椅子过来。

Lái tīng yǎnjiǎng de rén tài duō le, yǐzi bú gòu, nǐmen kuài qù bān jǐ bǎ yǐzi guòlái.

Too many people have come to listen to the speech; there are **not enough chairs**. Hurry and go move a couple more chairs over here.

In a **positive** sentence, **够了** is used. This 了 implies 已经.

今天的演讲，会有五十位听众；我们的椅子已经**够了**，可是点心、饮料还**不够**。

Jīntiān de yǎnjiǎng, huì yǒu wǔshí wèi tīngzhòng; wǒmen de yǐzi yǐjīng gòu le, kěshì diǎnxīn, yǐnliào hái bú gòu.

There will be 50 people in the audience for today's speech. We already have **enough chairs**, but there are **not enough** refreshments yet.

b. As an adjective, 够 can also appear **after the verb**; the function is to serve as the **complement of result**. Used in this pattern ('**verb + 够**'), 够 implies 'doing something **to one's heart's content**'.

(Scenario: Mrs Wang will not stop nagging at her son; her husband asks her to stop, but she refuses to.)

王先生:	你**说够**了没有？别再说了！
Wáng xiānsheng:	*Nǐ shuō gòu le méiyǒu? Bié zài shuō le.*
王太太:	我在骂儿子，你别插嘴。等我**骂够**了，我自然会停。
Wáng tàitai:	*Wǒ zài mà érzi, nǐ bié chāzuǐ. Děng wǒ mà gòu le, wǒ zìrán huì tíng.*
王先生:	你为什么要骂他？
Wáng xiānsheng:	*Nǐ wèi shénme yào mà tā?*

王太太:	他每天下了课就出去玩，**玩够**了才回家，所以我当然要骂他。
Wáng tàitai:	*Tā měitiān xià le kè jiù chūqù wán, **wán gòu** le cái huí jiā, suǒyǐ wǒ dāngrán yào mà tā.*
Mr Wang:	Have you **talked enough**? Stop talking!
Mrs Wang:	I am scolding our son. Don't interrupt. When I have **scolded** him **enough**, I naturally will stop.
Mr Wang:	Why did you want to scold him?
Mrs Wang:	Every day, he goes to have fun after school. He will only come home when he **has had enough fun**. So of course I wanted to scold him.

c. 够 is also an **adverb** that appears **before an adjective**. This usage shows a **reverse order** from its **counterpart in English**, and thus merits special attention.

学生:	老师，我的这篇文章，您给的分数很低，是不是因为**不够长**？
Xuéshēng:	*Lǎoshī, wǒde zhè piān wénzhāng, nín gěi de fēnshù hěn dī, shì bú shì yīnwèi bú gòu cháng?*
老师:	你写了两千个字，**够长**了，可是内容**不够好**。
Lǎoshī:	*Nǐ xiě le liǎng qiān ge zì, gòu cháng le, kěshì nèiróng bú gòu hǎo.*
Student:	Sir, you gave a low score for my essay. Was it because it was not **long enough**?
Teacher:	You wrote 2,000 characters; it was **long enough**, but the content was **not good enough**.

家长:	我的儿子想参加篮球队，您为什么拒绝他？
Jiāzhǎng:	*Wǒ de érzi xiǎng cānjiā lánqiú duì, nín wèi shénme jùjué tā?*
教练:	因为他**不够高**。
Jiàoliàn:	*Yīnwèi tā bú gòu gāo.*
Parent:	My son wanted to join the basketball team. Why did you reject him?
Coach:	Because he is **not tall enough**.

d. 够 can appear **before a verb**. The implication is that there is **enough (quantity, space, etc.) for consumption**. Therefore, the verbs that can be used in this pattern are limited.

妻子:	今天咱们请了十个客人，我做了八个菜；你觉得**够(吃)不够吃**？
Qīzi:	*Jīntiān zánmen qǐng le shí ge kèrén, wǒ zuò le bā ge cài; nǐ juéde gòu (chī) bú gòu chī?*

丈夫:	菜应该**够吃**。可是我只买了三瓶酒，酒可能会**不够喝**。
Zhàngfū:	*Cài yīnggāi gòu chī. Kěshì wǒ zhǐ mǎi le sān píng jiǔ, jiǔ kěnéng huì bú gòu hē.*
妻子:	我叫你买六瓶，你怎么只买了三瓶？
Qīzi:	*Wǒ jiào nǐ mǎi liù píng, nǐ zěnme zhǐ mǎi le sān píng?*
丈夫:	因为我带的钱只**够买**三瓶。
Zhàngfū:	*Yīnwèi wǒ dài de qián zhǐ gòu mǎi sān píng.*
Wife:	We invited ten guests today, and I made eight dishes. Do you think there is **enough** (food for ten people) **to eat**?
Husband:	The food should be **enough (for all the people) to eat**, but I only bought three bottles of wine. There probably won't be **enough** wine (for ten people) **to drink**.
Wife:	I told you to buy six bottles; how come you only bought three bottles?
Husband:	Because the money I had on me was only **enough to buy** three bottles.

这块地非常大，**够盖**三栋房子。

Zhè kuài dì fēicháng dà, gòu gài sān dòng fángzi.

This piece of land is very large. There is **enough space to build** three houses.

e. '**够** + verb' vs. 'verb + **够**': Based on the discussions above, 够 can appear either before or after a verb. However, these two patterns have **distinctly different** meanings. It is important to make the distinction between the two.

A:	六个人，三个披萨，**够吃**吗？（or 够不够吃？）
	Liù ge rén, sān ge pīsà, gòu chī ma? (or gòu bú gòu chī?)
B:	**够吃**，因为这三块披萨都是大的。
	Gòu chī, yīnwèi zhè sān kuài pīsà dōu shì dà de.
A:	There are six people and three pizzas. Is it **enough** (food for everyone) **to eat**?
B:	There is **enough** (for everyone) **to eat** because these three pizzas are large.

儿子:	我想吃一块蛋糕。
Érzi:	*Wǒ xiǎng chī yī kuài dàngāo.*
妈妈:	你已经吃了一碗牛肉面、十个饺子，你还没**吃够**吗？
Māma:	*Nǐ yǐjīng chī le yī wǎn niúròu miàn, shí ge jiǎozi, nǐ hái méi chī gòu ma?*
Son:	I want to eat a piece of cake.
Mother:	You already had a bowl of beef noodles and ten dumplings. Haven't you **eaten enough**?

f. 够 can be used as a **verb** that is **followed by a noun**. The noun is usually an abstract noun that is associated with **qualification**, **standard**, etc. 够 used this way can be translated as '**to reach**'; the implication is '**to be good enough**' for something.

小张想代表学校参加百米比赛，可是老师说他**不够资格**，因为他跑得**不够快**。

Xiǎo Zhāng xiǎng dàibiǎo xuéxiào cānjiā bǎi mǐ bǐsài, kěshì lǎoshī shuō tā bú gòu zīgé, yīnwèi tā pǎo de bú gòu kuài.

Little Zhang wanted to represent his school in the 100-meter dash; but the teacher said that he did **not meet the qualifications** (he is **not good enough** to run in the race) because he did not run **fast enough**.

老师: 你儿子还**不够条件**进一流大学，因为他成绩**不够好**。

Lǎoshī: Nǐ érzi hái bú gòu tiáojiàn jìn yī liú dàxué, yīnwèi tā chéngjī bú gòu hǎo.

家长: 成绩要多好才**够条件**呢？

Jiāzhǎng: Chéngjī yào duō hǎo cái gòu tiáojiàn ne?

Teacher: Your son does not yet **meet the requirements** to enter a first-rate college because his grades are **not good enough**.

Parent: How good do his grades need to be before he can **meet the requirements**?

关系 *guānxì*

As a stand-alone word, 关系 means 'relationship', 'relation' and sometimes 'connection'. But it is actually a word with implications that go beyond its basic definitions, and can be used in various expressions and contexts. This section discusses some of the most common uses of 关系.

a. Based on the definitions of 'relationship' and 'relation', numerous phrases with the word 关系 can be formed; for example, **人际关系** (*rénjì guānxì*: interpersonal relationship), **国际关系** (*guójì guānxì*: international relations), **亲子关系** (*qīnzǐ guānxì*: parent-child relationship), **因果关系** (*yīnguǒ guānxì*: the relationship between cause and effect) and so on.

b. Learners who are English speakers should be aware that the word 关系 **cannot** be used to refer to a **romantic relationship**.

   For example, the sentence 'Wang Xiaolan is **in a relationship with** Li Ming' cannot be directly translated into Chinese using the word 关系. One can only paraphrase it and say 'Wang Xiaolan is dating Li Ming' (王小兰跟李明在交往: *Wáng Xiǎolán gēn Lǐ Míng zài jiāowǎng*), 'Wang Xiaolan and Li Ming are boyfriend and girlfriend' (王小兰跟李明是男女朋友: *Wáng Xiǎolán gēn Lǐ Míng shì nán nǔ péngyǒu*) or another similar expression.

   Learners should further be aware that when the word 关系 is indeed used to suggest a **romantic relationship**, it actually subtly refers to a **sexual relationship**, as in the phrase 发生关系 (发生: *fāshēng* literally means 'to occur').

妈妈警告女儿，结婚以前绝对不可以和她男朋友**发生关系**。

Māma jǐnggào nǚ'ér, jiéhūn yǐqián juéduì bù kěyǐ hé tā nán péngyǒu fāshēng guānxì.

Mother warns her daughter that she absolutely cannot **have** (cannot **develop**) a **sexual relationship** with her boyfriend before getting married.

c. 关系 can also be defined as 'connection', which is actually a word that has **rich cultural connotations**. For example, the expression **讲关系** (*jiǎng guānxì*) is almost impossible to translate and must be understood as a **cultural and social phenomenon**. 关系 in the expression 讲关系 means '**social connections**' (社会关系: *shèhuì guānxì*); it is somewhat similar to the concept of 'networking' and emphasizes what one can achieve (not through legitimate channels, but) based on one's (personal) connections. Furthermore, 讲 does not mean 'to talk about'; instead, it implies 'to care about' or 'to be particular about'. In certain contexts, 讲关系 can also be interpreted as '**to make use of one's connections**'.

A: 李明连高中都没有毕业，他怎么有一份这么好的工作？
   Lǐ Míng lián gāozhōng dōu méiyǒu bìyè, tā zěnme yǒu yī fèn zhème hǎo de gōngzuò?

B: 靠**关系**啊！他岳父认识的人很多。
   Kào guānxì a! Tā yuèfù rènshì de rén hěn duō.

A: Li Ming did not even graduate from high school. How did he get such a good job?

B: Relying on connections! His father-in-law knows many people. (Implied: His father-in-law is well connected.)

A: 在中国，一个人如果没有**关系**，好像什么事都办不成。
   Zài Zhōngguó, yī ge rén rúguǒ méiyǒu guānxì, hǎoxiàng shénme shì dōu bàn bù chéng.

B: 不完全对。据我所知，有一件事，绝对不能**讲关系**。
   Bù wánquán duì. Jù wǒ suǒ zhī, yǒu yī jiàn shì, juéduì bù néng jiǎng guānxì.

A: 什么事？
   Shénme shì?

B: 进大学的高考。不管爸妈有什么样的**关系**，如果孩子成绩不好，还是进不了好大学。
   Jìn dàxué de gāokǎo. Bùguǎn bàmā yǒu shénme yàng de guānxì, rúguǒ háizi chéngjī bù hǎo, háishì jìn bù liǎo hǎo dàxué.

A: In China, if you do not have **connections**, it seems that you cannot get anything done.

B: It is not completely correct. As far as I know, there is one thing which you absolutely cannot **achieve by making use of your connections**.

A: What is that?

B: University entrance exams. No matter what kind of **connections** the parents have, if the child's academic performance is not good, he or she still cannot get into a good university.

d. It takes at least two entities to form a relationship. When both entities are mentioned, the pattern is 'A 跟 B(没)有关系'. 跟 can be replaced with 和 or the more formal word 与 (*yǔ*).

There are several ways to translate this expression: 'A and B are related (or unrelated)'; 'A has something (or nothing) to do with B'; and 'A and B have (or do not have) a relationship', etc.

The following examples show the variations of the pattern.

A: 有钱的人不一定快乐，所以财富**跟**快乐**没有关系**。
   Yǒu qián de rén bù yīdìng kuàilè, suǒyǐ cáifù gēn kuàilè méiyǒu guānxì.
B: 我不同意。我认为，财富**跟**快乐或许**没**有绝对的**关系**，但是**有**一定的**关系**。
   Wǒ bù tóngyì. Wǒ rènwéi, cáifù gēn kuàilè huòxǔ méiyǒu juéduì de guānxì, dànshì yǒu yīdìng de guānxì.
A: Rich people are not necessarily happy, so wealth **has nothing to do with** happiness.
B: I don't agree. I think that wealth **and** happiness may **not have** an absolute **relationship**, but they **have** a certain kind of **relationship**.

A: 这个小房子为什么比那个大房子贵这么多？
   Zhè ge xiǎo fángzi wèi shénme bǐ nà ge dà fángzi guì zhème duō?
B: 房价**跟**房子的地点**很有关系**，跟房子的大小不一定**有关系**。
   Fáng jià gēn fángzi de dìdiǎn hěn yǒu guānxì, gēn fángzi de dàxiǎo bù yīdìng yǒu guānxì.
A: Why is this small house so much more expensive than that big house?
B: Housing prices **have a lot to do with** the location of houses, and they are **not** necessarily **related to** the size of the houses.

A: 王太太的女儿为什么还没有男朋友？
   Wáng tàitai de nǚ'ér wèi shénme hái méiyǒu nán péngyǒu?
B: 她女儿有没有男朋友**跟你有什么关系**？(跟你有什么关系 is a rhetorical question that means 跟你没有关系.)
   Tā nǚ'ér yǒu méiyǒu nán péngyǒu gēn nǐ yǒu shénme guānxì?
C: 对！我们不应该去管**跟**自己**没有关系**的事。
   Duì! Wǒmen bù yīnggāi qù guǎn gēn zìjǐ méiyǒu guānxì de shì.
A: Why doesn't Mrs Wang's daughter have a boyfriend yet?
B: **What business is it of yours** (What does **it have to do with you**) whether her daughter has a boyfriend or not?
C: That's right! We should not concern ourselves with matters that **have nothing to do with** us.

e. Although 没关系 literally means 'unrelated', it is often used as a **stand-alone expression** that means 'it's OK', typically **a response to** 对不起 (*duì bù qǐ*: sorry), and 有 in 没有 is frequently omitted. In addition, it can mean 'it does not matter'.

(Scenario: Wang borrowed a book from Li, but he forgets it at home on the day he is supposed to return it.)

王: 啊，**对不起**，我忘了把你的书带来了。

Wáng: A, duì bù qǐ, wǒ wàng le bǎ nǐ de shū dài lái le.

李: **没关系**，你可以下次见面的时候还我。

Lǐ: Méi guānxì, nǐ kěyǐ xià cì jiànmiàn de shíhòu huán wǒ.

Wang: Ah, **sorry**! I forgot to bring your book.

Li: **It's OK**, you can return it to me next time when we meet.

(Scenario: Two friends arrive at the movie theater only to realize that the movie has already started.)

A: 糟糕，我们来晚了！怎么办？

Zāogāo, wǒmen lái wǎn le! Zěnme bàn?

B: **没关系**，先去附近的商店逛逛，看下一场。

Méi guānxì, xiān qù fùjìn de shāngdiàn guàng guàng, kàn xià yī chǎng.

A: Oh, no! We're late. What are we going to do?

B: **It doesn't matter**. Let's first go to the nearby shops to do some window shopping, and then we can see the next show.

(Scenario: A father is insisting that his son study accounting so that he can get a job after graduation. In this use, 都 **before** 没关系 **is required** since there are two options.)

儿子: 可是我对会计没有兴趣，我想学音乐。

Érzi: Kěshì wǒ duì kuàijì méiyǒu xìngqù, wǒ xiǎng xué yīnyuè.

爸爸: 一个人对自己的专业**有没有**兴趣**都没(有)关系**，最要紧的是以后找工作的问题。

Bàba: Yī ge rén duì zìjǐ de zhuānyè yǒu méiyǒu xìngqù dōu méi(yǒu) guānxì, zuì yǎojǐn de shì yǐhòu zhǎo gōngzuò de wèntí.

Son: But I am not interested in accounting. I want to study music.

Father: **Whether or not** one is interested in one's major **does not matter**. What's most important is the issue of getting a job in the future.

f. In certain expressions, 关系 cannot be literally interpreted as 'relationship'. What it really conveys is the '**impact**', '**effect**' or '**consequence**' of a situation.

(i) The phrase **关系重大** is a common expression which indicates that a certain situation has a major or far-reaching **impact**. It should be noted that although 关系 is a noun, 的 is nearly always omitted.

这件事(的)**关系重大**，进行的时候，我们应该小心谨慎。

Zhè jiàn shì (de) guānxì zhòngdà, jìnxíng de shíhòu, wǒmen yīnggāi xiǎoxīn jǐnshèn.

This matter has a major impact. When we proceed, we should be careful and cautious.

(ii) 关系 can be used as a **verb**. The expression is usually **关系到** or **关系着**.

政府的任何一个经济政策都**关系到**无数老百姓的生计。
Zhèngfǔ de rènhé yī ge jīngjì zhèngcè dōu guānxì dào wúshù lǎobǎixìng de shēngjì.
Any economic policy made by the government will **impact** numerous civilians' livelihood.

小孩子的成长环境**关系着**他们将来的人格发展，所以父母一定要做孩子的好榜样。
Xiǎo háizi de chéngzhǎng huánjìng guānxì zhe tāmen jiānglái de réngé fāzhǎn, suǒyǐ fùmù yīdìng yào zuò háizi de hǎo bǎngyàng.
The environment where children grow up **impacts** the future development of their personalities, so parents must be good role models for their children.

g. In the phrase '**因为 . . . 的关系**', 关系 does **not** have any literal meaning and **的关系 is actually optional**. When what follows 因为 is a simple word or a short sentence/phrase, 的关系 tends to be used. The word 所以 becomes omissible if 的关系 is used.

因为失业率太高**的关系**，社会上的穷人很多。(= **因为**失业率太高，**所以**社会上的穷人很多。)
Yīnwèi shīyè lǜ tài gāo de guānxì, shèhuì shàng de qióng rén hěn duō.
Because the unemployment rate is too high, there are many poor people in society.

因为缺钱**的关系**，（所以）王先生和他的未婚妻决定取消他们的蜜月旅行。
Yīnwèi quē qián de guānxì, (suǒyǐ) Wáng xiānsheng hé tā de wèihūnqī juédìng qǔxiāo tāmen de mìyuè lǚxíng.
Because they lack money, Mr Wang and his fiancée have decided to cancel their honeymoon trip.

Related expression

相干 *xiānggān*

'**A 跟 B 不相干**' has a similar meaning to '**A 跟 B 没有关系**', but is normally used in casual speech. Note that 关系 can be used in either a positive (有关系) or a negative (没有关系) phrase, but 相干 is generally **only used in 不相干**.

(Scenario: A work place situation.)

A: 王小兰今年为什么没有加薪？是不是**因为**她请了三个月产假**(的关系)**？我们应该去抗议。
Wáng Xiǎolán jīnnián wèi shénme méiyǒu jiā xīn? Shì bú shì yīnwèi tā qǐng le sān ge yuè chǎnjià (de guānxì)? Wǒmen yīnggāi qù kàngyì.

B: 这件事**跟**我们**不相干**，别管闲事。
Zhè jiàn shì gēn wǒmen bù xiānggān, bié guǎn xiánshì.

A: 这件事**跟**你或许**不相干**，但是**跟**我很**有关系**，因为我也怀孕了。(Do not say 跟我很相干。)
Zhè jiàn shì gēn nǐ huòxǔ bù xiānggān, dànshì gēn wǒ hěn yǒu guānxì, yīnwèi wǒ yě huáiyùn le.

A: Why did Wang Xiaolan not receive a pay raise this year? Was it **because** she took three months' maternity leave? We should protest.

B: This matter **has nothing to do with** us. Don't be nosy.

A: Perhaps this matter **has nothing to do with** you, but it **has a lot to do with** me because I am also pregnant.

还是 *háishì*

还是 is a word with several different meanings and uses, the most prominent of which is perhaps its definition of 'still'. Because of this, the proper use or interpretation of 还是 in a sentence is sometimes confusing to learners who are not familiar with other uses of this common word. This section provides explanations on the major uses of 还是.

a.　还是 is used to link the two options in an **alternative question**. If there are three options, 还是 is used between the last two, whereas an **enumerating comma** should be used to link the first two options.

(Scenario: A girl is shopping for new clothes with a friend at a store.)

A: 你想买裙子**还是**裤子？
Nǐ xiǎng mǎi qúnzi háishì kùzi?

B: 今天我想买一条裙子。
Jīntiān wǒ xiǎng mǎi yī tiáo qúnzi.

A: 这里有好几种颜色；你喜欢红的、蓝的**还是**绿的？(Note that an **enumerating comma** is used between the first two options.)
Zhèlǐ yǒu hǎo jǐ zhǒng yánsè; nǐ xǐhuān hóng de, lán de háishì lǜ de?

B: 我喜欢蓝的。
Wǒ xǐhuān lán de.

A: Do you want to buy a skirt **or** trousers?

B: I want to buy a skirt today.

A: There are quite a few colors (color choices) here. Do you like the red one, the blue one **or** the green one?

B: I like the blue one.

(i) When one does not want to make a choice, either because both (or all) options are valid or because neither (or none) are valid, one should **pre-pose the options** (if the options are the objects of the sentence) or **omit** them altogether if the choices are already clear from the context. The word 都 or 都不/都没有 **must be used** in the main sentence.

To pre-pose the object means to move the object **to the beginning** of the sentence. It is also acceptable to move it right **after the subject**. Learners should pay special attention to this word-order rule as well as the **use of punctuation**.

A: 你打算请小兰**还是**小英当你的伴娘？
   Nǐ dǎsuàn qǐng Xiǎolán háishì Xiǎoyīng dāng nǐ de bànniáng?
B: 小兰、小英，我**都不**打算请；我要请小文。(Do not say 我都不打算请小兰、小英。)
   Xiǎolán, Xiǎoyīng, wǒ dōu bù dǎsuàn qǐng; wǒ yào qǐng Xiǎowén.
A: Do you plan to ask Xiaolan **or** Xiaoying to be your bridesmaid?
B: I **don't** plan to ask Xiaolan **or** Xiaoying; I plan to ask Xiaowen.

A: 你看过中文版的《老人与海》**还是**英文版的？
   Nǐ kàn guo Zhōngwén bǎn de 'Lǎorén yǔ Hǎi' háishì Yīngwén bǎn de?
B: 中文版的跟英文版的，我**都**看过。你呢？(Do not say 我都看过中文版的跟英文版的. But it is correct to simply say 我都看过。)
   Zhōngwén bǎn de gēn Yīngwén bǎn de, wǒ dōu kàn guo. Nǐ ne?
A: 我（中文版的、英文版的，）**都没有**看过。
   Wǒ (Zhōngwén bǎn de, Yīngwén bǎn de,) dōu méiyǒu kàn guo.
A: Have you read the Chinese version of *The Old Man and the Sea* **or** the English version?
B: I have read **both** (the Chinese version and the English version). How about you?
A: I have read **neither** (the Chinese version nor the English version).

(ii) Since 还是 is simply translated as 'or' in an alternative question, learners often confuse it with 或者 (*huòzhě*), whose English counterpart is 'or' as well. However, 还是 implies '**whether . . . or**', whereas 或者 indicates '**either . . . or**'. They are used in different patterns and contexts.

→ See 或者 (*huòzhě*) for more information.

b. When 还是 is interpreted as '**still**', it suggests that a situation **remains unchanged**. In this use, 还是 is an **adverb** and appears before the verb (or verbal phrase) or an adjective. It is also possible for 还是 to appear before a sentence.

(i) It implies that a situation **remains unchanged** after a period of time or efforts to make it change. In more formal speech, 还是 can be replaced with **仍然** (*réngrán*) or **依旧** (*yījiù*). In addition, 还是 can be shortened to 还.

> A: 王大中发财以后，**还是**非常节省。他每天**还是**跟以前一样，骑自行车去上班。
> *Wáng Dàzhōng fācái yǐhòu, háishì fēicháng jiéshěng. Tā měitiān háishì gēn yǐqián yīyàng, qí zìxíngché qù shàngbān.*
> B: 那他**还是**住那栋旧房子吗？
> *Nà tā háishì zhù nà dòng jiù fángzi ma?*
> (The three 还是 can be replaced with **仍然/依旧**. They can also be shortened to **还**.)
> A: After making his fortune, Wang Dazhong is **still** very thrifty. He **still** rides his bicycle to work every day just like he used to.
> B: Then, does he **still** live in that old house?

(ii) It is often paired with **虽然** (*suīrán*: although/though) or **尽管** (*jǐnguǎn*: even though) to indicate that the situation **remains unchanged** or even is **opposite to** what may have been expected. 还是 in this usage is similar to the English words '**nonetheless**' or '**nevertheless**'.

Normally, 虽然 should be paired with 可是/但是. However, with the use of 还是 in the main sentence, 可是/但是 becomes optional. When 虽然/尽管 is used, 还是 is usually not shortened to 还.

> A: **虽然**(or **尽管**)今天刮大风、下大雨，飞机**还是**准时起飞了。
> *Suīrán (or jǐnguǎn) jīntiān guā dà fēng, xià dà yǔ, fēijī háishì zhǔnshí qǐfēi le.*
> B: 那为什么这班飞机最后**还是**延误了两小时才到达目的地呢？
> *Nà wèi shénme zhè bān fēijī zuìhòu háishì yánwù le liǎng xiǎoshí cái dàodà mùdìdì ne?*
> A: **Although** (or: **Even though**) there were strong winds and pouring rain today, the airplane **still** took off on time.
> B: Then why is it that this flight eventually was **still** delayed by two hours before it finally arrived at its destination?

> A: **虽然**(or **尽管**)王小兰认真地节食、努力地运动，她的体重**还是**没有下降。
> *Suīrán (or jǐnguǎn) Wáng Xiǎolán rènzhēn de jiéshí, nǔlì de yùndòng, tā de tǐzhòng háishì méiyǒu xiàjiàng.*
> B: 她**还是**(or **还**)跟以前一样胖吗？
> *Tā háishì gēn yǐqián yīyàng pàng ma?*
> A: **Although** (or: **Even though**) Wang Xiaolan has followed her diet conscientiously and exercised diligently, her weight **still** has not gone down.
> B: She is **still** as overweight as she used to be?

c.   The **distinction between** 还 **and** 还是 is frequently a source of confusion for learners because 还 is sometimes translated as 'still' as well. Despite their similarity in meaning, 还 and 还是 have **different connotations** and are used in different contexts. 还 implies that the situation **might or will change**, whereas 还是 indicates that the situation **remains the same**.

For example, when 还 is followed by a negative word, such as 不 or 没有, the expression (还不/还没有) means '**not yet**', implying that the situation **can change**. On the other hand, 还是不/还是没有 specifically indicates '**still not**', referring to **no change**. Learners should pay attention to the nuance and choose the proper word for 'still' after observing the context.

妹妹上高中的时候，想去中国学中文，可是爸爸说她**还**太小了，所以**还不**可以出国留学。没想到她上了两年大学以后，爸爸**还是**不让她去。

Mèimei shàng gāozhōng de shíhòu, xiǎng qù Zhōngguó xué Zhōngwén, kěshì bàba shuō tā hái tài xiǎo le, suǒyǐ hái bù kěyǐ chūguó liúxué. Méi xiǎngdào tā shàng le liǎng nián dàxué yǐhòu, bàba háishì bú ràng tā qù.

When my younger sister was in high school, she wanted to go to China to study Chinese, but our father said that she was **still** too young, and so she could **not** study abroad **yet**. Who would have thought that after she had been in college for two years, our father **still would not** let her go.

(Scenario: A boy was in the middle of cleaning his room when a friend called and asked him to go swimming.)

儿子: 我可不可以跟朋友去游泳？
Érzi: *Wǒ kě bù kěyǐ gēn péngyǒu qù yóuyǒng?*
妈妈: **还不**行，因为你**还没有**把房间打扫好。
Māma: *Hái bù xíng, yīnwèi nǐ hái méiyǒu bǎ fángjiān dǎsǎo hǎo.*
儿子: (Half an hour later.) 房间打扫好了，我现在可以去了吗？
Érzi: *Fángjiān dǎsǎo hǎo le, wǒ xiànzài kěyǐ qù le ma?*
妈妈: **还是**不行，因为我头疼，得去躺一下，你得在家看弟弟。
Māma: *Háishì bù xíng, yīnwèi wǒ tóu téng, děi qù tǎng yīxià, nǐ děi zài jiā kān dìdi.*
Son: Can I go swimming with my friends?
Mother: **Not yet**, because you have **not** finished cleaning your room **yet**. (Half an hour later.)
Son: I am done cleaning the room. Can I go now?
Mother: You **still cannot** go, because I have a headache and I have to go lie down for a while. You have to babysit your younger brother at home.

客人: 我该回家了！
Kèrén: *Wǒ gāi huí jiā le.*
主人: 才五点，**还**早嘛！
Zhǔrén: *Cái wǔ diǎn, hái zǎo ma!*
Guest: I should go home now.
Host: It's only five o'clock. It's **still** early.

还是 . . . （吧）! *háishì . . . (ba)!*

When there are two or more possible options, one can use 还是 . . . （吧）to indicate **the better (or the best) option** after weighing up the situation. Learners should not interpret 还是 as 'still' in such a context. In addition, 吧 is used when a suggestion is made.

a.   A verb/verbal phrase or a sentence can be used.

A: 小王和小李共同开创的科技公司大赚钱以后，小王变得很爱花钱，可是小李**还是**很节省，所以我很佩服小李。
Xiǎo Wáng hé Xiǎo Lǐ gòngtóng kāichuàng de kējì gōngsī dà zhuàn qián yǐhòu, Xiǎo Wáng biànde hěn ài huā qián, kěshì Xiǎo Lǐ háishì hěn jiéshěng, suǒyǐ wǒ hěn pèifú Xiǎo Lǐ.

B: 其实我觉得**还是**小王比较让人佩服，因为他捐了很多钱给慈善机构，可是小李的钱都在他的银行账户里。
Qíshí wǒ juéde háishì Xiǎo Wáng bǐjiào ràng rén pèifú, yīnwèi tā juān le hěn duō qián gěi císhàn jīgòu, kěshì Xiǎo Lǐ de qián dōu zài tā de yínháng zhàngfù lǐ.

A: Ever since the tech company Little Wang and Little Li had jointly started made big money, Little Wang has become extravagant in spending money, but Little Li is **still** frugal, so I really admire Little Li.

B: Actually, I think that, **(between the two of them,)** Little Wang is more admirable because he has donated a lot of money to charity organizations, but all of Little Li's money is in his bank account.

A: 谁去问老师明天可不可以不考试？
Shéi qù wèn lǎoshī míngtiān kě bù kěyǐ bù kǎoshì?

B: **还是**你去问**吧**! 老师比较喜欢你，你去问，她或许会说可以。
Háishì nǐ qù wèn ba! Lǎoshī bǐjiào xǐhuān nǐ, nǐ qù wèn, tā huòxǔ huì shuō kěyǐ.

A: Who will go ask the teacher if she can cancel the test tomorrow?

B: **It's best that** you go! The teacher likes you better. If you go ask her, perhaps she will say yes.

(Scenario: A couple has been looking to buy a house. They have looked at many houses and like two of them. They need to make a decision now.)

妻子: 你觉得我们应该买哪栋？
Qīzi: Nǐ juéde wǒmen yīnggāi mǎi nǎ dòng?

丈夫: （我们）**还是**买那栋小的**吧**! 地点比较好，价钱也很合理。
Zhàngfū: (Wǒmen) háishì mǎi nà dòng xiǎo de ba! Dìdiǎn bǐjiào hǎo, jiàqián yě hěn hélǐ.

Wife: Which one do you think we should buy?

Husband: **It's better that** we buy the smaller one. Its location is better, and the price is also reasonable.

b.   If the suggestion is indicated by a **negative** sentence, 别 or 不要 should be
used. To simply use 不 would not be correct.

(Scenario: A couple has a plan to go picnicking; the woman has packed a
basket of food.)

女: 吃的东西都准备好了！走吧！
Nǔ: *Chī de dōngxi dōu zhǔnbèi hǎo le! Zǒu ba!*
男: 你看，好像快下雨了！（我们）**还是别**(or **不要**) 去了**吧**！
Nán: *Nǐ kàn, hǎoxiàng kuài xià yǔ le! (Wǒmen) háishì bié* (or *bú yào*)
qù le ba!
Woman: The food is packed. Let's go!
Man: Look! It looks like it is about to rain. **It's better that** we don't go.

害（得） *hài(de)*

Although 害 literally means 'to harm', 害（得） can also be interpreted as 'to
make' or 'to cause'. It is similar to 使（得） (*shǐ(de)*) in meaning and usage, but
害（得） is only used to indicate an **unfortunate or bad event**. This means it is
only proper in certain contexts.

我昨天去看了一部恐怖电影，**害（得）我**晚上开着灯睡觉。
*Wǒ zuótiān qù kàn le yī bù kǒngbù diǎnyǐng, hài(de) wǒ wǎnshàng kāi zhe
dēng shuìjiào.*
I went to see a horror movie yesterday, which **made me leave** the lights on
when I went to sleep at night.

→ See 使 (*shǐ*) for more information.

好 *hǎo/hào*

Nearly every learner of Chinese is familiar with the character 好 when it is
defined as 'good', 'fine', 'OK', etc. The discussion below focuses on the use of
好 beyond these most basic definitions.

a.   好 used as a **complement of result** (verb + **好**): When 好 follows a verb
to indicate the result, there are two implications.

(i)   It implies that an action is done/handled **well, properly** or **securely**.

李先生的儿子是在美国生的，但是他要儿子把中文**学好**，所以天天
在家跟他说中文，还请老师来家里教他。
*Lǐ xiānsheng de érzi shì zài Měiguó shēng de, dànshì tā yào érzi bǎ
Zhōngwén xué hǎo, suǒyǐ tiāntiān zài jiā gēn tā shuō Zhōngwén, hái
qǐng lǎoshī lái jiā lǐ jiāo tā.*
Mr Li's son was born in the U.S., but he wants his son to **master** the
Chinese language, so he speaks Chinese with him at home every day;
he also hires a teacher to come to their house to teach him.

服务员把咖啡给他的时候，他没有**拿好**，所以咖啡杯掉在地上了。

Fúwùyuán bǎ kāfēi gěi tā de shíhòu, tā méiyǒu ná hǎo, suǒyǐ kāfēi bēi diào zài dìshàng le.

When the waiter handed him the coffee, he did not **hold** the coffee cup **properly**, so the cup dropped to the floor.

(ii) It implies that an action is **completed**, and the **completed work** can be shown.

妈妈:	碗**洗好**了没有？
Māma:	*Wǎn xǐ hǎo le méiyǒu?*
儿子:	还没有，还在洗呢！
Érzi:	*Hái méiyǒu, hái zài xǐ ne!*
Mother:	Are you **done washing** the dishes?
Son:	Not yet. I am still washing them.

老师:	请你们每个人填一张表，**填好**以后交给我。
Lǎoshī:	*Qǐng nǐmen měi ge rén tián yī zhāng biǎo, tián hǎo yǐhòu jiāo gěi wǒ.*
Teacher:	Everyone please fill out a form. After you have **completed** the form, please hand it to me.

b.   It is a **degree adverb** similar to 很 in meaning, but is used in **casual speech** and often implies a **mild exclamation**.

张:	上星期六老王在新房子请客，你去了吗？
Zhāng:	*Shàng xīngqī liù Lǎo Wáng zài xīn fángzi qǐngkè, nǐ qù le ma?*
李:	去了，还有**好多**老同学也都去了。大家都说**好久**没看到你了，不知道你为什么没去。
Lǐ:	*Qù le, hái yǒu hǎo duō lǎo tóngxué yě dōu qù le. Dàjiā dōu shuō hǎo jiǔ méi kàndào nǐ le, bù zhīdào nǐ wèi shénme méi qù.*
张:	唉！最近**好忙**，每天回家以后都觉得**好累**，所以周末只想在家休息。他的新房子怎么样？
Zhāng:	*Ài! Zuìjìn hǎo máng, měi tiān huí jiā yǐhòu dōu juéde hǎo lèi, suǒyǐ zhōumò zhǐ xiǎng zài jiā xiūxi. Tā de xīn fángzǐ zěnme yàng?*
李:	**好大**！有两层楼，还有一个**好漂亮**的花园！
Lǐ:	*Hǎo dà! Yǒu liǎng céng lóu, hái yǒu yī gè hǎo piàoliàng de huāyuán.*
Zhang:	Old Wang had a dinner party at his new house last Saturday; did you go?
Li:	I did; **many** of our old classmates also went. Everybody was saying that they had not seen you in **such a long time**, and we wondered why you did not go.
Zhang:	Sigh! I have been **so busy** lately. I feel **so tired** when I get home every day. So I only wanted to rest at home on the weekend. How is his new house?
Li:	It's **so big**! There are two stories. And there is also a **very pretty** garden!

It should be noted that 好 can only be used this way to describe something **one has experienced or is experiencing**. It should not be used to describe something that has yet to occur. For example, it is **inappropriate** to say 李明又聪明又肯努力，所以他**毕业以后**一定可以找到一个**好好的**工作。(*Lǐ Míng yòu cōngmíng yòu kěn nǔlì, suǒyǐ tā bìyè yǐhòu yīdìng kěyǐ zhǎodào yī gè hǎo hǎo de gōngzuò.* Li Ming is both smart and willing to work hard, so he will definitely be able to find a very good job after he graduates.) In this scenario, the expression 好好的工作 is inappropriate and should be **很好的**工作.

c. 好 can imply that **a task is easy**; therefore, it is similar to **容易** (*róngyì*: easy) in meaning, and 不好 means 难 (*nán*: difficult). 好 or 不好 appears **before the verb** that indicates the task.

(Scenario: A rich man scolds his son for spending too much money; his wife takes the son's side.)

爸爸:　你太浪费了！你以为钱是**好**(= **容易**)赚的吗？你自己去找个工作就知道钱**好不好**(= **容易不容易**)赚！

Bàba:　*Nǐ tài làngfèi le! Nǐ yǐwéi qián shì hǎo (= róngyì) zhuàn de ma? Nǐ zìjǐ qù zhǎo ge gōngzuò jiù zhīdào qián hǎo bù hǎo (= róngyì bù róngyì) zhuàn!*

妈妈:　现在经济不景气，**工作不好**(= **很难**)找，让他到你的公司去帮忙吧！

Māma:　*Xiànzài jīngjì bù jǐngqì, gōngzuò bù hǎo (= hěn nán) zhǎo, ràng tā dào nǐ de gōngsī qù bāngmáng ba!*

Father:　You are too wasteful! Do you think money is **easy to earn**? You go get a job yourself and you will know if money is **easy to earn**.

Mother:　There is a recession now. Jobs are **not easy to find**. Why don't you let him go help out in your company!

A:　为什么大家都不愿意跟小李合作？
　　Wèi shénme dàjiā dōu bú yuànyì gēn Xiǎo Lǐ hézuò?
B:　因为他很**不好相处**。
　　Yīnwèi tā hěn bù hǎo xiāngchǔ.
A:　Why is it that nobody is willing to work with Little Li?
B:　Because he is **not easy to get along** with.

d. 好 can **precede a verb** that indicates one's **sensory functions**, such as **吃** (*chī*: to taste), **喝** (*hē*: to drink), **听** (*tīng*: to listen) and 看 (*kàn*: to look at), and form an **adjective** that implies **pleasantness**. Therefore, 好吃 and 好喝 mean 'delicious'; 好看 can describe a pretty woman, a good novel, a good movie, etc., all of which involve the use of one's eyesight. 好听 can describe good music or songs. 好玩 (*hǎowán*), literally 'good play', means an activity is fun.

The opposite to 好 in this usage is either **不好 or 很难**; 难 should not be interpreted as 'difficult' when it is used this way.

A: 听说你去看了《北京和纽约》，你觉得这个电影**好看不好看**？

　　Tīngshuō nǐ qù kàn le 'Běijīng hé Niǔyuē', nǐ juéde zhè ge diànyǐng hǎokàn bù hǎokàn?

B: **不好看**！我真不懂，这么**难看**的电影，为什么这么受欢迎？

　　Bù hǎo kàn! Wǒ zhēn bù dǒng, zhème nánkàn de diànyǐng, wèi shénme zhème shòu huānyíng?

A: 电影里面的歌曲呢？**好不好听**？

　　Diànyǐng lǐmiàn de gēqǔ ne? Hǎo bù hǎotīng?

B: 歌曲倒**不难听**，也许这就是这个电影受欢迎的原因。(The implication of 倒 in this sentence is 'contrary to what one might expect'.)

　　Gēqǔ dǎo bù nántīng, yěxǔ zhè jiù shì zhè ge diànyǐng shòu huānyíng de yuányīn.

A: I heard that you went to see *Beijing and New York*. Do you think this movie was **good (entertaining)**?

B: It's **not good**. I really don't understand why such a **bad** movie would be so popular.

A: How about the songs in the movie? Were they **good (pleasant to hear)**?

B: The songs were **not bad**. Maybe this is the reason why this movie was so popular.

e. When 好 is pronounced in the 4th tone, it is **similar to 喜欢** (*xǐhuān*: to like; to be fond of) in meaning, but is usually used in words or expressions that describe one's **personality** or **characteristics**. Common words and expressions are: 好管闲事 (*hào guǎn xiánshì*: nosy), 好客 (*hàokè*: hospitable), 好动 (*hàodòng*: active and restless), 好奇 (*hàoqí*: curious), 好吃懒做 (*hàochī lǎn zuò*: gluttonous and lazy), etc. Note that these are all **adjectives**.

A: 奇怪！王家的女儿快三十了，不知道为什么还没有男朋友？

　　Qíguài! Wáng jiā de nǚ'ér kuài sānshí le, bù zhīdào wèi shénme hái méiyǒu nán péngyǒu?

B: 你为什么这么**好管闲事**？(好管闲事 literally means '**to like to** mind other people's business'.)

　　Nǐ wèi shénme zhème hào guǎn xiánshì?

A: 我不是**好管闲事**，只是有点**好奇**。

　　Wǒ bú shì hào guǎn xiánshì, zhǐ shì yǒudiǎn hàoqí.

A: Strange! The Wang family's daughter is almost 30 years old. I wonder why she does not have a boyfriend yet.

B: Why are you so **nosy**?

A: I am not **nosy**; I am just a bit **curious**.

A: 小英的男朋友一定是个很**好吃**的人。昨天王阿姨请客，我注意到他不停地吃。

　　Xiǎo Yīng de nán péngyǒu yídìng shì ge hěn hàochī de rén. Zuótiān Wáng āyí qǐngkè, wǒ zhùyì dào tā bùtíng de chī.

B: 那不见得表示他**好吃**；王阿姨做的菜实在太**好吃**了，我也吃了不少。(Note the two different meanings and pronunciations of 好吃 in this sentence.)

Nà bú jiànde biǎoshì tā hàochī; Wáng āyí zuò de cài shízài tài hǎochī le, wǒ yě chī le bù shǎo.

C: 王阿姨非常**好客**；客人吃得越多，她越高兴。

Wáng āyí fēicháng hàokè; kèrén chī de yuè duō, tā yuè gāoxìng.

A: Xiaoying's boyfriend must be a very **gluttonous** person. At Mrs Wang's dinner party yesterday, I noticed that he ate nonstop.

B: That does not necessarily mean he is **gluttonous**. Mrs Wang's cooking was truly **delicious**; I also ate a lot.

A: Mrs Wang is very **hospitable**. The more her guests eat, the happier she is.

好多 *hǎo duō* and 好几 *hǎo jǐ*

While both 好多 and 好几 are about quantity, they do not have the same meaning. 好 in 好多 can be replaced with 很 (see section b. of 好 above), whereas 很 cannot replace 好 in 好几.

好多 is a mild exclamation that means 很多 (many/much). 好几 means 'quite a few'. Since 几 means 'a few', 好几 suggests a number closer to ten.

→ See 几 (*jǐ*) for related information.

好了 *hǎo le*

Because 了 as a modal particle (appearing at the end of a sentence) often implies 已经 (*yǐjīng*: **already**) or a **change of situation**, there are at least three ways to interpret 好了.

a. It can mean one **has** (already) **recovered** from an illness.

王医生开的药真有效，我吃了两天就完全**好了**。

Wáng yīshēng kāi de yào zhēn yǒuxiào, wǒ chī le liǎng tiān jiù wánquán hǎo le.

The medicine Dr Wang prescribed was really effective. I only took it for two days and I **have** now completely **recovered**.

Because a sentence with 才 normally does not have 了 at the end, sometimes simply 好 (without 了) can imply one has recovered.

A: 你的感冒**好了**没有？

Nǐ de gǎnmào hǎo le méiyǒu?

B: 这次感冒真厉害，拖了两个星期**才好**。

Zhè cì gǎnmào zhēn lìhài, tuō le liǎng ge xīngqī cái hǎo.

A: Have you got over (**recovered from**) your cold?

B: This time my cold was really severe. It dragged on for two weeks before I **finally recovered**.

b. When 好 is used as the complement of result indicating '**completion**' (see section a.(ii) of 好 above), the **verb** is sometimes **omitted**. This results in only 好了 being used in a question or a (short) positive statement.

> A: 饭(做)**好了**没有?
> *Fàn (zuò) hǎo le méiyǒu?*
> B: **好了**。
> *Hǎo le.*
> A: Is dinner made (= **ready**)?
> B: It's **ready**.

c. As a stand-alone **exclamation**, 好了 can imply '**that's enough**' (meaning '**no more**') or '**stop**'. It is not unusual for the speaker to repeat it at least once to convey a sense of impatience or urgency.

> (Scenario: A mother keeps nagging at her son. Her husband tells her to stop.)
> 爸爸: **好了! 好了!** 别再说了!
> *Bàba:*   *Hǎo le! Hǎo le! Bié zài shuō le.*
> Father: **That's enough**! Don't nag anymore! (**Stop** nagging!)

> (Scenario: At a dinner, the host pours wine into a guest's glass, but the guest does not want to drink that much.)
> 客人: **好了，好了!** 我喝不了那么多。
> *Kèrén:*   *Hǎo le, hǎo le! Wǒ hē bù liǎo nàme duō.*
> Guest: That's plenty! (**Stop pouring!**) I cannot drink that much!

好(不)容易 *hǎo (bù) róngyì*

好(不)容易 + **verb**: As stated above (section c. of 好), 好 in the '好 + verb' pattern sometimes implies 容易; however, 好容易 is a stand-alone expression; also, 好 in 好容易 cannot be replaced with 很.

The negative form is 好不容易. It should be noted that both the **positive** form 好容易 and the **negative** form 好不容易 **have the same meaning**. Both indicate that a task is **finally done after much effort**. As such, 才 is often used.

> 昨天的数学功课又多又难，我做了五、六个小时，**好(不)容易才做完**。没想到今天老师说这个功课不用交。
> *Zuótiān de shùxué gōngkè yòu duō yòu nán, wǒ zuò le wǔ, liù ge xiǎoshí, hǎo (bù) róngyì cái zuò wán. Méi xiǎngdào jīntiān lǎoshī shuō zhè ge gōngkè búyòng jiāo.*
> Yesterday I had a lot of mathematics homework that was hard. I worked on it for five or six hours and I **finally finished it (after toiling through it)**. Who would have thought that today the teacher would say that we do not have to turn it in.

好意思 *hǎo yìsi*

Although the definition of 意思 is 'meaning', 好意思 cannot be interpreted literally. It is an expression used to **accuse or blame someone** because of their inappropriate behavior. It is a common expression; therefore, it is important to have an accurate understanding of its proper use.

→ See 意思 (*yìsi*) for more information.

会 *huì*

会 is a modal verb. This means it is followed by a regular verb (unless a short answer is given). It has two major functions: to indicate a **skill one can learn** and to show the **possibility of an event happening**. Therefore, the proper interpretation of 会 in a sentence depends on the context.

a. 会 indicates a **skill one can learn or acquire**, and is often translated as 'can' or 'to know how (to do something)'. For example, speaking a foreign language is an acquired skill, so the expression 'do you speak English?' should be 你**会不会**说英文? (*Nǐ huì bú huì shuō Yīngwén?*) literally 'do you **know how to** speak English?' instead of the common mistake made by learners who are English speakers: 你说不说英文?

我弟弟才一岁半，他还**不会**说话，可是已经**会**走路了。
Wǒ dìdi cái yī suì bàn, tā hái bú huì shuōhuà, kěshì yǐjīng huì zǒu lù le.
My little brother is only one-and-a-half years old; he **does not know how to** (= **has not learned to**) talk yet, but he already **can** (= **has learned how to**) walk.

(Scenario: Anna chances to meet a coworker at the park. The coworker has a little girl, who is her niece, with her. Anna asks the girl what her name is, but the little girl does not reply.)

安娜:　你侄女还**不会说**话吗?
Ānnà:　*Nǐ zhínǚ hái bú huì shuōhuà ma?*

同事:　她已经**会说**话了；可是她爸妈在家跟她说英文，所以她只**会说**英文，**不会说**中文。
Tóngshì:　*Tā yǐjīng huì shuōhuà le; kěshì tā bàmā zài jiā gēn tā shuō Yīngwén, suǒyǐ tā zhǐ huì shuō Yīngwén, bú huì shuō Zhōngwén.*

Anna:　Your niece **doesn't know how to talk** yet?

Coworker:　She **can** already **talk**; but her parents only speak English with her at home, so she **can** only **speak** English, she **doesn't know how to speak** Chinese.

b. As 会 indicates a skill, one of its implications is '**to be good at** some skill'. When 会 is used in this way, a **degree adverb** such as 很, 真, 非常 or 太 is used.

李阿姨**很会**做法国菜，可是她**不太会**做甜点。
Lǐ āyí hěn huì zuò Fǎguó cài, kěshì tā bú tài huì zuò tiándiǎn.
Mrs Li is **very good at** making French food, but she is **not very good at** making desserts.

(Scenario: An interaction between a teacher and her students in a Chinese-language class. Note that the two instances of 会 have different functions.)

学生:　　老师，请您教我们唱中国歌，好不好？
Xuéshēng:　Lǎoshī, qǐng nín jiāo wǒmen chàng Zhōngguó gē, hǎo bù hǎo?
老师:　　好啊，可是我**不太会**唱歌，你们别笑我。你们想学唱什么歌？
Lǎoshī:　Hǎo a, kěshì wǒ bú tài huì chàng gē, nǐmen bié xiào wǒ. Nǐmen xiǎng xué chàng shénme gē?
学生:　　请您教我们唱《我爱北京》。
Xuéshēng:　Qǐng nín jiāo wǒmen chàng 'Wǒ ài Běijīng'.
老师:　　《我爱北京》？我**不会**唱这个歌，我教你们唱别的歌吧！
Lǎoshī:　'Wǒ ài Běijīng'? Wǒ bú huì chàng zhè ge gē, wǒ jiāo nǐmen chàng biéde gē ba.
Students:　Teacher, will you please teach us to sing Chinese songs?
Teacher:　Sure! But I am **not very good at** singing, so don't laugh at me (at my singing). What songs do you want to learn to sing?
Students:　Please teach us how to sing 'I love Beijing'.
Teacher:　'I love Beijing'? I **don't know how to** sing this song. Why don't I teach you to sing another one!

小李**很会说话**，所以他应该去找一份推销员的工作。
Xiǎo Lǐ hěn huì shuō huà, suǒyǐ tā yīnggāi qù zhǎo yī fèn tuīxiāo yuán de gōngzuò.
Little Li is **very good at talking (= articulate and eloquent)**, so he should go find a job as a salesperson.

c. 会 can be used to indicate the **possibility** of something **happening in the future**.

A:　听说明天**会**下雨，你出门的时候，别忘了带伞。
Tīngshuō míngtiān huì xià yǔ, nǐ chūmén de shíhòu, bié wàng le dài sǎn.
B:　你放心，我**不会**忘的。
Nǐ fàngxīn, wǒ bú huì wàng de.
A:　I heard that it **will** rain tomorrow. When you leave the house, don't forget to take an umbrella with you.
B:　Don't worry. I **will not** forget.

When 会 is used in this context, its English counterpart is likely to be in **the future tense**. Learners should be aware of the difference between 要 and 会. 要 is generally used to indicate a future event that one **wills to happen or can make plans for**; whereas 会 is for an event that one does not consciously **control with one's will or plans**. Therefore, words such as 可能 (*kěnéng*), 大概 (*dàgài*) and 应该 (*yīnggāi*), which indicate possibility, often appear before 会.

A: 明天小李在家请客，你们**要不要**去？
　 Míngtiān Xiǎo Lǐ zài jiā qǐngkè, nǐmen yào bú yào qù?
B: 我和我女朋友都**要**去。
　 Wǒ hé wǒ nǚ péngyǒu dōu yào qù.
C: 我还没决定；不过我明天没有事，所以我**可能会**去。
　 Wǒ hái méi juédìng; búguò wǒ míngtiān méiyǒu shì, suǒyǐ wǒ kěnéng huì qù.
A: Tomorrow Little Li is having a dinner party at home. Are you going? (= **Will** you go?)
B: Both my girlfriend and I **will** go.
C: I have not decided yet. But I am free tomorrow, so I **will probably** go.

d.　会 can be used to indicate an event that **already took place**. It often implies the speaker's surprise because what happened was somewhat unexpected. This interpretation of 会 is closely related to **possibility**.

(Scenario: Xiaozhong's parents are displeased that he missed an important exam because he forgot about it.)
爸爸:　这么重要的事，你怎么**会**忘了？
Bàba:　*Zhème zhòngyào de shì, nǐ zěnme huì wàng le?*
妈妈:　怎么**不会**？比这更重要的事，他都**会**忘。
Māma:　*Zěnme bú huì? Bǐ zhè gèng zhòngyào de shì, tā dōu huì wàng.*
Father:　How **could** you have forgotten (literally: how was it **possible** for you to forget) such an important matter?
Mother:　Why not? (Literally: How was it **not possible**?) He **will** (**is likely to**) forget matters even more important than this.

e.　会 can sometimes be used to indicate the **possibility** of something happening **now** (at the time when the speech is uttered).

(Scenario: Two friends are taking a walk and find themselves to be in another friend's neighborhood.)
A: 小李住在这附近；你想他现在**会不会**在家？我们去找他聊天，好不好？
　 Xiǎo Lǐ zhù zài zhè fùjìn; nǐ xiǎng tā xiànzài huì bú huì zài jiā? Wǒmen qù zhǎo tā liáotiān, hǎo bù hǎo?

B: 现在七点，我想他应该**会**在家。可是他告诉我，他这星期都**会**很
忙，所以我们还是别去吧！

*Xiànzài qī diǎn, wǒ xiǎng tā yīnggāi huì zài jiā. Kěshì tā gàosù wǒ, tā
zhè xīngqī dōu huì hěn máng, suǒyǐ wǒmen háishì bié qù ba.*

A: Little Li lives in this neighborhood. Do you think he **is likely to** be
home now? Let's go and see if he is available for a chat, OK?

B: It's seven o'clock now; I think he should be home (= he is **likely to** be
home). But he told me that he **will be** busy all this week, so we had
better not go.

Related expressions

学会 *xué huì*

Because 会 (as a modal verb) is associated with skills one can learn, it is also
used as a **complement of result** following the verb 学. **学会** means to **actually
learn** to do something after making the effort to learn (学) it.

我和我弟弟一起开始**学**游泳，他很快就**学会**了，可是我**学**了很久还是没
学会。我不想**学**了，因为我想我大概永远**学不会**。

*Wǒ hé wǒ dìdi yīqǐ kāishǐ xué yóuyǒng, tā hěn kuài jiù xuéhuì le, kěshì wǒ
xué le hěn jiǔ háishì méi xuéhuì. Wǒ bù xiǎng xué le, yīnwèi wǒ xiǎng wǒ
dàgài yǒngyuǎn xué bú huì.*

My younger brother and I started to **take** swimming **lessons** together. He
quickly (= soon) learned, but I **tried to learn** for a long time and still I **have
not learned** (how to swim). Now I don't want to **try to learn** to swim anymore because I think I will probably **never be able to learn** (how to swim).

要是…会 *yàoshì … huì*

Because 会 can indicate the possibility or likelihood of an event, it is often used
in the expression 要是…会…, which describes a **hypothetical** situation.

A: 王大中做了这么不好的事；**要是**我是他爸爸，我**会**非常生气。

*Wáng Dàzhōng zuò le zhème bù hǎo de shì; yàoshì wǒ shì tā bàba, wǒ
huì fēicháng shēngqì.*

B: 这件事真的不能怪王大中；**要是**我是他，我也**会**这么做。

*Zhè jiàn shì zhēn de bù néng guài Wáng Dàzhōng; yàoshì wǒ shì tā,
wǒ yě huì zhème zuò.*

A: Wang Dazhong did such a bad thing. **If** I were his father, I **would be**
extremely angry.

B: We really can't blame Wang Dazhong for doing this. **If** I were him,
I **would** have done the same (= I would have also done it this way).

→ See 要是 (*yàoshì*) for more information.

或者 *huòzhě*

The difference between 或者 and 还是 (*háishì*) is a major source of confusion for learners. This is because both are translated as 'or' when no context is provided. The 者 in 或者 can be optional.

To be precise, **或者** means '**either . . . or . . .**', whereas **还是** is used in an **alternative question**, and it means '**whether . . . or . . .**'.

a.　还是 has several other meanings, but when it means 'whether . . . or . . .' it is always used in a question, which can be either a direct question or an indirect question.

> 男:　　　你的车是日本车**还是**美国车?
> *Nán:*　　*Nǐ de chē shì Rìběn chē háishì Měiguó chē?*
> 女:　　　都不是，是德国车。
> *Nǚ:*　　*Dōu bú shì, shì Déguó chē.*
> Man:　　Is your car a Japanese car **or** an American car?
> Woman:　Neither. It is a German car.

> (Scenario: Two teachers are talking about their class enrollments.)
> 丁老师:　　这学期我们班男生比女生多，你们班呢?
> *Dīng lǎoshī:*　*Zhè xuéqī wǒmen bān nán shēng bǐ nǚshēng duō, nǐmen bān ne?*
> 陈老师:　　我现在还不知道我们班男生多**还是**女生多。
> *Chén lǎoshī:*　*Wǒ xiànzài hái bù zhīdào wǒmen bān nánshēng duō háishì nǚshēng duō.*
> Teacher Ding:　This semester there are more boys than girls in my class. How about your class?
> Teacher Chen:　Right now I don't know yet **whether** there are more boys **or** more girls in my class.

b.　或(者) is usually used in a statement. When it is used in a question, it is always a **yes-no** question (either an **affirmative-negative** question or a question with **吗**).

> (Scenario: Bai visits Zhang at her house. Zhang offers Bai drinks.)
> 张:　　　喝点饮料吧! 你想喝什么? 茶**还是**咖啡?
> *Zhang:*　*Hē diǎn yǐnliào ba! Nǐ xiǎng hē shénme? Chá háishì kāfēi?*
> 白:　　　茶**或者**咖啡都可以。
> *Bai:*　　*Chá huòzhě kāfēi dōu kěyǐ.*
> (Zhang walks into the kitchen and then comes out without the drink.)
> 张:　　　啊! 真对不起，茶和咖啡都没有了。不过有可乐，也有啤酒，你**想不想**喝杯可乐**或者**啤酒?
> *Zhāng:*　*À! Zhēn duì bù qǐ, chá hé kāfēi dōu méiyǒu le. Búguò yǒu kělè, yě yǒu píjiǔ, nǐ xiǎng bù xiǎng hē kělè huòzhě píjiǔ?*

白:　啤酒和可乐，我今天都不想喝，我还是喝杯水吧！('还
　　　是 . . . 吧！' here means 'had better'.)

Bai:　*Píjiǔ hé kělè, wǒ jīntiān dōu bù xiǎng hē, wǒ háishì hē bēi shuǐ
　　　ba!*

Zhang:　Have a drink. What would you like? Tea **or** coffee?

Bai:　　**Either** tea **or** coffee would be fine.

Zhang:　Ah, I am really sorry, we've run out of both tea and coffee. But
　　　we have cola, and we also have beer. Would you like to have some
　　　cola **or** beer?

Bai:　　I don't feel like beer or cola today. I had better have a glass of
　　　water.

c.　When responding to an alternative question without making a choice, the
　　two options must be either **omitted** or **pre-posed**. If not omitted, the two
　　pre-posed options can be linked with 和, **或者** or an **enumerating comma**.

　　(Scenario: Gao is taking Li out for a meal.)

高:　昨天是你的生日，我没有送你东西，今天我请你吃晚饭，怎么
　　　样？

Gāo:　*Zuótiān shì nǐ de shēngrì, wǒ méiyǒu sòng nǐ dōngxi, jīntiān wǒ qǐng
　　　nǐ chī wǎnfàn, zěnme yàng?*

李:　好啊！谢谢！

Lǐ:　*Hǎo a! Xièxie.*

高:　你喜欢吃中国菜**还是**美国菜？

Gāo:　*Nǐ xǐhuān chī Zhōngguó cài háishì Měiguó cài?*

李:　中国菜**或者**(can be 和 or 、)美国菜，我都不太喜欢吃。

Lǐ:　*Zhōngguó cài huòzhě Měiguó cài, wǒ dōu bú tài xǐhuān chī.*

高:　那我们吃法国菜**或者**日本菜，好不好？你看，那儿有两家餐馆，
　　　一家法国餐馆，一家日本餐馆。你想吃法国菜**还是**日本菜？

Gāo:　*Nà wǒmen chī Fǎguó cài huòzhě Rìběn cài, hǎo bù hǎo? Nǐ kàn,
　　　nà'ér yǒu liǎng jiā cānguǎn, yī jiā Fǎguó cānguǎn, yī jiā Rìběn
　　　cānguǎn. Nǐ xiǎng chī Fǎguó cài háishì Rìběn cài?*

李:　法国菜太贵了，我们还是吃日本菜吧！

Lǐ:　*Fǎguó cài tài guì le. Wǒmen háishì chī Rìběn cài ba!*

Gao:　Yesterday was your birthday; I didn't give you a gift. How about if
　　　I take you out for dinner today?

Li:　　OK! Thanks.

Gao:　Do you like Chinese food **or** American food?

Li:　　I don't like Chinese food **or** American food very much.

Gao:　Then let's have **either** French food **or** Japanese food. Look, there
　　　are two restaurants over there. One is French and the other is Japa-
　　　nese. Do you feel like eating French food **or** Japanese food?

Li:　　French food is too expensive. Let's eat Japanese food.

→ See 还是 (*háishì*) for related information.

d. In certain contexts, 或者 is the same as **或许** (*huòxǔ*: **perhaps**). 或者 may
sound somewhat more formal than 或许.

(Scenario: Mrs Wang confides to Mrs Chen about her worries for her daughter.)
王: 我女儿跟小李交往了五年多了，还没谈婚事，我快急死了！

Wáng: *Wǒ nǚ'ér gēn Xiǎo Lǐ jiāowǎng le wǔ nián duō le, hái méi tán*
             hūnshì, wǒ kuài jí sǐ le.

陈: 你别急；**或者**他很快就会向你女儿求婚了呢。

Chén: *Nǐ bié jí; **huòzhě** tā hěn kuài jiù huì xiàng nǐ nǚ'ér qiúhūn le ne.*

Wang: My daughter and Little Li have been dating for over five years,
            and they have not talked about getting married. I am almost wor-
            ried to death.

Chen: Don't worry! **Perhaps** he will propose to your daughter very soon.

Related expression

或者 A 或者 B

In this pattern, A and B tend to be **sentences** or at least **verbal phrases**. If A
and B are pronouns or nouns, 或(者) should be used only once ('**A 或者 B**' or
'**A 或 B**'). It should be noted that 或者 in this pattern should not be shortened
to simply 或.

(Scenario: A manager is assigning different jobs to different employees.)
高: 经理，上海那件差事该派谁去？

Gāo: *Jīnglǐ, Shànghǎi nà jiàn chāishì gāi pài shéi qù?*

经理: 可以派王先生**或(者)**李先生去。不过下星期去北京的那件
            差事，一定得派张先生去。(Do not say 可以派**或者**王先生**或
            者**李先生去.)

Jīnglǐ: *Kěyǐ pài Wáng xiānsheng **huòzhě** Lǐ xiānsheng qù. Búguò xià*
             xīngqī qù Běijīng de nà jiàn chāishì, yīdìng děi pài Zhāng
             xiānsheng qù.

高: 可是张先生这星期休假，没有来上班。

Gāo: *Kěshì Zhāng xiānsheng zhè xīngqī xiūjià, méiyǒu lái shàngbān.*

经理: 那你**或者**给他打电话，**或者**给他发电子邮件；总之要跟他联
            系上。

Jīnglǐ: *Nà nǐ **huòzhě** gěi tā dǎ diànhuà, **huòzhě** gěi tā fā diànzǐ yóujiàn,*
             zǒngzhī yào gēn tā liánxì shàng.

Gao: Manager, who should be assigned to take care of the business
            in Shanghai?

Manager: We can assign **either** Mr Wang **or** Mr Li. But we must assign
            Mr Zhang to the job in Beijing next week.

Gao: But Mr Zhang is on holiday this week; he has not come to work.

Manager: Then **either** call him **or** send him an e-mail. In short, you have
            to get in touch with him.

即使 *jíshǐ*

The correct use and interpretation of 即使 (**even if**; **even**) may be confusing to learners, especially those who are English speakers. A common mistake is using 即使 when 尽管 (*jǐnguǎn*: **even though**) is the proper word. Such a mistake is perhaps caused by the fact that 'even if' and 'even though' are considered by some to be interchangeable in English. The following example illustrates the basic difference between 即使 and 尽管.

> (Scenario: Mr Wang's son was admitted to an expensive second-rate college. Two of his friends are discussing the situation.)
>
> A: **尽管**王先生没有钱，**还是**想办法把他儿子送去了那所大学。(This shows **a fact**.)
> *Jǐnguǎn Wáng xiānsheng méiyǒu qián, háishì xiǎng bànfǎ bǎ tā érzi sòng qù le nà suǒ dàxué.*
>
> B: **即使**我有钱**也**不会把儿子送去上那所大学。(This shows a **hypothetical situation**. The speaker, just like Mr Wang, does not have the money.)
> *Jíshǐ wǒ yǒu qián, yě bú huì bǎ érzi sòng qù shàng nà suǒ dàxué.*
>
> A: **Even though** Mr Wang didn't have the money, he **still** managed to send his son to that university.
>
> B: **Even if** I had the money, I would not send my son to that university.

→ See 尽管 (*jǐnguǎn*) for related information.

There are several connotations when 即使 is used. But one key point must be kept in mind: 也, which should not be literally interpreted as 'also', must be used in the **main sentence**.

a. 即使 . . . 也 . . . can denote a **hypothetical** or **counter-factual** situation; the main sentence (with 也) implies that the outcome would be the same regardless of the situation.

> A: 王中不诚实、不可靠，张小兰为什么要跟他结婚？我一定要去阻止她跟王中这种人结婚。
> *Wáng Zhōng bù chéngshí, bù kěkào, Zhāng Xiǎolán wèi shénme yào gēn tā jiéhūn? Wǒ yídìng yào qù zǔzhǐ tā gēn Wáng Zhōng zhè zhǒng rén jiéhūn.*
>
> B: 别去！**即使**你是她爸爸，**也**没有权利阻止她要跟谁结婚。
> *Bié qù! Jíshǐ nǐ shì tā bàba, yě méiyǒu quánlì zǔzhǐ tā yào gēn shéi jiéhūn.*
>
> A: Wang Zhong is not honest and not reliable. Why is Zhang Xiaolan going to marry him? I must go and stop her from marrying someone like Wang Zhong.
>
> B: Don't go! **Even if** you were her father, you would have no right to stop her from marrying whoever she wants to.

张文对数学没有兴趣，整个学期也没有认真地学习；下星期就是数学期末考了，**即使**他从今天开始每天只睡三个小时来准备这个考试，**也**一定不会及格的。

Zhāng Wén duì shùxué méiyǒu xìngqù, zhěng ge xuéqī yě méiyǒu rènzhēn de xuéxí; xià xīngqī jiù shì shùxué qīmòkǎo le, jíshǐ tā cóng jīntiān kāishǐ měi tiān zhǐ shuì sān ge xiǎoshí lái zhǔnbèi zhè ge kǎoshì, yě yídìng bú huì jígé de.

Zhang Wen is not interested in mathematics; and he did not study diligently during the entire semester. Next week there will be the final exam for mathematics; **even if** he were to sleep only three hours in order to study for the test starting today, he would definitely fail the exam.

b. 即使 . . . 也 . . . can refer to a **possible situation in the future**. The main sentence (with 也) indicates that the outcome would be the same regardless.

> A: 天气预报说，明天的天气会很坏；要是下雨，咱们还去不去呢？
> *Tiānqì yùbào shuō, míngtiān de tiānqì huì hěn huài; yàoshì xià yǔ, zánmen hái qù bú qù ne?*
> B: **即使**刮风、打雷、下冰雹，我**也**一定要去。
> *Jíshǐ guā fēng, dǎ léi, xià bīngbào, wǒ yě yídìng yào qù.*
> A: The weather forecast says that the weather tomorrow will turn very bad. Are we still going if it rains?
> B: **Even if** there is strong wind, thunder and hail, I will definitely go.

> A: 王中不诚实、不可靠；要是你跟他结了婚，将来恐怕会离婚。
> *Wáng Zhōng bù chéngshí, bù kěkào; yàoshì nǐ gēn tā jié le hūn, jiānglái kǒngpà huì líhūn.*
> B: **即使**以后离婚，我现在**也**一定要嫁给他。
> *Jíshǐ yǐhòu líhūn, wǒ xiànzài yě yídìng yào jià gěi tā.*
> A: Wang Zhong is not honest and not reliable. If you marry him, you will probably get a divorce in the future.
> B: **Even if** we divorce in the future, I will definitely marry him now.

c. 即使 . . . 也 . . . can refer to an **uncertain past situation**. The main sentence (with 也) indicates that the outcome would be or would have been the same regardless.

(Scenario: Two coworkers have been bad-mouthing their manager, and they suddenly notice that Wang Zhong is nearby.)

> A: 糟糕！不知道王中听到了没有？
> *Zāogāo! Bù zhīdào Wáng Zhōng tīngdào le méiyǒu?*
> B: 你放心，王中一向谨慎，**即使**他听到了**也**不会跟别人说。
> *Nǐ fàngxīn, Wáng Zhōng yīxiàng jǐnshèn, jíshǐ tā tīngdào le yě bú huì gēn biérén shuō.*
> A: Oh, no! I wonder if Wang Zhong heard us.
> B: Don't worry! Wang Zhong has always been discrete. **Even if** he heard us, he would not tell anybody.

It should be noted that, in English, 'if', instead of 'even if', is frequently used in this context. Learners who are English speakers should interpret 'if' in this context as 即使, not 要是 (*yàoshì*) or 如果 (*rúguǒ*).

(Scenario: Rumor has it that Wang Zhong's girlfriend is about to leave him for another man.)

没有人知道王中到底听到这个谣言没有；但是**即使**他听到了，**也**没有表现出特别不高兴的样子。

Méiyǒu rén zhīdào Wáng Zhōng dàodǐ tīngdào zhè ge yáoyán méiyǒu; dànshì jíshǐ tā tīngdào le, yě méiyǒu biǎoxiàn chū tèbié bù gāoxìng de yàngzi.

No one knew whether or not Wang Zhong had heard the rumor. But **(even) if** he had, he did not appear to be particularly unhappy.

d. 即使...也... can imply a '**concession**'. This means that one first accepts or reluctantly acknowledges something to be true, and then maintains that the outcome would not be affected by the situation.

(Scenario: Zhang Wen calls his teacher on the morning of a big test.)

张文:	老师，今天我不舒服，不能来学校。
Zhāng Wén:	*Lǎoshī, jīntiān wǒ bù shūfú, bù néng lái xuéxiào.*
老师:	**即使**不舒服你**也**得来，今天的考试太重要了。
Lǎoshī:	*Jíshǐ bù shūfú nǐ yě děi lái, jīntiān de kǎoshì tài zhòngyào le.*
Zhang Wen:	Teacher, I am not feeling well today. I cannot come to school.
Teacher:	Even if you're not feeling well, you have to come. Today's test is too important (for you to miss it).

(Scenario: A man and his wife are looking to buy a car. They have rejected three cars that they like because they cannot afford the price of 10,000 *kuai*. Now they are looking at a fourth car.)

妻子:	这辆车比较小，应该不要10,000块。
Qīzi:	*Zhè liàng chē bǐjiào xiǎo, yīnggāi bú yào yī wàn kuài.*
丈夫:	**即使**不要一万，最少**也**要八千，我们还是买不起。
Zhàngfū:	*Jíshǐ bú yào yī wàn, zuìshǎo yě yào bā qiān; wǒmen háishì mǎi bù qǐ.*
Wife:	This car is smaller; it shouldn't cost 10,000 *kuai*.
Husband:	**Even if** it does not cost 10,000, it will cost at least 8,000. We still cannot afford it.

e. 即使(是)...也 (or 都) can be used to show an **extreme situation**. The implication is that the outcome would not be affected by the extreme situation. Note that this is the only situation where the main sentence can have **either 也 or 都**. 即使(是) is normally translated as 'even'.

What follows 即使(是) is usually a **noun**, a **time phrase** or a **prepositional phrase**; it can be interchangeable with 连...也 (**or 都**).

A: 我要去阻止王小兰跟小李这种人结婚！

Wǒ yào qù zǔzhǐ Wáng Xiǎolán gēn Xiǎo Lǐ zhè zhǒng rén jiéhūn.

B: 这种事，**即使(是)**她爸爸**也**没有权力阻止(= **连**她爸爸**都**没有权力阻止)，你有什么权力阻止她？

Zhè zhǒng shì, jíshǐ (shì) tā bàba yě méiyǒu quánlì zǔzhǐ (= lián tā bàba dōu méiyǒu quánlì zǔzhǐ), nǐ yǒu shénme quánlì zǔzhǐ tā?

A: I am going to stop Wang Xiaolan from marrying someone like Little Li.

B: When it comes to this type of thing, **even** her father has no power to stop her. What power do you have to stop her?

张文是一个完美主义者；他做事的时候，**即使**是最小的细节，他**也**非常注意(= **连**最小的细节，他**都**非常注意)。

Zhāng Wén shì yī ge wánměi zhǔyì zhě; tā zuòshì de shíhòu, jíshǐ shì zuì xiǎo de xìjié, tā yě fēicháng zhùyì (= lián zuì xiǎo de xìjié, tā dōu fēicháng zhùyì).

Zhang Wen is a perfectionist. When he does things, he pays close attention to **even** the smallest detail.

A: 王中真没有礼貌，**即使(是)**在图书馆里，他**都**会大声说话。

Wáng Zhōng zhēn méiyǒu lǐmào, jíshǐ (shì) zài túshūguǎn lǐ, tā dōu huì dàshēng shuōhuà.

B: 他弟弟比他更没有礼貌，**即使(是)**老师在说话(的時候)，他**也**会插嘴。

Tā dìdi bǐ tā gèng méiyǒu lǐmào, jíshǐ (shì) lǎoshī zài shuōhuà (de shíhòu), tā yě huì chāzuǐ.

A: Wang Zhong is really rude. **Even** in the library, he would talk loudly.

B: His younger brother is even ruder than he is. **Even** when the teacher was talking, he would interrupt.

→ See 连 . . . 也/都 (*lián . . . yě/dōu*) for related information.

f.　就是 (*jiùshì*) and 就算 (*jiùsuàn*) are two words that are interchangeable with 即使. Although it is not uncommon to use 即使 in daily speech, it is considered a somewhat more formal word than either of these two words.

几 *jǐ*

几 is both an **interrogative pronoun** that means 'how many' and an **approximate number** that means 'a few'. Without a clear context, a spoken sentence with 几 can sometimes cause confusion due to the absence of punctuation. For example,

他有几个中国朋友？ means '**How many** Chinese friends does he have?'
他有几个中国朋友。 means 'He has **a few** Chinese friends.'

Regardless of its definition, 几 should be followed by a measure word (几+MW).

a. As an **interrogative pronoun**, 几+MW is similar to 多少 (*duōshǎo*) in meaning; both can be defined as 'how many?' However, 多少 can also mean 'how much', whereas 几 only means 'how many'. This is why 几 is followed by a measure word.

→ See 多少 (*duōshǎo*) for related information.

(i) When the expected answer is **around ten or smaller than ten**, one tends to use '几+MW' although 多少 is acceptable from a grammatical perspective.

(Scenario: A couple are looking to buy a new house. An agent is going to show them a house.)

丈夫:	这个房子有**几个**洗澡间?
Zhàngfū:	*Zhè ge fángzi yǒu jǐ ge xǐzǎo jiān?*
房地产商:	有三个。
Fángdìchǎn shāng:	*Yǒu sān ge.*
妻子:	只有三个?恐怕不够。
Qīzi:	*Zhǐ yǒu sān ge? Kǒngpà bú gòu.*
房地产商:	三个还不够?你们家有**几个**人?
Fángdìchǎn shāng:	*Sān ge hái bú gòu? Nǐmen jiā yǒu jǐ ge rén?*
妻子:	我们有五个女儿。
Qīzi:	*Wǒmen yǒu wǔ ge nǚ'ér.*
Husband:	**How many** bathrooms does this house have?
Real estate agent:	There are three.
Wife:	Only three? I am afraid that it's not enough.
Real estate agent:	Three is not enough? **How many** people are there in your family?
Wife:	We have five daughters.

为了准备今天的考试，我昨晚整个晚上没有睡觉，不停地喝咖啡，连我自己都不知道一共喝了**多少杯**(= 几杯)。
Wèile zhǔnbèi jīntiān de kǎoshì, wǒ zuówǎn zhěng ge wǎnshàng méiyǒu shuìjiào, bùtíng de hē kāfēi, lián wǒ zìjǐ dōu bù zhīdào yígòng hē le duōshǎo bēi (= jǐ bēi).
I stayed up all night last night in order to study for today's test, and I drank coffee nonstop. Even I myself do not know **how many cups** (of coffee) I drank.

(ii) When the expected answer is clearly **a large number**, only 多少 can be used. Using 几+MW would not be considered appropriate.

你知不知道这个大学有**多少**学生? (这个大学有几个学生 in this situation would sound odd.)
Nǐ zhī bù zhīdào zhè ge dàxué yǒu duōshǎo xuéshēng?
Do you know **how many** students there are at this university?

听说中国是全世界人口最多的国家；你知不知道中国到底有**多少**人？(中国有几个人 would not be an acceptable expression.)

Tīngshuō Zhōngguó shì quán shìjiè rénkǒu zuì duō de guójiā; nǐ zhī bù zhīdào Zhōngguó dàodǐ yǒu duōshǎo rén?

I have heard that China is the most populated country in the world. Do you know exactly **how many** people there are in China?

(iii) When there is **no clear expectation**, either 几 or 多少 is acceptable.

王老师:	李老师，这学期你教**几门**课？一共有**多少**学生？
Wáng lǎoshī:	*Lǐ lǎoshī, zhè xuéqī nǐ jiāo jǐ mén kè? Yīgòng yǒu duōshǎo xuéshēng?*
李老师:	我教三门课，一共有九十八个学生。
Lǐ lǎoshī:	*Wǒ jiāo sān mén kè, yīgòng yǒu jiǔshí bā ge xuéshēng.*
Teacher Wang:	Teacher Li, how many classes are you teaching this semester? How many students do you have altogether?
Teacher Li:	I am teaching three classes, and there are 98 students altogether.

(Scenario: A prospective employee asks the interviewer to repeat the annual salary of the job because he did not hear it clearly when it was mentioned.)

对不起，我没有听清楚，你可不可以再说一次，这个工作年薪**多少万**？(多少万 can be 几万. 万 means 'ten thousand'.)

Duìbuqǐ, wǒ méiyǒu tīng qīngchǔ, nǐ kě bù kěyǐ zài shuō yī cì, zhè ge gōngzuò niánxīn duōshǎo wàn?

Sorry, I did not hear you clearly. Can you tell me again how much (literally: **how many** *wàn*) the annual salary is for this job?

(iv) Before 千 (thousand) or 百 (hundred), only 几 is used. This is because only a number smaller than ten (1–9) can be used before them. But 万 can be preceded by a number larger than nine; thus, either 几 or 多少 can be used before 万.

(Scenario: A mother wants to find out how much money her daughter's boyfriend is making every month.)

妈妈:	小王一个月赚**多少万**？
Māma:	*Xiǎo Wáng yī ge yuè zhuàn duōshǎo wàn?*
女儿:	没有那么多；他一个月才赚**几千**。
Nǚ'ér:	*Méiyǒu nàme duō; tā yī ge yuè cái zhuàn jǐ qiān.*
妈妈:	才赚**几千**呢？到底**几千**呢？五千跟八、九千差很多呢！
	(几千 has two different meanings here.)
Māma:	*Cái zhuàn jǐ qiān? Dàodǐ jǐ qiān ne? Wǔ qiān gēn bā, jiǔ qiān chà hěn duō ne.*

Mother: **How many** *wan* (ten thousands) does Little Wang make each month?

Daughter: He doesn't make that much. He only makes **a few thousand** every month.

Mother: Only **a few thousand?** Exactly **how many thousands?** There is a big difference between 5,000 and 8–9,000!

b. As **an approximate number**, 几 strictly refers to **an integer number smaller than ten**, and is frequently translated as '**a few**' or sometimes '**several**'. The following are common expressions:

几 (a few): 2–9
十几 (ten plus): 11–19
二十几 (twenty-something): 21–29
几十 (several tens): 20–99
几百 (a few hundred; several hundred): 200–999
几千 (a few thousand; several thousand): 2,000–9,999
几万 (twenty thousand to ninety-nine thousand): 20,000–99,999
几十万 (two hundred thousand to nine hundred thousand): 200,000–999,999
几百万 (a few million; several million): 2,000,000–9,999,999
几千万 (twenty million to ninety-nine million): 20,000,000–99,999,999

When 几 **follows** 十, it is interchangeable with 多. Therefore, 十几, 二十几, 三十几, etc. can be 十多, 二十多, 三十多, etc. However, 几十 cannot be 多十 since 多十 is not a legitimate expression.

→ See 多 (*duō*) used as an approximate number for more information.

c. When the **expected answer** to a question is **a number**, 几 is used as the interrogative pronoun even if **a quantity is not involved**. In English, the word '**what**' or '**which**' is often used.

A: 请问，王先生的办公室在**几楼**?
    Qǐng wèn, Wáng xiānsheng de bàngōngshì zài jǐ lóu?
B: 在五楼。
    Zài wǔ lóu.
A: Excuse me, **which floor** is Mr Wang's office on?
B: It's on the fifth floor.

A: 今天是**几月几号**? **星期几**?
    Jīntiān shì jǐ yuè jǐ hào? Xīngqī jǐ?
B: 五月十号，星期三。
    Wǔyuè shí hào, xīngqī sān.
A: **What**'s today's date? **What** day of the week is today?
B: It is the tenth of May, Wednesday.

A:　你的电话是**几号**? (多少号 is also acceptable.)
　　Nǐ de diànhuà shì jǐ hào?
B:　是三九五二〇一四。
　　Shì sān jiǔ wǔ èr líng yī sì.
A:　**What** is your phone number?
B:　It's 3952014.

Related expressions

好几 *hǎo jǐ*

好几 and 几 (as an approximate number) share similarities in the sense that both refer to an integer number smaller than ten; however, 好几 implies that the number is at the **higher end** of the 2–9 range. As such, 好几 can be thought of as '**quite a few**'.

A:　昨天的考试，你考得怎么样?
　　Zuótiān de kǎoshì, nǐ kǎo de zěnme yàng?
B:　三十个问题，我只答错了**几个**，所以得到八十五分。你呢?
　　Sānshí ge wèntí, wǒ zhǐ dá cuò le jǐ ge, suǒyǐ dédào bāshí wǔ fēn. Nǐ ne?
A:　两个部分，我每个部分都答错**好几个**，所以几乎不及格。
　　Liǎng ge bùfèn, wǒ měi ge bùfèn dōu dá cuò hǎo jǐ ge, suǒyǐ jīhū bù jígé.
A:　How did you do on yesterday's test?
B:　Of the 30 questions, I answered **a few** of them wrong, so I got a score of 85. What about you?
A:　There were two parts, and I answered **quite a few** questions wrong in each part, so I almost failed.

A:　听说老王收藏了**几幅**名画，值不少钱，是真的吗?
　　Tīngshuō Lǎo Wáng shōucáng le jǐ fú míng huà, zhí bùshǎo qián, shì zhēn de ma?
B:　是真的。而且他收藏的不只是**几幅**，是**好几幅**；他的收藏值**好几**百万呢!
　　Shì zhēn de. Érqiě tā shōucáng de bùzhǐ shì jǐ fú, shì hǎo jǐ fú; tā de shōucáng zhí hǎo jǐ bǎiwàn ne!
A:　I have heard that Old Wang has collected **a few** famous paintings, and they are worth quite a lot of money. Is it true?
B:　It is true. Moreover, he has collected more than just **a few**; he has **quite a few**. His collection is worth **several (quite a few) million** dollars.

A similar expression to 好几 is **好多**, but they are **not interchangeable**. 好多 is a casual way to say 很多, which means '**many/much**' and can refer to a number **much larger than ten** or be used with an uncountable noun.

几时 *jǐshí*

几时 means 什么时候 (*shénme shíhòu*: **when**), but is usually used in **very casual, conversational speech**. 几时 should not be confused with 几点, which means '**what time?**'

> A: 你**几时**有空？来我家喝杯茶、聊聊天吧！
>   *Nǐ jǐshí yǒu kòng? Lái wǒ jiā hē bēi chá, liáo liáo tiān ba!*
> B: 好啊！我今天就有空。你要我**几点**来？
>   *Hǎo a! Wǒ jīntiān jiù yǒu kòng. Nǐ yào wǒ jǐdiǎn lái?*
> A: **When** are you free? Come to my house to have a cup of tea and chat!
> B: OK! I am free today. **What time** do you want me to come?

见 *jiàn* and 见面 *jiànmiàn*

The simple definitions of 见 ('to see') and 见面 ('to meet') do not provide adequate information about how to use them properly. Consequently, learners often make mistakes both in grammar patterns and contextual appropriateness. The focus of this section is on the distinction between 见 and 见面 as expressions used to refer to **seeing or meeting people**.

a.   **见面** means 'to meet (with) someone' or 'two or more people meeting' for a **specific purpose**, which can be **personal**, **social** or **business**. It is a **compound verb**. This means only 见 (meaning 'to see') is the verb, and 面 (meaning 'face') is a noun. It is incorrect to say, for example, 见面他女朋友; instead, it is 跟他女朋友见面. Furthermore, another word or expression can be inserted between 见 and 面.

> 王大中最近很忙，一个星期最多**跟**他女朋友**见**一次**面**；他女朋友很不高兴，所以他们**见**了**面**就吵架。
> *Wáng Dàzhōng zuìjìn hěn máng, yī ge xīngqī zuìduō gēn tā nǚ péngyǒu jiàn yī cì miàn; tā nǚ péngyǒu hěn bù gāoxìng, suǒyǐ tāmen jiàn le miàn jiù chǎojià.*
> Wang Dazhong has been busy lately; he can **meet (with)** his girlfriend at most once a week. His girlfriend is unhappy (about this situation), so they fight as soon as they **meet**.

b.   Although 认识 (*rènshì*) can be used to indicate two people meeting each other for the first time, it is only used when these two people become friends or acquaintances. When two people have met but did not subsequently develop a friendship or any kind of relationship, **见过**, rather than **认识**, is the proper word.

→ See 认识 (*rènshì*) for related information.

When 见过 is used in this context, there are **three patterns**:

(i) person + 跟 + person + 见过
   Example: 王先生不记得**他**以前**跟李明见过**。
   Wáng xiānsheng bú jìde tā yǐqián gēn Lǐ Míng jiàn guo.
   Mr Wang does not remember that **he** has **met Li Ming** before.

(ii) person 见过 + person
   Example: 李明到了文英家以后，发现**他**以前**见过**她**爸爸**。
   Lǐ Míng dào le Wényīng jiā yǐhòu, fāxiàn tā yǐqián jiàn guo tā bàba.
   After Li Ming arrived at Wenying's house, **he** realized that he **had met** her **father** before.

(iii) 我们/你们/他们 + 见过
   Example: **我们**去年在一个餐会**见过**，他大概不记得我了。
   Wǒmen qùnián zài yī ge cānhuì jiàn guo, tā dàgài bú jìde wǒ le.
   We met at a dinner party last year, (but) he probably does not remember me.

李明星期六要去**跟**他女朋友王英的爸妈**见面**，所以他天天都很紧张。星期六他到了王英家以后，发现他以前**见过**王英的爸爸，可是王先生不记得他**跟**李明**见过**。
Lǐ Míng xīngqī liù yào qù gēn tā nǔ péngyǒu Wáng Yīng de bàmā jiànmiàn, suǒyǐ tā tiān tiān dōu hěn jǐnzhāng. Xīngqī liù tā dào le Wáng Yīng jiā yǐhòu, fāxiàn tā yǐqián jiàn guo Wáng Yīng de bàba, kěshì Wáng xiānsheng bú jìde tā gēn Lǐ Míng jiàn guo.
Li Ming was going to **meet with** the parents of his girlfriend, Wang Ying, on Saturday; so he was nervous every day. On Saturday when he arrived at Wang Ying's house, he found out that he had **met** Wang Ying's father before. But Mr Wang did not recall that he had **met** Li Ming.

(Scenario: At a business party.)
王: 你**认识**周经理吗？要不要我介绍一下？
Wáng: Nǐ rènshì Zhōu jīnglǐ ma? Yào bú yào wǒ jièshào yīxià?
李: 其实我们去年在一个餐会**见过**，可是我想他大概不记得我了。
Lǐ: Qíshí wǒmen qùnián zài yī ge cānhuì jiàn guò, kěshì wǒ xiǎng tā dàgài bú jìde wǒ le.
Wang: Do you **know** Manager Zhou? Do you want me to introduce you?
Li: Actually we **met** at a dinner party last year, but I think he probably does not remember me.

c.   面 in 见面 is sometimes omitted when another word follows 见, or when 见面 is already used at least once in the context.

妈妈: 王明不是好人，以后不准你们**见面**。
Māma: *Wáng Míng bú shì hǎo rén, yǐhòu bù zhǔn nǐmen jiànmiàn.*
女儿: 他已经约了我明天在咖啡馆**见(面)**，请让我再**跟**他**见**最后一次**(面)**。
Nǚ'ér: *Tā yǐjīng yuē le wǒ míngtiān zài kāfēiguǎn jiàn (miàn), qǐng ràng wǒ zài gēn tā jiàn zuìhòu yī cì (miàn).*
Mother: Wang Ming is not a good person. From now on, I won't allow you two **to meet (to see each other)**.
Daugher: He already asked me to **meet** at a coffee shop tomorrow. Please let me **meet with him** for one last time.

d.   Sometimes 见 implies 再见 (*zàijiàn*). When the **specific time** or **location** is mentioned, 再 is no longer used; for example, 明天见 (*Míngtiān jiàn*: See you tomorrow), 下星期见 (*Xià xīngqī jiàn*: See you next week), 电影院门口见 (*Diànyǐng yuàn ménkǒu jiàn*: See you outside the movie theater), 图书馆见 (*Túshūguǎn jiàn*: See you at the library).

It is important to remember that 'you' in the phrase 'see you' cannot be translated; for example, it is incorrect to say 明天见你 for 'see you tomorrow'. On the other hand, it is correct to use the two people who will see each other again as the subject; for example, (我们)下星期见 ('See you next week') is correct.

A: 你明天有空吗？我想请你吃饭。
     Nǐ míngtiān yǒukòng ma? Wǒ xiǎng qǐng nǐ chī fàn.
B: 有啊！几点？在哪里？
     Yǒu a! Jǐdiǎn? Zài nǎlǐ?
A: 我六点下课，我们**在图书馆见**，然后一起去饭馆，好不好？
     Wǒ liù diǎn xià kè, wǒmen zài túshūguǎn jiàn, ránhòu yīqǐ qù fànguǎn, hǎo bù hǎo?
B: 好！**明天见**。(Do not say 明天见你。It is, however, acceptable to say 我们明天见。)
     Hǎo! Míngtiān jiàn.
A: **再见**。
     Zàijiàn.

A: Are you free tomorrow? I would like to take you out for a meal.
B: Sure! What time? Where?
A: I get out of class at six o'clock. We will **meet at the library**, and then go to the restaurant together; how's that?
B: OK! **See you tomorrow**.
A: **See you**.

e.　见 can be immediately followed by a person ('**Person A** 见 **Person B**') without 过. In this pattern, the purpose of the meeting is usually **not social** or **personal**, and the nature is **more formal**.

　　If **来 or 去** is used (or **implied** in the context), the connotation is that **Person B** is of a **superior** or **more authoritative position**. On the other hand, without **来** or **去**, **Person A** tends to be of a **superior status**. Such **nuance** merits attention.

(Scenario: Outside Manager Zhou's office.)

秘书:	李先生，有事吗？
Mìshū:	*Lǐ xiānsheng, yǒu shì ma?*
李:	我**来见**周经理，昨天他叫我今天下午**来见他**。(周经理/他 is of superior status.)
Lǐ:	*Wǒ lái jiàn Zhōu jīnglǐ, zuótiān tā jiào wǒ jīntiān xiàwǔ lái jiàn tā.*
秘书:	请等一等，我去看看**他**现在能不能**见你**。(你 is of inferior status.)
Mìshū:	*Qǐng děng yī děng, wǒ qù kàn kàn tā xiànzài néng bù néng jiàn nǐ.*
Secretary:	Mr Li, is there anything (I can help you with)?
Li:	**I came to see Manager Zhou.** Yesterday he asked me to **come and see him** this afternoon.
Secretary:	Please wait a moment. I will go take a look to see if **he can see you** now.

Related expressions

认识 *rènshì*

认识 is a word that can be translated as '**to meet**'; however, its connotation is very different from '见面' since 认识 (when defined as 'to meet') indicates that two (or more) people are meeting **for the first time**. Learners should observe the social context before choosing the proper word.

→ See 认识 (*rènshì*) for more information.

找 *zhǎo*

'**To see (someone)**' is among the various uses for 找; however, its connotation is different from 见. It is the context in which the utterance is made that decides which word is more appropriate.

→ See 找 (*zhǎo*) for more information.

叫 *jiào*

叫 is a word with various meanings, and it can be used in several different patterns. It is basically a **verb**, but is also considered a **preposition** when used in a **passive structure**. In general, it tends to be used in more casual speech.

a. It is used to **ask** or **give one's name** in an 'unmarked' passive structure. This means that the sentence is passive in meaning, but not in structure. 叫 in this pattern can be interpreted as 'to be called'. Learners should avoid the mistake of using 是 to introduce one's name.

> A: 你**叫**什么**名字**?
> *Nǐ jiào shénme míngzì?*
> B: 我姓王，**(名字)叫**王文生。你呢?
> *Wǒ xìng Wáng, (míngzì) jiào Wáng Wénshēng. Nǐ ne?*
> A: 我的**名字叫**张大中。(or: 我**叫**张大中。)
> *Wǒ de míngzì jiào Zhāng Dàzhōng. (or: Wǒ jiào Zhāng Dàzhōng.)*
> A: What is your **name**? (Literally: You **are called** what **name**?)
> B: My last name is Wang; my full **name is (called)** Wang Wensheng. How about you?
> A: My **name is (called)** Zhang Dazhong. (or: I **am called** Zhang Dazhong.)

b. A similar expression is **叫做**. It is usually used to explain a **term** or a **phrase** (such as a proverb). **做 is optional** and it implies 'as'.

(i) 叫做 in an unmarked passive structure sometimes can be translated as 'to be referred to as'.

> 在中国，农历年也**叫(做)**春节；春节时贴在门上的对联**叫(做)**春联。
> *Zài Zhōngguó, nónglì nián yě jiào zuò chūnjié; chūnjié shí tiē zài mén shàng de duìlián jiào zuò chūnlián.*
> In China, Lunar New Year **is** also **called (referred to as)** the Spring Festival; the couplets pasted on the doors during the festival time **are called (are referred to as)** spring couplets.

> A: 王大中非常无知，可是他却以为自己什么都懂。
> *Wáng Dàzhōng fēicháng wúzhī, kěshì tā què yǐwéi zìjǐ shénme dōu dǒng.*
> B: 这种人**叫(做)** "井底之蛙"。
> *Zhè zhǒng rén jiào zuò 'jǐng dǐ zhī wā'.*
> A: Wang Dazhong is extremely ignorant, but he thinks that he knows everything.
> B: This kind of person **is called** a 'frog in the well'.

(ii) 叫做 can be used in a 把 sentence.

中国人**把**住在海外的华人**叫做**"华侨"。
Zhōngguó rén bǎ zhù zài hǎiwài de Huárén jiào zuò 'Huá qiáo'.
Chinese **call** overseas Chinese 'Hua qiao'.

因为番茄的形状很像柿子，所以有些人**把**番茄**叫做**西红柿。
Yīnwèi fānqié de xíngzhuàng hěn xiàng shìzi, suǒyǐ yǒuxiē rén bǎ fānqié jiào zuò xīhóngshì.
Because the shape of a tomato very much resembles that of a persimmon, some people **call** tomatoes 'Western red persimmons'.

c. It is used in the 'A 叫 B + noun' pattern to indicate **how A addresses B**. 叫 in this pattern means 'to call'.

李家的两个兄弟都是我的好朋友；我**叫**哥哥大李，**叫**弟弟小李。
Lǐ jiā de liǎng ge xiōngdì dōu shì wǒ de hǎo péngyǒu; wǒ jiào gēge Dà Lǐ, jiào dìdi Xiǎo Lǐ.
Both of the two brothers of the Li family are my good friends; I **call** the older brother Big Li, and I **call** the younger brother Little Li.

A: 王先生，你好！
   Wáng xiānsheng, nǐ hǎo!
B: 我是你的老师，请(你)**叫**我王老师。
   Wǒ shì nǐ de lǎoshī, qǐng (nǐ) jiào wǒ Wáng lǎoshī.
A: Hello, Mr Wang.
B: I am your teacher; please **call** me Teacher Wang.

d. 叫 can imply 'to shout' and the 'A 叫 B' pattern indicates that **A loudly calls B** by B's name in order to get his or her attention.

你女朋友在街对面**叫**你，你快过去吧！
Nǐ nǚ péngyǒu zài jiē duìmiàn jiào nǐ, nǐ kuài guò qù ba!
Your girlfriend is **calling** you from across the street. Why don't you go over now!

我在小李家门口**叫**了他好几次，他才出来。
Wǒ zài Xiǎo Lǐ jiā ménkǒu jiào le tā hǎo jǐ cì, tā cái chūlái.
I **called (loudly shouted his name)** Little Li quite a few times from outside his house before he finally came out.

e. 叫 can mean 'to order' food (at or from a restaurant) or service.

妻子：   今天我不想做饭，我们打电话去**叫**外卖吧！
Qīzi: *Jīntiān wǒ bù xiǎng zuò fàn, wǒmen dǎ diànhuà qù jiào wàimài ba!*

丈夫: 想不想吃披萨？我们**叫**披萨来吃，怎么样？
Zhàngfū: *Xiǎng bù xiǎng chī pīsà? Wǒmen jiào pīsà lái chī, zěnme yàng?*
妻子: 好，也帮我**叫**一个沙拉。
Qīzi: *Hǎo, yě bāng wǒ jiào yī ge shālā.*
Wife: I don't feel like cooking today; why don't we call (make a phone call) and **order** take-out?
Husband: Do you feel like having pizza? How about if we **order** a pizza?
Wife: OK, and **order** a salad for me, too.

(Scenario: A hotel guest calls the front desk because he is about to check out and go to the airport.)
请帮我**叫**一辆车，我结账以后就要去机场。
Qǐng bāng wǒ jiào yī liàng chē, wǒ jiézhàng yǐhòu jiù yào qù jīchǎng.
Please **order** a car for me. I am going to the airport right after I check out.

f. In the '**A 叫 B + verb**' pattern, 叫 can be interpreted as 'to order' as well. However, this means '**A orders B to do something**'. Besides 'to order', 叫 in this pattern is frequently translated as 'to tell' as in '**A tells B to do something**'.

It should be noted that '**A 叫 B to not do something**' is '**A 叫 B 别 (or 不要) + verb**'. Using 不 would not be correct.

(i) 叫 used in this pattern is similar to 请 (*qǐng*) and 让 (*ràng*) in meaning. But in terms of connotations, 叫 is perhaps **the least polite** among the three, whereas 请 shows the highest level of politeness.

(Scenario: A father repeats to his children what their mother has told them to do or not to do.)
爸爸: 小中，妈妈已经**叫**你**别** (or **不要**) 再**看**电视了，你怎么还在看？小明，妈妈**叫**你**去**洗碗，你怎么还不去洗？
Bàba: *Xiǎozhōng, māma yǐjīng jiào nǐ bié (or bú yào) zài kàn diànshì le, nǐ zěnme hái zài kàn? Xiǎomíng, māma jiào nǐ qù xǐ wǎn, nǐ zěnme hái bú qù xǐ?*
Father: Xiaozhong, your mother has already **told** you **not to watch** any more TV. How come you are still watching? And Xiaoming, your mother **told** you **to go do** the dishes. How come you still haven't done it?

→ See 请 (*qǐng*) and 让 (*ràng*) for related information.

(ii) Learners, especially English speakers, often confuse 叫 in this pattern with 告诉, since 告诉 is also translated as 'to tell'. In general, 告诉 as 'to tell' means 'to give information', not 'to issue an order or command'. Therefore, what follows 'A 告诉 B' is a sentence or a noun/noun phrase, not a verb.

A: 你可不可以**告诉**我刚才王中跟你说什么？

Nǐ kě bù kěyǐ gàosù wǒ gāngcái Wáng Zhōng gēn nǐ shuō shénme?

B: 他说那是他的秘密，所以他**叫**我**不要**(or **别**)**告诉**别人。

Tā shuō nà shì tā de mìmì, suǒyǐ tā jiào wǒ bú yào (or *bié*) *gàosù biérén.*

A: Can you **tell** me what Wang Zhong said to you just now?

B: He said it was his secret, so he **told** me **not to tell** anybody else.

→ See 告诉 (*gàosù*) for related information.

g.　叫 can be interpreted as 'to make' or 'to cause' in the '**A 叫 B + adjective**' pattern. 觉得 (*juéde*: to feel) sometimes precedes the adjective.

(i)　'A' in the pattern can be either a person or an event, but 'B' is typically a person, or even simply 人 without specifically referring to whom.

王文生很粗鲁、没有礼貌，听他说话常常**叫人**(觉得)**很不舒服**。

Wáng Wénshēng hěn cūlǔ, méiyǒu lǐmào, tīng tā shuō huà chángcháng jiào rén (juéde) hěn bù shūfú.

Wang Wensheng is impertinent and rude. Listening to him talk often **makes one feel annoyed**.

(Scenario: A couple on the verge of breaking up puts me in a dilemma as to whom to believe. 叫 has two different meanings in the scenario, and the contrast between 告诉 and 叫 is illustrated.)

张太太**告诉**我这件事完全是张明的错，张明**叫**我**别**(or **不要**)相信他太太的话，这个情形**叫**我很为难。

Zhāng tàitai gàosù wǒ zhè jiàn shì wánquán shì Zhāng Míng de cuò, Zhāng Míng jiào wǒ bié (or *bú yào*) *xiāngxìn tā tàitai de huà; zhè ge qíngxíng jiào wǒ hěn wéinán.*

Mrs Zhang **told me that** the whole thing is completely Zhang Ming's fault; but Zhang Ming **told me not to** believe what his wife said. This situation really **makes** me 'wei nan' (not know whose side to take).

叫 can be replaced with 让 (*ràng*), 使 (*shǐ*) or 令 (*lìng*) in this pattern. Both 叫 and 让 tend to be used in casual speech, whereas 使 and 令 are more formal.

→ See 让 (*ràng*), 使 (*shǐ*) or 令 (*lìng*) for more information.

(ii)　In a specific **rhetorical question**, '**谁叫** person + verb?', 叫 is often translated as 'to tell'; however, its real function is '**to make**'. This is evidenced by the **negative form** '**不 + verb**', instead of '**别 + verb**'.

　　This rhetorical question means **nobody else is to blame** for a mistake or bad situation. 让 can be used to **replace** 叫, but 使 or 令 **cannot**.

A: 唉！这次考试又不及格；我爸爸说下个月不给我零用钱。
   Ài! Zhè cì kǎoshì yòu bù jígé; wǒ bàba shuō xià ge yuè bù gěi wǒ língyòng qián.

B: **谁叫你**自己**不**努力学习？
   Shéi jiào nǐ zìjǐ bù nǔlì xuéxí?

A: Sigh! I failed the test again. My father said that he is not going to give me my allowance next month.

B: **Who told you to (who made you) not** study hard? (Implied: It was your own fault to not have studied hard.)

(Scenario: Two friends are gossiping about Wang Xiaolan's failed romantic relationship with Zhang Ming. Note the use of 别 and 不 in the two sentences with 叫.)

A: 王小兰的好朋友都**叫她别**跟张明这种人交往，可是她不听，现在她很后悔。
   Wáng Xiǎolán de hǎo péngyǒu dōu jiào tā bié gēn Zhāng Míng zhè zhǒng rén jiāowǎng, kěshì tā bù tīng, xiànzài tā hěn hòuhuǐ.

B: **谁叫她不**听朋友的话？
   Shéi jiào tā bù tīng péngyǒu de huà?

A: All of Wang Xiaolan's good friends **told her not to** date someone like Zhang Ming; but she would not listen. Now she really regrets it.

B: **Who told her to (who made her) not** listen to her friends? (Implied: It was her own fault to not listen to her friends' advice.)

h.   叫 can be used in a **passive sentence**. It is interchangeable with 让 when used in this pattern.

(i)   In **very casual speech**, 叫 **can replace** 被 (*bèi*) in a passive sentence. It is considered a preposition in such a pattern.

张大中这次考试又不及格，所以他**叫**(= **被**)老师骂了一顿。
Zhāng Dàzhōng zhè cì kǎoshì yòu bù jígé, suǒyǐ tā jiào (= bèi) lǎoshī mà le yī dùn.
Zhang Dazhong failed the test again, so he **was scolded by** the teacher.

(Scenario: My mother is angry because I hung our laundry in the yard to air-dry even though the weather forecast predicted rain. 叫 is used twice with two different meanings.)

妈妈: 是**谁叫你**把洗好的衣服挂在院子里的？你看，所有的衣服都**叫**雨淋湿了。

Māma: *Shì shéi jiào nǐ bǎ xǐ hǎo de yīfú guà zài yuànzi lǐ de? Nǐ kàn, suǒyǒu de yīfú dōu jiào yǔ lín shī le.*

Mother: Who **told you** to hang the clean laundry in the yard? Look! All the clothes **have been soaked by** the rain.

(Scenario: A mother laments about the carelessness of her son. 叫 is used in four sentences with three different meanings.)

我儿子做的事有时候真**叫**我生气。我**叫**他**别**(or **不要**)把值钱的东西放在车里，可是他总不听。昨天车窗**叫**人打破了，他的手机和平板电脑也**叫**那个小偷偷走了。

Wǒ érzi zuò de shì yǒu shíhòu zhēn jiào wǒ shēngqì. Wǒ jiào tā bié (or *bú yào*) *bǎ zhíqián de dōngxi fàng zài chē lǐ, kěshì tā zǒng bù tīng. Zuótiān chē chuāng jiào rén dǎ pò le, tā de shǒujī hé píngbǎn diànnǎo yě jiào nà ge xiǎotōu tōu zǒu le.*

Sometimes what my son does really **makes** me mad. I have **told** him **not to** put valuable things in his car, but he never listens. Yesterday his car windows **were broken** (**by** someone), and his cellphone and tablet **were** also **stolen by** the burglar.

(ii) When the **performer** (the noun following 被/叫) in a **passive** sentence is **not** mentioned, 叫 can no longer be used; **only** 被 can.

A: 李小兰喜欢买便宜货，所以她常常**被骗**，买到假货。(Do not say 叫骗.)
   Lǐ Xiǎolán xǐhuān mǎi piányí huò, suǒyǐ tā chángcháng bèi piàn, mǎi dào jiǎ huò.

B: **谁叫她不**学教训？我也**叫**(or **被**)摊贩骗过好几次，所以我现在再也不买便宜货了。
   Shéi jiào tā bù xué jiàoxùn? Wǒ yě jiào (or *bèi*) *tānfàn piàn guo hǎo jǐ cì, suǒyǐ wǒ xiànzài zài yě bù mǎi piányí huò le.*

A: Li Xiaolan likes to buy cheap stuff, so she has often **been cheated** and bought fake merchandise.

B: **Who told her to (who made her) not** learn from her own lessons? I was also **cheated by** street vendors several times, so now I will never buy cheap stuff again.

唉！考试又不及格。今天回家又要**被骂**了！(Do not say 叫骂.)
Ài, Kǎoshì yòu bù jígé. Jīntiān huí jiā yòu yào bèi mà le!
Sigh! I failed the test again. I will **be scolded** again when I get home today.

尽管 *jǐnguǎn*

尽管 can be used as an **adverb** or as a **conjunction**. These two uses have distinctly different meanings. This section discusses these two uses.

a. When 尽管 is used as an **adverb**, it appears before the verb (or verbal phrase); it has no direct counterpart in English, and implies 'no limit or no restriction'.

(Scenario: A manager asks an employee to comment on the company's new policy. The employee is hesitant about providing his opinion.)

经理: 你**尽管**说，除了我以外，没有人会知道你说了什么。

Jīnglǐ: *Nǐ jǐnguǎn shuō, chúle wǒ yǐwài, méiyǒu rén huì zhīdào nǐ shuō le shénme.*

Manager: You can say **anything you want**. Except me, no one will know what you say.

(Scenario: A boy is excited to find that their dinner is dumplings.)

男孩: 太棒了！好久没有吃饺子了。一个人可以吃几个？

Nánhái: *Tài bàng le! Hǎo jiǔ méiyǒu chī jiǎozi le. Yī ge rén kěyǐ chī jǐ ge?*

妈妈: 今天我包了两百多个饺子，你**尽管**吃。

Māma: *Jīntiān wǒ bāo le liǎng bǎi duō ge jiǎozi, nǐ jǐnguǎn chī.*

Boy: Great! We haven't had dumplings in a long time. How many can each of us eat?

Mother: I made more than 200 dumplings today. You can eat **as many as you want**.

b. When 尽管 is used as a **conjunction**, it is similar to 虽然 (*suīrán*: although, though) in meaning, but is **stronger than 虽然** in tone; as such, 尽管 is often translated as 'even though', and it should be paired with 可是, 但是 or another similar word in the main sentence.

(i) Frequently, the main sentence will have an adverb such as 还是 or 却 to indicate that the situation remains the same (usually with 还是 or 却还是) or is opposite to what is expected (usually with 却).

尽管影评家都说这部电影非常好，**可是**愿意花钱买票去看的人**却**不多。

Jǐnguǎn yǐngpíng jiā dōu shuō zhè bù diànyǐng fēicháng hǎo, kěshì yuànyì huā qián mǎi piào qù kàn de rén què bù duō.

Even though all movie critics said that this movie was extremely good, not many people were willing to spend money on tickets to go and see it.

尽管王先生事业成功、家庭美满，**但是**他**却还是**很不快乐，因为他从小就有一种自己不如人的自卑感。

Jǐnguǎn Wáng xiānsheng shìyè chénggōng, jiātíng měimǎn, dànshì tā què háishì hěn bú kuàilè, yīnwèi tā cóngxiǎo jiù yǒu yī zhǒng zìjǐ bùrú rén de zìbēi gǎn.

Even though Mr Wang has a successful career and a happy family, he **still** feels unhappy, because ever since he was little, he has had an inferiority complex, which makes him feel that he is not as good as other people.

(ii) 可是 or 但是 can be omitted if an adverb is used.

我家就在大马路旁边；**尽管**我们在窗户上装了双层隔音玻璃，**(但是)却还是**挡不住噪音。

Wǒ jiā jiù zài dà mǎlù pángbiān; jǐnguǎn wǒmen zài chuānghù shàng zhuāng le shuāng céng géyīn bōlí, (dànshì) què háishì dǎng bú zhù zàoyīn.

My house is right next to a big street; **even though** we have installed double-pane soundproof glass in the windows, it **still** cannot keep the noise out.

尽管我家就在大马路旁边，**(可是)**屋子里**却**几乎听不见噪音，因为我们在窗户上装了双层隔音玻璃。

Jǐnguǎn wǒ jiā jiù zài dà mǎlù pángbiān, (kěshì) wūzi lǐ què jīhū tīng bú jiàn zàoyīn, yīnwèi wǒmen zài chuānghù shàng zhuāng le shuāng céng géyīn bōlí.

Even though my house is right next to a big street, we almost cannot hear any noise inside the house, because we have installed double-pane soundproof glass in the windows.

c. Many learners, especially English speakers, confuse 尽管 with 即使 (*jíshǐ*: even if), and tend to overuse 即使 when, in fact, 尽管 is the proper word. This mistake is perhaps due to the fact that 'even though' and 'even if' are used interchangeably by some English speakers.

   In Chinese, 尽管 shows a **fact** or an event that has already **taken place**, whereas 即使 shows a **hypothetical situation**, a **future situation** or an **uncertain situation**. For example,

尽管昨天雨下得很大，**可是**球赛**还是**如期举行了。(a past situation)

Jǐnguǎn zuótiān yǔ xià de hěn dà, kěshì qiúsài háishì rúqī jǔxíng le.

Even though it rained hard yesterday, the ball game **still** took place as scheduled.

即使明天下大雨，球赛**也**会如期举行。(a future situation)

Jíshǐ míngtiān xià dà yǔ, qiú sài yě huì rúqī jǔxíng.

Even if it rains hard tomorrow, the ball game will take place as scheduled.

尽管王小兰又聪明又漂亮，**可是**她的朋友**却**不多，因为她很骄傲。(a fact)

Jǐnguǎn Wáng Xiǎolán yòu cōngmíng yòu piàoliàng, kěshì tā de péngyǒu què bù duō, yīnwèi tā hěn jiāo'ào.

Even though Wang Xiaolan is both smart and pretty, she does not have many friends because she is arrogant.

A: 你要不要我给你介绍女朋友？你喜欢什么样的女孩？聪明的还是漂亮的？

Nǐ yào bú yào wǒ gěi nǐ jièshào nǚ péngyǒu? Nǐ xǐhuān shénme yàng de nǚhái? Cōngmíng de háishì piàoliàng de?

B: 我太忙了，没有时间交女朋友，所以**即使**有又聪明又漂亮的，我**也**不想认识。(hypothetical situation)

Wǒ tài máng le, méiyǒu shíjiān jiāo nǚ péngyǒu, suǒyǐ jíshǐ yǒu yòu cōngmíng yòu piàoliàng de, wǒ yě bù xiǎng rènshì.

A: Do you want me to set you up with someone? What kind of girl do you like? Smart ones or pretty ones?

B: I am too busy and I don't have time to date, so **even if** there is someone who is both smart and pretty, I do not want to meet her.

d. A similarity between 尽管 and 即使 lies in the fact that both can imply '**concession**', meaning 'in spite of the fact that . . .'. For example,

今天早上我不舒服，所以给经理打了一个电话说我不能去上班；可是经理说**即使**我不舒服**也**得去，因为今天有一个很重要的会，我必须参加。所以**尽管**我头疼得要命，**还是**去上班了。(Note that 也得去 shows a future event from the manager's point of view, whereas 去上班了 shows a past event from the narrator's point of view.)

Jīntiān zǎoshàng wǒ bù shūfú, suǒyǐ gěi jīnglǐ dǎ le yī ge diànhuà shuō wǒ bù néng qù shàng bān; kěshì jīnglǐ shuō jíshǐ wǒ bù shūfú yě děi qù, yīnwèi jīntiān yǒu yī ge hěn zhòngyào de huì, wǒ bìxū cānjiā. Suǒyǐ jǐnguǎn wǒ tóu téng de yàomìng, háishì qù shàngbān le.

This morning I did not feel well, so I called my manager and told him that I could not go to work. But the manager said that **even so** (**even if** I was not feeling well), I would have to go to work, because there was going to be a very important meeting that I must attend. Therefore, **even though** I had a terrible headache, I **still** went to work.

→ See 即使 (*jíshǐ*) for related information.

究竟 *jiūjìng*

究竟 and 到底 (*dàodǐ*) have the same meaning and usages. 究竟 is a **more formal word** and is often used in written communication, whereas 到底 is used in more casual speech.

→ See 到底 (*dàodǐ*) for more information.

就是 . . . 也 . . . *jiùshì . . . yě . . .*

就, as a stand-alone word, is extremely versatile in meaning. The accurate interpretation of a sentence with 就 can only be achieved by taking into consideration the context in which 就 appears. In addition, when 就是 is in a sentence, 是 may or may not be a stand-alone word. For example:

(Scenario: Wang has heard a lot about Gao from her friend Li, but has never met him.)

李:　　　 你看！高大明在那里！

Lǐ:　　　 *Nǐ kàn! Gāo Dàmíng zài nàlǐ!*

王:　　　 那**就是**高大明？你可不可以给我们介绍？(是 is a stand-alone word. 就 puts emphasis on 是.)

Wáng:　 *Nà jiù shì Gāo Dàmíng? Nǐ kě bù kěyǐ gěi wǒmen jièshào?*

Li:　　　 Look! Gao Daming is over there!

Wang:　　 That *IS* Gao Daming? Can you introduce us?

(Scenario: A real estate agent is showing Mr Li a house.)

房地产商:　　　　 李先生，你觉得这个房子怎么样？

Fángdìchǎn shāng:　 *Lǐ xiānsheng, nǐ juéde zhè ge fángzi zěnme yàng?*

李:　　　　　　　 地点、价钱都不错，**就是**院子太小了。我喜欢院子大一点的房子。(就是 is an expression; 是 is not a stand-alone word.)

Lǐ:　　　　　　　 *Dìdiǎn, jiàqián dōu búcuò, jiùshì yuànzi tài xiǎo le. Wǒ xǐhuān yuànzi dà yīdiǎn de fángzi.*

Real estate agent:　 Mr Li, what do you think of this house?

Li:　　　　　　　 Both the location and price are quite good, **except** the yard is too small. I like a house with a bigger yard.

When 也 appears in a sentence with 就是, it does not have a stand-alone meaning, and should not be literally translated as 'also'. 就是 . . . 也 . . . is a pair that means 'even if'; it has several connotations and is considered **interchangeable with 即使 . . . 也 . . .** (*jíshǐ . . . yě . . .*). However, 就是 is often used in **casual communication**; whereas 即使 may be a somewhat more formal word. In addition, 即使 can be followed by 是, but 就是 cannot. Learners who fail to take into consideration the presence of 也 in the sentence often find the expression hard to understand or even misinterpret it.

→ See 即使 (*jíshǐ*) for detailed information.

就算 . . . 也 . . . *jiùsuàn . . . yě . . .*

就算 . . . 也 . . . is **interchangeable with 就是 . . . 也 . . . .** The only minor difference is that 就是 cannot be followed by another 是, whereas 就算 can.

(Scenario: Wang asks Xie for a loan; but Xie says he does not have much money.)

王:　　　 我急需用钱；你借我多少都行。**就算是**二十块**也**可以 (= **就是**二十块**也**可以)。

Wáng:　 *Wǒ jí xū yòng qián; nǐ jiè wǒ duōshǎo dōu xíng. Jiùsuàn shì èrshí kuài yě kěyǐ.*

Wang:　　 I urgently need money; however much you can loan me would be fine. **Even** 20 *kuai* would be OK.

就要 . . . 了 *jiù yào . . . le*

就要 . . . 了 is very similar in meaning to 快 . . . 了 (*kuài . . . le*) and 快要 . . . 了 (*kuài yào . . . le*). All of them are used to indicate an **impending event** or a **point in time about to be reached**.

→ See 快 . . . 了 (*kuài . . . le*) and 快要 . . . 了 (*kuài yào . . . le*) for related information.

你**就要**当爸爸**了**，怎么还这么不成熟？
(就要当爸爸了 can be **快**当爸爸**了** or **快要**当爸爸**了**.)
Nǐ jiù yào dāng bàba le, zěnme hái zhème bù chéngshóu?
You are **going to** be a father **soon**; how come you are still so immature?

李太太的儿子**就要**三岁**了**，可是还不会说话，李太太急得要命。
(就要三岁了 can be **快**三岁**了** or **快要**三岁**了**.)
Lǐ tàitai de érzi jiù yào sān suì le, kěshì hái bú huì shuōhuà, Lǐ tàitai jí de yàomìng.
Mrs Li's son **is (soon) going to be** three years old, but he still cannot talk. Mrs Li is worried to death.

a. When a **time phrase** appears in the sentence, **only 就要 . . . 了** can be used. Neither 快 . . . 了 nor 快要 . . . 了 would be correct.

下星期**就要**期末考**了**，你为什么还没有开始准备？(下星期 is the time phrase.)
Xià xīngqī jiù yào qīmòkǎo le, nǐ wèishénme hái méiyǒu kāishǐ zhǔnbèi?
Final exams are **coming (soon)** next week. Why have you not started to study (to get ready for the exams)?

b. When **words** or **phrases** that function as **time phrases** appear in the sentence, **only 就要 . . . 了** can be used.

飞机还有半小时**就要**起飞**了**，可是李先生还没有到机场呢！(**还有半小时** functions as the time phrase.)
Fēijī hái yǒu bàn xiǎoshí jiù yào qǐfēi le, kěshì Lǐ xiānsheng hái méiyǒu dào jīchǎng ne!
The flight **will soon** depart in half an hour; but Mr Li still has not arrived at the airport.

你马上**就要**离家上大学**了**，应该学会照顾自己的日常生活。(**马上** is an adverb, but it functions as a time phrase in this structure.)
Nǐ mǎshàng jiù yào lí jiā shàng dàxué le, yīnggāi xué huì zhàogù zìjǐ de rìcháng shēnghuó.
You **will soon** leave home to go to college; you should learn to take care of business in your own daily life.

觉得 *juéde*

觉得 is used to express one's **feelings**, either **physical** or **mental**, as well as one's **opinions**. Because it is often translated as 'to feel', the accurate use of this word can sometimes cause confusion.

a. When expressing one's **physical feelings**, use an **adjective after 觉得**; e.g. 她**觉得**很**冷** (*Tā juéde hěn lěng*: She feels cold); 我**觉得**又**累**又**饿** (*Wǒ juéde yòu lèi yòu è*: I feel both tired and hungry). This is the basic usage of 觉得.

b. 'Person + 觉得 + adjective' can express a person's **mental feelings**.

小中的妈妈花了很多钱给他请家教，可是他的成绩还是很差，所以妈妈**觉得**非常**失望**。
Xiǎozhōng de māma huā le hěn duō qián gěi tā qǐng jiājiào, kěshì tā de chéngjī háishì hěn chà, suǒyǐ māma juéde fēicháng shīwàng.
Xiaozhong's mother has spent a lot of money hiring tutors for him, but his academic performance is still bad, so his mother **feels** extremely **disappointed**.

Sometimes the adjective after 觉得 is used to show the person's mental feelings about a **situation**. Because the situation is often omitted from the sentence, the **surface pattern** is still 'person + 觉得 + adjective'.

A: 昨天的考试难不难？
     Zuótiān de kǎoshì nán bù nán?
B: 我**觉得**很**难**。(The full sentence is 我觉得昨天的考试很难.)
     Wǒ juéde hěn nán.
A: Was yesterday's test difficult?
B: **I feel that it** was difficult. (Do not translate this as 'I feel difficult.')

(Scenario: A couple is shopping for furniture.)
丈夫: 这把椅子怎么样？
Zhàngfū: *Zhè bǎ yǐzi zěnme yàng?*
妻子: **我觉得不太舒服**。我想试一下那把。(不太舒服 is about **the chair**.)
Qīzi: *Wǒ juéde bú tài shūfú. Wǒ xiǎng shì yīxià nà bǎ.*
Husband: How's this chair?
Wife: **I feel that it is** not very comfortable. I would like to try that one.

(Scenario: Wang calls Li on phone because Li was absent from class.)
王: 小李，你今天怎么没来上课？
Wáng: *Xiǎo Lǐ, nǐ jīntiān zěnme méi lái shàngkè?*
李: 因为**我觉得不太舒服**。(不太舒服 is about the person and his physical feeling.)
Lǐ: *Yīnwèi wǒ juéde bú tài shūfú.*
Wang: Little Li, how come you did not come to class today?
Li: Because **I didn't feel well**. (**I feel unwell**.)

Misinterpretation may occasionally occur. For example, 我觉得很奇怪 (*Wǒ juéde hěn qíguài*) should not be literally interpreted as 'I feel strange'; instead, it means that 'I feel the situation is strange'. Therefore, one must pay attention to the context in order to arrive at the accurate interpretation of the '**person** + 觉得 + **adjective**' pattern.

c.   觉得 can be followed by a **sentence** to express one's **opinion**. In this pattern, 觉得 is often translated as 'to think'. **Using 想** (*xiǎng*) instead of 觉得 to express one's opinions is a **common mistake** made by learners who are English speakers. 想 is normally used to express one's **speculation** about a situation.

→ See 想 (*xiǎng*) for more information.

A: 你们吃过日本菜吗？
  Nǐmen chī guo Rìběn cài ma?
B: 我**没吃过**，可是我**想**日本菜**一定**很好吃。(speculation)
  Wǒ méi chī guo, kěshì wǒ xiǎng Rìběn cài yídìng hěn hǎochī.
C: 我**吃过**，我**觉得**日本菜又贵又不好吃。(opinion)
  Wǒ chī guo, wǒ juéde Rìběn cài yòu guì yòu bù hǎochī.
A: Have you tried Japanese food?
B: I haven't. But **I think** Japanese food **must be** delicious.
C: I have (tried it). **I think (I feel)** that Japanese food is both expensive and not tasty.

It should be noted that, from a grammatical stand-point, one's **mental feelings** and one's **opinions** about a situation are **not distinctively different**.

(Scenario: Two students are having a conversation upon finishing a big exam.)
A: 考完了！你现在**觉得**很轻松吧！
  Kǎo wán le! Nǐ xiànzài juéde hěn qīngsōng ba!
B: 我不但不**觉得**轻松 (mental feeling)，反而**觉得**很难过 (mental feeling)，因为我**觉得**这个考试太难了(opinion or mental feeling)，所以我**想**我的成绩一定很差 (speculation)。
  Wǒ búdàn bù juéde qīngsōng, fǎn'ér juéde hěn nánguò, yīnwèi wǒ juéde zhè ge kǎoshì tài nán le, suǒyǐ wǒ xiǎng wǒde chéngjì yídìng hěn chà.
A: The test is over! You must be **feeling** relaxed now.
B: Not only do I not **feel** relaxed, but also I **feel** sad. **I feel (I think)** this test was too difficult, so **I think (I guess)** my score must be bad.

d.   It is acceptable to use 觉得 to indicate one's **speculation** as long as words such as 一定 (*yídìng*: definitely), 应该 (*yīnggāi*: should), 会 (*huì*: would) and 大概 (*dàgài*: probably) are used. However, it is incorrect to use 想 to indicate one's opinion.

A:　我**觉得**（想 is not acceptable）昨天的考试其实不太难，可是我考得非常糟糕；我**觉得**（想 is acceptable）老师**一定会**很失望。
　　Wǒ juéde zuótiān de kǎoshì qíshí bú tài nán, kěshì wǒ kǎo de fēicháng zāogāo; wǒ juéde lǎoshī yīdìng huì hěn shīwàng.

B:　你**想**（觉得 is acceptable）她会不会骂你？
　　Nǐ xiǎng tā huì bú huì mà nǐ?

A:　不知道，我**觉得**（想 is acceptable）她**可能**会。
　　Bù zhīdào, wǒ juéde tā kěnéng huì.

A:　I **think (I feel)** that yesterday's test actually was not very difficult, but I did very poorly. I **think** the teacher **must be** disappointed.

B:　Do you **think** she will scold you?

A:　I don't know; I **think** she **probably** will.

e.　Another word, **认为** (*rènwéi*), is also used to express one's opinion. It is used in more formal situations, or when the topic being discussed is more serious.

(Scenario: Two people are discussing China's population policy. Grammatically, both 认为 can be replaced by 觉得.)

A:　你对中国"一家一个孩子"的人口政策有什么看法？
　　Nǐ duì Zhōngguó 'yī jiā yī ge háizi' de rénkǒu zhèngcè yǒu shénme kànfǎ?

B:　我**认为**这个政策违反了人权。
　　Wǒ rènwéi zhè ge zhèngcè wéifǎn le rénquán.

A:　我不同意；我**认为**人口太多是全国百姓的负担，所以必须控制人口的增长。
　　Wǒ bù tóngyì; wǒ rènwéi rénkǒu tài duō shì quán guó bǎixìng de fùdān, suǒyǐ bìxū kòngzhì rénkǒu de zēngzhǎng.

A:　What's your opinion about China's 'one child per family' population policy?

B:　I **think (I am of the opinion that)** this policy violates human rights.

A:　I disagree. I **think (I am of the opinion that)** the population being too large is the burden of the whole country's citizens, so they must control the increase in population.

→ See 认为 (*rènwéi*) for more examples.

f.　English speakers often use the phrase 'to **feel** like' in various contexts. It is important to know that this phrase **may or may not** involve the word 觉得 in Chinese.

(i)　**觉得像** (*juéde xiàng*)

我已经十八岁了，可是妈妈还是要我每晚十点回家，有时候我**觉得像**个小孩。
Wǒ yǐjīng shíbā suì le, kěshì māma háishì yào wǒ měi wǎn shí diǎn huí jiā, yǒushíhou wǒ juéde xiàng ge xiǎohái.
I am already 18 years old, but my mother still wants me to return home by ten o'clock every evening. Sometimes I **feel like** a child.

(ii) **好像会** (*hǎoxiàng huì*)

天色很暗，**好像会**下雨。

Tiānsè hěn àn, hǎoxiàng huì xiàyǔ.

The sky is dark; it **feels like (it might)** rain.

(iii) **想 + verb** (*xiǎng* + verb)

我又热又渴，所以现在**想喝**一瓶冰啤酒。(Do not say 想一瓶冰啤酒 or 我觉得一瓶冰啤酒.)

Wǒ yòu rè yòu kě, suǒyǐ xiànzài xiǎng hē yī píng bīng píjiǔ.

I am both hot and thirsty, so I **feel like (having)** a bottle of cold beer now.

开始 *kāishǐ*

To use 开始 as a verb or a noun is relatively straightforward since it can be directly translated as 'to begin/to start' or 'the beginning'. However, less attention has been paid to the use of **开始 as a time word**. Misunderstanding or incomprehension can occur if one fails to accurately interpret 开始 in a sentence.

a. 开始 can be used as a **noun** to mean 'beginning'.

(Scenario: Two parents are giving their son advice before he goes to school on the first day of a new semester.)

爸爸: 新学期就是一个新的**开始**，希望你能天天早起，上课不迟到。

Bàba: *Xīn xuéqī jiù shì yī ge xīn de kāishǐ, xīwàng nǐ néng tiān tiān zǎo qǐ, shàng kè bù chídào.*

妈妈: 爸爸说得很对！好的**开始**是成功的一半。

Māma: *Bàba shuō de hěn duì! Hǎo de kāishǐ shì chénggōng de yībàn.*

Father: A new semester is a new **beginning**. I hope you can get up early every day and not be late for class.

Mother: Your father said it right! A good **beginning** is halfway to success.

b. There are a few patterns involving the use of 开始 as a **verb**. These patterns are similar to English.

It should be noted that 开始 is considered an **instantaneous** verb. This means that the sentence frequently needs 了 if the action has already taken place.

(i) As a verb, 开始 can be followed by another **verb** or a **noun**.

爸爸: 你打算什么时候**开始**写毕业论文？

Bàba: *Nǐ dǎsuàn shénme shíhòu kāishǐ xiě bìyè lùnwén?*

妈妈: 更重要的是，你打算什么时候**开始**找工作？

Māma: *Gèng zhòngyào de shì, nǐ dǎsuàn shénme shíhòu kāishǐ zhǎo gōngzuò?*

Father: When do you plan to **start** writing your graduation thesis?

Mother: Even more important, when do you plan to **start** looking for a job?

他們一進入野生公園，就**開始了**一連串精彩有趣的冒險活動。
Tāmen yī jìnrù yěshēng gōngyuán, jiù kāishǐ le yī liánchùan jīngcǎi yǒuqù de màoxiǎn huódòng.
As soon as they entered the wildlife park, they immediately **started** a series of exciting and interesting adventurous activities.

(ii) The activity that has started or is to start can be the subject with 开始 being the verb. Note the use of 了 in the sentences.

A: 听说王小兰最新的减肥计划又**开始了**。
　　Tīngshuō Wáng Xiǎolán zuì xīn de jiǎnféi jìhuà yòu kāishǐ le.
B: 你听错了，她说这次要等过了新年才**开始**。
　　Nǐ tīng cuò le, tā shuō zhè cì yào děng guò le xīnnián cái kāishǐ.
A: I heard that Wang Xiaolan's latest weight-loss plan **has started** again.
B: You heard it wrong. She has said that this time she will wait until after the New Year before she **starts** it.

A: 电影几点**开始**？
　　Diànyǐng jǐdiǎn kāishǐ?
B: 哪部电影？《哈利波特》已经**开始了**；《钢铁人》两点半**开始**。
　　Nǎ bù diànyǐng? 'Hālì Bōtè' yǐjīng kāishǐ le; 'Gāngtiě rén' liǎng diǎn bàn kāishǐ.
A: What time does the movie start?
B: Which movie? *Harry Potter* **has** already **started**; *Ironman* **starts** at 2:30.

c. When 开始 is used as a **time word**, it means '**at the outset**' or '**initially**'. The implication is 'it was so **at the beginning**, but **later** it turned out differently'. Therefore, words such as 后来 (*hòulái*: later on), 最后 (*zuìhòu*: eventually) and 了 (indicating a change of situation) are often used to describe the situation.

When used this way, 开始 is actually a short form for **(刚)开始的时候**, literally 'when it first started'.

A: 听说你在学中文；你学了多久了？你觉得中文难不难？
　　Tīngshuō nǐ zài xué Zhōngwén; nǐ xué le duō jiǔ le? Nǐ juéde Zhōngwén nán bù nán?
B: 我学了三年多了。**(刚)开始(的时候)**，我觉得很难，现在觉得不难**了**。
　　Wǒ xué le sān nián duō le. (Gāng) kāishǐ (de shíhòu), wǒ juéde hěn nán, xiànzài juéde bù nán le.
A: I have heard that you are studying Chinese. How long have you been studying it? Do you think Chinese is difficult?
B: I have been studying it for more than three years. **When I first started**, I felt that it was difficult (**initially**, I felt that it was difficult); now I **no longer** feel it's difficult.

Since a time word can appear **after the subject**, **confusion** can easily occur if 开始 is mistakenly interpreted as a verb.

王小兰要跟李大中结婚，她爸妈**开始**很反对，因为她才二十岁；可是**后来**他们跟李大中见了面，觉得他会是一个好丈夫，所以就同意**了**。

Wáng Xiǎolán yào gēn Lǐ Dàzhōng jiéhūn, tā bàmā kāishǐ hěn fǎnduì, yīnwèi tā cái èrshí suì; kěshì hòulái tāmen gēn Lǐ Dàzhōng jiàn le miàn, juéde tā huì shì yī ge hǎo zhàngfū, suǒyǐ jiù tóngyì le.

Wang Xiaolan wanted to marry Li Dazhong. Her parents **initially (at the beginning)** were very much opposed to it because she was only 20 years old. But **later** they met Li Dazhong, and they felt that he would be a good husband; so they agreed.

To accurately interpret 开始, one must **pay special attention to the context.** The following example shows 开始 as a verb and as a time word.

A: 这个项目是什么时候**开始**接受报名的？(verb)
　　Zhè ge xiàngmù shì shénme shíhòu kāishǐ jiēshòu bàomíng de?
B: 去年十月就**开始了**。(verb)
　　Qùnián shíyuè jiù kāishǐ le.
A: 报名的人多不多？
　　Bàomíng de rén duō bù duō?
B: 大家**开始** (time word) 似乎没有什么兴趣；可是因为我们努力做宣传工作，所以慢慢**开始** (verb) 得到一般人的注意。
　　Dàjiā kāishǐ sìhū méiyǒu shénme xìngqù; kěshì yīnwèi wǒmen nǔlì zuò xuānchuán gōngzuò, suǒyǐ màn màn kāishǐ dédào yībān rén de zhùyì.
A: 最后有多少人参加？
　　Zuìhòu yǒu duōshǎo rén cānjiā?
B: **开始** (time word) 只有一百个，可是项目进行了两个月以后，就有三百多个人**了**。
　　Kāishǐ zhǐ yǒu yī bǎi ge, kěshì xiàngmù jìnxíng le liǎng ge yuè yǐhòu, jiù yǒu sān bǎi duō ge rén le.
A: When did this program **start** accepting registrations?
B: It **started** last October.
A: Were there many people who signed up?
B: **Initially (at the beginning)** people did not seem to have much interest. But because we worked hard on promotional work, slowly we **began** to receive attention from average folks.
A: Eventually how many people participated?
B: **Initially** there were only 100 people, but after the program had been in progress for two months, there were already over 300 people.

d.　从 ... 开始 is used to indicate the **initial point** of an activity. The initial point can either be a **time** or a **location**.

这次考试我考得很差，**从**今天**开始**，我一定要努力学习。

Zhè cì kǎoshì wǒ kǎo de hěn chà, cóng jīntiān kāishǐ, wǒ yīdìng yào nǔlì xuéxí.

I did poorly on this test. **From today on (starting today)**, I will definitely study hard.

我们**从**山脚**开始**往上爬，爬了三个多小时，还没有到山顶。

Wǒmen cóng shānjiǎo kāishǐ wàng shàng pá, pà le sān ge duō xiǎoshí, hái méiyǒu dào shān dǐng.

We **started** to climb **from** the bottom of the mountain. After climbing for over three hours, we still have not reached the top of the mountain.

可以 *kěyǐ*

Although 可以 is often simply translated as 'can' or 'to be able to', it has various connotations including **ability**, **possibility**, and **permission**. As it is generally considered a **modal verb**, 可以 is normally followed by a regular verb or is used to give a short answer to a yes-no question.

However, in certain situations, 可以 can be used as an **adjective**. Therefore, it is important to pay attention to the context in which it appears in order to arrive at the best interpretation.

Although 能 (*néng*) has the same definitions as 可以 and they share similarities in usage, they are not always interchangeable with each other. The discussions in this section include the most common uses of 可以, as well as **comparisons between 能 and 可以** when applicable.

→ See 能 (*néng*) for related information.

a.　Indicating **ability** and **possibility**

(i)　In a **positive** sentence, the distinction between ability and possibility can be vague since both can refer to 'potential'. **可以 and 能 are interchangeable**.

李明一次**可以(or 能)**做两百个伏地挺身，真惊人！

Lǐ Míng yī cì kěyǐ (or néng) zuò liǎng bǎi ge fúdì tǐngshēn, zhēn jīngrén!

Li Ming **can (is able to)** do 200 push-ups at once. This is really amazing.

我知道一个秘方，不用节食，不用运动，就**可以**成功地减肥。

Wǒ zhīdào yī ge mìfāng, búyòng jiéshí, búyòng yùndòng, jiù kěyǐ chénggōng de jiǎnféi.

I know a secret. You don't have to diet, and you don't have to exercise, but you **can (will be able to)** successfully lose weight.

(ii)　It should be noted that the **negative form is not 不可以**, which specifically refers to 'no permission' (see section c. below). Therefore, **不能** should be used.

A: 王经理病了，所以他今天**不能**来开会。(Do not use 不可以.)
Wáng jīnglǐ bìng le, suǒyǐ tā jīntiān bù néng lái kāi huì.

B: 那他**可不可以**(or **能不能**)从家里打电话来参加讨论？
Nà tā kě bù kěyǐ (or néng bù néng) cóng jiā lǐ dǎ diànhuà lái cānjiā tǎolùn?

A: 他喉咙痛，根本**不能**说话。(Do not use 不可以.)
Tā hóulóng tòng, gēnběn bù néng shuō huà.

A: Manager Wang is sick, so he **cannot** come to the meeting today.

B: Then **can** he call from home to participate in the discussions?

A: He has a sore throat. He **cannot** talk at all.

(iii) When making a **request**, both 可以 and 能 can be used.

A: 你现在**可不可以**(or **能不能**)来我家跟我练习一下英语对话？我明天有一个口语考试。
Nǐ xiànzài kě bù kěyǐ (or néng bù néng) lái wǒ jiā gēn wǒ liànxí yīxià Yīngyǔ duìhuà? Wǒ míngtiān yǒu yī ge kǒuyǔ kǎoshì.

B: 我**可以**来你家，可是我大概**不能**(cannot be 不可以)帮忙你准备考试，因为我的英文也说得不太好。
Wǒ kěyǐ lái nǐ jiā, kěshì wǒ dàgài bù néng bāngmáng nǐ zhǔnbèi kǎoshì, yīnwèi wǒ de Yīngwén yě shuō de bú tài hǎo.

A: **Can** you come to my house now to practice English conversation with me? I have an oral exam tomorrow.

B: I **can** come to your house, but I probably **cannot** help you get ready for the test because I don't speak English too well, either.

(iv) The **short positive response** to the request can either be 可以 or 行 (*xíng*), but 能 is not a good choice. For a **negative response**, use 不行; either 不可以 or 不能 is improper.

学生: 这段话，我不太懂；您**可不可以**(or **能不能**)解释一下？
Xuéshēng: *Zhè duàn huà, wǒ bú tài dǒng; nín kě bù kěyǐ (or néng bù néng) jiěshì yīxià?*

老师: **可以**(or **行**)，但是我现在没有时间。你下午**能不能**到我的办公室来一趟？
Lǎoshī: *Kěyǐ (or xíng), dànshì wǒ xiànzài méiyǒu shíjiān. Nǐ xiàwǔ néng bù néng dào wǒ de bàngōngshì lái yī tàng?*

Student: I don't quite understand this passage. **Can** you explain it?

Teacher: Yes, I **can**, but I don't have time now. **Can** you come to my office in the afternoon?

A: 我想请王小兰去看电影，你**可不可以**告诉我她的电话号码？
Wǒ xiǎng qǐng Wáng Xiǎolán qù kàn diànyǐng, nǐ kě bù kěyǐ gàosù wǒ tā de diànhuà hàomǎ?

B: 对不起，**不行**！因为她是我哥哥的女朋友。
Duì bù qǐ, bù xíng! Yīnwèi tā shì wǒ gēge de nǚ péngyǒu.

A: I would like to invite Wang Xiaolan to a movie. **Can** you tell me her phone number?

B: Sorry, I **can't**, because she is my older brother's girlfriend.

b. Indicating the **potential use** of something

Both 可以 and 能 can be used in positive sentences or questions, but the **negative** for this use is **不能** (or 不行 for a short answer), not 不可以.

A: 王小兰出门的时候，总是带着伞；晴天**可以**遮太阳；下雨的时候**可以**挡雨。

Wáng Xiǎolán chūmén de shíhòu, zǒngshì dài zhe sǎn; qíngtiān kěyǐ zhē tàiyáng; xià yǔ de shíhòu kěyǐ dǎng yǔ.

B: 她的伞是布做的，**可以**遮太阳，但是**不能**挡雨。(不能 cannot be 不可以.)

Tā de sǎn shì bù zuò de, kěyǐ zhē tàiyáng, dànshì bù néng dǎng yǔ.

A: When Wang Xiaolan goes out, she always carries a parasol. On sunny days, it **can** (be used to) block the sun; when it is raining, it **can** (be used to) shield the rain.

B: Her parasol is made of cloth. It **can** (be used to) block the sun, but it **cannot** (be used to) shield the rain.

A: 椰子油有什么功能？

Yézǐ yóu yǒu shénme gōngnéng?

B: **可以**炒菜，也**可以**润肤。

Kěyǐ chǎo cài, yě kěyǐ rùn fū.

A: **可(以)不可以**(or **能不能**)给地板打蜡？

Kě (yǐ) bù kěyǐ (or néng bù néng) gěi dìbǎn dǎlà?

B: **不行**。

Bù xíng.

A: What functions does coconut oil have?

B: It **can** be used for cooking, and it **can** also be used to moisturize skin.

A: **Can** it be used to polish the floor?

B: No, it **can't**.

c. Indicating **permission**

Both 能 and 可以 can be used to ask for permission, but 可以 may sound **somewhat more polite** than 能. Use **(不)可以** or **(不)行** for a short answer.

A: 我**可不可以**用一下你的电脑？

Wǒ kě bù kěyǐ yòng yīxià nǐ de diànnǎo?

B: **可以**(or **行**)。

Kěyǐ (or xíng).

A: **May I** use your computer for a while?

B: Yes, you **may**.

(Scenario: A boy receives a phone call from a friend, asking him to go to a movie. He needs his mother's permission to go.)

儿子:	我**可不可以**跟朋友去看电影？
Érzi:	*Wǒ kě bù kěyǐ gēn péngyǒu qù kàn diànyǐng?*
妈妈:	**不行**。今天晚上我们有客人来，你要在家帮忙打扫屋子。
Māma:	*Bù xíng. Jīntiān wǎnshàng wǒmen yǒu kèrén lái, nǐ yào zài jiā bāngmáng dǎsǎo wūzi.*
儿子 (to his friend):	我妈妈说我**不可以**去。
Érzi:	*Wǒ māma shuō wǒ bù kěyǐ qù.*
Son:	**Can** I go to a movie with my friend?
Mother:	No, you **can't**. We have guests coming this evening; you have to stay home and help clean up the house.
Son:	My mother says that I **cannot (I am not allowed** to) go.

In a negative sentence, 不能 is more flexible in meaning, whereas **不可以** specifically refers to '**no permission**'; therefore, 不可以 means 'to be not allowed' or 'to be forbidden'.

A: 我们的英文老师说，上课的时候，**不可以**说中文。
   Wǒmen de Yīngwén lǎoshī shuō, shàng kè de shíhòu, bù kěyǐ shuō Zhōngwén.
B: 我们下课以后也**不能**跟英文老师说中文，因为她一句中文也不懂。
   Wǒmén xià kè yǐhòu yě bù néng gēn Yīngwén lǎoshī shuō Zhōngwén, yīnwèi tā yī jù Zhōngwén yě bù dǒng.
A: Our English teacher says that we **cannot (are not allowed to)** speak Chinese in class.
B: We also **cannot** speak Chinese with our English teacher after class, because she does not understand any Chinese.

d. Indicating **acceptability**
    When 可以 is not followed by a verb, it is no longer considered a modal verb but an **adjective**. It can be **replaced with** 行, but 能 cannot be used in this structure. 不可以 and 不能 cannot be used as its negative form, but **不行** can.

    (i) 可以 can be used as an adjective to say something is neither very good nor very bad, and is **merely so-so**. Used as a **predicate**, the expression is **还可以**, although 还 does not have a stand-alone meaning here and should not be interpreted as 'still' or another similar word.

(Scenario: Two retired old friends are catching up over the phone.)

A: 最近身体怎么样？

    Zuìjìn shēntǐ zěnme yàng?

B: **还可以**(or **还行**)。

    Hái kěyǐ (or *hái xíng*).

A: 打麻将的手气呢？(麻将 is a Chinese gambling game.)

    Dǎ májiàng de shǒuqì ne?

B: 也**还可以**，有输有赢。

    Yě hái kěyǐ, yǒu shū yǒu yíng.

A: How has your health been lately?

B: It's OK (**so-so**).

A: How about your luck in playing *majiang*?

B: It's also **so-so**. I win some and I lose some.

(ii) It can indicate something is **acceptable**. In this case, 还 **is not used**.

(Scenario: At a shoe store.)

店员: 这双**可以**吗？要不要试一双大一点的？

Diànyuán: *Zhè shuāng kěyǐ ma? Yào bú yào shì yī shuāng dà yīdiǎn de?*

顾客: **可以**，**可以**，不用再试了；我买这双。

Gùkè: *Kěyǐ, kěyǐ, búyòng zài shì le; wǒ mǎi zhè shuāng.*

Store clerk: **Will** this pair **do**? Do you want to try on another pair that is larger in size?

Customer: It **will do**. (It's **fine**. I will take it.) No need to try another pair. I will buy this pair.

The expression can be **可以了** to indicate 'it is good enough (and can stop) now'. 了 in this context implies 'already'.

(Scenario: A man is pouring wine at the dinner table for his guest.)

客人: **可以了**！**可以了**！我喝不了那么多。

Kèrén: *Kěyǐ le! Kěyǐ le! Wǒ hē bù liǎo nàme duō.*

Guest: **Good enough**! **Good enough**! (Don't pour me any more of the wine.) I cannot drink that much.

Related expressions

可以不 *kěyǐ bù*

Because 可以不 seems to suggest '**can + not**', learners often misinterpret it to literally mean 'cannot' or have difficulty using it properly. Actually, 可以 in this expression implies '**permission**', and 不 should be considered part of the verb that follows it. Therefore, the correct interpretation is '**to be allowed not to do something**', meaning '**to not have to**' or '**no need to**'.

(Scenario: A boy is getting ready to climb into bed.)

妈妈: 小中，你还**不可以**去睡觉，因为你还没有洗澡。

Māma: Xiǎozhōng, nǐ hái bù kěyǐ qù shuìjiào, yīnwèi nǐ hái méiyǒu xǐzǎo.

爸爸: 你看他这么累，我觉得他今天**可以不**洗澡。

Bàba: Nǐ kàn tā zhème lèi, wǒ juéde tā jīntiān kěyǐ bù xǐzǎo.

Mother: Xiaozhong, you **cannot (are not allowed to)** go to bed yet because you have not taken a shower.

Father: Look at him! He is so tired. I think he **is allowed to not (he does not have to)** take a shower today.

(Scenario: A workplace situation.)

A: 唉！又得去开会！

Ài, yòu děi qù kāi huì!

B: 其实我们**可以不**去，因为秘书告诉我，这次没有签到表。不过你**不可以**告诉别人。要是大家都不去，主管会不高兴。

Qíshí wǒmen kěyǐ bú qù, yīnwèi mìshū gàosù wǒ, zhè cì méiyǒu qiāndào biǎo. Búguò nǐ bù kěyǐ gàosù biérén. Yàoshì dàjiā dōu bú qù, zhǔguǎn huì bù gāoxìng.

A: Sigh! We have to go to a meeting again!

B: Actually we **don't have to go**, because the secretary has told me that there won't be a sign-up sheet this time. But you **cannot (mustn't)** tell other people about this. If nobody goes, the manager will be upset.

不可不 *bù kě bù*

Since 可以不 means 'no need to', 不可不 is its opposite and means '**must**' or '**to have to**'. Usually, it is used to give a **warning** or **advice**, and the tone tends to be **more formal**. Note that 以 is omitted.

小李是一个表里不一的人；跟这种人来往，**不可不**防。

Xiǎo Lǐ shì yī ge biǎo lǐ bù yī de rén; gēn zhè zhǒng rén láiwǎng, bù kě bù fáng.

Little Li is a duplicitous person. When you deal with this type of people, you **have to** be on guard.

到了北京，有几个**不可不**去的地方，长城就是其中之一。

Dào le Běijīng, yǒu jǐ ge bù kě bú qù de dìfāng; Chángchéng jiù shì qízhōng zhī yī.

When you arrive in Beijing, there are a few places that you **must** go; the Great Wall is one of them.

可以说 *kěyǐ shuō*

The surface meaning of 可以说 does not completely convey its meaning; therefore, when the subject is a person, confusion or misunderstanding sometimes arises. It is important to pay attention to the context in order to arrive at the correct interpretation.

(Scenario: At a dinner party, a precocious boy impresses the guests. 可以 说 has two different interpretations in this scenario.)

客人: 听说中国的人口政策改变了；新的政策跟原来的有什么不同 呢？

Kèrén: *Tīngshuō Zhōngguó de rénkŏu zhèngcè găibiàn le; xīn de zhèngcè gēn yuánlái de yŏu shénme bùtóng ne?*

男孩: 我知道，我知道，**我可以说**吗？(可以 indicates 'permission'.)

Nánhái: *Wŏ zhīdào! Wŏ zhīdào! Wŏ kěyĭ shuō ma?* (The boy proceeds to give a good explanation.)

客人: 王先生，你儿子**可以说**是我见过最聪明的小孩。(可以 indicates 'possibility'.)

Kèrén: *Wáng xiānsheng, nĭ érzi kěyĭ shuō shì wŏ jiàn guo zuì cōngmíng de xiăohái.*

Guest: I have heard that China's population policy has changed. What are the differences between the new one and the original one?

Boy: I know; I know. **May I say** it?

Guest: Mr Wang, your son **can be said to be** the smartest child I have ever met.

课 *kè*

课 is a word that has several definitions, the majority of which are related to school activities. Each usage requires a different measure word. The focus of this section is on the use of the **measure words** for 课.

a. 课 can mean '**course**' or '**class**', and the proper measure word is 门 (*mén*). It is important to know that, when defined as 'class', 课 refers to the **content** or **subject matter** of a class, not the people in the class (班: *bān*).

→ See 班 (*bān*) for related information.

A: 你这学期上**几门**课？
   Nĭ zhè xuéqī shàng jĭ mén kè?

B: **四门**。**两门**数学(**课**)、**一门**英文(**课**)，还有**一门**音乐(**课**)。
   Sì mén. Liăng mén shùxué (kè), yī mén Yīngwén (kè), háiyŏu yī mén yīnyuè (kè).

A: How many classes (= **courses**) are you taking this semester?

B: Four. Two mathematics classes, an English class and a music class.

b. 课 can refer to '**class period**', and the measure word is either 节 (*jié*) or 堂 (*táng*). Because its English translation is often simply 'class', it is important to distinguish between 一门课 and 一节 (or 堂) 课.

A: 你今天有**几节**课？

    Nǐ jīntiān yǒu jǐ jié kè?

B: 有**两节**。上午有**一节**英文**课**，下午有**一节**数学**课**；**每节课**都是七十五分钟。

    Yǒu liǎng jié. Shàngwǔ yǒu yī jié Yīngwén kè, xiàwǔ yǒu yī jié shùxué kè; měi jié kè dōu shì qīshí wǔ fēnzhōng.

A: How many classes (= **periods of class**) do you have today?

B: I have two. In the morning I have **an (a period of) English class**; in the afternoon, I have **a (period of)** mathematics **class**. **Each class (period)** is 75 minutes.

李老师教**三门**课，所以她一个星期有**九堂**课；王老师教**两门**课，所以她一个星期只有**六堂**课。

Lǐ lǎoshī jiāo sān mén kè, suǒyǐ tā yī ge xīngqī yǒu jiǔ táng kè; Wáng lǎoshī jiāo liǎng mén kè, suǒyǐ tā yī ge xīngqī zhǐ yǒu liù táng kè.

Teacher Li teaches **three classes (courses)**, so she has **nine classes (periods of class)** every week. Teacher Wang teaches **two classes**, so she only has **six periods of class** every week.

c.   课 can refer to 'lesson', as in lessons in a textbook. There is **no measure word** when 课 is used this way.

这本书一共有**二十课**，现在我们在学**第十课**；老师说，这学期我们要学**十五课**。

Zhè běn shū yīgòng yǒu èrshí kè, xiànzài wǒmen zài xué dì shí kè; lǎoshī shuō, zhè xuéqī wǒmen yào xué shíwǔ kè.

This book has **20 lessons** altogether; right now we are studying **Lesson 10 (the tenth lesson)**. The teacher has said that we will study **15 lessons** during the semester.

Related expressions

上课 *shàng kè*

上课 generally refers to being engaged in **classroom activities**. This means that 上课 can mean either the **teacher teaching** or the **students attending classes**.

王老师: 各位同学，明天我有事，不能来，所以我请了一位李老师来**给你们上课**。

Wáng lǎoshī: *Gèwèi tóngxué, míngtiān wǒ yǒu shì, bù néng lái, suǒyǐ wǒ qǐng le yī wèi Lǐ lǎoshī lái gěi nǐmen shàng kè.*

Teacher Wang: Everyone, I have something to do tomorrow, and I cannot come; so I have asked a Teacher Li to come and **teach the class**.

妈妈:　　小中，都九点了，你为什么还在睡觉？你今天不**去上课**了吗？

Māma:　*Xiǎozhōng, dōu jiǔ diǎn le, nǐ wèi shénme hái zài shuìjiào? Nǐ jīntiān bú qù shàng kè le ma?*

Mother:　Xiaozhong, it's already nine o'clock; why are you still sleeping? Are you not **going to (attend) classes** today?

上课的时候，老师站在教室前面讲课，学生坐在座位上听。

Shàng kè de shíhòu, lǎoshī zhàn zài jiàoshì qiánmiàn jiǎng kè, xuéshēng zuò zài zuòwèi shàng tīng.

During **class time**, the teacher stands in the front of the classroom and lectures; the students sit on their seats and listen.

下课 *xià kè*

下课 means 'class is over'. From a grammatical perspective, 上课 and 下课 have different basic usages because **上课 is an action that can last**, whereas **下课 is an instantaneous verb**; the action referred to by **下课 cannot last**.

　　Thus, a period of time follows the verb 上 (not 上课) to indicate that, during that time period, the class is/was going on. The same distinction exists between 上班 (*shàng bān*) and 下班 (*xià bān*).

→ See 上班 (*shàng bān*) and 下班 (*xià bān*) for related information.

今天我**上**了八小时(的)**课**，累死我了。(Do not say 今天我上课了八小时。)

Jīntiān wǒ shàng le bā xiǎoshí (de) kè, lèi sǐ wǒ le.

Today I attended classes (I was in classes) for eight hours. I am tired to death.

Conversely, a period of time follows 下课; it does not follow 下.

下课半个小时了，可是还有很多学生在问老师问题，所以老师还不能离开教室。(Do not say 下了半小时的课了。)

Xià kè bàn ge xiǎoshí le, kěshì hái yǒu hěn duō xuéshēng zài wèn lǎoshī wèntí, suǒyǐ lǎoshī hái bù néng líkāi jiàoshì.

The **class has been over** for half an hour, but many students are still asking the teacher questions. So the teacher cannot leave the classroom yet.

王大中在教室里**上**了半小时的**课**才发现他走错教室了，可是他不好意思马上离开，所以一直等到**下课**才走。

Wáng Dàzhōng zài jiàoshì lǐ shàng le bàn xiǎoshí de kè cái fāxiàn tā zǒu cuò jiàoshì le, kěshì tā bù hǎo yìsi mǎshàng líkāi, suǒyǐ yìzhí děng dào xià kè cái zǒu.

Wang Dazhong only discovered that he was in (had walked into) the wrong classroom after he **had been in class (attending the class) for half an hour**, but he could not bring himself to leave right away, so he waited until **the class was over** before he (finally) left.

快 *kuài*

Although 快 is frequently associated with **fast speed**, it has different meanings in different contexts. This section presents various patterns and uses of 快 that go beyond its basic definition.

The basic meaning of 快 is 'quick' or 'fast'; its antonym is 慢 (*màn*: slow).

> 小张写字写得太**快**，所以他的字写得很不好看；小李写字写得太**慢**，所以考试的时候，他总觉得时间不够。
>
> *Xiǎo Zhāng xiě zì xiě de tài kuài, suǒyǐ tā de zì xiě de hěn bù hǎokàn; Xiǎo Lǐ xiě zì xiě de tài màn, suǒyǐ kǎoshì de shíhòu, tā zǒng juéde shíjiān bú gòu.*
>
> Little Zhang writes characters too **fast**; therefore, his characters are ugly. Little Li writes characters too **slowly**; therefore, he always feels that he does not have enough time when taking a test.

a. **快 + verb**

  (i) When 快 appears before a verb, it is typically in an **imperative** sentence used to urge the other person to '**hurry (and not to delay)**'. 快一点 and **快点** are its variations. Therefore, its focus is not on 'speed' but on '**haste**'. Its implication is '**Do it now (or immediately)!**'

  > **快**进去！(= 快一点进去！ or 快点进去！) 下雨了！
  > *Kuài jìnqù! (= Kuài yīdiǎn jìnqù! or Kuài diǎn jìnqù!) Xià yǔ le!*
  > **Hurry** and go inside! (Go inside **now**!) It is raining!

  > 已经十二点了，你怎么还在看电视？**快** (or 快点/快一点) 去睡觉。
  > *Yǐjīng shí'èr diǎn le, nǐ zěnme hái zài kàn diànshì? Kuài (or kuài diǎn/ kuài yīdiǎn) qù shuìjiào.*
  > It's already 12 o'clock; how come you are still watching TV? **Hurry** and go to bed. (Go to bed **now**.)

  > 花瓶是不是你打破的？**快**说！
  > *Huāpíng shì bú shì nǐ dǎpò de? Kuài shuō!*
  > Did you break the vase? Tell me **now** (no delay)!

  (ii) Because '快 + verb' is not about speed, one cannot substitute 快 with 慢 and arrive at the opposite meaning in the above two examples. In other words, 慢进去 or 慢去睡觉 is not a legitimate expression in Chinese. The proper expression would be **等一下再进去** or **等一下再去睡觉**. The **implication** is 'Don't do it now. **Wait for a moment** before you do it.'

  In certain contexts, it is correct to say **慢走** (used when a guest is leaving) or **慢用** (used to ask someone to enjoy the food). But these are

fixed expressions, and 慢 in these expressions is a shortened form for 慢慢（地）. It is about **speed**.

b. **很快就 + verb and 很快地 + verb**

(i) '很快**就** + verb' implies that it did not or will **not take long** for something to happen. Both 很 and 就 are **not optional** in this expression. Although this phrase can be translated as 'very quickly', it means '**very soon**' or '**before long**'. Therefore, it is once again **not about speed** but about **immediacy (short time)**.

今天的功课不多，只要写十个生词，所以虽然我一个字一个字慢慢地写，还是**很快就**写完了。
Jīntiān de gōngkè bù duō, zhǐ yào xiě shí ge shēngcí, suǒyǐ suīrán wǒ yī ge zì yī ge zì màn màn de xiě, háishì hěn kuài jiù xiě wán le.
There was not much homework today; we only needed to write ten new vocabulary words. Therefore, although I wrote them slowly character by character, it still **didn't take me long** to finish (I **soon** finished it).

想看那个电影吗？**快**（点）**去**买票！这么好看的电影，大家都想看，票**很快就**会卖完。**快**（点）去！**快**（点）去！
Xiǎng kàn nà ge diànyǐng ma? Kuài (diǎn) qù mǎi piào! Zhème hǎokàn de diànyǐng, dàjiā dōu xiǎng kàn, piào hěn kuài jiù huì mài wán. Kuài (diǎn) qù! Kuài (diǎn) qù.
Do you want to see that movie? **Hurry and go** buy the tickets. (**Go buy the tickets now.**) It's such a good movie; everybody wants to see it. The tickets will be sold out **very soon. Hurry! Hurry!**

(ii) **很快地** is an **adverbial modifier** that is used before a verb. '很快**地** + verb' is about **speed** and should not be confused with '很快**就** + verb'.

今天老师晚了十分钟下课，所以下课以后，我**很快地跑**到车站去，可是还没有到车站车就开走了。我以为得等很久，没想到下一班车**很快就来**了。
Jīntiān lǎoshī wǎn le shí fēnzhōng xià kè, suǒyǐ xià kè yǐhòu, wǒ hěn kuài de pǎo dào chēzhàn qù, kěshì hái méiyǒu dào chēzhàn chē jiù kāi zǒu le. Wǒ yǐwéi děi děng hěn jiǔ, méi xiǎngdào xià yī bān chē hěn kuài jiù lái le.
Today the teacher dismissed the class ten minutes later than usual, so I **ran fast** to the bus stop after class. But before I reached the bus stop, the bus had already gone. I had thought that I would have to wait for a long time; I didn't expect that the next bus would come **shortly after (very soon)**.

(iii) It is possible to **combine speed and immediacy**, resulting in '**很快地就** + verb'.

很快(地)就 王明和李英认识的时候，年纪都不小了，所以他们**很快(地)就**结婚了。没想到他们结婚以后，发现个性不合，所以差不多天天吵架，大家都觉得，他们大概**很快就**会离婚。

Wáng Míng hé Lǐ Yīng rènshì de shíhòu, niánjì dōu bù xiǎo le, suǒyǐ tāmen hěnkuài (de) jiù jiéhūn le. Méi xiǎngdào tāmen jiéhūn yǐhòu, fāxiàn gèxìng bù hé, suǒyǐ chàbùduō tiān tiān chǎojià , dàjiā dōu juéde, tāmen dàgài hěn kuài jiù huì líhūn.

When Wang Ming and Li Ying met, neither of them were young, so they **quickly (shortly after they met)** got married. Who would have thought that they would find out that they had incompatible personalities after they got married, so they have been fighting almost every day. Everybody thinks that they will probably get a divorce **very soon**.

音乐会一结束，几千个观众**很快地就**散了。

Yīnyuè huì yī jiéshù, jǐ qiān ge guānzhòng hěnkuài de jiù sàn le.

As soon as the concert was over, several thousand audience members **quickly (and immediately)** dispersed.

c. **快** + **number**

快 can be used to indicate that a situation is **close to a certain point**. The point is represented by an expression with a number in it. It is frequently translated as '**almost**'. Although it shares some similarities with **差不多** (*chàbùduō*), '快 + number' and '差不多 + number' should not be considered equivalent. 差不多 means 'approximately'.

李美文的男朋友比她大了**快**二十岁，所以她爸妈反对他们结婚。

Lǐ Měiwén de nán péngyǒu bǐ tā dà le kuài èrshí suì, suǒyǐ tā bàmā fǎnduì tāmen jiéhūn.

Li Meiwan's boyfriend is **almost (but not quite)** 20 years her senior, so her parents object to their getting married.

王老师：	你这学期有几个学生？
Wáng lǎoshī:	*Nǐ zhè xuéqī yǒu jǐ ge xuésheng?*
李老师：	**快**五十个。你呢？
Lǐ lǎoshī:	*Kuài wǔshí gè. Nǐ ne?*
王老师：	**差不多**三十五、六个。
Wáng lǎoshī:	*Chàbùduō sānshí wǔ, liù ge.*
Teacher Wang:	How many students do you have this semester?
Teacher Li:	**Almost** 50 (but not quite). How about you?
Teacher Wang:	**About (approximately)** 35 or 36.

快 . . . 了 *kuài . . . le* and 快要 . . . 了 *kuài yào . . . le*

快 . . . 了 has two important functions. First, it indicates **an impending event**, meaning the event is going to happen very soon. It is interchangeable with 快要 . . . 了 or 要 . . . 了. Second, it indicates a **point in time soon to be reached**; 快要 . . . 了 can be used in this context as well.

a. When the impending event is indicated by a verb in its **positive form**, 快 . . . 了 can be interchangeable with 快要 . . . 了 or 要 . . . 了.

快下雨了，你为什么还在外面站着，快进来吧！ (快下雨了 can be replaced by 快要下雨了 or 要下雨了.)
Kuài xià yǔ le, nǐ wèi shénme hái zài wàimiàn zhàn zhe? Kuài jìn lái ba!
It's **about to** rain. (It's going to rain **very soon**.) Why are you still standing outside? **Hurry** (Don't delay) and come in!

快要考试了，你怎么还整天上网、看电视？快去准备考试！ (快要考试了 can be replaced by 快考试了 or 要考试了.)
Kuài yào kǎoshì le, nǐ zěnme hái zhěngtiān shàngwǎng, kàn diànshì? Kuài qù zhǔnbèi kǎoshì!
The test is coming **soon**; how come you are still surfing the Internet and watching TV all day long? **Hurry** and go study for the test. (Go study **now**.)

b. When the impending event is indicated by a word in its **negative form**, either 快 . . . 了 or 快要 . . . 了 can be used. 要 . . . 了 is normally not the best choice.

哎呀，汽车快(要)没油了，快找一个加油站加油吧！
Āiya! Qìchē kuài (yào) méi yóu le, kuài zhǎo yī ge jiāyóu zhàn jiā yóu ba!
Oh no! The car is **about to run out** of gas. **Hurry** (don't delay) and find a gas station to get some gas. (Find a gas station **now**.)

八号病房的病人好像快(要)不行了！快去请医生来看看吧！ (不行 in this context implies 死 *sǐ*: to die.)
Bā hào bìngfáng de bìngrén hǎoxiàng kuài (yào) bù xíng le! Kuài qù qǐng yīshēng lái kàn kàn ba!
It seems that the patient in Room #8 is **about to die**. **Hurry** and go ask the doctor to come and take a look! (Go get a doctor **now**.)

c. The impending event can be represented by an **adjective**.

李先生住了两个多星期医院，医生说，他的病快(要)好了。
Lǐ xiānsheng zhù le liǎng ge duō xīngqī yīyuàn, yīshēng shuō, tā de bìng kuài (yào) hǎo le.
Mr Li has been hospitalized for more than two weeks. The doctor says that he is going to recover (get well) **very soon**.

上星期买的那些水果**快要**坏**了**，我今天就得把它们吃了，否则太浪费。
(**快要**坏**了** can be **快**坏**了** or **要**坏**了**.)

Shàng xīngqī mǎi de nàxiē shuǐguǒ kuài yào huài le, wǒ jīntiān jiù děi bǎ tāmen chī le, fǒuzé tài làngfèi.

The fruit I bought last week is **going to be bad (rotten) soon**. I will have to eat them today. Otherwise, it would be too wasteful.

d. The **point in time soon to be reached** in the 快 . . . 了 or 快要 . . . 了 structure often involves a **number**.

(Scenario: Mrs Li is a pregnant woman who is interested in chatting with other women with children. Today she chances to meet another woman, Mrs Zhang, at the park with a little girl.)

李: 这是你女儿吗？好可爱！多大了？
Lǐ: Zhè shì nǐ nǚ'ér ma? Hǎo kě'ài! Duō dà le?

张: **快(要)**五岁**了**！
Zhāng: Kuài (yào) wǔ suì le.

李: 那**快(要)**上幼儿园**了**，对吗？
Lǐ: Nà kuài (yào) shàng yòu'ér yuán le, duì ma?

张: 你几个月了？
Zhāng: Nǐ jǐ ge yuè le?

李: **快(要)**八个月**了**。
Lǐ: Kuài (yào) bā ge yuè le.

张: 啊！那**快(要)**生**了**！
Zhāng: À! Nà kuài (yào) shēng le.

Li: Is this your daughter? So cute! How old is she?
Zhang: She is **going to be** five **soon**.
Li: Then she is **about to** start kindergarten, right?
Zhang: How many months (pregnant) are you?
Li: **Almost (but not quite)** eight months.
Zhang: Ah! Then you are **about to** give birth.

e. The point in time soon to be reached can be a **noun** that indicates a **season**, a **calendar time** or an event with a **fixed schedule**. Note that there is **no need to use a verb**.

妈妈: **快**十二点**了**，你怎么还不去睡觉？
Māma: Kuài shí'èr diǎn le, nǐ zěnme hái bú qù shuìjiào?

儿子: **快**期末考**了**，我得努力学习。(期末考 is a noun and an event with a fixed schedule.)
Érzi: Kuài qīmò kǎo le, wǒ děi nǔlì xuéxí.

Mother: It's **almost** 12 o'clock. How come you are still not in bed?
Son: Final exams are **coming soon**. (The exam is **imminent**). I have to study hard.

快冬天**了**，天气渐渐冷起来了。
Kuài dōngtiān le, tiānqì jiànjiàn lěng qǐlái le.
Winter is **coming (soon)**. It is gradually starting to get cold.

快十一月**了**，怎么还这么热？
Kuài shíyī yuè le, zěnme hái zhème rè?
It's **almost** November; how come it is still so hot?

f.   了 is not used when the impending event or point about to be reached is in a **relative clause** or is followed by an **expression with** 的.

昨天的百米比赛，小李本来跑得最**快**，可是**快**到终点**的**时候，摔了一跤，所以只得到第三名。
Zuótiān de bǎi mǐ bǐsài, Xiǎo Lǐ běnlái pǎo de zuì kuài, kěshì kuài dào zhōngdiǎn de shíhòu, shuāi le yī jiāo, suǒyǐ zhǐ dédào dì sān míng.
In yesterday's 100-meter dash, Little Li originally ran the **fastest**. But when he was **about to** reach the finish line, he fell, so he was only placed the third.

(Scenario: Mrs Chen takes her son to a toddler group.)

工作人员:	你的宝宝多大？
Gōngzuò rényuán:	*Nǐ de bǎobao duō dà?*
陈:	**快**一岁**了**。
Chén:	*Kuài yī suì le.*
工作人员:	那请你带他去参加那组。那组都是**快**一岁**的**小孩。(Do not say 快一岁了的小孩。)
Gōngzuò rényuán:	*Nà qǐng nǐ dài tā qù cānjiā nà zǔ. Nà zǔ dōu shì kuài yī suì de xiǎohái.*
Staff:	How old is your baby?
Mrs Chen:	**Almost** one. (He is **about to** turn one.)
Staff:	Then please take him to join that group. All those in that group are children **who are about to** be one year old.

今天我上午九点半有课，**快**九点**的**时候，我从家里出来去车站等公共汽车。可是我等了**快**四十分钟车才来，所以我到教室的时候，已经**快**十点**了**。
Jīntiān wǒ shàngwǔ jiǔ diǎn bàn yǒu kè, kuài jiǔ diǎn de shíhòu, wǒ cóng jiā lǐ chūlái qù chēzhàn děng gōnggòngqìchē. Kěshì wǒ děng le kuài sìshí fēnzhōng chē cái lái, suǒyǐ wǒ dào jiàoshì de shíhòu, yǐjīng kuài shí diǎn le.
Today I had a class at 9:30. When it was **about to be** 9:00 (a little before 9:00), I left my house and went to the bus stop to wait for the bus. But I waited for **almost** 40 minutes before the bus finally came; therefore, when I arrived at the classroom, it was **almost** 10:00 already.

g.　When a **time phrase** is used in the impending event or point in time soon
to be reached, 快 . . . 了, 快要 . . . 了 can no longer be used. Instead, the
correct expression is 就要 . . . 了.

李太太下个月**就要**生**了**，所以她现在又兴奋又紧张。(下个月 is a time
phrase.)
Lǐ tàitai xià ge yuè jiù yào shēng le, suǒyǐ tā xiànzài yòu xīngfèn yòu jǐnzhāng.
Mrs Li **is (soon) going to** give birth next month. So she is both excited and
nervous now.

→ See 就要 . . . 了 (*jiù yào . . . le*) for related information.

来 *lái*

来 has a simple definition of 'to come', and it is generally considered the opposite
to 去 (*qù*: to go); therefore, 来 and 去 share many grammatical features. In terms
of expressions, however, 来 and 去 frequently are two unrelated words. This
section discusses some of the common expressions with 来; in these expressions,
来 does not literally mean 'to come'.

→ See 去 (*qù*) for related information.

a.　In casual speech, 来 can be used to imply '**here and now**'. Learners should
be aware that when 来 is used this way, neither (or none) of the people in
the conversation are expected to physically move. It has **no counterpart in
English**, and should not be literally translated as 'to come'.

(Scenario: Li brings his girlfriend to visit Wang at Wang's house. Wang has
not met his girlfriend before.)
王：　　(He opens the door.) 啊！小李，是你！请进！
Wáng:　*À! Xiǎo Lǐ, shì nǐ! Qǐng jìn!*
李：　　谢谢！(He and his girlfriend enter Wang's house.) 小王，这是我
　　　　女朋友；你们还没见过吧！我**来**介绍一下。
Lǐ:　　*Xièxie! Xiǎo Wáng, zhè shì wǒ nǚ péngyǒu; nǐmen hái méi jiàn guo*
　　　　ba! Wǒ lái jièshào yīxià.
(Li and his girlfriend have sat down. Wang comes out from the kitchen with
drinks.)
王：　　**来，来**，喝点饮料！
Wáng:　*Lái, lái, hē diǎn yǐnliào!*
Wang:　　Ah! Little Li, it's you! Come in, please.
Li:　　　Thanks! Little Wang, this is my girlfriend; you two haven't met,
　　　　have you? Let me introduce you **(now)**.
Wang:　　**Here, here**, have some drink.

(Scenario: At a casual get-together where several young people are chatting.
来 **is optional** in either sentence, but is often used.)

张:　　　　小谢，听说你很会跳舞，你**来**表演一下吧!

Zhāng:　　Xiǎo Xiè, tīngshuō nǐ hěn huì tiàowǔ, nǐ lái biǎoyǎn yīxià ba!

谢:　　　　哪里，其实我舞跳得不好。我**来**唱个歌吧!

Xiè:　　　Nǎlǐ, qíshí wǒ wǔ tiào de bù hǎo. Wǒ lái chàng ge gē ba!

Zhang:　　Little Xie, I have heard that you are very good at dancing. Why
　　　　　 don't you perform a dance **(here and now)**?

Xie:　　　 Not at all. Actually I am not a good dancer. (I don't dance well.)
　　　　　 Why don't I sing a song **(here and now)**?

b.　来 is often used to **order food at an eatery**.

服务员:　　准备点菜了吗?

Fúwùyuán:　Zhǔnbèi diǎn cài le ma?

顾客:　　　**来**半只烤鸭、一盘炒青菜跟一碗酸辣汤。

*Gùkè:　　　Lái bàn zhī kǎo yā, yī pán chǎo qīngcài gēn yī wǎn suānlà
　　　　　　　tāng.*

服务员:　　要不要**来**个小菜?

Fúwùyuán:　Yào bú yào lái ge xiǎocài?

顾客:　　　好! **来**一个腌黄瓜。

Gùkè:　　　Hǎo! Láo yī ge yān huángguā.

服务员:　　要喝什么饮料?

Fúwùyuán:　Yào hē shénme yǐnliào?

顾客:　　　**来**一瓶啤酒。

Gùkè:　　　Lái yī píng píjiǔ.

Waiter:　　 Are you ready to order?

Customer:　**Bring me (I want)** half a roast duck, a plate of sautéed green
　　　　　　 vegetables and a bowl of hot and sour soup.

Waiter:　　 Would you like to **order** an appetizer?

Customer:　OK! **Bring me (I want)** an order of pickled cucumber.

Waiter:　　 What drink would you like to have?

Customer:　**Bring me (I want)** a bottle of beer.

c.　来 can **follow a period of time**. The implication is **the current time is the
　ending point** of the said period of time. It is used to describe what has
　happened during this period of time. An **optional** 这 can be used before the
　period of time.

小张离开北京已经半年了；(这)**半年来**，他只给他女朋友打过一次
电话、发过两个电子邮件。

*Xiǎo Zhāng líkāi Běijīng yǐjīng bàn nián le; zhè bàn nián lái, tā zhǐ gěi tā
nǚ péngyǒu dǎ guo yī cì diànhuà, fā guo liǎng ge diànzǐ yóujiàn.*

It's been half a year since Little Zhang left Beijing. **In the past half year**,
he has only called his girlfriend once and e-mailed her twice.

中国人一向"重男轻女"；**五千多年来，**这个传统的观念一直没有改变。

Zhōngguó rén yīxiàng 'zhòng nán qīng nǚ'; wǔ qiān duō nián lái, zhè ge chuántǒng de guānniàn yīzhí méiyǒu gǎibiàn.

The Chinese have always been 'valuing boys and thinking lightly of girls'. **In the past 5,000-plus years**, this traditional concept has never changed.

连 . . . 也/都 *lián . . . yě/dōu*

连 . . . 也/都 is used as an **emphatic expression**. Either 也 or 都 can be used before the verb in the main sentence. Its function is to use an **extreme situation** to emphasize one's point; therefore, it is similar to **甚至** (*shènzhì*) in meaning; it also shares certain similarities with 甚至 in terms of sentence patterns.

→ See 甚至 (*shènzhì*) for related information.

a. What follows 连 is typically **a noun or a noun phrase** which shows the extreme situation.

  (i) The noun phrase can be the subject of the sentence.

王中的数学是全班最好的，可是这次考试实在太难了，所以**连**王中**都**考得很差。

Wáng Zhōng de shùxué shì quán bān zuì hǎo de, kěshì zhè cì kǎoshì shízài tài nán le, suǒyǐ lián Wáng Zhōng dōu kǎo de hěn chà.

Wang Zhong's mathematics ability is the best in the entire class. But this test was truly too hard, so **even** Wang Zhong did poorly.

这是一个**连**三岁小孩**都**懂的常识，你怎么不懂？

Zhè shì yī ge lián sān suì xiǎohái dōu dǒng de chángshì, nǐ zěnme bù dǒng?

This is common knowledge that **even** a three-year-old child understands. How come you don't?

  (ii) A 连 . . . 也/都 sentence can be an '**inverted**' sentence; this means that what follows 连 is the **object of the verb**, resulting in the **object appearing before the verb**.

  The alternative to using the inverted sentence is to use **甚至** as an **adverb** (before the verb).

李明进了大学以后，只喜欢玩，很少学习，所以虽然已经上了一年大学，可是**连**学校的图书馆在哪里**都**不知道 (or 他**甚至**不知道学校的图书馆在哪里) 。

Lǐ Míng jìn le dàxué yǐhòu, zhǐ xǐhuān wán, hěnshǎo xuéxí, suǒyǐ suīrán yǐjīng shàng le yī nián dàxué, kěshì lián xuéxiào de túshūguǎn zài nǎlǐ dōu bù zhīdào.

Since Li Ming entered college, he has enjoyed having fun and has rarely studied. Therefore, although he has been in college for a year, he does not **even** know where the school's library is.

张先生的儿子才十六、七岁，可是最近开始跟一些坏朋友混在一起，有时候晚上**连**家**都**不回(or **甚至**不回家)，张先生常常担心得**连**觉**都**睡不着(or 担心得**甚至**睡不着觉)。

Zhāng xiānsheng de érzi cái shíliù, qī suì, kěshì zuìjìn kāishǐ gēn yīxiē huài péngyǒu hùn zài yīqǐ, yǒu shíhòu wǎnshàng lián jiā dōu bù huí, Zhāng xiānsheng chángcháng dānxīn de lián jiào dōu shuì bù zháo.

Mr Zhang's son is only 16 or 17 years old, but lately he has started to hang out with bad friends; sometimes he does not **even** come home at night. Mr Zhang is often worried to the point that he cannot **even** sleep.

(iii) 一 can follow 连 in a **negative sentence** to mean '**nothing at all**'. **连 is optional** in this pattern and is, in fact, often omitted.

A: 小李，可不可以借我二十块？
Xiǎo Lǐ, kě bù kěyǐ jiè wǒ èrshí kuài?
B: 二十块？我今天**(连)**一块**都**没有。
Èrshí kuài? Wǒ jīntiān (lián) yī kuài dōu méiyǒu.
A: Little Li, can you loan me 20 *kuai*?
B: 20 *kuai*? I **don't even have one** *kuai* today. (I **don't have any** money today.)

我刚到北京的时候，**(连)**一句中国话**都**不会说，所以**(连)**一个朋友**也**没有。
Wǒ gāng dào Běijīng de shíhòu, (lián) yī jù Zhōngguó huà dōu bú huì shuō, suǒyǐ (lián) yī ge péngyǒu yě méiyǒu.
When I first arrived at Beijing, I could **not even** speak **one** Chinese sentence (I didn't know how to speak **any** Chinese), and so I **didn't have even one** friend (I **had no** friends).

b. Sometimes what follows 连 can be a **verb**, but it is typically used in one of the two following patterns:

(i) The verb after 连 is **followed by a noun** to indicate an **activity**.

王小兰刚到美国的时候，**连**用电锅煮饭**也**不会；来了美国才五年，现在她**连**修车**都**会了(can be 连车都会修了)。
Wáng Xiǎolán gāng dào Měiguó de shíhòu, lián yòng diànguō zhǔ fàn dōu bú huì; lái le Měiguó cái wǔ nián, xiànzài tā lián xiū chē dōu huì le.
When Wang Xiaolan first arrived in the U.S., she did not **even** know how to cook rice with an electric rice cooker. After being here for only five years, she **even** knows how to fix cars now.

(ii) When the verb after 连 is not followed by a noun, it must be the **same verb in the main sentence**, and the sentence must be a **negative** one; that is, the pattern is '连 verb 都/也 + negative verb'. 连 **is optional** and is often omitted when used in this pattern.

> A: 你坐过高铁没有？
> *Nǐ zuò guo gāo tiě méiyǒu?*
> B: 高铁？高铁是什么？我**(连)听都没听**过，怎么可能会坐过？
> *Gāo tiě? Gāo tiě shì shénme? Wǒ (lián) tīng dōu méi tīng guo, zěnme kěnéng huì zuò guo?*
> A: Have you ridden the high-speed train?
> B: High-speed train? What is the high-speed train? I have **never even** heard of it. How could I possibly have ridden it?

> A: 听说昨天王小英请你去她家吃牛排，好吃不好吃？
> *Tīngshuō zuótiān Wáng Xiǎoyīng qǐng nǐ qù tā jiā chī niúpái, hǎochī bù hǎochī?*
> B: 唉！别提了，硬得像牛皮，**(连)嚼都嚼不**动。
> *Ài! Bié tí le, yìng de xiàng niúpí, (lián) jiáo dōu jiáo bú dòng.*
> A: I heard that Wang Xiaoying invited you to her house to have steak yesterday. Was it good (delicious)?
> B: Oh! Don't mention it. Her steak was as tough as leather. I could **not even** chew it.

c. In an inverted 连 . . . 也/都 sentence, the **subject** can be either before 连 or before 也/都.

> A: 你跟你女朋友的祖父母见过面没有？
> *Nǐ gēn nǐ nǚ péngyǒu de zǔ fùmǔ jiàn guo miàn méiyǒu?*
> B: **我连**她爸妈**都**还没见过呢！(= **连**她爸妈**我都**还没见过呢！)
> *Wǒ lián tā bàmā dōu hái méi jiàn guo ne! (= Lián tā bàmā wǒ dōu hái méi jiàn guo ne!)*
> A: Have you met your girlfriend's grandparents?
> B: I have **not even** met her parents.

我跟王大中早就分手了，可是他还是常常给我发短信，昨天又发了一个来；**连看我都不想看**，(= **我连看都不想看**)，一收到就删掉了。
Wǒ gēn Wáng Dàzhōng zǎo jiù fēnshǒu le, kěshì tā háishì chángcháng gěi wǒ fā duǎnxìn, zuótiān yòu fā le yī ge lái; lián kàn wǒ dōu bù xiǎng kàn, yī shōudào jiù shān diào le.
I broke up with Wang Dazhong a long time ago, but he still texts me frequently; yesterday he sent me a message again. I did **not even** want to take a look at it, and I deleted it as soon as I received it.

令 *lìng*

令 and 使 (*shǐ*) are considered interchangeable in the 'A 令 B + verb/adjective' pattern. In this pattern, 令 is defined as 'to cause' or 'to make'. Although 让 (*ràng*) and 叫 (*jiào*) can be used in the same pattern, 令 and 使 are somewhat more formal than both 让 and 叫.

→ See 叫 (*jiào*), 让 (*ràng*) and 使 (*shǐ*) for more information.

李先生的收入不多，但是他每个月都把薪水的一半捐给慈善机构；他的爱心实在**令人 (or 使人，让人，叫人)佩服**。

Lǐ xiānsheng de shōurù bù duō, dànshì tā měi ge yuè dōu bǎ xīnshuǐ de yíbàn juān gěi císhàn jīgòu; tā de àixīn shízài lìng rén (or *shǐ rén, ràng rén, jiào rén*) *peìfú.*

Mr Li does not have a high income, but he donates half of his salary to charity organizations every month. His kindness is truly **admirable** (truly **makes one admire him**).

另外 *lìngwài* and 别的 *biéde*

While 另外 and 别的 share similarities in meaning, they are used in different contexts. Therefore, the proper use for each of these words often confuses learners. 另外 is similar to 'the other' in English, whereas 别的 means 'others' or 'someone/something else'. Therefore, it is extremely important to observe the context in order to decide on the proper word to use.

In terms of grammatical usage, **另外** usually does not appear immediately before a noun but is followed by '**a number/那 + measure word + noun**'. In addition, it can be used as an adverb or a conjunction.

On the other hand, **别的** is followed by a **noun**, and the noun can be omitted when the context makes it clear what it is. This indicates that **when a number is necessary** in the expression, the choice of word should be **另外**, not 别的.

a. **另外**

It is used when **the entire group** has been mentioned.

(i) It implies 'the remaining one(s)'. Therefore, it is often interpreted as '**the other + noun**'.

A: 我想请你帮我做三件事。第一件是请你把这把椅子搬到楼上去。
Wǒ xiǎng qǐng nǐ bāng wǒ zuò sān jiàn shì. Dì yī jiàn shì qǐng nǐ bǎ zhè bǎ yǐzi bān dào lóushàng qù.

B: 好，没问题。**另外两件**呢？
Hǎo, méi wèntí. Lìngwài liǎng jiàn ne?

A: I would like you to help me do three things. The first one is to please move this chair upstairs.

B: OK, no problem. What about **the other two** things?

A: 你不是说一共来了十个人吗？我怎么只看到五、六个？

Nǐ bú shì shuō yīgòng lái le shí ge rén ma? Wǒ zěnme zhǐ kàndào wǔ, liù ge?

B: **另外几个**都在楼上。

Lìngwài jǐ ge dōu zài lóushàng.

A: Didn't you say that altogether ten people have come? How come I only saw five or six?

B: **The other (few)** people are upstairs.

(ii) When 另外 is followed by '那 + **measure word**', the expression specifically means '**the other one**'.

那里有两个人，一个是王明，我认识他。**另外那个**人是谁？

Nàlǐ yǒu liǎng ge rén, yī ge shì Wáng Míng, wǒ rènshì tā. Lìngwài nà ge rén shì shéi?

There are two people over there. One is Wang Ming; I know him. Who is **the other** person?

(Scenario: Xiaozhong has brought a friend home after school, and they want to eat some snacks.)

小中: 妈，冰箱里有三块蛋糕，我和我的朋友可以吃吗？

Xiǎozhōng: *Mā, bīngxiāng lǐ yǒu sān kuài dàngāo, wǒ hé wǒ de péngyǒu kěyǐ chī ma?*

妈妈: 你们一个人可以吃一块。**另外那块**要留给爸爸吃。

Māma: *Nǐmen yī ge rén kěyǐ chī yī kuài. Lìngwài nà kuài yào liú gěi bàba chī.*

Xiaozhong: Mother, there are three pieces of cake in the refrigerator. Can my friend and I eat them?

Mother: Each of you can eat a piece. We have to save **the other piece** for your father.

b. **别的**

When 别的 is used, the implication is 'else' (i.e. **anything or anyone other than the one** that was mentioned).

A: 你这个周末忙不忙？

Nǐ zhè ge zhōumò máng bù máng?

B: 不忙，不过星期六下午要去看我儿子打球。

Bù máng, búguò xīngqī liù xiàwǔ yào qù kàn wǒ érzi dǎ qiú.

A: 要是你没有**别的事**，星期六晚上来我家吃饭吧！

Yàoshì nǐ méiyǒu biéde shì, xīngqī liù wǎnshàng lái wǒ jiā chī fàn ba!

A: Are you busy this weekend?

B: No, but I have to go watch my son play in a ball game Saturday afternoon.

A: If you don't have **anything else (other things to do)**, why don't you come over to my house Saturday evening for dinner!

老师:	高大中，这次考试，**别的同学**都考得不错，只有你不及格。
Lǎoshī:	*Gāo Dàzhōng, zhè cì kǎoshì, biéde tóngxué dōu kǎo de búcuò, zhǐyǒu nǐ bù jígé.*
Teacher:	Gao Dazhong, all the **other students** did quite well on this test; only you failed.

c. In certain scenarios, '另外 + 一 + measure word' and 别的 can be considered interchangeable. This is because both expressions are used to imply 'a **different** one', meaning '**not this one**, but another one (or **a different one**)'.

It must be kept in mind that a number should follow 另外; whereas the noun directly follows 别的.

(Scenario: A father comforts his son, who is sad because his application for admission to a first-rate university has just been rejected.)

爸爸:	没关系，全国有这么多大学，上**别的**(= **另外一个**)**大学**也可以，不一定要上这个大学。
Bàba:	*Méi guānxì, quán guó yǒu zhème duō dàxué, shàng biéde (= lìngwài yī ge) dàxué yě kěyǐ, bù yīdìng yào shàng zhè ge dàxué.*
儿子:	可是**别的同学**都要上这个大学。
Érzǐ:	*Kěshì biéde tóngxué dōu yào shàng zhè ge dàxué.*
Father:	It's OK; there are so many universities in the entire country; it would be fine if you go to **another university** (a **different university**). You don't necessarily have to go to this one.
Son:	But **everyone else** is going to this university. (But **others/other students** are going to this university.)

A:	王先生刚从乡下搬到上海的时候，觉得他好像到了**另外一个**国家(= **别的**国家)。
	Wáng xiānsheng gāng cóng xiāngxià bān dào Shànghǎi de shíhòu, juéde tā hǎoxiàng dào le lìngwài yī ge guójiā (= biéde guójiā).
B:	我了解这种感觉。我刚到美国的时候，觉得自己是来自**另外一个**星球(= **别的**星球)的人。
	Wǒ liǎojiě zhè zhǒng gǎnjué. Wǒ gāng dào Měiguó de shíhòu, juéde zìjǐ shì lái zì lìngwài yī ge xīngqiú (= biéde xīngqiú) de rén.
A:	When Mr Wang first moved to Shanghai from a rural area, he felt like he had arrived in **another** country.
B:	I understand this feeling. When I first arrived in the U.S., I felt like I was a person who came from **another** planet.

Related expressions

另外 as an adverb

另外 can appear before a verb or verbal phrase to imply '**additionally**'. 又 (*yòu*) or 再 (*zài*) is often used either before or after 另外.

昨天是李小兰的生日；她男朋友请花店送了一打玫瑰花给她，**另外又**买了一个大蛋糕带到她家。

Zuótiān shì Lǐ Xiǎolán de shēngrì; tā nán péngyǒu qǐng huādiàn sòng le yī dǎ méiguī huā gěi tā, lìngwài yòu mǎi le yī ge dà dàngāo dài dào tā jiā.

Yesterday was Li Xiaolan's birthday. Her boyfriend asked the florist to deliver a dozen roses to her, and **additionally** (he) brought a big cake to her house.

It should be noted that there is often **no direct English translation** for this usage, and the word '**another**' is often used **before the noun**.

A:　糟糕！筷子掉在地上了。
　　Zāogāo! Kuàizi diào zài dì shāng le!
B:　没关系，请服务员**另外再**拿一双来。
　　Méi guānxì, qǐng fúwùyuán lìngwài zài ná yī shuāng lái.
A:　Oh no! I dropped the chopsticks on the floor.
B:　It's OK. We will ask the waiter to bring **another** pair.

A:　这个星期六你有没有空？来我家吃饭、聊天吧！
　　Zhè ge xīngqī liù nǐ yǒu méiyǒu kòng? Lái wǒ jiā chī fàn, liáotiān ba!
B:　恐怕不行，这个周末我岳母要来；我们**另外找**一天吧！
　　Kǒngpà bù xíng, zhè ge zhōumò wǒ yuèmǔ yào lái; wǒmen lìngwài zhǎo yī tiān ba!
A:　Are you free this Saturday? Come over to my house to have dinner and chat.
B:　I am afraid that I can't. My mother-in-law is coming this weekend. Let's find **another** day.

另外 as a conjunction

As a conjunction, 另外 appears **between two sentences**. It is used to **add another point** or to **push the point further**. Words such as 此外 (*cǐwài*) and 还有 (*háiyǒu*) are considered interchangeable with 另外 when used as a conjunction. 此外 may be somewhat more formal than either 另外 or 还有.

(Scenario: Judges for an English speech contest are discussing who should be awarded the first place.)
A:　李明的发音虽然不如张文好，可是他说得比较流利，所以他应该是第一名。
　　Lǐ Míng de fāyīn suīrán bùrú Zhāng Wén hǎo, kěshì tā shuō de bǐjiào liúlì, suǒyǐ tā yīnggāi shì dì yī míng.
B:　我同意；**另外**，我觉得他的演说内容也比张文的好。
　　Wǒ tóngyì; lìngwài, wǒ juéde tā de yǎnshuō nèiróng yě bǐ Zhāng Wén hǎo.
A:　Although Li Ming's pronunciation is not as good as Zhang Wen's, he spoke more fluently, so he should take first place.
B:　I agree. **In addition** (moreover; furthermore), I feel that the content of his speech was better than Zhang Wen's.

其他 *qítā*

其他 is similar to both 另外 and 别的 because it can be followed by 'a number + measure word' or directly by a noun.

a.   Similar to '**另外** + **number** + **measure word**'

三个小偷破门而入；警察来的时候，只抓到一个，**其他两个(=另外两个)** 跑掉了。
Sān ge xiǎotōu pò mén ér rù; jǐngchá lái de shíhòu, zhǐ zhuā dào yī ge, qítā liǎng ge (= lìngwài liǎng ge) pǎo diào le.
Three burglars broke in. When the police arrived, they only caught one; **the other two** ran away.

It should be noted that 另外 can be followed by '那 + measure word', but 其他 cannot.

b.   Similar to '**别的** + **noun**'
An optional 的 is sometimes used, especially when the noun is omitted.

我们班上，只有王美美没有英文名字，**其他(的)人**都有。
Wǒmen bān shàng, zhǐ yǒu Wáng Měiměi méiyǒu Yīngwén míngzì, qítā (de) rén dōu yǒu.
In our class, only Wang Meimei does not have an English name; all **the others** do.

A: 你去过欧洲没有？
     Nǐ qù guo Ōuzhōu méiyǒu?
B: 我只去过法国，没有去过**其他(的)国家**。
     Wǒ zhǐ qù guo Fǎguó, méiyǒu qù guo qítā (de) guójiā.
A: Have you been to Europe?
B: I have only been to France. I have not been to **the other** (European) **countries**.

(Scenario: At a department store, Wang Xiaowen has tried on several dresses before making a purchase.)
店员: 这几件都很好看，您想买哪几件呢？
Diànyuán: *Zhè jǐ jiàn dōu hěn hǎokàn, nín xiǎng mǎi nǎ jǐ jiàn ne?*
王: 我只喜欢这件蓝的，**其他的**我都不喜欢。
Wáng: *Wǒ zhǐ xǐhuān zhè jiàn lán de, qítā de wǒ dōu bù xǐhuān.*
Store clerk: All these dresses are pretty. Which ones would you like to buy?
Wang: I only like this blue one. I don't like **(any of) the others**.

哪里 *nǎlǐ*

哪里, an interrogative pronoun which literally means 'where', can convey more meanings than a simple inquiry about a physical location.

a. It can be used in a **rhetorical question** to make a **negative statement**. When used this way, 哪里 replaces words such as 没 and 不. An exclamation mark is frequently used instead of a question mark at the end of the rhetorical question.

Another interrogative pronoun, 怎么 (*zěnme*), has a similar function.

→ See 怎么 (*zěnme*) for related information.

(Scenario: After a day's shopping, a wife suggests that they go have dinner at a restaurant.)

妻子: 逛了一天，好累！找家餐馆吃一顿吧！

Qīzi: *Guàng le yī tiān, hǎo lèi! Zhǎo jiā cānguǎn chī yī dùn ba!*

丈夫: 你买了一个皮包、两双鞋、一件大衣。咱们**哪里**还**有**钱上馆子？(= 已经**没有**钱上馆子了。)

Zhàngfū: *Nǐ mǎi le yī ge píbāo, liǎng shuāng xié, yī jiàn dàyī. Zánmen nǎlǐ hái yǒu qián shàng guǎnzi (= yǐjīng méiyǒu qián shàng guǎnzi le).*

Wife: We have been shopping all day; I am so tired! Let's find a restaurant and have a meal.

Husband: You bought a handbag, two pairs of shoes and a coat. **Where are we going to get** the money to go eat at a restaurant? (= **We don't have** any more money.)

(Scenario: Wang and Zhang have been debating about an economic issue; neither will relent, so they ask Li to give his opinion. But Li declines to offer his opinion.)

王: 老李，你说，我的看法对还是老张的看法对？

Wáng: *Lǎo Lǐ, nǐ shuō, wǒ de kànfǎ duì háishì Lǎo Zhāng de kànfǎ duì?*

李: 别问我！我是学音乐的，我**哪里**懂经济？(= 我**不懂**经济。)

Lǐ: *Bié wèn wǒ! Wǒ shì xué yīnyuè de, wǒ nǎlǐ dǒng jīngjì? (= wǒ bù dǒng jīngjì.)*

Wang: Old Li! You be the judge! Is my opinion correct or Old Zhang's opinion correct?

Li: Don't ask me! I study music. **How would I know** anything about economics? (= **I don't know anything** about economics.)

b. In a sentence with a **potential complement**, 哪里 does not directly replace the negative word 不 in a rhetorical question; instead, it converts the positive form into the negative form.

(Scenario: A son comes home when everybody else has already had dinner.)

妈妈: 今天我们吃饺子，还剩三十个，你把它们都吃了吧！

Māma: *Jīntiān wǒmen chī jiǎozi, hái shèng sānshí ge, nǐ bǎ tāmen dōu chī le ba!*

儿子: 我一个人**哪里吃得了**三十个饺子！(= 我一个人**吃不了**三十个饺子。)

Érzi: *Wǒ yī ge rén nǎlǐ chī dé liǎo sānshí ge jiǎozi!* (= *Wǒ yī ge rén chī bù liǎo sānshí ge jiǎozi.*)

Mother: We had dumplings today; there are still 30 left. Why don't you eat them all!

Son: **How can I (= I cannot) eat** 30 dumplings all by myself?

c. 哪里 is considered interchangeable with 哪儿 (*nǎ'ér*); however, as a **response to a compliment or 'thank you'**, only 哪里 can be used. Using 哪儿 would sound odd.

The reason 哪里 is used in these situations is to show **humbleness** or **humility** by using an indirect way to reject the compliment or gratitude. It is similar to saying '**not at all**', without actually using a negative word such as 不. A question mark should not be used in this case.

A: 你的中文说得真好！学了很多年了吧！

Nǐ de Zhōngwén shuō de zhēn hǎo! Xué le hěn duō nián le ba!

B: **哪里**！还有很多该学的呢！

Nǎlǐ! Hái yǒu hěn duō gāi xué de ne!

A: You speak Chinese really well! You must have studied it for many years!

B: *Nǎlǐ!* (My Chinese is **really not** that good!) I still have much to learn.

d. Besides making an inquiry about a physical location, 哪里 can be used to ask about **a point** one makes **in an argument**, **a speech**, etc. When used this way, 哪里 is equivalent to 什么地方 (*shénme dìfāng*). 地方 can also mean '(abstract) point' or 'feature' besides a physical location.

→ See 地方 (*dìfāng*) for related information.

A: 王先生刚说的那段话非常不合理。

Wáng xiānsheng gāng shuō de nà duàn huà fēicháng bù hélǐ.

B: 哦，是吗？我觉得他的观点都挺好的；你觉得**哪里**不合理？

O, shì ma? Wǒ juéde tā de guāndiǎn dōu tǐng hǎo de; nǐ juéde nǎlǐ bù hélǐ?

A: Those words Mr Wang just said were extremely unreasonable.

B: Oh, is that so? I think his points were all quite good. **Which points** do you think were unreasonable?

能 *néng*

Both 能 and 可以 (*kěyǐ*) are often translated as 'can' or 'to be able to', suggesting that these two words share similarities in meaning and uses. Comparisons between them can be found in the 可以 section. This section, therefore, discusses the features of 能 that are not shared by 可以.

→ See 可以 (*kěyǐ*) for related information.

a.   Although both 能 and 可以 can indicate 'ability', 能 can be **preceded by a degree adverb**, e.g. 很 and 非常, whereas 可以 cannot. It is usually a **general statement** to imply a **special ability**.

(Scenario: A couple has invited a friend to their house for dinner. The husband has gone and bought three bottles of wine.)

妻子:	只请老王一个人，为什么买三瓶酒？太多了吧！
Qīzi:	*Zhǐ qǐng Lǎo Wáng yī ge rén, wèi shénme mǎi sān píng jiǔ? Tài duō le ba!*
丈夫:	放心，老王**很能喝**。他一个晚上**能**(or **可以**) 喝两瓶。(很能喝 is a general statement; 可以喝两瓶 or 能喝两瓶 is more specific and thus cannot be preceded by 很.)
Zhàngfū:	*Fàngxīn, Lǎo Wáng hěn néng hē, tā yī ge wǎnshàng néng (or kěyǐ) hē liǎng píng.*
妻子:	是吗？我只知道他**很能吃**，所以我做了八个菜。
Qīzi:	*Shì ma! Wǒ zhǐ zhīdào tā hěn néng chī, suǒyǐ wǒ zuò le bā ge cài.*
Wife:	We only invited Old Wang (and no one else). Why did you buy three bottles of wine? Won't it be too much?
Husband:	Don't worry. Old Wang **can really drink**. He **can** drink two bottles in one evening.
Wife:	Is that so? I only knew that he **can really eat (a lot)**, so I made eight dishes.

b.   Although both 能 and 可以 can indicate 'permission', 不可以 specifically indicates 'to be not allowed' or 'to be forbidden', whereas 不能 is more flexible in meaning. Therefore, observing the context is necessary in order to arrive at the proper interpretation of an utterance.

(Scenario: Xiaoying cannot stop eating the delicious dumplings her mother has made. Her mother tells her not to overeat.)

妈妈:	小英，你**不能**再吃了！(不可以 is acceptable but might be too strong in tone.)
Māma:	*Xiǎoyīng, nǐ bù néng zài chī le!*
小英:	为什么？
Xiǎoyīng:	*Wèi shénme?*

妈妈:	你已经吃了五十个了！要是你再吃，等一下你一定会肚子疼。
Māma:	*Nǐ yǐjīng chī le wǔshí ge le! Yàoshì nǐ zài chī, děng yīxià nǐ yīdìng huì dùzi téng.*
Mother:	Xiaoying, you **cannot** eat any more!
Xiaoying:	Why (not)?
Mother:	You have already eaten 50 (of the dumplings). If you eat more, you will definitely get a stomachache later.

小中:	妈妈，还有没有饺子？我还想再吃几个。
Xiǎozhōng:	*Māma, hái yǒu méiyǒu jiǎozi? Wǒ hái xiǎng zài chī jǐ ge.*
妈妈:	你**不可以**再吃了！要是你再吃，爸爸的晚餐就不够了。
	(不能 is acceptable but might not be strong enough in tone.)
Māma:	*Nǐ bù kěyǐ zài chī le! Yàoshì nǐ zài chī, bàba de wǎncān jiù bú gòu le.*
Xiaozhong:	Mother, are there more dumplings? I want to eat a few more.
Mother:	You **cannot (are not allowed to)** eat more. If you eat more, your father will not have enough for dinner.

主人:	今天包了几百个饺子，你再吃几个吧！
Zhǔrén:	*Jīntiān bāo le jǐ bǎi ge jiǎozi, nǐ zài chī jǐ ge ba!*
客人:	我**不能**再吃了！要是我再吃，肚子恐怕要爆炸了！(不可以 is not proper since 不能 in this sentence refers to 'possibility' not 'permission'.)
Kèrén:	*Wǒ bù néng zài chī le! Yàoshì wǒ zài chī, dùzi kǒngpà yào bàozhà le.*
Host:	We made several hundred dumplings today. Why don't you have some more!
Guest:	I **cannot** eat any more. If I eat more, I am afraid that my stomach will explode.

Related expressions

不能不 *bù néng bù*

Although there are two negative words 不, 不能不 is not equal to 能, but is instead used to indicate '**must**' or '**to have to**'. It is similar to 不可不 (*bù kě bù*), but is less formal in tone. In addition, 不可不 is often used to give warnings or advice, whereas 不能不 may not always have this connotation.

→ See 不可不 (*bù kě bù*) for related information

(Scenario: Li had agreed to go to Xie's house for a *majiang* game, which requires four people to play.)

李:　老谢，我还有点事，恐怕**不能**来了！

Lǐ:　*Lǎo Xiè, wǒ hái yǒu diǎn shì, kǒngpà **bù néng** lái le.*

谢:　你**可以**晚点来，可是**不能不**来，我们三个人在等你呢！

Xiè:　*Nǐ **kěyǐ** wǎn diǎn lái, kěshì **bù néng bù** lái, wǒmen sān ge rén zài děng nǐ ne!*

Li:　Old Xie, I still have some business to attend to. I am afraid that I **cannot (won't be able to)** come (as I originally said I would).

Xie:　You **can** come (**It's OK** if you come) a little late, but you **have to** come. The three of us are waiting for you (to start the game).

(Scenario: Zhang is a new employee. A coworker gives him some advice about surviving in the company.)

张:　　明天王先生请客，你们去不去？

Zhāng:　*Míngtiān Wáng xiānsheng qǐngkè, nǐmen qù bú qù?*

高:　　你是新来的，你大概还不知道吧！王先生的岳父是公司的老板，我们**不能**得罪他。他请客，我们**不能不**去。

Gāo:　*Nǐ shì xīn lái de, nǐ dàgài hái bù zhīdào ba! Wáng xiānsheng de yuèfù shì gōngsī de lǎobǎn, wǒmen **bù néng** dézuì tā. Tā qǐngkè, wǒmen **bù néng bú** qù.*

Zhang:　Mr Wang is hosting a dinner party tomorrow. Are you going?

Gao:　You are new here, (so) you probably didn't know that Mr Wang's father-in-law is our company's owner; we **cannot** offend him. When he has parties, we **have to** go.

能不 . . . 吗 *néng bù . . . ma*

能不 and 可以不 are similar in meaning to a certain extent, but are generally used in different contexts. **可以不 implies 'it is OK not to** do something', whereas 能不 is often used in a **rhetorical question: 能不 . . . 吗**? and it has two possible connotations.

a.　能 implies '**possibility**'. 能不 . . . 吗 means **it is not possible** for something to **not** occur (= it's bound to happen).

A:　什么事让你这么生气？生气对你身体不好，别气了！

Shénme shì ràng nǐ zhème shēngqì? Shēngqì duì nǐ shēntǐ bù hǎo, bié qì le!

B:　我儿子这星期的考试全部不及格，你说我**能不生气吗**？

*Wǒ érzi zhè xīngqī de kǎoshì quánbù bù jígé, nǐ shuō wǒ **néng bù shēngqì ma**?*

A:　What makes you so angry? Being angry is not good for your health. Don't be angry anymore!

B:　My son failed all the tests this week. You tell me, **how can I not** get angry? (Literally: **Is it possible that I don't** get angry?)

b.　能 implies '**permission**', 能不 . . . 吗 means '**must**' or '**to have to**'. The connotation is one **is obligated** to do something.

(Scenario: A man tells his wife he is going to Mr Wang's house because Mr Wang and two other people need a fourth person to play a *majiang* game.)

妻子:　　你**可不可以**跟他说你有事，**不能**去？

Qīzi:　　*Nǐ kě bù kěyǐ gēn tā shuō nǐ yǒu shì, bù néng qù?*

丈夫:　　王先生是我的老板，他叫我去，我**能不去吗**？

Zhàngfū:　*Wáng xiānsheng shì wǒ de lǎobǎn, tā jiào wō qù, wǒ néng bú qù ma?*

Wife:　　**Can** you tell him that you will be occupied and so you **cannot** go?

Husband:　Mr Wang is my boss. When he tells me to go, I **have to** go. (Literally: **Can** I **not** go?)

宁可 *nìngkě*

宁可 is used to state **the choice one makes** after evaluating the advantages and disadvantages of **two options**. Therefore, it is usually not a stand-alone word. When it appears in a sentence as a stand-alone word, the option one decides not to choose is already clearly implied in the context.

a.　'**宁可 A 也不要 B**' is a pattern used to imply that **neither** option A **nor** option B **is an ideal choice**. However, after evaluating the situation, one decides that **option A** is still **less undesirable** than option B. If option A is a longish sentence, a comma is used after it.

老百姓**宁可**死**也不要**过着没有自由的生活。

Lǎobǎixìng nìngkě sǐ yě bú yào guò zhe méiyǒu zìyóu de shēnghuó.

Civilians **would rather** die **than** live a life without freedom.

(Scenario: Zhang explains the meaning of a Chinese proverb to Wang.)

王:　　什么叫做 '**宁**为鸡首，**不**为牛后'？

　　　　Shénme jiàozuò 'nìng wéi jī shǒu, bù wéi niú hòu'?

张:　　这句中国成语的意思是，我**宁可**做一只在小池塘里的大鱼，**也不要**做一只在大池塘里的小鱼。

　　　　Zhè jù Zhōngguó chéngyǔ de yìsi shì, wǒ nìngkě zuò yī zhī zài xiǎo chítáng lǐ de dà yú, yě bú yào zuò yī zhī zài dà chítáng lǐ de xiǎo yú.

Wang:　What does '**rather** be chicken head **not** be cow tail' mean?

Zhang:　This Chinese proverb means that I **would rather** be a big fish in a small pond **than** be a small fish in a big pond.

Option A that follows 宁可 can be a **negative** sentence. But **option B** is normally a **positive** one since it follows the negative word 也不要.

妈妈说，如果小中不去整理房间，晚饭以后就不准他吃甜点。可是小中**宁可不**吃甜点**也不要**去整理房间。

Māma shuō, rúguǒ Xiǎozhōng bú qù zhěnglǐ fángjiān, wǎnfàn yǐhòu jiù bù zhǔn tā chī tiándiǎn. Kěshì Xiǎozhōng nìngkě bù chī tiándiǎn, yě bú yào qù zhěnglǐ fángjiān.

Xiaozhong's mother says that if he does not go clean up his room, he will not be allowed to have dessert after dinner. But Xiaozhong **would rather not** eat dessert **than** go clean up his room.

(Scenario: Two people are discussing Mrs Li's domestic plight.)
A: 李先生根本不爱他太太了，我真不懂李太太为什么不愿意离婚。

　　Lǐ xiānsheng gēnběn bú ài tā tàitai le, wǒ zhēn bù dǒng Lǐ tàitai wèi shénme bú yuànyì gēn tā líhūn.

B: 李太太告诉我，她**宁可**自己痛苦，**也不要**孩子在一个破碎的家庭里长大。

　　Lǐ tàitai gàosù wǒ, tā nìngkě zìjǐ tòngkǔ, yě bú yào háizi zài yī ge pòsuì de jiātíng lǐ zhǎngdà.

A: 要是我是他们的孩子，我**宁可没有**爸爸或者妈妈，**也不要**我爸妈为了我而过着没有爱情的日子。

　　Yàoshi wǒ shì tāmen de háizi, wǒ nìngkě méiyǒu bàba huòzhě māma, yě bú yào wǒ bàmā wèile wǒ ér guò zhe méiyǒu àiqíng de rìzi.

A: Mr Li does not love his wife anymore. I really don't understand why Mrs Li is unwilling to divorce.

B: Mrs Li has told me that she **would rather** suffer the pain herself **than** have her children grow up in a broken family.

A: If I were their child, I **would rather be without** my father or mother **than** have my parents live a loveless life for the sake of me.

b. **'宁可 A 也要 B'** suggests that while option A does not offer an ideal situation, or is undesirable, option B is something one is determined to do.

李小兰**宁可**每天只吃一餐，**也要**把钱省下来买化妆品。

Lǐ Xiǎolán nìngkě měi tiān zhǐ chī yī cān, yě yào bǎ qián shěng xiàlái mǎi huàzhuāng pǐn.

Li Xiaolan **would rather** eat only one meal a day, but she **must** save the money to buy cosmetics.

(Scenario: Two women are gossiping about another friend's personal life.)
A: 听说王美英的爸妈强烈反对她跟李大中结婚，可是她还是决定要嫁给李大中。

　　Tīngshuō Wáng Měiyīng de bàmā qiángliè fǎnduì tā gēn Lǐ Dàzhōng jiéhūn, kěshì tā háishì juédìng yào jià gěi Lǐ Dàzhōng.

B: 她说**宁可**跟爸妈断绝关系，**也一定要**跟李大中结婚。

　　Tā shuō nìngkě gēn bàmā duànjué guānxì, yě yīdìng yào gēn Lǐ Dàzhōng jiéhūn.

A: I heard that Wang Meiying's parents are strongly against her marriage to Li Dazhong, but she has still decided to marry him.

B: She says that she **would rather** sever the relationship with her parents, but she **must** marry Li Dazhong.

c. It is possible for a sentence to have **only 宁可 without 也不要 or 也要** if the **context** gives clear indications what has been omitted.

A: 有汉堡，也有热狗，你想吃哪个？
  Yǒu hànbǎo, yě yǒu règǒu, nǐ xiǎng chī nǎ ge?
B: 我是吃素的，我**宁可**饿肚子。
  Wǒ shì chī sù de, wǒ nìngkě è dùzi.
A: There are hamburgers and also hot dogs. Which do you feel like?
B: I am a vegetarian; I **would rather** go hungry.

自己一个人住，虽然房租比较贵，可是跟同屋合住，麻烦总是比较多；所以我**宁可**一个人住。
Zìjǐ yī ge rén zhù, suīrán fángzū bǐjiào guì, kěshì gēn tóngwū hé zhù, máfán zǒngshì bǐjiào duō; suǒyǐ wǒ nìngkě yī ge rén zhù.
Although my rent is higher if I live by myself, there is always more trouble if I live with a roommate; therefore, I **would rather** live by myself.

→ See 与其 (*yǔqí*) for related expressions.

瓶 *píng* and other 'container' words

As straightforward as the definition of 瓶 (bottle) is, its actual use often confuses learners, especially English speakers. This is because 瓶 can be both a **noun** and a **measure word**. In fact, all other words that indicate 'containers' have the same uses. These words include 杯 (*bēi*: cup or glass), 碗 (*wǎn*: bowl), 盘 (*pán*: plate), 碟 (*dié*: dish), 壶 (*hú*: kettle or pot) 锅 (*guō*: cooking pot), 盒 (*hé*: box), 罐 (*guàn*: can) and so on. Examples given in this section will include many of these 'container' words and will not be limited to 瓶.

a. Container words used as **measure words**

(i) When used as a measure word, a container word gives information about the **content** (or the **quantity**) of what is being held in the container.

A: 桌上怎么有**两瓶**酒？是你买的吗？
  Zhuō shàng zěnme yǒu liǎng píng jiǔ? Shì nǐ mǎi de ma?
B: 今天是你的生日，**这瓶**红酒是小李送你的；**那瓶**白酒是我买的。我们开**哪瓶**？
  Jīntiān shì nǐ de shēngrì, zhè píng hóng jiǔ shì Xiǎo Lǐ sòng nǐ de; nà píng bái jiǔ shì wǒ mǎi de. Wǒmen kāi nǎ píng?
A: 现在我口渴，先给我**一罐**可乐吧！
  Xiànzài wǒ kǒu kě, xiān gěi wǒ yī guàn kělè ba!

A: How come there are **two bottles of** wine on the table? Did you buy them?

B: Today is your birthday. **This bottle of** red wine is for you from Little Li; and I bought **that bottle of** white wine. **Which bottle** should we open?

A: I am thirsty now. Give me **a can of** cola first.

(Scenario: A man has come home after a long day's work; his wife has his dinner ready.)

女: 桌上有**两盘**饺子、**一碗**汤，那是我给你准备的晚餐。

Nǚ: *Zhuō shàng yǒu liǎng pán jiǎozi, yī wǎn tāng, nà shì wǒ gěi nǐ zhǔnbèi de wǎncān.*

男: 太好了！我饿死了！

Nán: *Tài hǎo le! Wǒ è sǐ le!*

女: 我去给你拿**一碟**醋和**一碟**酱油来。...**这碟**是醋，**这碟**是酱油。

Nǚ: *Wǒ qù gěi nǐ ná yī dié cù hé yī dié jiàngyóu lái. . . . Zhè dié shì cù, zhè dié shì jiàngyóu.*

男: 谢谢。

Nán: *Xièxie.*

女: 今天我还买了**一盒**点心，你吃了晚餐以后，可以一边喝咖啡一边吃甜点。

Nǚ: *Jīntiān wǒ hái mǎi le yī hé diǎnxīn, nǐ chī le wǎncān yǐhòu, kěyǐ yībiān hē kāfēi yībiān chī tiándiǎn.*

男: 我今天下午已经喝了**三杯**咖啡，所以我想喝茶。

Nán: *Wǒ jīntiān xiàwǔ yǐjīng hē le sān bēi kāfēi, suǒyǐ wǒ xiǎng hē chá.*

女: 好，我现在就去给你泡**一壶**茶。

Nǚ: *Hǎo, wǒ xiànzài jiù qù gěi nǐ pào yī hú chá.*

Woman: There are **two plates of** dumplings and **a bowl of** soup on the table. That's the dinner I have made for you.

Man: Great! I am starving.

Woman: I will go get you **a dish of** vinegar and **a dish of** soy sauce . . . **This (dish)** is vinegar and **this (dish)** is soy sauce.

Man: Thank you.

Woman: I also bought **a box of** pastries today. After you have had your dinner, you can have coffee while having some dessert.

Man: I already had **three cups of** coffee this afternoon, so I would like to drink tea.

Woman: OK, I will go make you **a pot of** tea right now.

(ii) Although an **adjective** is usually not placed immediately before the measure word, 大 or 小 is sometimes used **when the measure word is a container word**. In such cases, 大 or 小 is usually not meant to specifically describe the size of the container, but to refer to the **large or small quantity** of the contents in the container.

王先生平常很少喝酒，可是因为今天是他七十岁的生日，他的儿子
请了很多朋友来家里吃饭，所以王先生就喝了**一小杯**。

Wáng xiānsheng píngcháng hěnshǎo hē jiǔ, kěshì yīnwèi jīntiān shì tā
qīshí suì de shēngrì, tā de érzi qǐng le hěn duō péngyǒu lái jiā lǐ chī
fàn, suǒyǐ Wáng xiānsheng jiù hē le yī xiǎo bēi.

Ordinarily Mr Wang rarely drinks (alcohol); but today is his 70th birthday, and his son has invited many friends to their house for dinner, so
Mr Wang **drank a small glass** (he drank **a small amount)** of alcohol.

我是这家餐厅的常客，所以每次我来这里吃饭，老板都会给我满满
一大碗白饭，不另收费。

Wǒ shì zhè jiā cāntīng de chángkè, suǒyǐ wǒ měi cì lái zhèlǐ chī fàn,
lǎobǎn dōu huì gěi wǒ mǎn mǎn yī dà wǎn bái fàn, bú lìng shōu fèi.

I am a regular at this restaurant, so every time I come here to eat, the
owner gives me **a full bowl** (**a generous portion, a huge amount**) of
rice with no extra charge.

b. Container words used as **nouns**

With the exception of 碗, container words usually have **at least two
characters** when they are used as nouns. If the type of container is not
mentioned, the character 子 (*zi*) is used after the container word; e.g. 瓶子,
杯子, 盘子, 盒子, etc.

　　The **measure word** for these containers is **个**.

A: 这里为什么有**六个啤酒瓶**？你今天喝了**六瓶啤酒**吗？

　　Zhèlǐ wèi shénme yǒu liù ge píjiǔ píng? Nǐ jīntiān hē le liù píng píjiǔ
　　ma?

B: 你再看一下，这**六个瓶子**都是啤酒瓶吗？

　　Nǐ zài kàn yīxià, zhè liù ge píngzi dōu shì píjiǔ píng ma?

A: 啊！对！只有**三个**是**啤酒瓶**，另外**三个**是可乐的**瓶子**（or **可乐瓶**）。

　　A! Duì! Zhǐ yǒu sān ge shì píjiǔ píng, lìngwài sān ge shì kělè de píngzi
　　(or *kělè píng*).

A: Why are there **six beer bottles**? Did you have **six bottles of beer** today?

B: Take another look. Are all these **six bottles** beer bottles?

A: Ah, you are right! Only **three** are **beer bottles**; the other **three** are **cola
bottles**.

A: **这个盒子**里是什么？

　　Zhè ge hézi lǐ shì shénme?

B: 是我新买的茶具。这套茶具有**一个茶壶**、**六个茶杯**，还有**六个小碟
子**。

　　Shì wǒ xīn mǎi de chájù. Zhè tào chájù yǒu yī ge chá hú, liù ge chá
　　bēi, hái yǒu liù ge xiǎo diézi.

A: 嗯，很不错！**这个茶壶**很大，一次最少可以泡**六杯茶**。

　　Èn, hěn búcuò. Zhè ge chá hú hěn dà, yī cì zuìshǎo kěyǐ pào liù bēi
　　chá.

A: What is inside this **box**?

B: It's the new tea set that I just bought. This tea set has **one teapot, six teacups** and also **six saucers**.

A: Mmm, not bad! **This teapot** is big. We can make at least **six cups of tea** each time.

昨天我买了**一个**新**锅子**，所以今天做了**一锅**牛肉面；你去拿**两个碗**来，现在我们可以一个人吃**一碗**。

Zuótiān wǒ mǎi le yī ge xīn guōzi, suǒyǐ jīntiān zuò le yī guō niúròu miàn; nǐ qù ná liǎng ge wǎn lái, xiànzài wǒmen kěyǐ yī ge rén chī yī wǎn.

Yesterday I bought **a** new **cooking pot**, so I made **a pot of** beef noodle soup today. Go get **two bowls**. Each of us can have **a bowl (of** noodles) right now.

(Scenario: Wang is trying a new cake recipe at Li's house. He needs to measure flour. The word '**spoon**' is used as both a **noun** and a **measure word**.)

王: 你家有没有**量杯**？

Wáng: Nǐ jiā yǒu méiyǒu liángbēi?

李: 以前有**一个**，后来摔破了。抽屉里有**几个**汤匙，你用汤匙量吧。**八匙**就是**半杯**。

Lǐ: Yǐqián yǒu yī ge, hòulái shuài pò le. Chōutì lǐ yǒu jǐ ge tāngchí, nǐ yòng tāngchí liáng ba! Bā chí jiù shì bàn bēi.

Wang: Do you have a **measuring cup**?

Li: I had **one** before, but then I broke it. There are **a few** soup spoons in the drawer. Why don't you use the soup spoon to measure it. **Eight spoons** is equal to **half a cup**.

c. Container words are often used when one orders food or drinks **at an eatery**. The words 大, 中, or 小 often appear **before the container word to refer to the size of the order**; either 个 or the **container word** can be the **measure word** for food orders.

(Scenario: At a restaurant.)

服务员: 准备点菜了吗？

Fúwùyuán: Zhǔnbèi diǎn cài le ma?

男: **一个大碗**的酸辣汤、**两盘**牛肉炒面。

Nán: Yī ge dà wǎn de suān là tāng, liǎng pán niúròu chǎomiàn.

女: 酸辣汤点**小碗**的吧！我不想喝汤，我要**一杯**冰奶茶。

Nǚ: Suān là tāng diǎn xiǎo wǎn de ba! Wǒ bù xiǎng hē tāng, wǒ yào yī bēi bīng nǎichá.

服务员: 好，奶茶要**大杯**的还是**小杯**的？

Fúwùyuán: Hǎo, nǎichá yào dà bēi de háishì xiǎo bēi de?

男: 来**两个大杯**的，我们一个人**一杯**。

Nán: Lái liǎng ge dà bēi de, wǒmen yī ge rén yī bēi.

服务员: 要点**两个小菜**吗？我们的小菜不错。

Fúwùyuán: Yào diǎn liǎng ge xiǎocài ma? Wǒmen de xiǎocài búcuò.

女:	**两个**太多了，来一个腌黄瓜吧！
Nǚ:	*Liǎng ge tài duō le. Lái yī ge yān huángguā ba!*
Waiter:	Are you ready to order?
Man:	**A large (order of)** hot and sour soup and **two (plates of)** beef fried noodles.
Woman:	Let's order **a small one** for the hot and sour soup. I don't feel like having soup; I would like to have **a glass of** iced milk tea.
Waiter:	OK! Do you want **a large one** or **a small one** for the milk tea?
Man:	Let's have **two large ones**. Each of us will have **a glass**.
Waiter:	Would you like to order **two** appetizers? Our appetizers are quite good.
Woman:	**Two** appetizers are too much. Let's have **a (an order of)** pickled cucumber.

其实 *qíshí*

Although the use of 其实 is not complicated, learners, especially English speakers, frequently misuse it because its English translation causes confusion. While 其实 can be, and frequently is, translated as '**in fact**', '**actually**' or other similar phrases, its main function is to imply that a **previous statement** or a **certain situation** is **incorrect or untrue**, and, at the same time, to **offer the correct version** (i.e. the fact or the truth).

The phrase 'in fact' in English can be used to either strengthen/support a previous statement or to contradict/correct a previous statement, but 其实 in Chinese only has one function, to **contradict/correct**. For this reason, English speakers tend to overuse 其实.

For example, the word 其实 cannot be used to translate the phrase '**in fact**' in the sentence 'Mr Li owns a very small business; in fact, his company has only two employees.' But 其实 can be used to translate 'in fact' in the sentence 'Mr Li always tells others that he is the owner of the business; in fact, his father-in-law owns the business.' (王先生总告诉别人他是公司的老板；**其实**他岳父才是老板。 *Wáng xiānsheng zǒng gàosù biérén tā shì gōngsī de lǎobǎn, qíshí tā yuèfù cái shì lǎobǎn.*)

It should be noted that when 'in fact' is used to strengthen or support a previous statement in English, the phrase does not have a direct counterpart in Chinese. The following discussions focus on the use of 其实 in various contexts.

a. 其实 is used to **contradict or correct a previous statement**.

公司主管告诉员工，新的制度是为了提升工作效率；**其实**员工都知道，真正的目的是为了提高利润。
Gōngsī zhǔguǎn gàosù yuángōng, xīn de zhìdù shì wèile tíshēng gōngzuò xiàolǜ; qíshí yuángōng dōu zhīdào, zhēnzhèng de mùdì shì wèile tígāo lìrùn.
The company's executives tell the employees that the new system is (in order) to raise work efficiency; **actually**, all employees know that its real purpose is to increase profits.

许多人都认为，喝无糖汽水不会让人发胖；**其实**不少研究结果指出，喝了无糖汽水让人更想吃甜食，所以常喝无糖汽水的人还是会发胖。

Xǔduō rén dōu rènwéi, hē wútáng qìshuǐ bú huì shǐ rén fā pàng; qíshí bùshǎo yánjiū jiéguǒ zhǐchū, hē le wútáng qìshuǐ huì ràng rén gèng xiǎng chī tiánshí, suóyǐyǐ cháng hē wútáng qìshuǐ de rén háishì huì fā pàng.

Many people think that drinking sugarless soda will not cause them to gain weight; **actually** the results of many research studies have pointed out that drinking sugarless soda makes one want to eat sweets even more; so people who often drink sugarless soda still gain weight.

王中跟妈妈说他不舒服，所以妈妈就给老师打了一个电话，跟老师说王中今天不能去上课。**其实**王中根本没有不舒服，他是因为没有准备好今天的考试而想逃课。

Wáng Zhōng gēn māma shuō tā bù shūfú, suǒyǐ māma jiù gěi lǎoshī dǎ le yī ge diànhuà, gēn lǎoshī shuō Wáng Zhōng jīntiān bù néng qù shàng kè. Qíshí Wáng Zhōng gēnběn méiyǒu bù shūfú, tā shì yīnwèi méiyǒu zhǔnbèi hǎo jīntiān de kǎoshì ér xiǎng táo kè.

Wang Zhong told his mother that he was not feeling well, so his mother called the teacher and said that Wang Zhong could not go to class today. **Actually** Wang Zhong was not sick at all. He wanted to skip class because he did not prepare for today's test.

b. 其实 often follows a sentence with expressions such as 以为 (*yǐwéi*: to mistakenly think), 表面上 (*biǎomiàn shàng*: on the surface) and 看起来 (*kàn qǐlái*: to look like) in order to correct the misconception or false impression.

王中很少笑，所以**看起来**是一个很严肃的人，**其实**认识他的人都知道，他非常有幽默感。

Wáng Zhōng hěnshǎo xiào, suǒyǐ kàn qǐlái shì yī ge hěn yánsù de rén; qíshí rènshì tā de rén dōu zhīdào, tā fēicháng yǒu yōumò gǎn.

Wang Zhong rarely smiles, so he **looks like** a very stern person. **Actually** all those who know him know that he has a great sense of humor.

张文的女朋友爱上了别人，所以跟他分手了；张文**表面上**不在乎，**其实**他心里非常痛苦。

Zhāng Wén de nǚ péngyǒu ài shàng le biérén, suǒyǐ gēn tā fēnshǒu le; Zhāng Wén biǎomiàn shàng bú zàihū, qíshí tā xīn lǐ fēicháng tòngkǔ.

Zhang Wen's girlfriend had fallen in love with someone else, so she broke up with him. **On the surface**, Zhang Wen does not care; **actually** he is in great pain inside.

李明非常有钱，可是他吃的、用的都很简陋，开的是十年的老车，住的是一幢小房子，所以大家都**以为**李明很小气。可是**其实**他每年都匿名捐很多钱给慈善机构。

Lǐ Míng fēicháng yǒuqián, kěshì tā chī de, yòng de dōu hěn jiǎnlòu, kāi de shì shí nián de lǎo chē, zhù de shì yī zhuàng xiǎo fángzi, suǒyǐ dàjiā dōu yǐwéi Lǐ Míng hěn xiǎoqì. Kěshì qíshí tā měi nián dōu nìmíng juān hěn duō qián gěi císhàn jīgòu.

Li Ming is very wealthy, but what he eats and what he uses are very plain and simple. He drives a ten-year-old car and lives in a small house, so everybody **(mistakenly) thinks** that Li Ming is stingy. But **actually** he anonymously donates a lot of money to charities every year.

c. When a **misconception exists or is implied in the premise**, 其实 can be used without the misconception being specifically mentioned.

    A: 学中文难不难？
        Xué Zhōngwén nán bù nán?
    B: **其实**不难，只要肯多花时间就一定能学好。(The connotation is people generally perceive learning Chinese to be hard.)
        Qíshí bù nán, zhǐyào kěn duō huā shíjiān jiù yīdìng néng xué hǎo.
    A: Is studying Chinese hard?
    B: **Actually** it's not hard. As long as one is willing to spend more time, one can definitely learn it very well (master it).

    A: 听说王先生出院了。(The connotation is Mr Wang has recovered from his illness.)
        Tīngshuō Wáng xiānsheng chū yuàn le.
    B: 对，可是**其实**他的病还没有好，他请了私人护士来家里照顾他。
        Duì, kěshì qíshí tā de bìng hái méiyǒu hǎo, tā qǐng le sīrén hùshì lái jiā lǐ zhàogù tā.
    A: I heard that Mr Wang has been discharged from the hospital.
    B: That's correct, but **actually** he has not recovered (he is still sick). He has hired a private nurse to come to his house to care for him.

d. 才 often appears in the sentence with 其实 to directly contradict the false part in the statement and **offer the correct version at the same time**.

    A: 听说张文**是**全班英文说得最好的人。
        Tīngshuō Zhāng Wén shì quán bān Yīngwén shuō de zuì hǎo de rén.
    B: **其实**李明说得比他更好。(or **其实**李明**才是**全班英文说得最好的人。)
        Qíshí Lǐ Míng shuō de bǐ tā gèng hǎo. (or *Qíshí Lǐ Míng cái shì quán bān Yīngwén shuō de zuì hǎo de rén.*)
    A: I heard that Zhang Wen **is** the person who speaks the best English in the whole class.
    B: **Actually** Li Ming speaks English even better than he. (or: **Actually**, Li Ming **IS** the person who speaks the best English in the whole class.)

公司的主管说，提升效率**是**推行新制度的原因，**其实**提高利润**才是**真正
的原因。

*Gōngsī de zhǔguǎn shuō, tíshēng xiàolǜ shì tuīxíng xīn zhìdù de yuányīn,
qíshí tígāo lìrùn cái shì zhēnzhèng de yuányīn.*

The company's executives say that raising efficiency **is** the reason why they
implemented the new system; **actually** increasing profits **IS** the real reason.

e. In certain contexts, 其实 has the connotation of **虽然** (*suīrán*: although)
    because a sentence with 可是 ensues. What 其实 contradicts is implied.

老师问谁会回答这个问题，**其实**我会回答，**可是**因为我觉得自己的英文
不好，所以我不好意思举手回答。

*Lǎoshī wèn shéi huì huídá zhè ge wèntí, qíshí wǒ huì huídá, kěshì yīnwèi
wǒ juéde zìjǐ de Yīngwén bù hǎo, suǒyǐ wǒ bù hǎo yìsi jǔshǒu huídá.*

The teacher asked who knew how to answer this question; **actually** I knew
how to answer it, but because I felt that my English was not good, I was
too embarrassed to raise my hand to answer it.

王经理说的笑话**其实**一点都不好笑，**可是**他说完以后，他的属下都哈哈
大笑。

*Wáng jīnglǐ shuō de xiàohuà qíshí yīdiǎn dōu bù hǎoxiào, kěshì tā shuō wán
yǐhòu, tā de shǔxià dōu hāhā dà xiào.*

The joke Manager Wang just told was **actually** not funny at all, but once
he finished telling it, all his subordinates laughed heartily.

Related expression

事实上 *shìshí shàng*

事实上 is generally considered to have the same meaning and usage as 其实.
Therefore, the two expressions are interchangeable. **事实上 is a more formal
expression** than 其实; and is not often used in casual, conversational speech.

其他 *qítā*

其他 is similar to both 另外 (*lìngwài*) and 别的 (*biéde*) in meaning and in usage,
and can frequently substitute either one in a sentence.

→ See 另外 (*lìngwài*) and 别的 (*biéde*) for more information.

请 *qǐng*

请 is a word that is typically used to convey a message **with politeness**. Although
certain verbs, such as 请客 (*qǐng kè*: to invite guests), 请假 (*qǐng jià*: to ask for
leave of absence) and 请安 (*qǐng'ān*: to pay respect to an elder), include the
character 请, the focus of this section is on the use of 请 as a stand-alone word

and its grammatical features. In addition, other words that have the same uses and meaning (without the implied politeness) will be compared against 请.

a. 请 can be used at the beginning of an **imperative sentence** (giving a command or making a request) to convey **politeness**. It is the same as the word 'please' in English, but 请 should never be placed at the end of the imperative sentence.

请先填表，再去排队交钱。
Qǐng xiān tián biǎo, zài qù páiduì jiāo qián.
Please fill out the form first, and then go get in line to pay.

这是图书馆，**请**别大声说话。
Zhè shì túshǔguǎn, qǐng bié dàshēng shuō huà.
This is the library. Don't talk loudly, **please**.

The subject, 你 or 你们, in an imperative sentence, although optional, is often used, and 请 can appear either before or right after 你 or 你們 depending on the context.

(i) To politely make a **request** or give a **command**, 请 appears **before** 你 or 你们。

经理:	李小姐，**请(你)**给张先生打一个电话，问他什么时候有空。
Jīnglǐ:	*Lǐ xiǎojiě, qǐng (nǐ) gěi Zhāng xiānsheng dǎ yī ge diànhuà, wèn tá shénme shíhòu yǒu kòng.*
Manager:	Miss Li, **please** call Mr Zhang and ask him when he is free.

老师:	**请(你们)**别忘了在出席表上写下自己的名字。
Lǎoshī:	*Qǐng (nǐmen) bié wàng le zài chūxí biǎo shàng xiě xià zìjǐ de míngzì.*
Teacher:	**Please** don't forget to write your name down on the attendance sheet.

(ii) Occasionally, one might start an imperative sentence with **你们请**. But such a sentence may have the **undertone of an 'invitation'**. Therefore, when **giving a command politely**, it is best to avoid using 你(们)请. Instead, use **请你(们)**。

(Scenario: A couple's teenage son has brought a group of friends to their house for dinner. His parents are very hospitable.)

男主人:	**请你们**别客气。(or **你们请**别客气。)
Nán zhǔrén:	*Qǐng nǐmen bié kèqì.*
女主人:	是啊! **你们请**尽量吃(or **请你们**尽量吃)，今天我做了很多菜。
Nǚ zhǔrén:	*Shì a! Nǐmen qǐng jìnliàng chī, jīntiān wǒ zuò le hěn duō cài.*

| Host: | **Please** don't be polite. |
| Hostess: | Yes! **Please** eat as much as you want. I made a lot of dishes today. |

b. 请 can be used as a **verb**; as such, it has two main uses.

   (i) It can be **followed by a noun** (which typically refers to a person or people) to mean '**to invite**' or '**to treat**' (meaning 'paying for someone's entertainment'). 请 in the word 请客 (客 literally means 'guest') is used in this pattern.

     A: 听说昨天你在家**请客**；**请**了哪些**人**？
       Tīngshuō zuótiān nǐ zài jiā qǐng kè; qǐng le nǎ xiē rén?
     B: **请**了五、六个老**同学**。
       Qǐng le wǔ, liù ge lǎo tóngxué.
     A: 你**请王大中**了没有？
       Nǐ qǐng Wáng Dàzhōng le méiyǒu?
     B: 我没有**请他**，因为他现在在外国。
       Wǒ méiyǒu qǐng tā, yīnwèi tā xiànzài zài wàiguó.
     A: I heard that you **invited people (for a meal)** to your house yester-day. Whom did you **invite**?
     B: I **invited** five or six old classmates.
     A: Did you **invite** Wang Dazhong?
     B: I did not **invite** him because he is overseas.

     A: 下午想不想一起去看电影？
       Xiàwǔ xiǎng bù xiǎng yīqǐ qù kàn diànyǐng?
     B: 好啊！谁**请**谁？(or 谁**请客**？)
       Hǎo a! Shéi qǐng shéi? (or Shéi qǐng kè?)
     A: 我**请你**吧！因为上次你**请**了**我**。
       Wǒ qǐng nǐ ba! Yīnwèi shàng cì nǐ qǐng le wǒ.
     A: Would you like to go to a movie together in the afternoon?
     B: Sure! **Whose treat**? (Who pays?)
     A: Let me **treat you** because you **treated me** last time.

  (ii) As a verb, 请 is often used in the '**A 请 B + verb**' pattern to indicate that **A asks or invites B to do something**. It is either a **polite request** or an **invitation**.

     今天有一个朋友**请我**和我先生**吃**晚饭，所以我们**请我妈妈来**我们家帮我们看孩子。
     Jīntiān yǒu yī ge péngyǒu qǐng wǒ hé wǒ xiānsheng chī wǎnfàn, suǒyǐ wǒmen qǐng wǒ māma lái wǒmen jiā bāng wǒmen kān háizi.
     Today a friend has **invited me** and my husband **to dinner**, so we have **asked** my **mother to come** to our house to babysit for us.

王经理**请张小姐**下班以后在办公室**等**他一下，因为他要**请张小姐去**看电影。

Wáng jīnglǐ qǐng Zhāng xiǎojiě xià bān yǐhòu zài bàngōngshì děng tā yīxià, yīnwèi tā yào qǐng Zhāng xiǎojiě qù kàn diànyǐng.

Manager Wang has **asked Miss Zhang to wait** for him in the office after work because he is going to **take her to (see)** a movie (treat her to a movie).

男:	李小姐，你现在有空吗？我想**请你去**喝杯咖。
Nán:	*Lǐ xiǎojiě, nǐ xiànzài yǒu kòng ma? Wǒ xiǎng qǐng nǐ qù hē bēi kāfēi.*
女:	你也**请**我**妹妹**(一起**去**)，好不好？
Nǚ:	*Nǐ yě qǐng wǒ mèimei (yīqǐ qù), hǎo bù hǎo?*
Man:	Miss Li, do you have time now? I would like to **invite you to have** a cup of coffee (I would like to take you out for a cup of coffee).
Woman:	Can you **treat my younger sister** (to coffee), too?

It should be noted that a **noun cannot follow 'A 请 B'**. This is a **common mistake** made by English speakers since 'A treats B to something' or 'A takes B out to something' is a common expression in English.

妈妈:	小中，快开始写功课。你写了功课以后，爸爸要**请我们去**吃冰淇淋。(Do NOT say 爸爸要请我们冰淇淋。)
Māma:	*Xiǎozhōng, kuài kāishǐ xiě gōngkè. Nǐ xiě le gōngkè yǐhòu, bàba yào qǐng wǒmen qù chī bīngqílín.*
Mother:	Xiaozhong, (hurry and) start your homework now. After you are done with your homework, your father is going to **treat us to some ice cream** (take us out for ice cream).

王文生又有钱又大方，常常**请朋友吃**晚饭、**看**电影、**看**球赛；每次都是他**请客**，从来不要他的朋友出钱。(Do Not say 请朋友晚饭、电影、球赛。)

Wáng Wénshēng yòu yǒuqián yòu dàfāng, chángcháng qǐng péngyǒu chī wǎnfàn, kàn diànyǐng, kàn qiúsài; měi cì dōu shì tā qǐng kè, cónglái bú yào tā de péngyǒu chū qián.

Wang Wensheng is both rich and generous; he often **treats his friends to dinners**, movies and ball games. He **pays for them (treats them)** every time, and he never wants them to pay.

In addition, because 请 can mean 'to treat' as well as 'to invite', it is important to pay attention to the context in order to know whether it is **only an invitation** or an **actual treat**.

A: 李中**请我**这星期六去他家吃晚饭，可惜我不能去，因为我那天要去北京。

    Lǐ Zhōng qǐng wǒ zhè xīngqī liù qù tā jiā chī wǎnfàn, kěxí wǒ bù nèng qù, yīnwèi wǒ nà tiān yào qù Běijīng.

B: 是吗？他为什么要**请你**吃饭？

    Shì ma? Tā wèi shénme yào qǐng nǐ chī fàn?

A: 因为上星期我**请他**看了一场电影。

    Yīnwèi shàng xīngqī wǒ qǐng tā kàn le yī chǎng diànyǐng.

A: Li Zhong **has invited me** to his house for dinner this Saturday; too bad I cannot go because I am going to Beijing that day.

B: Is that so? Why was he going to **treat you** to dinner?

A: Because I **treated him** to a movie last week.

c. If A politely asks B to **NOT do something**, the pattern is 'A 请 B 别 + verb'. A very common mistake made by learners is to use 不 when 别 is the accurate word. 别 in this use is **interchangeable with 不要**; but to only use 不 would be a mistake.

(Scenario: A passenger on a flight cannot understand the announcement made by the flight attendant.)

A: 请告诉我那个广播说什么？

    Qǐng gàosù wǒ nà ge guǎngbō shuō shénme?

B: 她说，机长**请我们别忘**了(= **不要忘**了)把安全带系好。

    Tā shuō, jīzhǎng qǐng wǒmen bié wàng le (= bú yào wàng le) bǎ ānquán dài jì hǎo.

A: Please tell me what the announcement said.

B: She said that the pilot **asked us not to forget** to fasten the seat belt.

A: 王大中昨天为什么**请你吃**饭？

    Wáng Dàzhōng zuótiān wèi shénme qǐng nǐ chī fàn?

B: 因为我看到他跟张小兰一起去看电影，他**请我别**(or **不要**)**告诉**他女朋友。

    Yīnwèi wǒ kàndào tā gēn Zhāng Xiǎolán yīqǐ qù kàn diànyǐng, tā qǐng wǒ bié (or bú yào) gàosù tā nǚ péngyǒu.

A: Why did Wang Dazhong **treat you to a meal** yesterday?

B: Because I saw him going to a movie with Zhang Xiaolan, and he has **asked me not to tell** his girlfriend.

Related expressions

问 *wèn*

A **very common mistake** made by learners, particularly English speakers, is to use 问 instead of 请 to make a polite request. This is because 请 in this use is translated as 'to ask'. 问 is strictly used to **ask a question**, not to make a request.

今天我打算**请**我的**邻居**王阿姨**来**帮我看孩子，所以我得去**问她**晚上**有没有**空。

Jīntiān wǒ dǎsuàn qǐng wǒ de línjū Wāng āyí lái bāng wǒ kān háizi, suǒyǐ wǒ děi qù wèn tā wǎnshàng yǒu méiyǒu kòng.

Today I plan to **ask my neighbor**, Auntie Wang, **to come** and babysit for me, so I have to go **ask her if** she is free in the evening.

(Scenario: A group needs one more member to join their project.)
A: 我们还需要一个人。
   Wǒmen hái xūyào yī ge rén.
B: 我去**问**王先生**愿意不愿意**来参加我们的小组？
   Wǒ qù wèn Wáng xiānsheng yuànyì bú yuànyì lái cānjiā wǒmen de xiǎo zǔ?
A: 王先生已经参加另外一個小组了。
   Wáng xiānsheng yǐjīng cānjiā lìngwài yī ge xiǎo zǔ le.
C: 那我可以去**请**李先生**来**参加。我想他应该会愿意。
   Nà wǒ kěyǐ qù qǐng Lǐ xiānsheng lái cānjiā. Wǒ xiǎng tā yīnggāi huì yuànyì.
A: We still need one person.
B: I will go **ask** Mr Wang **if** he is willing to join our group.
A: Mr Wang has already joined another group.
C: Then I can go **ask** Mr Li **to join** us. I think he should be willing to.

请问 *qǐng wèn*

a. 请问 should not always be interpreted based on its surface meaning. It does not literally mean 'please ask', but is instead a **preamble for a question**. Therefore, it means '**may I please ask** . . .' or, sometimes, 'excuse me' (before asking a question).

(Scenario: A telephone conversation.)
A: **请问**（，）王文生在吗？
   Qǐng wèn(,) Wáng Wénshēng zài ma?
B: 我就是，你是小李吧！有什么事吗？
   Wǒ jiù shì, nǐ shì Xiǎo Lǐ ba! Yǒu shénme shì ma?
A: 张小姐**请**我打电话来**问**你，今天**为什么**没有来上班？
   Zhāng xiǎojiě qǐng wǒ dà diànhuà lái wèn nǐ, jīntiān wèi shénme méiyǒu lái shàng bān?
B: 你们还不知道吗？我已经辞职了。
   Nǐmen hái bù zhīdào ma? Wǒ yǐjīng cízhí le.
A: **May I please ask** if Wang Wensheng is in?
B: This is he. You must be Little Li. Do you have something on your mind?
A: Miss Zhang **asked** me to call and **ask you why** you did not come to work today.
B: Didn't you know that I had already resigned?

(Scenario: A tourist mistakes another tourist for a local person.)

A:　**请问**(，)火车站在哪里？

　　　 Qǐngwèn(,) huǒchē zhàn zài nǎlǐ?

B:　不好意思，我也是观光客。(Pointing at someone else.) **请**你去**问**那个人，他应该是本地人。

　　　 Bù hǎo yìsi, wǒ yě shì guānguāng kè. Qǐng nǐ qù wèn nà ge rén, tā yīnggāi shì běndì rén.

A:　**Excuse me (May I please ask)**, where is the train station?

B:　Sorry, I am also a tourist. **Please go ask** that person. He should be a local.

b.　请问 can be an expression to make 问 more polite, especially when one is directly addressing another person. Even though 请 is optional grammar-wise, its necessity is context-dependent.

王小姐，我想**请问你**，星期六晚上**有没有**空？要是你有空，我想**请你去**看电影。

Wáng xiǎojiě, wǒ xiǎng qǐng wèn nǐ, xīngqī liù wǎnshàng yǒu méiyǒu kòng? Yàoshì nǐ yǒu kòng, wǒ xiǎng qǐng nǐ qù kàn diànyǐng.

Miss Wang, I would like to **ask you if** you are free Saturday evening. If you are, I would like to **invite you to** a movie (I would like to take you to a movie).

叫 *jiào*

叫 has several meanings, one of which is to **give a command**. Because it does not have the connotation of politeness that 请 does, the more appropriate translation for 叫 is '**to tell**'. The pattern is '**A 叫 B + verb**'. It is usually used when A is in a position to give B orders.

→ See 叫 (*jiào*) for more information.

(Scenario: Wang was absent from class; one of his classmates, Gao, calls him in the evening.)

王:　　　小高，有什么事？

Wáng:　　*Xiǎo Gāo, yǒu shénme shì?*

高:　　　老师**叫我打**电话**问**你，今天**为什么**没有来上课？

Gāo:　　*Lǎoshī jiào wǒ dǎ ge diànhuà wèn nǐ, jīntiān wèi shénme méiyǒu lái shàng kè?*

王:　　　我不舒服。今天老师有没有交待功课？

Wáng:　　*Wǒ bù shūfú. Jīntiān lǎoshī yǒu méiyǒu jiāodài gōngkè?*

高:　　　有。他**叫我们**把第三课的课文**抄**两遍。

Gǎo:　　*Yǒu. Tā jiào wǒmen bǎ dì sān kè de kèwén chāo liǎng biàn.*

Wang: Little Gao, why did you call? (Literally: Is there any specific business?)

Gao: The teacher **told me to call** and **ask** you **why** you did not come to class today.

Wang: I was not feeling well. Did the teacher assign any homework today?

Gao: Yes, he did. He **told us to copy** the text of Lesson Three twice.

妻子: 医生**叫你别**喝酒，你为什么又在喝？

Qīzi: *Yīshēng jiào nǐ bié hē jiǔ, nǐ wèi shénme yòu zài hē?*

丈夫: 医生没有**叫我别**喝酒，他只**叫我**少**喝**一点。

Zhàngfū: *Yīshēng méiyǒu jiào wǒ bié hē jiǔ, tā zhǐ jiào wǒ shǎo hē yīdiǎn.*

Wife: The doctor **told you not to drink.** Why are you drinking again?

Husband: The doctor did not **tell me not to drink.** He only **told me to drink** a little less.

让 *ràng*

Although 让 is frequently associated with 'to let' or 'to allow', it is acceptable to use it in the 'A 让 B + verb' pattern to indicate that A asks B to do something. **In terms of politeness, 让 is between 请 and 叫.** In other words, it is neutral in tone. Politeness is not necessary, but it is not an order, either.

→ See 让 (*ràng*) for more information.

(Scenario: Two managers are discussing whom they should assign a job to.)

A: 你认为，我们应该**让王先生**还是李先生**去**跟客户协调这件事？

   Nǐ rènwéi, wǒmen yīnggāi ràng Wáng xiānsheng háishì Lǐ xiānsheng qù gēn kèhù xiétiáo zhè jiàn shì?

B: 我觉得我们应该**让王先生去**，他的英文比李先生好。

   Wǒ juéde wǒmen yīnggāi ràng Wáng xiānsheng qù, tā de Yīngwén bǐ Lǐ xiānsheng hǎo.

A: Do you think we should **ask Mr Wang** or Mr Li **to negotiate** this business with the client?

B: I think we should **ask Mr Wang to do** it; his English is better than Mr Li's.

李明昨天跟同学打架；可是老师没有骂他，只**让他回**家去反省一下这种行为。

Lǐ Míng zuótiān gēn tóngxué dǎjià, kěshì lǎoshī méiyǒu mà tā, zhǐ ràng tā huí jiā qù fǎnxǐng yīxià zhè zhǒng xíngwéi.

Li Ming had a fist fight with a classmate yesterday, but the teacher did not scold him; she only **asked him to go** home and self-reflect on this kind of behavior.

去 *qù*

The simple definition of 去 ('to go') does not provide a full picture of its uses. The discussion in this section focuses on the differences between the use of 去 and the use of the verb 'to go' in English so as to help learners, especially those who are English speakers, avoid making mistakes when using this basic vocabulary word.

a.　去 must be followed by either a **place** or a **verb** (indicating an activity). It **cannot** be directly followed by a pronoun or a noun that does not indicate a place.

　　　(Scenario: Two friends are discussing what to do after work.)
　　A:　下班以后我们**去看**电影，怎么样？(Do NOT say 去电影. 电影 cannot follow 去.)
　　　　Xià bān yǐhòu, wǒmen qù kàn diànyǐng, zěnme yàng?
　　B:　我不喜欢看电影。我们**去吃**晚饭，好吗？(Do NOT say 去晚饭.)
　　　　Wǒ bù xǐhuān kàn diànyǐng. Wǒmen qù chī wǎnfàn, hǎo ma?
　　A:　好！**去哪儿**吃？(哪儿 indicates a location; it can follow 去.)
　　　　Hǎo! Qù nǎ'ér chī?
　　B:　**去四海饭馆**吧！那儿的菜不错。吃了晚饭，咱们**去打**保龄球，好不好？(Sihai Restaurant is a location; it can follow 去.)
　　　　Qù Sìhǎi fànguǎn ba! Nà'ér de cài búcuò. Chī le wǎnfàn, zánmen qù dǎ bǎolíng qiú, hǎo bù hǎo?
　　A:　How about if we **go to (see)** a movie after work?
　　B:　I don't like to watch movies. Let's **go to (have)** dinner, OK?
　　A:　OK! **Where** should we **go** (to have dinner)?
　　B:　Why don't we go to Sihai Restaurant! Food there is not bad. How about if we **go bowling** after dinner?

b.　Sometimes, an English sentence does not have an obvious word 'to go', but its counterpart in Chinese needs 去. The verb 请 (*qǐng*: to invite) provides a good example for this rule, and the basic pattern is '**A invites B to a place**'. While there is no obvious need for the word 去 due to the lack of 'to go' in the English sentence, it would be a mistake to omit 去 before the place.

　　A:　昨天王文生**请我吃**饭。(吃 is a verb; 吃饭 can follow 请我.)
　　　　Zuótiān Wáng Wénshēng qǐng wǒ chī fàn.
　　B:　是吗？他**请你去哪里**吃？(哪里 is a location; 去 must be used after 请你.)
　　　　Shì ma? Tā qǐng nǐ qù nǎlǐ chī?
　　A:　他**请我去**一家高级**饭馆**吃牛排。(Do not say 他请我一家高级饭馆.)
　　　　Tā qǐng wǒ qù yī jiā gāojí fànguǎn chī niúpái.
　　A:　Yesterday Wang Wensheng treated me to a meal (literally: **invited me to eat**).
　　B:　Is that so? **Where** did he **take (= invite) you** to eat?
　　A:　He **took me (invited me) to** a high-end **restaurant** to have steak.

c. An English sentence can have a person (pronoun, noun or proper noun) directly after 'to go', but **a person cannot follow** 去 in Chinese. In this case, the word 那儿 (*nà'ér*) or 那里 (*nàlǐ*) must be added to make the expression grammatical. The pattern is '**去 person + 那里/那儿**'. However, exactly what is referred to by 那儿/那里 is vague and is usually understood by the listener(s).

下课以前，老师说，有问题的人，下午可以**去他那里**问问题。
Xià kè yǐqián, lǎoshī shuō, yǒu wèntí de rén, xiàwǔ kěyǐ qù tā nàlǐ wèn wèntí.
Before class was over, the teacher said that those who had questions could **go to him** in the afternoon to ask their questions.

(Scenario: A group of coworkers are discussing where they will hold their monthly dinner get-together this month.)

高: 上次的餐会是在小张家办的，所以这次应该**去老王那里**办。

Gāo: *Shàng cì de cānhuì shì zài Xiǎo Zhāng jiā bàn de, suǒyǐ zhè cì yīnggāi qù Lǎo Wáng nàlǐ bàn.*

李: 老王上星期过生日，已经**请**了咱们**去他家**吃饭，这次别**去他那儿**了吧！

Lǐ : *Lǎo Wáng shàng xīngqī guò shēngrì, yǐjīng qǐng le zánmen qù tā jiā chī fàn, zhè cì bié qù tā nà'ér le ba!*

高: 那**去谁那里**呢？

Gāo: *Nà qù shéi nàlǐ ne?*

王: **去我那儿**，没关系。我喜欢做菜。

Wáng: *Qù wǒ nà'ér, méi guānxì. Wǒ xǐhuān zuò cài.*

Gao: The dinner was held at Little Zhang's house last time, so this time we should **go to Old Wang's place** to have it.

Li: When Old Wang celebrated his birthday last week, he already **invited** us **to his house** for dinner. Let's not **go to his place** this time.

Gao: Then **whose place** shall we **go** to?

Wang: **Go to my place**. It will be all right. I like to cook.

d. 来 (*lái*: to come) and 去 are similar in usage, but 这儿 (*zhè'ér*)/这里 (*zhèlǐ*) should be used in place of 那儿/那里 when the verb is 来.

(Scenario: A couple's one-year-old daughter is learning to walk. They enjoy encouraging her.)

妈妈: 来！来！**来妈妈这里**！ (Do NOT say 来妈妈。)

Māma: *Lái! Lái! Lái māma zhèlǐ.*

爸爸: 别**去妈妈那里**！**来爸爸这里**！爸爸跟你玩！

Bàba: *Bié qù māma nàlǐ. Lái bàba zhèlǐ. Bàba gēn nǐ wán.*

Mother: Come here! Come here! **Come to Mama.**

Father: Don't **go to Mama**. **Come to Papa.** Papa will play with you.

→ See 来 (*lái*) for related information.

e. Sometimes the expression '**to go to + a place**' in English does not take the verb 去 in Chinese; instead, the verb 上 (*shàng*) is used. In this case, 'to go' does not merely indicate physically going somewhere, but indicates going to a place **for the activities specifically for such a place**.

Examples are 上图书馆 (*shàng túshūguǎn*: to go to the library), 上厕所 (*shàng cèsuǒ*: to go use the toilet), 上大学 (*shàng dàxué*: to go to college), 上教堂 (*shàng jiàotáng*: to go to church), etc.

(Scenario: Wang describes what his student life is like to Li. Note the difference between the uses of 去 and 上, both of which are translated as 'to go'.)

王: 你上哪个**大学**？

Wáng: Nǐ shàng nǎ ge dàxué?

李: 我明年才要**上大学**呢！你呢？

Lǐ: Wǒ míngnián cái yào shàng dàxué ne! Nǐ ne?

王: 我已经**上**了两年**大学**了。**上大学**没什么意思，功课好多，我每天都得**上图书馆**，准备大考试的时候，会连**上厕所**的时间都没有。

Wáng: Wǒ yǐjīng shàng le liǎng nián dàxué le. Shàng dàxué méi shénme yìsi, gōngkè hǎoduō, wǒ měi tiān dōu děi shàng túshūguǎn; zhǔnbèi dà kǎoshì de shíhòu, huì lián shàng cèsuǒ de shíjiān dōu méiyǒu.

李: 那你周末做什么？

Lǐ: Nà nǐ zhōumò zuò shénme?

王: 我每个星期天都**上教堂**；星期六晚上常常**上馆子**吃顿饭。

Wáng: Wǒ měi ge xīngqī tiān dōu shàng jiàotáng. Xīngqī liù wǎnshàng chángcháng shàng guǎnzi chī dùn fàn.

李: 我现在想**去**你们学校的**图书馆**参观一下，你可不可以陪我去？

Lǐ: Wǒ xiànzài xiǎng qù nǐmen xuéxiào de túshūguǎn cānguān yīxià; nǐ kě bù kěyǐ péi wǒ qù?

王: 行！不过我想先**去厕所**洗一下手，你在这里等一下。

Wáng: Xíng! Búguò wǒ xiǎng xiān qù cèsuǒ xǐ yīxià shǒu; nǐ zài zhèlǐ děng yīxià.

Wang: Which **college** do you **go to**?

Li: I won't **go to a college** until next year. How about you?

Wang: I have been **going to college** (meaning: being a college student) for two years already. **Going to college** is not much fun. I have so much homework. I have to **go to the library** (meaning: to study or to do research) every day. When studying for a big exam, I don't even have time to **go to the bathroom**.

Li: Then what do you do on the weekend?

Wang: I **go to church** every Sunday. I often **go to a restaurant** to have a meal on Saturday evenings.

Li: I would like to **go to** your school's **library** to look around. Can you go with me?

Wang: Sure! But I want to first **go to the bathroom** to wash my hands. Please wait for me here.

却 *què*

却 is an **adverb**, and its basic definition is '**however**' or '**yet**'. This suggests that it is used to express a situation or idea that is **contrary to** what might normally be expected.

The **correct word order** in a sentence with 却 needs special attention. Although 却 can be interpreted as 'however', it cannot be placed before the subject of the sentence because it is an adverb.

For example, the Chinese sentence for 'I like Li Xiaolan very much; **however, she** does not know' **cannot** be 我很喜欢李小兰，**却她**不知道. One can either say 可是她不知道 or 她却不知道.

Therefore, a common mistake learners must avoid is to use 却 and 可是 (or 但是/不过) interchangeably. Since 可是 **is a conjunction**, and 却 **is an adverb**, each occupies a different location in a sentence in terms of word order. In other words, they do not replace each other, but **can coexist**.

a.   Normally, when 虽然 (*suīrán*: although/though) is used, the main sentence should have 可是. However, when 却 **is used**, 可是 **becomes optional**. If both 可是 and 却 are missing, the sentence is considered grammatically incorrect.

In terms of word order, 可是 (a conjunction) appears before the subject of the sentence; 却 (an adverb) **appears after the subject** (and the time phrase, if any), but before the verb or adjective.

虽然今天是星期六，而且天气很不错，**(可是)**小李**却**不想出去玩，因为他觉得不太舒服。
Suīrán jīntiān shì xīngqī liù, érqiě tiānqì hěn búcuò, (kěshì) Xiǎo Lǐ què bù xiǎng chūqùwán, yīnwèi tā juéde bú tài shūfú.
Although today is Saturday, and also the weather is not bad, Little Li, **however**, does not want to go out to have fun because he is not feeling well.

高文生跟李小兰**虽然**已经交往了八年，**(可是)**两个人**却**没有结婚的打算。
Gāo Wénshēng gēn Lǐ Xiǎolán suīrán yǐjīng jiāowǎng le bā nián, (kěshì) liǎng ge rén què méiyǒu jiéhūn de dǎsuàn.
Although Gao Wensheng and Li Xiaolan have already been dating for eight years, the two of them, **however**, don't have plans to get married.

Sometimes, 可是 and 却 may ostensibly appear to be interchangeable, but this is only because the subject in the main sentence is omitted (to avoid redundancy).

他虽然有钱，**可是却**很小气。 (The subject 他 is not repeated in the main sentence with 可是.)
Tā suīrán yǒu qián, kěshì què hěn xiǎoqì.
= 他虽然有钱，**可是**很小气。= 他虽然有钱，**却**很小气。
Although he is wealthy, he, **however**, is stingy.

Even when the sentence does not have 虽然, the rule is the same.

(Scenario: A friend asks Mr Wang how he is enjoying his retirement. He says:)

退休以前，想出去玩**(可是)却**没有时间；退休以后，**(虽然)**时间多了，**(可是)却**没有体力了。

Tuìxiū yǐqián, xiǎng chūqù wán, (kěshì) què méiyǒu shíjiān; tuìxiū yǐhòu, (suīrán) shíjiān duō le, (kěshì) què méiyǒu tǐlì le.

Before I retired, I wanted to go out to have fun, **but** I, **however**, didn't have the time; since I retired, **although** I have had more time, I, **however**, don't have the energy anymore.

Sometimes, both 虽然 and 可是 are omitted, and **却 alone** can show the **two opposite situations**, particularly when the two situations are indicated by **two adjectives**.

A: 王小英是我们班上最聪明漂亮**却**最不受欢迎的同学。
   Wáng Xiǎoyīng shì wǒmen bān shàng zuì cōngmíng piàoliàng què zuì bú shòu huānyíng de tóngxué.
B: 你的意思是，她**(虽然)**很出色，**(可是)却**没有朋友，对吗？
   Nǐ de yìsi shì, tā (suīrán) hěn chūsè, (kěshì) què méiyǒu péngyǒu, duì ma?
A: 对！因为她太骄傲了。
   Duì! Yīnwèi tā tài jiāo'ào le.

A: In our class, Wang Xiaoying is the student that is the smartest and prettiest **yet** the least popular.
B: What you meant is that, **although** she is outstanding, she, **however**, does not have any friends, right?
A: That's right! It's because she is too arrogant.

b. 却 can imply a **contradiction** that exists between two situations or ideas.

   (i) The contradiction exists between **what seems to be and what actually is**. A good interpretation for 却 used this way is '**actually**' (其实: *qíshí*), instead of 'however'.

   儿子从战场回到家，妈妈只说"你瘦了。"一句**简单**的话**却**包含了**无尽**的母爱。(The contradiction is between 简单 and 无尽。)
   Érzi cóng zhànchǎng huí dào jiā, māma zhǐ shuō 'Nǐ shòu le.' Yī jù jiǎndān de huà què bāohán le wújìn de mǔ'ài.
   The son came home from the war; his mother only said, 'You are thinner.' A **simple** sentence **actually** contained **boundless** mother's love.

谁都想不到，这个表面上**幸福快乐**的家庭背后**却**有许多**矛盾与冲突**。(The contradiction is between 幸福快乐 and 矛盾冲突.)

Shéi dōu xiǎng bú dào, zhè ge biǎomiàn shàng xìngfú kuàilè de jiātíng bèihòu què yǒu xǔduō máodùn yǔ chōngtú.

No one had expected that this ostensibly (= seemingly) **happy** family **actually** had many **conflicts and fights** behind closed doors.

(ii) The contradiction exists between **what is supposed to be and what actually turns out to be**. There is often **no direct counterpart in English** for 却 used this way. To literally translate it into 'however' may distort the meaning of the sentence.

王大中看到张美兰，对她说：“好久不见，你好像又胖了。”一个无心的玩笑**却**让张美兰难过了很久。

Wáng Dàzhōng kàndào Zhāng Měilán, duì tā shuō: 'Hǎo jiǔ bú jiàn, nǐ hǎoxiàng yòu pàng le.' Yī ge wúxīn de wánxiào què ràng Zhāng Měilán nánguò le hěn jiǔ.

When Wang Dazhong saw Zhang Meilan, he said to her, 'long time no see. You seem to have gained weight again.' An unintentional joke made Zhang Meilan feel hurt for quite a long time.

老师：　这么容易的问题**却**没有一个人会回答，这是怎么回事？

Lǎoshī:　*Zhème róngyì de wèntí què méiyǒu rén huì huídá, zhè shì zěnme huí shì?*

Teacher:　Such an easy question, **yet** no one can answer it. What's going on?

让 *ràng*

让 has several definitions, each of which is used in a different pattern. This section focuses on five of its main uses.

a.　让 can indicate '**to yield**' or '**to relinquish**'. It means **to give way** or **to give up** something. There are usually no direct translations in English when 让 is used for this definition. Therefore, this use of 让 often confuses learners or escapes their attention.

(i)　A noun (or a pronoun) sometimes follows 让; in addition, it is often **reduplicated** or **followed by** 一下.

(Scenario: On a busy sidewalk, a delivery man is pushing a cartload of merchandise and he is being blocked by other pedestrians.)

不好意思，不好意思，请**让一让**(or 请**让路**)。

Bù hǎo yìsi, bù hǎo yìsi, qǐng ràng yī ràng (or qǐng ràng lù).

Excuse me, excuse me. Please **make way**. (Implied: Please **yield the path** to me.)

(Scenario: A boy and his younger sister are having a fight.)

妈妈:	你们两个，别再吵了。小中，你**让她一下**吧！
Māma:	*Nǐmen liǎng ge, bié zài chǎo le. Xiǎozhōng, nǐ ràng tā yīxià ba!*
小中:	为什么要我**让她**？
Xiǎozhōng:	*Wèi shénme yào wǒ ràng tā?*
妈妈:	哥哥**让妹妹**是应该的。
Māma:	*Gēge ràng mèimei shì yīnggāi de.*
Mother:	The two of you, stop fighting. Xiaozhong, why don't you **give her a break**!
Xiaozhong:	Why do I have to **give her a break**?
Mother:	An older brother **giving his younger sister a break** – that is the way it's supposed to be.

在公共汽车上看到老人或者怀孕的妇女，我们应该**让座**。

Zài gōnggòng qìchē shàng kàndào lǎorén huòzhě huáiyùn de fùnǚ, wǒmen yīnggāi ràng zuò.

When we see senior citizens or pregnant women on public transportation, we should **yield our seats** (give our seats to them).

(ii) **让给** is used when the object to be yielded and the receiver are both mentioned. The receiver immediately follows 给; therefore, it can be used in a 把 sentence.

在公共汽车上，我们应该把座位**让给**老人或者怀孕的妇女。

Zài gōnggòng qìchē shàng, wǒmen yīnggai bǎ zuòwèi ràng gěi lǎorén huòzhě huáiyùn de fùnǚ.

On public transportation, we should **yield** our seats **to** senior citizens or pregnant women.

If the object is indefinite, the pattern '让 something 给 someone' is often used.

我有五张球赛的票，可是我家只有三个人，所以我就**让了两张给**李明，因为他只有一张票，可是他的两个儿子也都想去看这场比赛。(让 in this sentence does not say Li Ming received the tickets for free or had to pay for them.)

Wǒ yǒu wǔ zhāng qiúsài de piào, kěshì wǒ jiā zhǐ yǒu sān ge rén, suǒyǐ wǒ jiù ràng le liǎng zhāng gěi Lǐ Míng, yīnwèi tā zhǐ yǒu yī zhāng piào, kěshì tā de liǎng ge érzi yě xiǎng qù kàn zhè chǎng bǐsài.

I had five tickets for the ball game, but there are only three people in my family, so I **gave up two** of my tickets (and let Li Ming have them), because he only had one ticket, but both of his sons wanted to see this game, too.

b. 让 means '**to let**' or '**to allow**'. This is one of the most common uses of 让.

(i) In the 'A 让 B + verb' pattern, 让 implies 'permission' or sometimes 'no interference'. If **no permission** is given, **不让** is used.

A: 我爸妈非常开明，从小他们就**让我**自由**发展**自己的兴趣。
Wǒ bàmā fēicháng kāimíng, cóngxiǎo tāmen jiù ràng wǒ zìyóu fāzhǎn zìjǐ de xìngqù.

B: 我真羡慕你；从小我爸妈就**不让我做**自己喜欢做的事，我一定得听他们的安排。
Wǒ zhēn xiànmù nǐ; cóngxiǎo wǒ bàmā jiù bú ràng wǒ zuò zìjǐ xǐhuān zuò de shì, wǒ yīdìng děi tīng tāmen de ānpái.

A: My parents are very open-minded. Ever since I was little, they have **let me (allowed me to) freely develop** my own interests.

B: I really envy you. Ever since I was little, my parents have **not let me do** things I like to do; I have to obey their arrangements.

A: 大中，我们都在等你，你怎么还不来？
Dàzhōng, wǒmen dōu zài děng nǐ, nǐ zěnme hái bù lái?

B: 上次考试考得太差了，所以这个周末我妈妈**不让我出**门。
Shàng cì kǎoshì kǎo de tài chà le, suǒyǐ zhè ge zhōumò wǒ māma bú ràng wǒ chūmén.

A: Dazhong, we are all waiting for you. How come you have not come yet?

B: I did really poorly on the last test, so my mother **won't allow me to go** out this weekend.

妈妈: 你为什么跟同学打架？
Māma: Nǐ wèi shénme gēn tóngxué dǎjià?
爸爸: 我想他跟同学打架的原因是 . . .
Bàba: Wǒ xiǎng tā gēn tóngxué dǎjià de yuányīn shì . . .
妈妈: **(你)让他**自己**说**，我要听他怎么说。(This implies 'no interference'.)
Māma: (Nǐ) ràng tā zìjǐ shuō, wǒ yào tīng tā zěnme shuō.
Mother: Why did you fight with your classmates?
Father: I think the reason why he fought with his classmates is . . .
Mother: **Let him say** it. I want to hear how he explains it.

(ii) As 'to let', 让 can be used in expressions similar to 'let us' or 'let me'. However, it is not used in common daily speech to make casual suggestions, but in **more formal situations** to declare one's **intention or wish**.

(Scenario: A company is celebrating its 50th anniversary. Employees and management are having a party.)

经理: 　　　　　　　现在**让我们**一起**举**杯庆祝。
Jīnglǐ: 　　　　　*Xiànzài ràng wǒmen yīqǐ jǔ bēi qìngzhù.*
执行主管: 　　　　　**让我们**共同为公司的未来**努力**。
Zhíxíng zhǔguǎn: 　*Ràng wǒmen gòngtóng wèi gōngsī de wèilái nǔlì.*
Manager: 　　　　　Now **let us raise** our glasses and celebrate together.
Executive: 　　　　　**Let us work hard** together for the future of the company.

It should be noted that, when making a **suggestion** in a casual manner, one might use 'let's . . .' in English, but 让 is **not used** in Chinese in such a situation. 吧 or 怎么样 is more appropriate.

A: 今天晚上有没有事？
　　Jīntiān wǎnshàng yǒu méiyǒu shì?
B: 没有。
　　Méiyǒu.
A: 那我们**去**啤酒馆喝两杯**吧**！
　　Nà wǒmen qù píjiǔ guǎn hē liǎng bēi ba!
B: 最近身体不太好，医生**不让我喝**酒。去看电影，**怎么样**？
　　Zuìjìn shēntǐ bú tài hǎo, yīshēng bú ràng wǒ hē jiǔ. Qù kàn diànyǐng, zěnme yàng?
A: 好吧！
　　Hǎo ba!

A: Are you free this evening?
B: Yes.
A: Then **let's go** to a pub to have a couple of drinks.
B: Recently my health has not been very good. My doctor does **not allow me to drink. Let's go** see a movie, **how's that**?
A: OK!

c. 让 means '**to ask**' or '**to tell**'. The pattern is '**A 让 B + verb**', which indicates that **A asks (or tells) B to do something**. Although the pattern appears similar to the one above when 让 means 'to let', a major difference lies in the **negative forms** of these two patterns.

让 used in this pattern is similar to 请 (*qǐng*) and 叫 (*jiào*) with different degrees of **politeness**.

→ See 请 (*qǐng*) and 叫 (*jiào*) for related information.

(Scenario: Wang's friends are waiting for him to start a basketball game, but he cannot go. Note the two **different negative patterns** when 让 is used.)
A: 王大中，我们都在等你，你怎么还不来？
　　Wáng Dàzhōng, wǒmen dōu zài děng nǐ, nǐ zěnme hái bù lái?

B:　你们别等了，我妈妈**不让我去**。
　　Nǐmen bié děng le, wǒ māma bú ràng wǒ qù.
A:　为什么？
　　Wèi shénme?
B:　今天晚上我们要请客，所以**她让我别出**门，在家帮忙准备。
　　Jīntiān wǎnshàng wǒmen yào qǐng kè, suǒyǐ tā ràng wǒ bié chū mén,
　　zài jiā bāngmáng zhǔnbei.
A:　Wang Dazhong, we are all waiting for you. How come you are not here yet?
B:　Don't wait anymore. My mother **will not allow me to go**.
A:　Why?
B:　We have guests for dinner this evening, so she **told me not to go out** and help get things ready at home.

(Scenario: A man cannot get any of his coworkers to go have a drink with him after work. 让 is used in various patterns here.)
王：　下班以后，一起去那家新开的啤酒馆喝两杯**吧**！
Wáng:　*Xià bān yǐhòu, yīqǐ qù nà jiā xīn kāi de píjiǔ guǎn hē liǎng bēi ba!*
李：　最近身体不太好，医生**让我别喝**酒。
Lǐ:　*Zuìjìn shēntǐ bú tài hǎo, yīshēng ràng wǒ bié hē jiǔ.*
白：　我太太**让我**下了班就**回家**去帮忙看孩子。
Bái:　*Wǒ tàitai ràng wǒ xià le bān jiù huí jiā qù bāngmáng kān háizi.*
王：　小张，你呢？你去不去？
Wáng:　*Xiǎo Zhāng, nǐ ne? Nǐ qù bú qù?*
张：　我也不能去，因为我女朋友**不让我喝**酒。
Zhāng:　*Wǒ yě bù néng qù, yīnwèi wǒ nǚ péngyǒu bú ràng wǒ hē jiǔ.*
Wang:　**Let's go** to that new pub to have a couple of drinks after work.
Li:　My health has not been very good lately. My doctor has **told me not to drink**.
Bai:　My wife has **told me to go home** right after work to help her babysit the children.
Wang:　Little Zhang, how about you? Are you going?
Zhang:　I cannot go, either, because my girlfriend does **not allow me to drink**.

d.　让 means '**to make**' (or 'to cause'). **让 and 叫** (when defined as 'to make' or 'to cause') are **interchangeable** when used in the '**A 让 (or 叫) B + adjective**' pattern.

The verb 觉得 sometimes appears before the adjective. Learners should not confuse this pattern with the '**A 让/叫 B + verb**' (**A tells B to do something**) even though their **surface structures appear to be the same**.

Two other words, **令** (*lìng*) and **使** (*shǐ*), share the same meaning and use with 叫 and 让; but 叫 and 让 are normally used in casual speech, whereas 令 and 使 are used in **more formal situations**.

→ See 叫 (*jiào*), 令 (*lìng*) and 使 (*shǐ*) for more information.

张大中在学校不听老师的话，在家常常跟爸妈吵架、顶嘴，这种行为实在**让人**很**生气**。(很 can appear before 让人: 很让人生气.)

Zhāng Dàzhōng zài xuéxiào bù tīng lǎoshì de huà, zài jiā chángcháng gēn bàmā chǎojià, dǐngzuǐ, zhè zhǒng xíngwéi shízài ràng rén hěn shēngqì.

Zhang Dazhong disobeys the teacher in school, and he often fights with and talks back to his parents at home. This kind of behavior really **makes one angry**.

The negative form for this pattern is usually 不 **before the adjective**, not before 让.

我女儿下个月就要去外地上大学了，这是她第一次离开家，真**让我不放心**。

Wǒ nǚ'ér xià ge yuè jiù yào qù wàidì shàng dàxué le, zhè shì tā dì yī cì líkāi jiā, zhēn ràng wǒ bú fàngxīn.

My daughter is going out of town for college next month. This will be her first time away from home, and it really **makes me worried**.

e. 让 and 叫 share another similarity in meaning and use; that is, they can both **replace 被** in a **passive sentence** when the **performer is mentioned**.

爸爸发现妈妈包的饺子都**让**(= 被 or 叫)弟弟吃完了；这**让**(= 叫 or **使** or **令**)**爸爸很不高兴**；他说他晚上**不让**弟弟**看**电视，可是妈妈**让**(= 叫 or **请**)爸爸**别生气**，因为冰箱里还有几十个呢。

Bàba fāxiàn māma bāo de jiǎozi dōu ràng (= bèi or jiào) dìdi chī wán le; zhè ràng (= jiào, shǐ or lìng) bàba hěn bù gāoxìng; tā shuō tā wǎnshàng bú ràng dìdi kàn diànshì, kěshì māma ràng (= jiào or qǐng) bàba bié shēngqì, yīnwèi bīngxiāng lǐ hái yǒu jǐ shí ge ne.

My father found out that all the dumplings my mother made had **been finished by** my younger brother, and this **made him upset**. He said he would **not allow** my younger brother **to watch** TV in the evening. But my mother **asked my father to not get mad** because there were still dozens of dumplings in the refrigerator.

我儿子今年申请了全国最有名的一所大学，可是没有**被**接受。(让 or 叫 cannot be used to replace 被 since the 'performer' is not mentioned.)

Wǒ érzi jīnnián shēngqǐng le quán guó zuì yǒumíng de yī suǒ dàxué, kěshì méiyǒu bèi jiēshòu.

This year my son applied for admission to one of the most reputable universities in the country, but he **was not accepted**.

认得 *rènde*

认得 and 认识 are interchangeable when both are used to indicate knowing (being **acquainted with**) or being **familiar with** someone or something. 认得 may sound **more casual** than 认识.

→ See 认识 (*rènshì*) for related information.

a. 认得 also means 'to recognize'. Its implication is to have the ability to **identify** someone or something based on one's **familiarity** with them or from one's **memory**. In this sense, 认得 may not be replaced with 认识.

(Scenario: Li asks Zhang to deliver something to Wang's house.)

李: 你**认得**(= 认识)路吗？要不要我给你画个地图？

Lǐ: *Nǐ rènde (rènshì) lù ma? Yào bú yào wǒ gěi nǐ huà ge dìtú?*

张: 不用。老王的家，我去过一次；到了那条街，我就**认得** (cannot be 认识) 他的房子。

Zhāng: *Búyòng. Lǎo Wáng de jiā, wǒ qù guo yī cì; dào le nà tiáo jiē, wǒ jiù rènde tā de fángzi.*

Li: Do you **know** your way? (Are you **familiar with** the way to his house?) Do you want me to draw you a map?

Zhang: It's not necessary. I have been to Old Wang's house once. When I get to his street, I will **recognize** his house.

(Scenario: Wang is proud of his son, whereas Li is disappointed with his. Note that 认识 might be acceptable in this scenario, but 认得 is better.)

王: 我儿子才两岁，已经**认得**一百多个汉字了。

Wáng: *Wǒ érzi cái liǎng suì, yǐjīng rènde yī bǎi duō gè Hànzì le.*

李: 唉！我儿子在大学学了半年的中文，只**认得**"大、中、小"三个字。

Lǐ: *Ài! Wǒ érzi zài dàxué xué le bàn nián de Zhōngwén, zhǐ rènde 'dà, zhōng, xiǎo' sān ge zì.*

Wang: My son is only two years old, and he already **recognizes** over 100 Chinese characters.

Li: Sigh! My son studied Chinese in college for half a year, and he only **recognizes** three characters – big, middle and small.

b. **不认得** means 'to **not** recognize'; **认不得** means 'being **unable to** recognize'. (It should be noted that 认识 can never have 不 inserted between 认 and 识.)

(Scenario: Mr Wang goes back to his old high school for the 30th reunion.)

王: 李大中，三十年不见了，你还**认得**我吗？

Wáng: *Lǐ Dàzhōng, sānshí nián bú jiàn le, nǐ hái rènde wǒ ma?*

李: 啊！**认得**，**认得**，你是王明！我们当年是最好的朋友，怎么会**不认得**？

Lǐ: *À! Rènde, rènde, nǐ shì Wáng Míng! Wǒmen dāngnián shì zuì hǎo de péngyǒu, zěnme huì bú rènde?*

王: 是啊！老朋友我差不多都还**认得**，倒是校园变了很多，我几乎**认不得**了。

Wáng: *Shì a! Lǎo péngyǒu wǒ chàbùduō dōu hái rènde, dǎo shì xiàoyuán biàn le hěn duō, wǒ jīhū rèn bù dé le.*

Wang: Li Dazhong, we haven't seen each other in 30 years. Do you still **recognize** me?

Li: Ah, yes, yes, I **recognize** you. You are Wang Ming. We were best friends in those days; how is it possible for me to **not recognize** you?

Wang: Yeah! I still **recognize** almost all the old friends. But it is the campus that has changed so much, and I almost **cannot recognize** the place.

认识 *rènshì*

认识 is a word with various implications although its basic definition can simply be 'to know'. 认识 is usually used to talk about people although occasionally things that one is **familiar with** can follow 认识 as well. What is important is for learners to be aware of the difference between 认识 and 知道 (*zhīdào*), which is also defined as 'to know'.

→ See 知道 (*zhīdào*) for related information.

a. As 'to know', 认识 means 'to be acquainted (with)'. When two or more people know （认识） one another, these people can be the **subject** of the sentence; the actual word 'one another' is not necessary.

王:　　小张，你**认识**李先生吗？要不要我介绍一下？

Wáng: Xiǎo Zhāng, nǐ rènshì Lǐ xiānsheng ma? Yào bú yào wǒ jièshào yīxià?

张:　　不用，**我们认识**。

Zhāng: Bú yòng, wǒmen rènshì.

Wang: Little Zhang, do you **know** Mr Li? Do you want me to introduce you?

Zhang: It's not necessary. We **know each other**.

b. In order to be acquainted with someone, one must first **meet** that person; 认识 can also be used as a verb that indicates an action, meaning 'to meet (someone **for the first time**)'.

李:　　老王，你**认识**张小姐吗？可不可以介绍一下？

Lǐ: Lǎo Wáng, nǐ rènshì Zhāng xiǎojiě ma? Kě bù kěyǐ jièshào yīxià?

王:　　你想**认识**她吗？没问题，我**认识**她，我给你们介绍。

Wáng: Nǐ xiǎng rènshì tā ma? Méi wèntí, wǒ rènshì tā, wǒ gěi nǐmen jièshào.

Li: Old Wang, do you **know** Miss Zhang? Can you introduce us?

Wang: You want to **meet** her? No problem! I **know** her. I'll introduce you.

c. Since 认识, when defined as '**to be acquainted**', does not indicate an action, its **negative form** should be **不认识**, whether it is referring to a **current** situation or a **previous** situation.

On the other hand, when 认识 is used to indicate '**to meet** (someone for the first time)', its **negative** form is **没有认识**.

我去中国以前，一个中国人也**不认识**；我总以为到了中国就会**认识**很多**中国朋友**。可是我在北京住了半年，竟然**没有认识**任何中国人。

Wǒ qù Zhōngguó yǐqián, yī ge Zhōngguó rén yě bú rènshì; wǒ zǒng yǐwéi dào le Zhōngguó jiù huì rènshì hěn duō Zhōngguó péngyǒu. Kěshì wǒ zài Běijīng zhù le bàn nián, jìngrán méiyǒu rènshì rènhé Zhōngguó rén.

Before I came to China, I **did not know** any Chinese (people). I had always thought that I would **meet** many Chinese once I arrived at China. But I have lived in Beijing for half a year, and surprisingly I **have not met** any Chinese.

A: 你和你妻子是上大学的时候**认识**的吗？
    Nǐ hé nǐ qīzi shì shàng dàxué de shíhòu rènshì de ma?
B: 不是，虽然我们俩上的是同一个大学，可是那时候**我们不认识**。
    Búshì, suīrán wǒmen liǎ shàng de shì tóng yī gè dàxué, kěshì nà shíhòu wǒmen bú rènshì.
A: **Did** you and your wife **meet** when you were in college?
B: No. Although we attended the same college, **we did not know each other** then.

d. Similarly, 认识 as 'to be acquainted with' (no action indicated) should not be followed by 了 whether or not the acquaintance exists **now** or existed **previously**.

我上大学的时候，并**不认识**我现在的妻子，我只**认识**她妹妹。
Wǒ shàng dàxué de shíhòu, bìng bú rènshì wǒ xiànzài de qīzi; wǒ zhǐ rènshì tā mèimei。
When I was in college, I **did not know** my current wife; I only **knew** her younger sister.

As a verb indicating **an action ('to meet' someone)**, 认识 can be followed by 了 if the action took place in a **past time frame**.

我在北京留学的时候，**认识了**我现在的未婚妻。
Wǒ zài Běijīng liúxué de shíhòu, rènshì le wǒ xiànzài de wèihūnqī.
When I was studying abroad in Beijing, I **met** my current fiancée.

e. Although 认识 can indicate two people meeting for the first time, the word 朋友 (*péngyǒu*: friend) is sometimes used in this situation. The implication of '认识 + 朋友' is that two people have met (for the first time) and they will **subsequently become friends**.

高: 昨天我在图书馆**认识了**一个中国**朋友**，他说他**认识**你。
Gāo: *Zuótiān wǒ zài túshūguǎn rènshì le yī ge Zhōngguó péngyǒu, tā shuō tā rènshì nǐ.*

陈:　　是吗？我**认识**好几个中国人。他姓什么？

Chén:　Shì ma? Wǒ rènshì hǎo jǐ ge Zhōngguó rén. Tā xìng shénme?

高:　　姓周。

Gāo:　Xìng Zhōu.

陈:　　啊！老周！对，我们是去年在北京**认识**的。(了 is not used in the '是 . . . 的' structure.)

Chén:　À! Lǎo Zhōu! Duì, wǒmen shì qùnián zài Běijīng rènshì de.

Gao:　　Yesterday I **met** a Chinese at the library. He said that he **knew (was acquainted with)** you.

Chen:　　Is that so? I **know** quite a few Chinese. What's his last name?

Gao:　　His last name is Zhou.

Chen:　　Ah! Old Zhou! That's correct! We **met** in Beijing last year.

f.　Since 见面 (*jiànmiàn*) is also translated as **'to meet' in certain contexts**, it should not be confused with 认识. There are two main differences between 认识 and 见面:

(i)　认识 indicates two people, who hitherto did not know each other, '**meeting (making an acquaintance) for the first time**'. 见面 indicates two people 'meeting **for a specific purpose**' whether or not it is for the first time.

我很荣幸今天能有这个机会**认识**您。('Meeting' for the first time.)
Wǒ hěn róngxìng jīntiān néng yǒu zhè ge jīhuì rènshì nín.
I am honored to have the opportunity to **make your acquaintance** today.

明天张大中要去**跟**他女朋友的爸妈**见面**，所以他现在有点紧张。('Meeting' for a specific purpose.)
Míngtiān Zhāng Dàzhōng yào qù gēn tā nǚ péngyǒu de bàmā jiànmiàn, suǒyǐ tā xiànzài yǒu diǎn jǐnzhāng.
Tomorrow Zhang Dazhong is going to meet (with) his girlfriend's parents, so he is a little nervous right now.

(ii)　见面 is a compound verb. This means only 见 is the verb; 面 is a noun. It is incorrect to say, for example, 见面他女朋友的家人; instead, it should be 'A 跟 B 见面'.
　　认识 is a two-character verb. Although the preposition 跟 can be used with 认识 (i.e. A 跟 B 认识), the person normally follows 认识 (A 认识 B). For example, both 小张跟小李认识 and 小张认识小李 mean 'Little Zhang and Little Li know each other'.

→ See 见 (*jiàn*) and 见面 (*jiànmiàn*) for more information.

g.　Although all examples provided above are about people, 认识 can also be used to suggest one's **familiarity with non-person objects** or **information**. But the pattern is limited to '**A 认识 B**'.

李文生只学了半年中文，可是已经**认识了**五百个汉字。

Lǐ Wénshēng zhǐ xué le bàn nián Zhōngwén, kěshì yǐjīng rènshì le wǔ bǎi ge Hànzì.

Li Wensheng has only been studying Chinese for half a year, but he already knows 500 Chinese characters. (了 in 认识了 implies that he 'has acquired' these characters.)

A: 你**认不认识**这几个字？
   Nǐ rèn bú rènshì zhè jǐ ge zì?
B: **不认识**。你呢？
   Bú rènshì. Nǐ ne?
A: 一个星期以前，我也**不认识**这几个字，现在我不但**认识**而且还会写呢！
   Yī ge xīngqī yǐqián, wǒ yě bú rènshì zhè jǐ ge zì. Xiànzài wǒ búdàn rènshì, érqiě hái huì xiě ne.
A: Do you **know** these characters?
B: I **don't know** them. How about you?
A: A week ago, I **did not know** them, either. Now I not only **know** them but also know how to write them.

h. In the 'A 认识 B' ('A is acquainted with B') pattern, 认识 can be replaced with **认得** (*rènde*). But 认得 may sound more casual than 认识. Also, 认得 carries the connotation of 'to recognize'.

A: 那个人是谁？
   Nà ge rén shì shéi?
B: 我也**不认得**他。
   Wǒ yě bú rènde tā.
A: Who is that person?
B: I **don't know** him, either.

→ See 认得 (*rènde*) for related information.

认为 *rènwéi*

认为 is a word used to express one's opinion. Grammatically, **觉得** (*juéde*) can replace 认为. However, 觉得 tends to be used in casual conversations, whereas 认为 is often used in discussing **more serious issues** or in **more formal situations**.

→ See 觉得 (*juéde*) for more information.

a. Although 认为 is often translated as '**to think**', one should not use 想 (*xiǎng*) to indicate one's opinion. This is because 想, as 'to think', indicates one's **assumption or speculation**, not opinion.

→ See 想 (*xiǎng*) for related information.

(Scenario: A manager is consulting two coworkers about a workplace decision. 觉得 can replace 认为, but 认为 is more appropriate in this context.)

经理: 你们**认为**我应该不应该给王小姐加薪？

Jīnglǐ: *Nǐmen rènwéi wǒ yīnggāi bù yīnggāi gěi Wáng xiǎojiě jiā xīn?*

张先生: 王小姐跟李先生做一样的工作，可是她的薪水却比李先生低，所以我**认为**给她加薪是很合理的。

Zhāng xiānsheng: *Wáng xiǎojiě gēn Lǐ xiānsheng zuò yīyàng de gōngzuò, kěshì tā de xīnshuǐ què bǐ Lǐ xiānsheng dī, suǒyǐ wǒ rènwéi gěi tā jiā xīn shì hěn hélǐ de.*

周先生: 我**认为**王小姐**不**应该加薪，因为她的工作表现很差。

Zhōu xiānsheng: *Wǒ rènwéi Wáng xiǎojiě bù yīnggāi jiā xīn, yīnwèi tā de gōngzuò biǎoxiàn hěn chà.*

Manager: Do you **think** I should give Miss Wang a salary increase?

Mr Zhang: Miss Wang and Mr Li do the same kind of work, but her salary is lower than Mr Li's; therefore, I **think** to give her a salary increase is reasonable (justifiable).

Mr Zhou: I **don't think** Miss Li should get a salary increase, because her work performance is poor.

b. 认为 should be **followed by a sentence**. But sometimes the subject of the sentence is omitted, resulting in **an adjective following 认为**.

A: 你**认为**只给王小姐加薪，不给李先生加合理不合理？
   Nǐ rènwéi zhǐ gěi Wáng xiǎojiě jiā xīn, bù gěi Lǐ xiānsheng jiā hélǐ bù hélǐ?

B: 我**认为很合理**。(= 我认为**这个做法**很合理。)
   Wǒ rènwéi hěn hélǐ.

A: Do you **think** it is justifiable to only give Miss Wang a salary increase without giving Mr Li one?

B: I **think it is** justifiable.

c. In a negative sentence to show one does not hold a certain opinion, there are two possible word orders (using 不). However, they may have slightly different connotations.

(i) Normally 不 appears in the sentence that follows 认为. Learners who are English speakers should not directly translate phrases such as 'I don't think . . .' as 我不认为.

A: 你对中国的人口政策有什么看法？
   Nǐ duì Zhōngguó de rénkǒu zhèngcè yǒu shénme kànfǎ?

B: 我**认为**中国政府**不应该**改变目前的政策。(Do not say 我不认为中国政府应该 . . . .)
   Wǒ rènwéi Zhōngguó zhèngfǔ bù yīnggāi gǎibiàn mùqián de zhèngcè.

A: What is your opinion on China's population policy?

B: I **think** (I **am of the opinion**) that the Chinese government **should not** change the current policy.

(ii) In certain contexts, 不认为 is an acceptable expression. It is used to **negate or rebut a previous mentioned opinion**.

A: 很多人**认为**中国政府应该改变目前的人口政策；你**认为**呢？

  Hěn duō rén rènwéi Zhōngguó zhèngfǔ yīnggāi gǎibiàn mùqián de rénkǒu zhèngcè; nǐ rènwéi ne?

B: 我**不认为**中国的人口政策**需要**改变。（Can be 我**认为**中国的人口政策**不需要**改变。）

  Wǒ bú rènwéi Zhōngguó de rénkǒu zhèngcè xūyào gǎibiàn.

A: Many people **think (are of the opinion)** that the Chinese government should change their current population policy. What do you **think**? (What is **your opinion**?)

B: I **don't think** China's population policy needs to change.

Related expression

在 + person + 看来 *zài* + person + *kàn lái*

在 + person + 看来 is used to **express one's opinion**. It is similar to 认为 in that both tend to be used in **more formal discussions** of issues. 在 + person + 看来 is an **interpolation** because it can be inserted inside a sentence.

离婚，**在我看来**，不是解决问题的办法。

Líhūn, zài wǒ kàn lái, bú shì jiějué wèntí de bànfǎ.

= **在我看来**，离婚不是解决问题的看法。

In my opinion, divorce is not a way to solve the problem.

→ See 在 + person + 看来 (*zài* + person + *kàn lái*) for more information.

仍然 *réngrán*

仍然 means 'still' and is interchangeable with 还是 (*háishì*) in certain patterns. However, 仍然 is a formal word and is used in writing. In less formal situations or casual speech, 还是 is used.

→ See 还是 (*háishì*) for more information.

如果 *rúguǒ*

如果 means 'if' and is interchangeable with 要是 (*yàoshì*).

→ See 要是 (*yàoshì*) for more information.

如何 *rúhé*

如何 is similar to both 怎么 (*zěnme*) and 怎么样 (*zěnme yàng*) in meaning; all three of them can be translated as 'how', but 如何 is a **more formal word**. Also, it is not always interchangeable with either 怎么 or 怎么样 in usage. In general, 怎么/怎么样 can be used in more expressions than 如何.

→ See 怎么 (*zěnme*) and 怎么样 (*zěnme yàng*) for more information.

少 *shǎo*

少, when referring to **quantity or amount**, can be considered an **antonym to 多** (*duō*); thus, 很多 can be considered a synonym to 不少. Likewise, both 不多 and 很少 mean 'not many/much'.

This section discusses the **differences and similarities between 多 and 少** in usage.

→ See 多 (*duō*) for related information.

a. 很多 can appear before a noun, whereas 很少, with rare exceptions (see section b. below), usually does not modify a noun. 很少 typically appears **after the subject** to serve as the **predicate** of the sentence.

For example, to say 'Wang Meilan **has many** friends', either 王美兰有**很多朋友** or 王美兰的**朋友很多** is correct. However, to say 'Zhang Xiaowen **does not have many** friends', one should not say 张小文有很少朋友; instead, one would say 张小文的**朋友很少**.

It should be noted that 很 in 很少 does not literally mean 'very'. **很少** simply means '**not much**' or '**not many**'. Using 少 without 很 or another degree adverb is not correct (unless a **comparison** is implied.)

我们班，男生**多**，女生**少**。(This sentence implies a comparison.)
Wǒmen bān, nánshēng duō, nǚshēng shǎo.
There are **more** male students **than** female students in our class. (or: There are **more** male students and **fewer** female students.)

(Scenario: Two teachers are discussing class enrollment.)
A: 这学期来报名上中文课的人**很少**，只有八、九个。
Zhè xuéqī lái bàomíng shàng Zhōngwén kè de rén hěn shǎo, zhǐ yǒu bā, jiǔ ge.
B: 希望开学以前还有人来报名。要是学生**太少**，这门课就会被取消。
Xīwàng kāixué yǐqián hái yǒu rén lái bàomíng. Yàoshì xuéshēng tài shǎo, zhè mén kè jiù huì bèi qǔxiāo.
A: There are **not many** students who have registered for the Chinese class this semester; there are only about eight or nine students.
B: I hope there will be more people coming to register before the semester starts. If there are **too few** students (**the number** of students **is too small**), the class will be canceled.

b.　As noted above, 很少 normally does not appear before a noun. However, it is acceptable to **start a sentence with '很少 + noun'**.

很少人知道周先生成名以前是做什么的。
Hěn shǎo rén zhīdào Zhōu xiānsheng chéng míng yǐqián shì zuò shénme de.
Not many people know what Mr Zhou did before he became famous.

c.　'不少 + **noun**' is a common expression; whereas '不多 + **noun**' is inappropriate. (不多 should be used after the noun **as the predicate**.)

A:　你买这幢房子，大概花了**不少钱**吧！
　　Nǐ mǎi zhè zhuàng fángzi, dàgài huā le bùshǎo qián ba.
B:　买房子花的**钱不多**，但是买了房子以后，又买了**不少家具**，所以
　　一共花了**很多钱**(= 不少钱)。
　　Mǎi fángzi huā de qián bù duō, dànshì mǎi le fángzi yǐhòu, yòu mǎi le
　　bùshǎo jiājù, suǒyǐ yīgòng huā le hěn duō qián (= bùshǎo qián).
A:　You must have spent **a lot of money** buying this house.
B:　I did **not** spend **much money** buying the house. (Literally: Money spent on buying the house was **not much**.) But after buying the house, I bought **lots of furniture**, so altogether I have spent **lots of money**.

d.　很少 can be used as a **frequency adverb**, which must appear **before the verb**. It is often translated as 'rarely', 'seldom', or 'hardly'.

我爸爸差不多每天都走路去上班，他**很少开车**去。
Wǒ bàba chàbùduō měi tiān dōu zǒu lù qù shàng bān, tā hěnshǎo kāi chē qù.
My father walks to work almost every day; he **seldom drives** (to his office).

In the following dialogue, 很少 has two different meanings.

A:　这个地区冬暖夏凉，气候很不错；为什么居民**这么少**？
　　Zhè ge dìqū dōng nuǎn xià liáng, qìhòu hěn búcuò; wèi shénme jūmín
　　zhème shǎo?
B:　这个地区**很少** (adverb)**下雨**。因为每年的雨量**很少**，所以不太适合
　　居住。
　　Zhè ge dìqū hěnshǎo xiàyǔ. Yīnwèi měi nián de yǔliàng hěnshǎo, suǒyǐ
　　bú tài shìhé jūzhù.
A:　This area has warm winters and cool summers; the climate is pretty good. Why is it that there are **so few** residents?
B:　It **rarely rains** here. Since the amount of annual rainfall is **not much**, it is not suitable for inhabiting.

It should be noted that 很多 cannot be used as an antonym to 很少 to indicate 'frequently'. The proper word for 'frequently' is 常常 (*chángcháng*) or 经常 (*jīngcháng*), even though in casual English the expression 'a lot' can be used.

最近**常常下**雨；即使是不下雨的时候，也是阴天，**很少出**太阳。(Do not say 最近下雨很多.)

Zuìjìn chángcháng xià yǔ; jíshǐ shì bú xià yǔ de shíhòu, yě shì yīntiān; hěnshǎo chū tàiyáng.

It has **been raining a lot** lately. Even when it is not raining, it is cloudy; the sun **rarely** comes out. (There is **rarely** sunshine.)

e.　'**少 + verb**' is similar to '**多 + verb**' in usage (see section c. of 多) but opposite in meaning. 少 in this pattern indicates doing an action **less often**.

(Scenario: A boy has failed several exams in school; his parents are trying to discipline him.)

妈妈:　从今天开始，你得**少看**电视、**少上**网。

Māma:　Cóng jīntiān kāishǐ, nǐ děi shǎo kàn diànshì, shǎo shàngwǎng.

爸爸:　还要**少玩**电子游戏。

Bàba:　Hái yào shǎo wán diànzǐ yóuxì.

Mother:　From now on, you have to **watch less** TV, and **go online less often**.

Father:　Also, you have to **play fewer** video games (play video games **less often**).

(Scenario: A wife has made a new dish she has never made before.)

妻子:　怎么样？好不好吃？

Qīzi:　Zěnme yàng? Hǎo bù hǎochī?

丈夫:　还不错，不过下次最好**少放(一)点**盐，**多放点**辣椒。

Zhàngfū:　Hái búcuò, búguò xià cì zuìhǎo shǎo fàng (yī) diǎn yán, duō fàng diǎn làjiāo.

Wife:　How is it? Is it delicious?

Husband:　Not bad, but it'd be best if you **put a little less** salt and **a little bit more** hot pepper next time.

甚至 *shènzhì*

The basic function of 甚至 is to **emphasize** or **strengthen** one's point. The expressions such as 'even' and 'even go so far as to...' are usually its counterparts in English. It can be used as a stand-alone **adverb** or used as a **conjunction**, which must be paired with 也 or 都.

a.　甚至 ... 也/都 is interchangeable with **连 ... 也/都**. Both are used to emphasize one's point by showing an **extreme situation**. Basically, a **noun** or a **noun phrase** follows 甚至.

这个小城在高山上，有时候**甚至**六、七月的时候**都**会下雪。

Zhè ge xiǎo chéng zài gāo shān shàng, yǒu shíhòu shènzhī liù, qī yuè de shíhòu dōu huì xià xuě.

This small town is on a high mountain; sometimes it snows **even** in June or July.

王大中做了严重违法的事，现在**甚至**他爸爸**也**不能原谅他。

Wáng Dàzhōng zuò le yánzhòng wéifǎ de shì, xiànzài shènzhì tā bàba yě bù néng yuánliàng tā.

Wang Dazhong committed a severely illegal act; now **even** his father cannot forgive him.

甚至 and 连 can be **used together** to make a strong statement. 甚至 must appear **before** 连.

王太太去做了脸部整容手术以后，几乎变成另外一个人，**甚至连**她自己的儿女都认不出她来。

Wáng tàitai qù zuò le liǎn bù zhěngróng shǒushù yǐhòu, jīhū biànchéng lìngwài yī ge rén, shènzhì lián tā zìjǐ de érnǚ dou rèn bù chū tā lái.

Since Mrs Wang had plastic surgery done on her face, she has almost turned into another person. **Even** her own children cannot recognize her.

Note that the object of the verb can appear after 甚至连, resulting in an **inverted** sentence (**object before the verb**).

王老先生最近记忆越来越差，现在**甚至连**自己是哪年生的**都**想不起来了。

Wáng lǎo xiānsheng zuìjìn jìyì yuè lái yuè chà, xiànzài shènzhì lián zìjǐ shì nǎ nián shēng de dōu xiǎng bù qǐlái le.

The old gentleman Mr Wang's memory has been deteriorating (getting worse and worse); now he cannot **even** recall in which year he was born.

A:　你计划什么时候买车？

　　Nǐ jìhuà shénme shíhòu mǎi chē?

B:　买车？我现在**甚至连**自行车**都**还买不起，天天坐公共汽车；谁知道我什么时候才能买车？

　　Mǎi chē? Wǒ xiànzài shènzhì lián zìxíngchē dōu hái mǎi bù qǐ, tiān tiān zuò gōnggòng qìchē; shéi zhīdào wǒ shénme shíhòu cái néng mǎi chē?

A:　When do you plan to buy a car?

B:　Buy a car? I cannot **even** afford to buy a bicycle now, and I ride on public transport every day. Who knows when I will be able to buy a car.

→ See 连 . . . 都／也 (*lián . . . dōu/yě*) for related information.

b. When the point to be emphasized is an **event or action** (e.g. a **verb**), 甚至 is used as an **adverb** before the verb. Such a sentence would not be an inverted sentence, and **都 or 也 is not used**.

> A: 这家餐馆远近驰名，每天都大排长龙，有时候**甚至**要等两个小时才有桌子。
> *Zhè jiā cānguǎn yuǎn jìn chímíng, měi tiān dōu dà pái cháng lóng, yǒu shíhòu shènzhì yào děng liǎng ge xiǎoshí cái yǒu zhuōzi.*
> B: 我听说，**甚至**有人从外地开几个小时的车来这里吃饭。
> *Wǒ tīngshuō, shènzhì yǒu rén cóng wàidì kāi jǐ xiǎoshí de chē lái zhèlǐ chī fàn.*
> C: 还有人**甚至**从外国坐飞机来这里吃一顿。
> *Hái yǒu rén shènzhì cóng wàiguó zuò fēijī lái zhèlǐ chī yī dùn.*
> A: This restaurant is famous near and far. Every day there is a long line (literally: people line up like a long dragon). Sometimes, one **even** has to wait two hours before there is a table.
> B: I have heard that some people **even (go so far as to)** drive several hours to come here from out of town for a meal.
> C: There are also people who **even (go so far as to)** fly from a foreign country to have a meal here.

> 医生跟王中说，动手术以前十二个小时，不能吃任何东西，**甚至**不能喝水 (can be an inverted sentence: **甚至连**水**也**不能喝)。
> *Yīshēng gēn Wáng Zhōng shuō, dòng shǒushù yǐqián shí'èr ge xiǎoshí, bù néng chī rènhé dōngxi, shènzhì bù néng hē shuǐ.*
> The doctor has told Wang Zhong that, for 12 hours prior to his surgery, he cannot eat anything; he cannot **even** drink water.

c. 甚至 can be used to **push a point even further**. What follows 甚至 is a parallel structure to the original point; therefore, a verb, a noun, an adjective, etc., can follow 甚至 in this use.

> 李先生对他儿子实在太严厉了。儿子犯了一点错，他就会大声地**骂他，甚至罚他**不许吃饭；所以他儿子每天都过着**紧张的，甚至恐怖的**日子。
> *Lǐ xiānsheng duì tā érzi shízài tài yánlì le. Érzi fàn le yīdiǎn cuò, tā jiù huì dàshēng de mà tā, shènzhì fá tā bù xǔ chī fàn; suǒyǐ tā érzi měi tiān dōu guò zhe jǐnzhāng de, shènzhì kǒngbù de rìzi.*
> Mr Li is really too strict and harsh on his son. When his son makes a minor mistake, he loudly **scolds him, and even (goes so far as to) punishes him** by not allowing him to eat. So his son leads an **anxious, even fearful**, life every day.

> 专家认为，**三岁的小孩，甚至更小的**，就可以开始学写字了。
> *Zhuānjiā rènwéi, sān suì de xiǎohái, shènzhì gèng xiǎo de, jiù kěyǐ kāishǐ xué xiě zì le.*
> Experts are of the opinion that **three-year-old** children, **even** those who are **still younger**, can start to learn to write characters.

甚至于 *shènzhìyú*

甚至于 is considered identical to 甚至 in both meaning and usage. In other words, they are interchangeable.

→ See 甚至 (*shènzhì*) for more information.

使 *shǐ*

This section focuses on the use of 使 when it is defined as '**to cause**' or '**to make**'. The pattern is '**A 使 B + verb/adjective**'.

a.   Although 使 is considered **interchangeable with** 叫 (*jiào*) or 让 (*ràng*), two differences must be noted. First, **使** tends to be used in **more formal** situations, whereas 叫 or 让 are usually used in casual speech. Second, 叫 or 让, when used in the 'A 叫/让 B + verb' pattern, have other interpretations (e.g. 'to tell', 'to allow', etc.), but 使 only means 'to cause' or 'to make'.
   On the other hand, 令 (*lìng*) and 使 have the same meaning, and both are often used when the speech style is more formal.

→ See 叫 (*jiào*), 让 (*ràng*) and 令 (*lìng*) for related information.

政府的新政策**使**低收入的**老百姓**也有能力购买房产。('**A 使 B + verb**')
Zhèngfǔ de xīn zhèngcè shǐ dī shōurù de lǎobǎixìng yě yǒu nénglì gòumǎi fángchǎn.
The government's new policy **makes** low-income **civilians have** the ability to purchase properties, too.

人类智慧的结合**使**科技的**发展**日新月异。
Rénlèi zhìhuì de jiéhé shǐ kējì de fāzhǎn rì xīn yuè yì.
The combined effort of human intelligence has **made** the **development** of science and technology **progress** rapidly.

在那部电影里，坏人最后逍遥法外，这个结局**使观众**大失所望。('**A 使 B + adjective**')
Zài nà bù diànyǐng lǐ, huài rén zuìhòu xiāoyáo fǎ wài, zhè ge jiéjú shǐ guānzhòng dà shī suǒ wàng.
In that movie, the bad person eventually got away and was not punished by law. This ending **made the audience** greatly **disappointed**.

同样的非法行为，穷人坐牢，富人罚款，这种现象**使人**怀疑司法的公平性。
Tóngyàng de fēifǎ xíngwéi, qióng rén zuòláo, fù rén fákuǎn, zhè zhǒng xiànxiàng shǐ rén huáiyí sīfǎ de gōngpíng xìng.
For the same illegal behavior, poor people go to prison and rich people pay fines. This phenomenon **makes one doubt** the fairness of the justice system.

b. Because 使 is often translated as 'to make', learners who are English speakers should avoid making the following **two mistakes**:

(i) Do **not** use 使 in the English pattern 'A makes B + noun'. The accurate pattern in Chinese that represents this pattern in English is to use the verb **成为** (*chéngwéi*), **成了** (*chéng le*) or **变成** (*biànchéng*), all of which mean '**to become**', before the noun.

This pattern ('**A 使 B 成为**') is sometimes translated as '**A turns B into . . .**'. Learners should be aware of the need to use 使 in this pattern.

那部卖座的电影**使张龙**一夜之间**成为**最受欢迎的大**明星**。
Nà bù màizuò de diànyǐng shǐ Zhāng Lóng yī yè zhījiān chéngwéi zuì shòu huānyíng de dà míngxīng.
That box office success movie has **made Zhang Long** the most popular movie **star** overnight.

连年旱灾**使农田**都**变成**了**荒地**。
Lián nián hànzāi shǐ nóngtián dōu biànchéng le huāngdì.
Drought in consecutive years has **turned** farmland **into** wasteland.

(ii) Do **not** use 使 in the English pattern 'A makes B **do something**'. There is no direct counterpart in Chinese for 'to make' in the English pattern. Either 'A tells (叫: *jiào*) B to do something' or 'A forces (逼: *bī*) B to do something' can be used to represent a similar situation.

我正在看电视的时候，妈妈**叫我去**打扫房间，这**使我**非常**不愉快**。
Wǒ zhèng zài kàn diànshì de shíhòu, māma jiào wǒ qù dǎsǎo fángjiān, zhè shǐ wǒ fēicháng bù yúkuài.
While I was watching TV, my mother **made me go** clean up my room. This **made me** very **unhappy**.

王小英不爱张先生，可是她爸妈**逼她接受**张先生的求婚。
Wáng Xiǎoyīng bú ài Zhāng xiānsheng, kěshì tā bàmā bī tā jiēshòu Zhāng xiānsheng de qiúhūn.
Wang Xiaoying does not love Mr Zhang, but her parents **made her accept** Mr Zhang's marriage proposal.

使得 *shǐ de*

使得 and 使 share the same meaning and usage; however, when what follows 使 is simply 人 (implying 'everybody'), 使得 is normally not used.

炎热的天气**使人**昏昏欲睡。	= 炎热的天气**使(得)我**昏昏欲睡。
Yánrè de tiānqì shǐ rén hūn hūn yù shuì.	= *Yánrè de tiānqì shǐ (de) wǒ hūn hūn yù shuì.*
The searing hot weather **makes one** sleepy.	= The searing hot weather **makes me** sleepy.

成功常常**使人**骄傲自满。

Chénggōng chángcháng shǐ rén jiāo'ào zìmǎn.

Success often **makes one** arrogant and complacent.

Compare:

成功**使(得)张龙**骄傲自满。

Chénggōng shǐ (de) Zhāng Lóng jiāo'ào zìmǎn.

Success has **made Zhang Long** arrogant and complacent.

Related expressions

害(得) *hài (de)*

害(得) and 使(得) are very similar in meaning and usage, except that 害(得) is only used in **casual, conversational speech**. Also, what follows 害(得) must be **negative in meaning**.

A: 你怎么现在才来？

   Nǐ zěnme xiànzài cái lái?

B: 对不起，闹钟坏了，**害(得)我**睡过头了。

   Duì bù qǐ, nàozhōng huài le, hài (de) wǒ shuì guòtóu le.

A: 我以为你出事了，**害(得)我**担心得要命。

   Wǒ yǐwéi nǐ chūshì le, hài (de) wǒ dānxīn de yàomìng.

A: How come you only came now? (Why are you late?)

B: Sorry, my alarm clock was not working, **causing me** to oversleep.

A: I had thought you had an accident. It **made me** very worried (worry to death).

造成 *zàochéng*

Since 造成 is often translated as 'to cause', learners who are English speakers often use 使 where 造成 is the accurate word. A major distinction between 使 and 造成 is the fact that **a noun can follow 造成** to indicate the consequence or result of a certain action or event. Therefore, 造成 can also be translated as 'result in'. On the other hand, 使 is followed by 'noun + verb/adjective' (see section a. of 使 above).

大台风带来的豪雨**造成**了严重的**水灾** (Do not use 使 or 使得)，**使(得)**很多**人无家可归**。

Dà táifēng dàilái de háo yǔ zàochéng le yánzhòng de shuǐzài, shǐ (de) hěnduō rén wú jiā kě guī.

The heavy rain brought by the strong typhoon has **caused (resulted in)** severe **floods**, **causing** many people **to have** no home to return to.

酒后开车容易**造成车祸**；严重的车祸会**使人受伤**或丧命，所以我们无论如何不可以酒后开车。

Jiǔ hòu kāi chē róngyì zàochéng chēhuò; yánzhòng de chēhuò huì shǐ rén shòushāng huò sàngmìng, sunzhòng de chlùn rúhé bù kěyǐ jiǔ hòu kāi chē.

Driving after drinking (alcohol) can easily **cause (result in) accidents**. Severe accidents will **cause people to be** injured or lose their lives, so we cannot drink and drive, no matter what.

事实上 *shìshí shàng*

事实上 and 其实 (*qíshí*) have the same meaning and usage. 事实上 is a somewhat more formal word than 其实, which is more often used in casual conversation.

→ See 其实 (*qíshí*) for more information.

舒服 *shūfú*

Without context, 舒服 is simply defined as 'comfortable'. This section puts more emphasis on the discussion of the implications of **不舒服** since 'uncomfortable' is not always an accurate interpretation.

a. Both 舒服 and 不舒服 can be used to describe **an environment or an object**, as well as the **physical feeling** one may have.

(Scenario: Someone is shopping for a new chair.)
A: 这把椅子太硬了，坐起来很**不舒服**。
  Zhè bǎ yǐzi tài yìng le, zuò qǐlái hěn bù shūfú.
B: 那你试试这把，看这把**舒服**不舒服？
  Nà nǐ shì shì zhè bǎ, kàn zhè bǎ shūfú bù shūfú?
A: 嗯，这把不错，相当**舒服**。
  Èn, zhè bǎ búcuò, xiāngdāng shūfú.
A: This chair is too hard. It is **uncomfortable** sitting in it.
B: Then try this one, and see if it is **comfortable or not**.
A: Mmm, this one is not bad; it is pretty **comfortable**.

我在健身房运动以后，洗了一个冷水澡，现在全身**觉得很舒服**。
Wǒ zài jiànshēnfáng yùndòng yǐhòu, xǐ la yī ge lěngshuǐ zǎo, xiànzài quánshēn juéde hěn shūfú.
After I worked out at the gym, I took a cold shower. Now my whole body feels wonderful.

A: 王先生的爸妈住在北京，可是他去北京出差的时候，总是住旅馆，他觉得**旅馆**比他爸妈家**舒服**。
  Wáng xiānsheng de bàmā zhù zài Běijīng, kěshì tā qù Běijīng chūchāi de shíhòu, zǒngshì zhù lǚguǎn, tā juéde lǚguǎn bǐ tā bàmā jiā shūfú.

B:　为什么？
　　Wèi shénme?
A:　他爸妈家不大，而且只有一个厕所，所以**他**每次在那里都住得**不太
　　舒服**。
　　*Tā bàmā jiā bú dà, érqiě zhǐ yǒu yī ge cèsuǒ, suǒyǐ tā měi cì zài nàlǐ
　　dōu zhù de bú tài shūfú.*

A:　Mr Wang's parents live in Beijing; but when he goes to Beijing on
　　business, he always stays at a hotel; he feels that **hotels** are more
　　comfortable than his parents' house.
B:　Why?
A:　His parents' house is not big; besides, there is only one bathroom, so
　　every time he goes there, **he** feels that staying there is **not comfortable**.

b.　不舒服 is not always the direct opposite to 舒服 in terms of connotation.
　　The following examples illustrate this point.

(i)　不舒服 can be used to refer to **physical ailment**. When one is **not feel-
　　ing well** (typically a minor illness), the expression is **不舒服**. However,
　　to recover (from illness) is generally **not 舒服**, but **好了**. When one's
　　symptoms are lessened, either 舒服 or 好 can be used.

医生:　　哪里**不舒服**？
Yīshēng:　*Nǎlǐ bù shūfú?*
病人:　　头痛、喉咙痛。
Bìngrén:　*Tóu tòng, hóulóng tòng.*
医生:　　可能是感冒。吃两天药，应该就会**好了**。
Yīshēng:　*Kěnéng shì gǎnmào. Chī liǎng tiān yào, yīnggāi jiù huì
　　　　hǎo le.*
病人:　　**胃**也常常**不舒服**，尤其是饭后。
Bìngrén:　*Wèi yě chángcháng bù shūfú, yóuqí shì fàn hòu.*
医生:　　那我给你开一种胃药，**不舒服**的时候，吃一粒，就会觉
　　　　得**舒服一点**了。
Yīshēng:　*Nà wǒ gěi nǐ kāi yī zhǒng wèi yào; bù shūfú de shíhòu, chī
　　　　yī lì, jiù huì juéde shūfú yīdiǎn le.*
Doctor:　What is wrong? (Literally: What part is **not feeling well**?)
Patient:　Headache and sore throat.
Doctor:　It's probably a cold. Take medicine for two days and you
　　　　should **feel fine** (**recover** from it).
Patient:　Also I often have an **upset stomach**, especially after a meal.
Doctor:　Then I will prescribe a stomach medicine for you. When you
　　　　are **not feeling well**, take one pill, and then you will **feel a
　　　　little better**.

Learners should avoid the mistake of using 觉得不好 for 'not feeling
well'.

(Scenario: A manager notices that an employee is napping at his desk. Note that 不舒服 in the scenario has two different interpretations.)

经理: 小张，现在是上班时间，你怎么在睡觉？

Jīnglǐ: *Xiǎo Zhāng, xiànzài shì shàng bān shíjiān, nǐ zěnme zài shuìjiào?*

张: 经理，对不起，**我今天不太舒服**。我可不可去那张沙发上躺一下？

Zhāng: *Jīnglǐ, duìbuqǐ, wǒ jīntiān bú tài shūfú. Wǒ kě bù kěyǐ qù nà zhāng shāfā shàng tǎng yīxià?*

经理: 躺在沙发上太**不舒服**了，你回家去休息吧！

Jīnglǐ: *Tǎng zài shāfā shàng tài bù shūfú le, nǐ huí jiā qù xiūxi ba.*

张: 不用，那张**沙发**其实相当**舒服**，我想我躺半个小时以后就会**好**一点**了**。

Zhāng: *Búyòng. Nà zhāng shāfā qíshí xiāngdāng shūfú, wǒ xiǎng wǒ tǎng bàn ge xiǎoshí yǐhòu jiù huì hǎo yīdiǎn le.*

Manager: Little Zhang, this is work time. How come you are taking a nap?

Zhang: Sorry, Manager. **I am not feeling very well** today. May I go lie down on that couch?

Manager: Lying on the couch is too **uncomfortable**. Why don't you go home to rest?

Zhang: There is no need. That **couch** is actually quite **comfortable**. I think I would **feel a little better** after lying down for half an hour.

(ii) When 不舒服 is used to describe one's **emotional or mental feelings**, it is **often misinterpreted**, especially by learners who are English speakers. This is because 不舒服 does not literally mean 'uncomfortable', which normally describes an awkward or uneasy feeling.

不舒服 in Chinese implies that one is **irritated, annoyed or upset** by another's words or acts, but does not explicitly show the irritation or annoyance. Therefore, the expression is often **心里不舒服** (*xīnlǐ bù shūfú*).

高文生的同屋常做一些让他很**不舒服**的事；比方说，昨天他同屋看到冰箱里有高文生从餐馆里带回来的剩菜，没有问他，就把它吃了。

Gāo Wénshēng de tóngwū cháng zuò yīxiē ràng tā hěn bù shūfú de shì; bǐfāngshuō, zuótiān tā tóngwū kàndào bīngxiāng lǐ yǒu Gāo Wénshēng cóng cānguǎn lǐ dài huílái de shèng cài, méiyǒu wèn tā, jiù bǎ tā chī le.

Gao Wensheng's roommate often does things that annoy him; for example, yesterday his roommate saw the leftover food Gao Wensheng had brought back from a restaurant; he just ate it without asking him (for permission).

王大中的女朋友在他家吃完饭以后，就跟他一起坐在客厅看电视，没有帮忙收桌子、洗碗筷，大中的妈妈**心里很不舒服**。

Wáng Dàzhōng de nǚ péngyǒu zài tā jiā chī wán fàn yǐhòu, jiù gēn tā yīqǐ zuò zài kètīng kàn diànshì, méiyǒu bāngmáng shōu zhuōzi, xǐ wǎnkuài; Dàzhōng de māma xīnlǐ hěn bù shūfú.

After Wang Dazhong's girlfriend ate dinner at his house, she just sat and watched TV with him in the living room. She did not help clear the table or do the dishes. Dazhong's mother was irritated (implied: but she did not show her irritation).

(iii) To describe an **awkward, uneasy feeling**, one should **not use 不舒服**, although the expression is **'being uncomfortable'** in English. This is a **common mistake** made by learners who are English speakers. There is, in fact, **no direct counterpart** for this expression in Chinese. The proper expression depends on the contexts or the actual situations.

我跟王大中刚认识，他就告诉了我很多他的私事，我不好意思打断他，这个情况让我**坐立难安**，不知道该怎么办。

Wǒ gēn Wáng Dàzhōng gāng rènshì, tā jiù gàosù le wǒ hěn duō tā de sīshì, wǒ bù hǎo yìsi dǎduàn tā; zhè ge qíngkuàng ràng wǒ zuò lì nán ān, bù zhīdào gāi zěnme bàn.

I only just met Wang Dazhong, but he has been telling me a lot of his private matters. I cannot bring myself to stop him. This situation makes me feel **uncomfortable**, and I don't know what to do.

我是这个讨论会里唯一的男性。我走进会场的时候，大家都瞪着我，让我**觉得很不自在**。

Wǒ shì zhè ge tǎolùn huì lǐ wéiyī de nánxing. Wǒ zǒu jìn huìchǎng de shíhòu, dàjiā dōu dèng zhe wǒ, ràng wǒ juéde hěn bú zìzài.

I am the only male at this discussion forum. When I walked into the meeting place, everybody was staring at me, making me **feel uncomfortable**.

说 *shuō* and 说话 *shuō huà*

The difference in usage between 说 and 说话 confuses many learners because they both mean 'to speak' or 'to talk'. What is clear is the fact that only 说 can be followed by a noun, such as 英文 (*Yīngwén*: English) and 故事 (*gùshì*: story), whereas 说话 cannot. Since 话 (spoken words) itself is a noun, 说话 cannot be followed by another noun. This section explains the differences in usage between 说 and 说话.

a. When 说话 is used, the **topic** or the **content** is **not specified**, and can be anything. This is because the noun in a compound verb (verb + noun) is **indefinite** and general.

在电影院里看电影的时候，不可以**说话**。
Zài diànyǐngyuàn lǐ kàn diànyǐng de shíhòu, bù kěyǐ shuō huà.
When seeing a movie in the movie theater, you must not **talk**.

老师在**说话**的时候，学生都应该注意听。
Lǎoshī zài shuō huà de shíhòu, xuéshēng dōu yīnggāi zhùyì tīng.
When the teacher is **talking**, all students should pay attention.

小英跟她的同屋合不来，所以她们现在**不说话**了。
Xiǎoyīng gēn tā de tóngwū hé bù lái, suǒyǐ tāmen xiànzài bù shuō huà le.
Xiaoying cannot get along with her roommate, so they **no longer talk** now.

b. The **preposition** frequently used with 说话 is **跟** (*gēn*: with), although the expression, when translated into English, is often 'A talks **to** B'. This is because 跟 in Chinese suggests some type of **interaction**.

昨天我去参加了一个很无聊的派对，因为我一个人也不认识，没有人**跟我说话**。
Zuótiān wǒ qù cānjiā le yī ge hěn wúliáo de pàiduì, yīnwèi wǒ yī ge rén yě bú rènshì, méiyǒu rén gēn wǒ shuō huà.
Yesterday I went to a very boring party because I did not know anybody and no one **talked to me**.

c. When there is a **specific topic or content**, **only** 说 can be used. Usually the topic or content is indicated in the context.

A: 这个问题只有王先生才能解决，可是他已经退休了，不知道他愿不愿意来帮忙。
Zhè ge wèntí zhǐyǒu Wáng xiānsheng cái néng jiějué, kěshì tā yǐjīng tuìxiū le, bù zhīdào tā yuàn bú yuànyì lái bāngmáng.
B: 王先生是我的好朋友，我去**跟他说**，他一定愿意。
Wáng xiānsheng shì wǒ de hǎo péngyǒu, wǒ qù gēn tā shuō, tā yīdìng yuànyì.
A: Only Mr Wang can solve this problem. But he has retired already; I wonder if he is willing to come and help.
B: Mr Wang is a good friend of mine. I will go **talk to him** (meaning: **to let him know** that we need his help); he will definitely be willing to help us.

d. 'A 跟 B 说' can be used as an expression similar in meaning to 告诉 (*gàosù*: to tell).

A: 刚才我看到你**跟**李明在**说话**，你们在**说什么**？

Gāngcái wǒ kàndào nǐ gēn Lǐ Míng zài shuō huà, nǐmen zài shuō shénme?

B: 他**跟我说**他明天要请一天假，因为他妈妈住院了。

Tā gēn wǒ shuō tā míngtiān yào qǐng yī tiān jià, yīnwèi tā māma zhùyuàn le.

A: 哦，是吗？他妈妈得了什么病？

O, shì ma? Tā māma dé le shénme bìng?

B: 他没有**跟我说**。

Tā méiyǒu gēn wǒ shuō.

A: I saw you **talking to (with)** Li Ming just now. **What** were you **talking about**?

B: He **told me** that he will have to take a day off tomorrow because his mother is in the hospital.

A: Oh, is that so? What is wrong with his mother? (Literally: What illness does his mother have?)

B: He did not **tell me**.

Related expressions

'A 跟 B 说' vs. 'A 跟 B 谈 (*tán*)'

谈 (*tán*) and 谈话 (*tán huà*) are two words that are also usually translated as 'to talk'. Therefore, the difference between 说 and 谈 merits some attention.

In situations where 谈 is used, the implication is '**to discuss**'. This means that the interlocutors have a **specific topic** to talk about (**to discuss**). The preposition is **跟**; however, '**A 跟 B 说**' and '**A 跟 B 谈**' have slightly different connotations. '**A 跟 B 说**' suggests that **A conveys the message to B** (see section d. of 说 above); whereas '**A 跟 B 谈**' implies **more interaction and discussion**.

(Scenario: Two teachers are concerned about a student's class performance and behavior. Note that 说 would not be the appropriate verb in this scenario.)

李老师: 最近王大中常常迟到，考试也都考得很差。

Lǐ lǎoshī: *Zuìjìn Wáng Dàzhōng chángcháng chídào, kǎoshì yě dōu kǎo de hěn chà.*

张老师: 那你应该找他来**谈话**。

Zhāng lǎoshī: *Nà nǐ yīnggāi zhǎo tā lái tán huà.*

李: 我已经**跟**他**谈**了好几次了，可是情况还是一样。

Lǐ: *Wǒ yǐjīng gēn tā tán le hǎo jǐ cì le, kěshì qíngkuàng háishì yīyàng.*

张: 那恐怕得**跟**他父母**谈**了。

Zhāng: *Nà kǒngpà děi gēn tā fùmǔ tán le.*

李: 我已经**跟**他**说**了，要是他再不改进，我就要给他爸妈打电话，请他们来**谈**了。

Lǐ: *Wǒ yǐjīng gēn tā shuō le, yàoshi tā zài bù gǎijìn, wǒ jiùyào gěi tā bàmā dǎ diànhuà, qǐng tāmen lái tán le.*

Teacher Li:	Recently Wang Dazhong has often been late to classes, and he has also done poorly on all the tests.
Teacher Zhang:	Then you should ask him to come and **have a talk** (come **for a discussion**).
Li:	I have already **talked (discussed this)** with him quite a few times, but the situation remains the same.
Zhang:	Then I am afraid that you will have to **talk to (discuss this with)** his parents.
Li:	I have already told him that if he does not improve, then I will call his parents and ask them to **come and talk (to discuss** his problems).

→ See 谈 (*tán*) and 谈话 (*tán huà*) for related information.

说不定 *shuō búdìng*

说不定 and 不一定 (*bù yīdìng*) both suggest uncertainty, but they are distinctly different in meaning. **说不定** indicates that **there is a possibility** for something to happen; whereas 不一定 means something **may not** happen. It is important to know the distinction between the two so as to avoid misinterpretation of the message.

→ See 一定 (*yīdìng*) for more information.

太 . . . （了）*tài . . . (le)*

Without context, 太 is simply translated as 'too' to be **followed by an adjective**. However, to use 太 accurately and properly, one must take into consideration the context in which the utterance is made. In addition, whether or not a modal particle 了 should be used along with 太 merits a discussion. (Note: A modal particle appears at the end of the sentence.)

a. In a **positive sentence**, the surface meaning of 太 ('too') suggests that the adjective used to describe a noun has a **negative quality** from the speaker's point of view. In this situation, modal particle 了 **is optional** but is frequently used, especially in **casual speech**.

(Scenario: A real estate agent is showing Mr and Mrs Wang a house.)

房地产商:	这个房子，你们觉得怎么样？
Fángdìchǎn shāng:	*Zhè ge fángzi, nǐmen juéde zěnme yàng?*
王太太:	我觉得厨房、厕所都**太小（了）**。
Wáng tàitai:	*Wǒ juéde chúfáng, cèsuǒ dōu tài xiǎo (le).*
王先生:	可是院子却**太大（了）**。
Wáng xiānsheng:	*Kěshì yuànzi què tài dà (le).*
房地产商:	哦？是吗？您为什么不喜欢大院子。
Fángdìchǎn shāng:	*O? Shì ma? Nín wèi shénme bù xǐhuān dài yuànzi?*

王先生:	浇花、保养草地要用**太多水（了）**。
Wáng xiānsheng:	*Jiāo huā, bǎoyǎng cǎodì yào yòng **tài duō shuǐ** (le).*
王太太:	是啊！**太浪费（了）**。
Wáng tàitai:	*Shì a! **Tài làngfèi** (le).*
房地产商:	价钱呢！
Fángdìchǎn shāng:	*Jiàqián ne?*
王先生:	价钱也**太贵（了）**。
Wáng xiānsheng:	*Jiàqián yě **tài guì** (le).*
房地产商:	那我带你们去看另外一个房子吧！
Fángdìchǎn shāng:	*Nà wǒ dài nǐmen qù kàn lìngwài yī ge fángzi ba!*
Real estate agent:	What do you think of the house?
Mrs Wang:	I think both the kitchen and the bathroom are **too small**.
Mr Wang:	But the yard is **too big**.
Real estate agent:	Oh? Is that so? Why do you not like a big yard?
Mr Wang:	Watering the flowers and maintaining the lawn require **too much** water.
Mrs Wang:	Yes, it's **too wasteful**.
Real estate agent:	What about the price?
Mr Wang:	It is also **too expensive**.
Real estate agent:	Then let me take you to see another house.

However, it should be noted that the adjective after 太 can have the word 不. Structure-wise, the sentence is still considered positive; thus 了 remains optional.

(Scenario: Three people are discussing China's 'one child per family' policy.)

A: 在中国，一家只能有一个孩子，我认为这个政策实在**太不合理（了）**。

*Zài Zhōngguó, yī jiā zhǐ néng yǒu yī ge háizi, wǒ rènwéi zhè ge zhèngcè shízài **tài bù hélǐ** (le).*

B: 这是因为中国的人口**太多（了）**。只有这个办法才能控制人口的增长。

*Zhè shì yīnwèi Zhōngguó de rénkǒu **tài duō** (le). Zhǐyǒu zhè ge bànfǎ cái néng kòngzhì rénkǒu de zēngzhǎng.*

C: 你们两个都**太不了解**中国的现状**（了）**。从现在开始，一家可以有两个孩子了。

*Nǐmen liǎng ge dōu **tài bù liǎojiě** Zhōngguó de xiànzhuàng (le). Cóng xiànzài kāishǐ, yī jiā kěyǐ yǒu liǎng ge háizi le.*

A: In China, each family can have only one child. I think this policy is truly **too unreasonable**.

B: This is because China's population is **too large**. Only this method can control the increase in population.

C: Both of you are way **too unfamiliar** with (**unaware of**) China's current situation. From now on, each family can have two children.

b. A sentence with 太 is considered negative when 不 **appears before** 太. In such a sentence, 了 **can no longer be used**.

'不太 + **adjective**' (literally '**not too + adjective**') means '**not very**' in Chinese. In other words, 不很, although acceptable, is not as common as 不太.

A: 你去过王先生家没有？他家离这里远不远？
   Nǐ qù guo Wáng xiānsheng jiā méiyǒu? Tā jiā lí zhèlǐ yuǎn bù yuǎn?
B: **不太远**，打车去也**不太贵**，只要十块钱。
   Bú tài yuǎn, dǎ chē qù yě bú tài guì, zhǐyào shí kuài qián.
A: 他明天请客，你去不去？
   Tā míngtiān qǐng kè, nǐ qù bú qù?
B: 我**不太想**去。
   Wǒ bú tài xiǎng qù.
A: 为什么？
   Wèi shénme?
B: 因为他家**不太大**，可是他每次都请很多人；而且他做的菜也**不太好吃**。你呢？你去不去？
   Yīnwèi tā jiā bú tài dà, kěshì tā měi cì dōu qǐng hěn duō rén; érqiě tā zuò de cài yě bú tài hǎochī. Nǐ ne? Nǐ qù bú qù?
A: 我现在还**不太能**确定。最近**太忙（了）**，常常得加班；要是明天不用加班，我就去。
   Wǒ xiànzài hái bú tài néng quèdìng. Zuìjìn tài máng (le), chángcháng děi jiābān; yàoshi míngtiān búyòng jiābān, wǒ jiù qù.
A: Have you been to Mr Wang's house? Is it far from here?
B: It's **not very** far. Also, it is **not very** expensive if you take a taxi; it costs only 10 *kuai*.
A: He is having a dinner party tomorrow. Are you going?
B: I **don't very much** feel like going.
A: Why? (Note: Chinese seldom say 'why not?')
B: Because his house is **not very** big, but he always invites many people. Besides, his cooking is **not very** delicious. How about you? Are you going?
A: I **cannot be too sure** yet. Lately, I have been **too busy**, and I often have to work overtime. If I don't have to work overtime, then I will go.

c.   An alternative for **不太** is **不怎么**. Either sounds better than 不很.

A: 昨天的考试难不难？
   Zuótiān de kǎoshì nán bù nán?
B: **不怎么难**，可是我考得**不太好**。
   Bù zěnme nán, kěshì wǒ kǎo de bú tài hǎo.
A: 为什么？
   Wèi shénme?
B: 因为虽然问题都**不太难**，可是题目**太多（了）**，所以时间**不怎么够**。
   Yīnwèi suīrán wèntí dōu bú tài nán, kěshì tímù tài duō (le), suǒyǐ shíjiān bù zěnme gòu.
A: Was yesterday's test hard?
B: It was **not very** hard. But I did **not** do **very well**.

A: Why?

B: Although the questions were **not very** hard, there were **too many** items, so the time was **not quite** enough.

→ See 不怎么 (*bù zěnme*) for more examples.

d. When 太 . . . 了 is used to express an **exclamation**, three points merit attention.

(i) 了 must always be used and is **no longer optional**.

(ii) The **adjective** may not carry a negative connotation; it is, in fact, **frequently positive**.

(iii) It is not **appropriate to translate 太 as 'too'**, especially when the adjective does not carry a negative connotation.

(Scenario: About Mr Wang's moral character.)

A: 王先生的为人实在太正直了，他见义勇为而且扶助弱小，自己的收入不多，可是常常捐款给慈善机构。

Wáng xiānsheng de wéirén shízài tài zhèngzhí le. Tā jiàn yì yǒng wéi, érqiě fú zhù ruòxiǎo; zìjǐ de shōurù bù duō, kěshì chángcháng juānkuǎn gěi císhàn jīgòu.

B: 这种人**太令人佩服了**！

Zhè zhǒng rén tài lìng rén pèifú le.

A: Mr Wang is truly an honest and upright man. He is courageous in doing what is just and kind in helping the weak. He does not make much money, but he often donates money to charity organizations.

B: People like this are **truly admirable**!

(Scenario: About ballgames.)

A: 昨天那场球赛怎么样？

Zuótiān nà chǎng qiúsài zěnme yàng?

B: **太精彩了**！

Tài jīngcǎi le!

A: 明天的比赛我有两张票，你想不想一起去看？

Míngtiān de bǐsài wǒ yǒu liǎng zhāng piào. Nǐ xiǎng bù xiǎng yīqǐ qù kàn?

B: 真的吗？**太棒了**！

Zhēn de ma? Tài bàng le!

A: How was yesterday's ballgame?

B: It was **splendid**!

A: I have two tickets for tomorrow's game. Would you like to go with me?

B: Really? That's **fantastic**!

(Scenario: About an earthquake.)

A: 昨天晚上有一场大地震，听说有一栋大楼塌了。

Zuótiān wǎnshàng yǒu yī chǎng dà dìzhèn; tīngshuō yǒu yī dòng dàlóu tā le.

B: 哎呀！**太**可怕**了**！
   Āiya! Tài kěpà le.

A: There was a huge earthquake last night. I heard that a tall building collapsed.

B: Oh no! That's **so** horrible!

e. Because 了 is a modal particle (a.k.a. sentence-final particle), it is **not used** if the expression with 太 is a modifier **before a noun**.

房地产商:	您喜欢什么样的房子？
Fángdìchǎn shāng:	*Nín xǐhuān shénme yàng de fángzi?*
李先生:	**太**贵**的**、**太**大**的**，我都不喜欢。还有，厨房**太**小**的**房子，我也不喜欢。
Lǐ xiānsheng:	*Tài guì de, tài dà de, wǒ dōu bù xǐhuān. Háiyǒu, chúfáng tài xiǎo de fángzi, wǒ yě bù xǐhuān.*
房地产商:	地区呢？
Fángdìchǎn shāng:	*Dìqū ne?*
李先生:	离市中心**太**远**的**地区也**不太好**。
Lǐ xiānsheng:	*Lí shì zhōngxīn tài yuǎn de dìqū yě bú tài hǎo.*
房地产商:	好！大安路上有一个**不太贵**的房子，我带你去看。
Fángdìchǎn shāng:	*Hǎo! Dà'ān Lù shàng yǒu yī ge bú tài guì de fángzi, wǒ dài nǐ qù kàn.*
Real estate agent:	What kind of house do you like?
Mr Li:	I don't like houses that are **too expensive** or **too big**. I also don't like a house in which the kitchen is **too small**.
Real estate agent:	What about location?
Mr Li:	Areas that are **too far** away from downtown are **not very good**, either.
Real estate agent:	OK! There is house on Da'an Road that is **not too expensive**. Let me take you to see it.

f. The expression 'a little bit' can be combined with the use of 太 . . . 了 to mean '**a little bit too . . .**'. There are two ways to do so:

(i) **有（一）点太 . . . 了**

这个房子，我很喜欢；可是我觉得价钱**有（一）点太**高**了**。
Zhè ge fángzi, wǒ hěn xǐhuān; kěshì wǒ juéde jiàqián yǒu (yī) diǎn tài gāo le.
I like this house very much. But I feel that the price is **a little bit too** high.

(ii) **太 . . . 了（一）点**

这篇文章写得不错，可是**太**短**了（一）点**。
Zhè piān wénzhāng xiě de búcuò, kěshì tài duǎn le (yī) diǎn.
This essay is well written, but it is **a bit too** short.

谈 *tán* **and** 谈话 *tán huà*

A common mistake learners make is to use 说 where 谈 is the proper word. This is likely due to the fact that both are translated as 'to talk' and that 说 is a more prevalent word than 谈.

→ See 说 (*shuō*) and 说话 (*shuō huà*) for related information.

For example, the objects of 说 can be nouns of various natures, such as 英文 (*Yīngwén*: English) and 故事 (*gùshì*: story); whereas 谈 is usually only followed by words such as 事情 (*shìqíng*: matter) or the specific topic to be discussed. In addition, 说 can mean 'to say that . . .' and **be followed by a complete sentence**; whereas 谈 does not have this function.

谈 implies that the interlocutors have a **specific issue to discuss**. Also, when 谈话 is used, the implication is that two people have **something to discuss**; the discussion topic is either clear from the context or not known. On the other hand, 说话 does not suggest any specific content or topic. Two people having any kind of oral interaction is 说话.

The proper preposition used with both 说 and 谈 is 跟 (*gēn*: with).

今天请来的专家要**跟**我们**谈**一下饮食跟健康的关系。

Jīntiān qǐng lái de zhuānjiā yào gēn wǒmen tán yīxià yǐnshí gēn jiànkāng de guānxì.

The expert we have invited here today is going to **talk to us about** the relationship between diet and health.

(Scenario: A teacher is concerned about one of her students and plans to talk to him about the situation.)

高文生好像一个朋友也没有，我从来没有看过他**跟**任何一个同学**说话**；我很担心，所以打算找他来我的办公室**谈谈**。

Gāo Wénshēng hǎoxiàng yī ge péngyǒu yě méiyǒu, wǒ cónglái méiyǒu kàn guo tā gēn rènhé yī ge tóngxué shuō huà; wǒ hěn dānxīn, suǒyǐ dǎsuàn zhǎo tā lái wǒ de bàngōngshì tán tán.

Gao Wenzhong does not seem to have any friends; I have never seen him **talking with** any classmates of his. I am worried, so I plan to ask him to my office to **talk (to discuss this situation)**.

老师:	高大中，李明，下课以后到我的办公室来一下，我要**跟**你们**谈**一件**事情**。
Lǎoshī:	*Gāo Dàzhōng, Lǐ Míng, xià kè yǐhòu dào wǒ de bàngōngshì lái yīxià, wǒ yào gēn nǐmen tán yī jiàn shìqíng.*
高:	老师为什么叫我们去她的办公室**谈话**？
Gāo:	*Lǎoshī wèi shénme jiào wǒmen qù tā de bàngōngshì tánhuà?*
李:	糟糕，一定是上次我们考试作弊被她发现了！
Lǐ:	*Zāogāo, yīdìng shì shàng cì wǒmen kǎoshì zuòbì bèi tā fāxiàn le!*

Teacher:	Gao Dazhong, Li Ming, come to my office after class. I want to **talk to you** about a certain **matter**.
Gao:	Why did the teacher ask us to her office **to talk (for a talk)**?
Li:	Oh, no. It must be because she has found out that we cheated on the last test.

万一 *wànyī*

万一 and 要是 (*yàoshì*) share certain similarities in meaning. Both can be used to indicate the **possibility** of an event happening **in the future**, but 万一 is used **when the possibility is slim**. It is thus often translated as 'in case'.

→ See 要是 (*yàoshì*) for related information.

(Scenario: A mother urges her daughter to take a parasol/umbrella with her when she is leaving the house. Note that both 'parasol' and 'umbrella' are 伞 in Chinese.)

妈妈:	太阳这么大，带把伞吧！**万一**下午下雨，还可以挡雨。
Māma:	*Tàiyáng zhème dà, dài bǎ sǎn ba! Wànyī xiàwǔ xià yǔ, hái kěyǐ dǎng yǔ.*
Mother:	It is so sunny! Why don't you take a parasol with you! **In case** (or: **On the off-chance**) it rains in the afternoon, you can also use it for rain (literally: to shield from the rain).

(Scenario: Mr Wang, a married man, invites a female coworker for lunch, but she declines.)

女同事:	对不起，我不能去。**万一**被别人看到我们一起吃饭，我怕他们会说闲话。
Nǚ tóngshì:	*Duìbuqǐ, wǒ bù néng qù. Wànyī bèi biérén kàndào wǒmen yīqǐ chīfàn, wǒ pà tāmen huì shuō xiánhuà.*
Female coworker:	Sorry, I cannot go. **In case** we are seen by others having a meal together, I am concerned that they would gossip about us.

唯一 *wéiyī*

唯一 means 'only' and it is an **adjective** which only **appears before a noun**. Learners often underuse 唯一 since most are more familiar with the word 只 (*zhǐ*). Although the definition of 只 is also 'only', it must be kept in mind that 只 cannot immediately appear before a noun because it is an adverb.

It should be noted that 的 follows 唯一, thus, '**唯一的** + noun'.

安娜是一个孤儿；她**唯一的**亲人是她妹妹。
Ānnà shì yī ge gū'ér; tā wéiyī de qīnrén shì tā mèimei.
Anna is an orphan; her **only relative** is her younger sister.

→ See 只 (*zhǐ*) for more information.

未必 *wèibì*

未必 and 不见得 (*bú jiànde*) are considered interchangeable. Both mean '**not necessarily**' and are usually used to show one's skepticism about a particular situation that has been deemed true or possible. 未必 is frequently used in both writing and speaking, whereas 不见得 tends to be used in casual communication.

→ See 不见得 (*bú jiànde*) for more information.

问 *wèn*

问 has a simple definition: 'to ask', and it is used to **ask questions** (A asks B a question), not to make a request, which is also 'to ask' in English (A asks B to do something). Therefore, a **common mistake** made by learners who are English speakers is to use 问 to make a request. To **indicate a request**, the proper verb is 请 (*qǐng*).

→ See 请 (*qǐng*) for related information.

无论 *wúlùn*

无论 and 不管 (*bùguǎn*: when defined as 'no matter' or 'regardless') are considered interchangeable, except that 无论 is a somewhat more formal word than 不管. Also, the word 不论 (*búlùn*) can be used to replace 无论.

→ See 不管 (*bùguǎn*) for related information.

Related expression

无论如何 *wúlùn rúhé*

Since 如何 (*rúhé*: how) is a formal or written expression for 怎么样 (*zěnme yàng*), **无论如何** and **不管怎么样** have the same meaning of '**no matter what**'. The implication is 'under all circumstances'. However, in terms of usage, 无论如何 is often a stand-alone expression; as such, **it is acceptable to omit 都 or 也** in the main sentence when 无论如何 is used this way.

A: 这是我的秘密，你**不管怎么样都**(or 也)不能告诉别人。(都 or 也 is necessary when 不管怎么样 is used.)
   Zhè shì wǒ de mìmì, nǐ bùguǎn zěnme yàng dōu (or yě) bù néng gàosù biérén.
B: 你放心，**无论如何**，我一定替你保密。
   Nǐ fàngxīn, wúlùn rúhé, wǒ yīdìng tì nǐ bǎomì.
A: This is my secret. You cannot tell anybody, **no matter what**.
B: Don't worry. I will definitely keep your secret **under any circumstances**.

A: 小李，你这个星期迟到了三次，经理非常不高兴；明天你**无论如何**不能再迟到了。

　　Xiǎo Lǐ, nǐ zhè ge xīngqī chídào le sān cì, jīnglǐ fēicháng bù gāoxìng; míngtiān nǐ wúlùn rúhé bù néng zài chídào le.

B: 你不用替小李担心。他是老板的侄子，他可以天天迟到。经理**无论如何**不会把他解聘的。

　　Nǐ búyòng tì Xiǎo Lǐ dānxīn. Tā shì lǎobǎn de zhízi, tā kěyǐ tiān tiān chídào. Jīnglǐ wúlùn rúhé bú huì bǎ tā jiěpìn de.

A: Little Li, you have been late three times this week; the manager is very unhappy. Tomorrow you cannot be late again **under any circumstances**.

B: You don't have to be worried about Little Li. He is the owner's nephew; he can be late every day. The manager won't fire him, **no matter what**.

相干 *xiānggān*

相干 is used in the '**A 跟 B 不相干**' pattern to indicate that 'A has nothing to do with B'; therefore, it means the same as '**A 跟 B 没(有)关系**'. Although both 不相干 and 没(有)关系 are frequently used in casual speech, 不相干 is rarely used in writing and is largely considered a spoken form.

→ See 关系 (*guānxi*) for more information.

想 *xiǎng*

When 想 appears without any context, the definition that usually comes to one's mind is 'to think'. However, 想 actually has several other definitions and can be used as a verb or a modal verb (which is followed by a regular verb). The proper use and interpretation of 想 can only be achieved by observing the context in which it appears.

In addition, there are words that share similarities with 想 but have different interpretations. Discussions in this section will be on the various uses of 想, as well as comparisons of uses between 想 and similar words.

a. '**想 + noun**': In this pattern, 想 is a verb, meaning 'to miss', such as 'I miss my mother' (我想我妈妈). It is possible to have a **degree adverb**, such as 很 or 非常, preceding it.

A: 你来中国三年了，**想不想家**？

　　Nǐ lái Zhōngguó sān nián le, xiǎng bù xiǎng jiā?

B: **想**。我**想**家里的每一个人，也**很想**我的狗。

　　Xiǎng. Wǒ xiǎng jiā lǐ de měi yī ge rén, yě hěn xiǎng wǒ de gǒu.

A: You have been in China for three years already; do you **miss home**? (= Are you homesick?)

B: Yes, **I do**. I **miss** everyone in my family; I also **miss** my dog **very much**.

b. As a verb, 想 is frequently defined simply as 'to think'. Learners who are English speakers often misuse it by associating it with one's opinion (see section d. below.) It is best to think of 想 as '**to think about**' or '**to ponder on**' something. '在 + 想' can be used to indicate that 想 is an **action in progress**.

A: 我跟你说话，你好像没听见；你**在想**什么？
Wǒ gēn nǐ shuō huà, nǐ hǎoxiàng méi tīngjiàn; nǐ zài xiǎng shénme?
B: 我**在想**今年我们应该去哪里度假。
Wǒ zài xiǎng jīnnián wǒmen yīnggāi qù nǎlǐ dùjià.
A: I was talking to you, and you acted like you did not hear me. What were you **thinking about**?
B: I was **thinking about** where we should go for our holiday this year.

It can be **reduplicated** (想想, 想一想, 想了想, 想一下), particularly when the issue to be pondered on does not directly follow 想, because it is either **pre-posed** to the beginning of the sentence or **clear in the context**.

老师: 这两个问题，请你们回家去**想一想**。(Issue is **pre-posed**.)
Lǎoshī: *Zhè liǎng ge wèntí, qǐng nǐmen huí jiā qù xiǎng yī xiǎng.*
Teacher: Please go home and **think about** these two questions.

女: 今天晚上在家吃还是出去吃？
Nǚ: *Jīntiān wǎnshàng zài jiā chī háishì chūqù chī?*
男: 让我**想想**。(Issue is **clear in the context**.)
Nán: *Ràng wǒ xiǎng xiǎng.*
Woman: Are we eating at home or going out to eat this evening?
Man: Let me **think about it for a while**.

小李告诉了服务员他要点的菜以后，**想了想**，又点了一瓶酒。
Xiǎo Lǐ gàosù le fúwùyuán tā yào diǎn de cài yǐhòu, xiǎng le xiǎng, yòu diǎn le yī píng jiǔ.
After Little Li told the waiter the dishes he wanted to order, he **thought for a moment**, and ordered a bottle of wine.

c. As 'to think', 想 can be **followed by a sentence** (or even a short paragraph) to indicate **one's thought**. This usually implies that one is 'talking to oneself without saying the words out loud'. The expression is often 心想 (*xīn xiǎng*) or 心里想 (*xīnlǐ xiǎng*) and is followed by a comma.

小王在超市买了两块牛排以后，**他想**，吃牛排应该有好酒，所以又买了一瓶红酒。
Xiǎo Wáng zài chāo shì mǎi le liǎng kuài niúpái yǐhòu, tā xiǎng, chī niúpái yīnggāi yǒu hǎo jiǔ, suǒyǐ yòu mǎi le yī píng hóng jiǔ.
After Little Wang bought two steaks at the supermarket, **he said to himself that** there should be good wine when having steak, and so he bought a bottle of red wine.

d. When 想 is **followed by a sentence**, it is used to indicate one's **speculation**, not opinion. While what is being expressed might be akin to one's opinion, it is something which one **cannot be sure of** or an event that **has not taken place yet**.

(i) When 想 is used in this context, a word such as 会 (*huì*: would), 应该 (*yīnggāi*: should), 大概 (*dàgài*: probably) and 可能 (*kěnéng*: probably) is almost always used.

(Scenario: Li tells his friend he is going to see a movie called *1911* the next day.)

朋友: 《一九一一》？为什么看这个电影？
Péngyǒu: *'Yī jiǔ yī yī'? Wèi shénme kàn zhè ge diànyǐng?*
李: 因为我喜欢历史故事，所以我**想**这个电影**应该**很好看。
Lǐ: *Yīnwèi wǒ xǐhuān lìshǐ gùshì, suǒyǐ wǒ xiǎng zhè ge diànyǐng yīnggāi hěn hǎokàn.*
Friend: *1911*? Why see this movie?
Li: Because I like historical stories, I **think** this movie **should be** good.

To inquire about another person's speculation about a situation ('do you think . . .'), 想不想 should not be used. In addition, to give a negative answer, 不想 should not be used. Learners who are English speakers should avoid making these mistakes.

A: 你**想**今天**会不会**下雨？(It is incorrect to say 你想不想今天会下雨.)
Nǐ xiǎng jīntiān huì bú huì xià yǔ?
B: 我**想不会**。(Do not say 我不想会.)
Wǒ xiǎng bú huì.
A: Do you think it will rain today?
B: I don't think so. (I think not.)

(ii) To actually **indicate one's opinion** (instead of one's speculation), 觉得 (*juéde*) or 认为 (*rènwéi*) is the proper word. Since both words can also be translated as 'to think', using 想 to state one's opinions is a **very common mistake** made by learners who are English speakers.

→ See 觉得 (*juéde*) and 认为 (*rènwéi*) for more information.

(Scenario: Li has seen the movie *1911*.)

朋友: 《一九一一》怎么样？好不好看？
Péngyǒu: *'Yī jiǔ yī yī' zěnme yàng? Hǎo bù hǎokàn?*
李: 我**觉得**很好看。(我想很好看 would be incorrect since he has seen the movie and is expressing his opinion now.)
Lǐ: *Wǒ juéde hěn hǎokàn.*

Friend: How was *1911*? Was it good?

Li: I **think** it was good.

e. 想 is also a **modal verb**; this means that it is **immediately followed by a
    verb** (or a verbal phrase). It is used to indicate one's **desire** or **intention to
    do something**.

A: 你以后**想做**什么工作？
    Nǐ yǐhòu xiǎng zuò shénme gōngzuò?

B: 我**想当**医生。
    Wǒ xiǎng dāng yīshēng.

A: What kind of work do you **want to do** in the future?

B: I **want to be** a doctor.

As a modal verb, 想 shares similarities with 要 (*yào*) both in terms of usage
and meaning, but 想 is **not as strong as 要** in conveying one's desire or
intention.

→ See 要 (*yào*) for related information.

要 is for an event that **is going to take place**; whereas 想 is for an event
that **one hopes will take place**.

A: 我下学期**要去**中国学中文。
    Wǒ xià xuéqī yào qù Zhōngguó xué Zhōngwén.

B: 我真羡慕你；我**也想去**中国，可是我爸妈不让我去。
    *Wǒ zhēn xiànmù nǐ; wǒ yě xiǎng qù Zhōngguó, kěshì wǒ bàmā bú ràng
    wǒ qù.*

A: I **am going to (will go to)** China to study Chinese next semester.

B: I really envy you. I also **want to go** to China; but my parents will not
    let me.

There are several phrases used to translate 想, all of which are related to
one's desire or intention to do something. A **degree adverb**, such as 很 or
非常, **can precede** 想. (But a degree adverb cannot precede 要.)

(i) 想 is often translated as '**would like**'.

A: 我今天晚上**要**跟几个朋友去跳舞，你**想不想**跟我们一起去？
    *Wǒ jīntiān wǎnshàng yào gēn jǐ ge péngyǒu qù tiàowǔ, nǐ xiǎng bù
    xiǎng gēn wǒmen yīqǐ qù?*

B: 我**很想**去，可是明天有一个大考试，我得在家学习。
    *Wǒ hěn xiǎng qù, kěshì míngtiān yǒu yī ge dà kǎoshì, wǒ děi zài
    jiā xuéxí.*

A: I **am going** dancing with a few friends this evening; **would you like** to go with us?

B: I **would very much like to** go, but I have a big test tomorrow; I have to study at home.

我**想**去中国留学，可是我爸妈不让我去；我**真想**跟他们说，我已经是大学生了，应该可以做自己**想**做的事，可是我不敢说。

Wǒ xiǎng qù Zhōngguó liúxué, kěshì wǒ bàmā bú ràng wǒ qù; wǒ zhēn xiǎng gēn tāmen shuō, wǒ yǐjīng shì dàxuéshēng le, yīnggāi kěyǐ zuò zìjǐ xiǎng zuò de shì, kěshì wǒ bù gǎn shuō.

I **would like to** go to China to study, but my parents will not let me go. I **would really like to (really want to)** tell them that I am already a college student, and I should be able to do things that I **would like to** do. But I dare not say it.

The usage of 想 (as 'would like') is somewhat different from the usage of the phrase 'would like' in English. This is because 想 is a modal verb, which must be followed by a verb. Learners who are English speakers should pay special attention to the differences.

For example, 想 **cannot** be used in the 'would like + person + verb' pattern. The accurate word for 'would like' in this pattern is 要.

For example, '**I would like to ask you** a question' is 我**想问你**一个问题 (*Wǒ xiǎng wèn nǐ yī ge wèntí*); whereas '**I would like you to answer** this question' is 我**要你回答**这个问题 (*Wǒ yào nǐ huídá zhè ge wèntí*). It would be incorrect to say 我想问你回答这个问题.

In addition, 'would like' in English can be followed by a noun, but 想 must be followed by a verb (or a verbal phrase), it cannot be followed by a noun.

主人：　你**想喝**点什么？

Zhǔrén: Nǐ xiǎng hē diǎn shénme?

客人：　我**想喝**杯咖啡。(It is incorrect to say 我想一杯咖啡.)

Kèrén: Wǒ xiǎng hē bēi kāfēi.

Host:　What **would you like to drink**?

Guest:　I **would like (to drink)** a cup of coffee.

However, 想要 can be used in this pattern. '**想要 + noun**' is acceptable.

A: 这两本《红楼梦》都是你的吗？可不可以给我一本？

Zhè liǎng běn 'Hóng Lóu Mèng' dōu shì nǐ de ma? Kě bù kěyǐ gěi wǒ yī běn?

B: 好啊！你**想要**哪本？（can be 你要哪本？, but cannot be 你想哪本？）

Hǎo a! Nǐ xiǎng yào nǎ běn?

A: 我**想要**这本繁体字的。
  Wǒ xiǎng yào zhè běn fántǐzì de.
A: Are both of these copies of *Dream of the Red Chamber* yours? Can you give me a copy?
B: OK! Which one **would** you **like**?
A: I **would like** this one in traditional characters.

(ii) It is possible for 想 to be translated as '**to feel like** (doing something)'.

男: 你今天晚上**想吃**哪国菜？**想不想去**吃日本菜？
Nán: *Nǐ jīntiān wǎnshàng xiǎng chī nǎ guó cài? Xiǎng bù xiǎng qù chī Rìběn cài?*
女: 好久没吃牛排了，今天我**想吃**牛排。
Nǔ: *Hǎo jiǔ méi chī niúpái le, jīntiān wǒ xiǎng chī niúpái.*
Man: What kind of (which country) food do you **feel like having** this evening? Do you **feel like going** to have Japanese food?
Woman: I haven't had steak in quite a while. I **feel like having** steak today.

(iii) 想 as a modal verb can be translated as '**to be planning on doing something**'.

A: 这个周末有什么计划？
  Zhè ge zhōumò yǒu shénme jìhuà?
B: 最近学会了几道菜，所以我**想请**几个朋友来吃饭。
  Zuìjìn xué huì le jǐ dào cài, suǒyǐ wǒ xiǎng qǐng jǐ ge péngyǒu lái chī fàn.
A: What plans do you have for this weekend?
B: Recently I have learned to cook a few dishes; so I **plan to invite** a few friends to come for dinner.

f. Although **想 and 要** are both used to express one's desire or intention to do something, **不想** is considered the **negative form for both**. This is because: (i) 不要 is **very strong** in its negativity, and may not be proper in most social situations; and (ii) 不要 is basically an **alternative for 别** used in the **negative imperative sentence**.

A: 这个周末的棒球赛，我有两张票，你**要不要**一起去？
  Zhè ge zhōumò de bàngqiú sài, wǒ yǒu liǎng zhāng piào, nǐ yào bú yào yīqǐ qù?
B: 谢谢，不过我**不想**去，因为我对棒球没有兴趣。
  Xièxie, búguò wǒ bù xiǎng qù, yīnwèi wǒ duì bàngqiú méiyǒu xìngqù.
A: I have two tickets for this weekend's baseball game. **Would you like to go together?**
B: Thanks, but I **don't want to** go because I am not interested in baseball.

今年暑假，我的同学都**要**出国；有的**要**去学外语，有的**要**去旅游，只有我哪里也**不想**去，我只**想**在家多陪陪我妈妈。

Jīnnián shǔjià, wǒ de tóngxué dōu yào chū guó; yǒude yào qù xué wàiyǔ, yǒude yào qù lǚyóu, zhǐyǒu wǒ nǎlǐ yě bù xiǎng qù, wǒ zhǐ xiǎng zài jiā duō péi péi wǒ māma.

This summer, all of my classmates **are going** abroad; some **will go** study foreign languages; some **will** go traveling; I am the only one who doesn't **want** to go anywhere; I only **want** to be home to spend more time with my mother.

g. Because 想 can be translated as '**would like**', learners who are English speakers often confuse 想 and 喜欢 (*xǐhuān*: **to like**), and tend to use 喜欢 when 想 is the correct word.

喜欢 is used to express one's '**fondness**', whereas 想 is used to express one's **intention or desire**. For example, it is possible for someone who **generally enjoys** (likes) Chinese food to not **feel like eating** a Chinese meal on a certain day. 我很**喜欢吃**中国菜，可是我今天**不想吃**中国菜，**想去吃**日本菜。(*Wǒ hěn xǐhuān chī Zhōngguó cài, kěshì wǒ jīntiān bù xiǎng chī Zhōngguó cài, xiǎng qù chī Rìběn cài.* I **like to eat** Chinese food very much, but I **don't feel like eating** Chinese food today; I **would like to eat** Japanese food.)

(Scenario: A man is trying to find out what his girlfriend would like to do that evening.)

男:	今天晚上**想**去跳舞还是看电影？
Nán:	*Jīntiān wǎnshàng xiǎng qù tiàowǔ háishì kàn diànyǐng?*
女:	我**不喜欢**跳舞，去看电影吧！
Nǚ:	*Wǒ bù xǐhuān tiàowǔ, qù kàn diànyǐng ba!*
男:	好！这个星期有一个外国电影，**想不想**去看？
Nán:	*Hǎo! Zhè ge xīngqī yǒu yī ge wàiguó diànyǐng, xiǎng bù xiǎng qù kàn?*
女:	外国电影？我最**不喜欢**看外国电影，我**不想**去！
Nǚ:	*Wàiguó diànyǐng? Wǒ zuì bù xǐhuān kàn wàiguó diànyǐng, wǒ bù xiǎng qù!*
男:	那你自己说，**想**做什么？
Nán:	*Nà nǐ zìjǐ shuō, xiǎng zuò shénme?*
女:	我**喜欢**听音乐，我们去听爵士乐吧！
Nǚ:	*Wǒ xǐhuān tīng yīnyuè, wǒmen qù tīng juéshì yuè ba!*
Man:	**Would** you **like** to go dancing or see a movie this evening?
Woman:	I **don't like** dancing. Let's go see a movie.
Man:	OK! There is a foreign movie this week; **would** you **like** to go see it?
Woman:	Foreign movie? I **dislike** foreign movies the most. (I really hate foreign movies.) I **don't want** to go.

Man:　　　Then you tell me what you **would like** to do.
Woman:　I **like** to listen to music. Why don't we go listen to some jazz music!

向来 *xiànglái* and 一向 *yīxiàng*

向来 and 一向 can be considered interchangeable. Both mean 'all along', implying '**from the beginning and all the time**'. They are similar to the English word 'hitherto' in meaning, although they are often translated as '**always**' in a positive sentence and '**never**' in a negative one.

It should be noted that they are **adverbs**, not time words. As such, they do not appear at the beginning of the sentence before the subject.

向来 and 一向 share similarities with 从来 (*cónglái*), but there are also some significant differences. The following section is a comparison between 向来/一向 and 从来.

→ See 从来 (*cónglái*) for related information.

a.　从来 is nearly always followed by a negative word, such as 不 or 没有, whereas 向来/一向 can be used in either a positive or a negative sentence.

在我家，做饭**向来**(or 一向)是我妈妈的工作；我爸爸几乎**从来不**进厨房。
Zài wǒ jiā, zuò fàn xiànglái (or *yīxiàng*) *shì wǒ māma de gōngzuò; wǒ bàba jīhū cónglái bú jìn chúfáng.*
At my house, cooking **has always been** my mother's job; my father almost **never** enters the kitchen.

王大中**一向**(or 向来)不喜欢吃海鲜，所以他**从来没有**去他岳父开的海鲜餐厅吃过饭。
Wáng Dàzhōng yīxiàng (or *xiànglái*) *bù xǐhuān chī hǎixiān, suǒyǐ tā cónglái méiyǒu qù tā yuèfù kāi de hǎixiān cāntīng chī guo fàn.*
Wang Dazhong **has always hated** seafood; therefore, he **has never been to** the seafood restaurant opened by his father-in-law for a meal.

b.　There is **no specific beginning point when** 向来 **or** 一向 **is used** because the implication is 'all the time and to this day'. This indicates that, when **a specific time frame** is mentioned, only 从来 is appropriate. When there is no specific time frame, any of these three words can be used.

张文的学习态度非常认真，他上课**向来不迟到**(= 从来不迟到)。
Zhāng Wén de xuéxí tàidù fēicháng rènzhēn; tā shàng kè xiànglái bù chídào (= *cónglái bù chídào*).
Zhang Wen has a very serious learning attitude; he **is never** late for class.

A: 王中跟张文**一向**合不来，他**从来**(can be **向来** or **一向**)不愿意去张
文家；为什么上星期张文过生日在家请客，王中也去了呢？
*Wáng Zhōng gēn Zhāng Wén yīxiàng hé bù lái, tā cónglái bú yuànyì
qù Zhāng Wén jiā; wèi shénme shàng xīngqī Zhāng Wén guò shēngrì
zài jiā qǐng kè, Wáng Zhōng yě qù le ne?*

B: 你还不知道吗？**自从**王中发现张文有一个漂亮的妹妹**以后** (Note: This
is the beginning point)，就**从来**(cannot be **向来** or **一向**)**不**放弃任何
一个去他家的机会。
*Nǐ hái bù zhīdào ma? Zìcóng Wáng Zhōng fāxiàn Zhāng Wén yǒu yī
ge piàoliàng de mèimei yǐhòu, jiù cónglái bú fàngqì rènhé yī ge qù tā
jiā de jīhuì.*

A: 那你去了吗？
Nà nǐ qù le ma?

B: 我当然去了。我**从来**(can be **向来** or **一向**)不放弃任何一个吃中国
菜的机会。
*Wǒ dāngrán qù le. Wǒ cónglái bú fàngqì rènhé yī ge chī Zhōngguó cài
de jīhuì.*

A: Wang Zhong **never** gets along with Zhang Wen, and he is **never** willing to go to Zhang Wen's house. Why did he go to Zhang Wen's house
last week when Zhang Wen had a birthday dinner at home?

B: Didn't you know? **Ever since** Wang Zhong found out that Zhang Wen
has a pretty younger sister, he **has never** passed up any opportunity of
going to his house.

A: Then did you go?

B: Of course I went; I **never** pass up any opportunity to eat Chinese food.

c. '**向来/一向** + 没有' vs. '**从来没有**': Although **ostensibly similar**, these
two patterns convey quite different meanings. This is because a **noun**
follows '**向来/一向** + 没有', but '**verb** + 过' usually follows 从来没有.

李明**向来没有**责任感，他**从来不**认真地做事，可是也**从来没有**被老板骂
过，因为这家公司**一向没有**制度。(责任感 and 制度 are nouns.)
*Lǐ Míng xiànglái méiyǒu zérèn gǎn, tā cónglái bú rènzhēn de zuò shì, kěshì
yě cóngláiméiyǒu bèi lǎobǎn mà guo, yīnwèi zhè jiā gōngsī yīxiàng méiyǒu
zhìdù.*

Li Ming **never has** any sense of responsibility; he **never does** anything
conscientiously, but he **has never been** scolded by his boss, because this
company **never has** any system.

王中**一向没有**什么朋友，他也**从来没有**想**过**他可以到网上的聊天室去交
朋友。
*Wáng Zhōng yīxiàng méiyǒu shénme péngyǒu, tā yě cónglái méiyǒu xiǎng
guo tā kěyǐ dào wǎng shàng de liáotiān shì qù jiāo péngyǒu.*

Wang Zhong **never has** many friends, and it **has never** occurred to him that
he could go to online chat rooms to make friends.

Related expression

一直 *yīzhí*

'Doing something continuously (nonstop)' is one of the several definitions and uses of 一直; therefore, 一直 and 一向/向来 share similarities in meaning. The difference between them in usage lies in the mention of a **specific time frame** in the sentence. When a specific time frame is indicated in the sentence, 一向/向来 is not used and 一直 might be the proper choice of word.

→ See 一直 (*yīzhí*) for more information.

晓得 *xiǎode*

晓得 is the same as 知道 (*zhīdào*) in meaning and usage, but is only used in very casual, conversational speech.

→ See 知道 (*zhīdào*) for related information.

些 *xiē*

些 is generally not considered a stand-alone word, but a character that appears after certain characters (or words) to form words. Therefore, it functions as a **suffix**. When 些 does appear as a stand-alone word, it is, in fact, a short form for 一些, and is used in casual speech.

Basically, 些 can be defined as 'some'. The noun following it can be either a countable noun, such as 人 (*rén*: person), or an uncountable noun, such as 水 (*shuǐ*: water). Once 些 is used, a **measure word is no longer used**. If a measure word is necessary, then 些 cannot be used.

This section provides the uses of common expressions that include the character 些.

a.　As vocabulary words, **这些**, **那些** and **哪些** are often translated as 'these', 'those' and 'which (+ plural)' respectively. However, such definitions are misleading because these three words can be followed by uncountable nouns as well.

　　(i)　When 这些, 那些 or 哪些 is followed by a countable noun, **a number can no longer be used**. For example, the expression 'these three people (这三个人: *zhè sān ge rén*)' does not involve the use of 些. It is incorrect to say 这些三个人. One can only say 这些人 (these people) without indicating the actual number. To use a number after one of these words is a **common mistake** made by learners who are English speakers.

　　　　The noun (if clear in context) after 些 is omissible.

(Scenario: Li is looking at some photos in Wang's photo album.)

李: **这些**人是谁？

Lǐ: *Zhèxiē rén shì shéi?*

王: **哪些**人？

Wáng: *Nǎxiē rén?*

李: **这两张**照片里的**这些**（人）。

Lǐ: *Zhè liǎng zhāng zhàopiàn lǐ de zhèxiē (rén).*

王: 哦，**这三个**是我弟弟，**那些**都是我的同学。

Wáng: *O, zhè sān ge shì wǒ dìdi, nàxiē dōu shì wǒde tóngxué.*

Li: Who are **these** people?

Wang: **Which** people?

Li: **These** (people) in **these two** photos.

Wang: Oh, **these three** are my younger brothers; all of **those** are my classmates.

Because 些 is associated with the word 'some', to interpret 这些, 那些 or 哪些 as 'these few', 'those few', or 'which few' is a **common mistake** made by learners. In actuality, 这些, 那些 or 哪些 can indicate **any number**.

很多人批评中国的人口政策，我认为，**这些人**完全不了解中国的人口问题有多严重。

Hěn duō rén pīpíng Zhōngguó de rénkǒu zhèngcè, wǒ rènwéi, zhèxiē rén wánquán bù liǎojiě Zhōngguó de rénkǒu wèntí yǒu duō yánzhòng. Many people criticize China's population policy. I am of the opinion that **these people** have no idea (completely do not understand) how serious China's population problem is.

(ii) **Uncountable nouns** can follow 這些, 那些 and 哪些 as well. In this case, the function of 些 is similar to that of a measure word because a noun should not follow 这, 那 or 哪 without a measure word.

(Scenario: A mother has found **some money** in her son's knapsack, and she wants to know the source of the money.)

妈妈: **这些钱**是谁给你的？

Māma: *Zhèxiē qián shì shéi gěi nǐ de?*

儿子: **哪些**钱？（什么钱？would also be correct in this context.）

Érzi: *Nǎxiē qián? (Shénme qián?)*

妈妈: 你背包里的**这些**。

Māma: *Nǐ bēibāo lǐ de zhèxiē.*

儿子: **那些**是我自己打工赚来的钱，你别动！

Érzi: *Nàxiē shì wǒ zìjǐ dǎgōng zhuàn lái de qián, nǐ bié dòng!*

Mother: Who gave you **this money**?

Son: **Which** money? (What money?)

Mother: **The money** in your knapsack.

Son: **That** is money I earned from working on odd jobs. Don't touch it!

(Scenario: Mr Zhou is training a new employee, Mr Gao. He shows Mr Gao two piles of documents.)

周: **这些**资料是公开的，**那些**是机密的。

Zhōu: Zhèxiē zīliào shì gōngkāi de, nàxiē shì jīmì de.

高: **哪些**是可以带回家研究的？

Gāo: Nǎxiē shì kěyǐ dài huí jiā yánjiū de?

周: 都不可以。

Zhōu: Dōu bù kěyǐ.

Zhou: **This** (pile of) **information** is open-to-the-public; **that** (pile of) **information** is confidential.

Gao: **Which** can be taken home to work on?

Zhou: Neither.

b. Although 有些 is simply translated as '**some**', it actually has **three different functions** depending on the **context** as well as the **sentence structure**. Therefore, the proper use of 有些 is often a source of confusion for many learners. What must be kept in mind is the fact that 有些 should **not** be treated as being **synonymous with 'a few (几 + measure word)'**.

(i) 有些 must appear **at the beginning of a sentence**; it means '**certain**', referring to **unidentified people or things**. The number it refers to can go way beyond simply 'a few'. It is interchangeable with 有的.

   In addition, 有 should **not** be considered **a separate word from** 些.

   A: **有些人**(= **有的人**)喜欢一边开车，一边用手机打电话，真危险！

   Yǒuxiē rén (= yǒude rén) xǐhuān yībiān kāi chē, yībiān yòng shǒujī dǎ diànhuà, zhēn wēixiǎn!

   B: **有些人**(= **有的人**)酒后开车，更危险！

   Yǒuxiē rén (= yǒude rén) jiǔ hòu kāi chē, gèng wēixiǎn!

   A: **Some people** (meaning: **certain people**) like to drive while talking on their cell phones. It's really dangerous.

   B: **Some people** drive after drinking (alcohol). It's even more dangerous.

   In the following example, which continues the previous dialogue, 有 **is a separate word** from 些; 些 means 一些 and can be interchangeable with '几 + measure word'. Therefore, 有 + 些 in this usage is not interchangeable with 有的.

   C: 是啊！现代社会确实**有些**(= **有一些** or **有几个**)以前没有的问题。

   Shì a! Xiàndài shèhuì quèshí yǒu xiē (= yǒu yīxiē or yǒu jǐ ge) yǐqián méiyǒu de wèntí.

   C: Yeah! Modern society indeed **has some (a few)** problems that we did not have before.

(ii) 有些 can be defined as '**some of . . .**' referring to a **sub-group** of a larger group. It is interchangeable with 有的.

The larger group must be made clear (or pre-existent in the context) before 有些 can be used.

桌上**有**十几本**书**，**有些**(= **有的**)是中文的，**有些**(= **有的**)是英文的。
Zhuō shàng yǒu shí jǐ běn shū, yǒuxiē (= yǒude) shì Zhōngwén de, yǒuxiē (= yǒude) shì Yīngwén de.
There are more than ten **books** on the table; **some (of them)** are in Chinese; **some** are in English.

When 有些 is used this way, it must appear **at the beginning of the sentence** even though the sub-group might be **the object of the verb**, resulting in an **inverted** sentence – object before the verb.

老师:	现在大家注意看黑板上的**这些句子**，**有些**我来给你们**翻译**，**有些**我要请李同学来**翻译**。(Do not say 我来给你们翻译有些 or 我要请李同学来翻译有些.)
Lǎoshī:	*Xiànzài dàjiā zhùyì kàn hēibǎn shàng de zhèxiē jùzi, yǒuxiē wǒ lái gěi nǐmen fānyì, yǒuxiē wǒ yào qǐng Lǐ tóngxué lái fānyì.*
Teacher:	Now everyone pay attention to **these** sentences on the blackboard. I will **translate some of them** for you, and I will ask Student Li to **translate some** others.

(iii) 有些 can appear **before an adjective** to mean '**a little bit**'; it can also been interpreted as '**somewhat** + adjective'. It is interchangeable with 有(一)点.

小李整个周末都在看球赛，没有帮忙做家事，所以他妻子**有些**(= 有一点)不高兴。
Xiǎo Lǐ zhěng ge zhōumò dōu zài kàn qiúsài, méiyǒu bāngmáng zuò jiāshì, suǒyǐ tā qīzi yǒuxiē (= yǒu yīdiǎn) bù gāoxìng.
Little Li has been watching ballgames all weekend long; he has not helped with any housework; so his wife is **a little (somewhat)** upset.

明天有一个大考试，老师说，这个考试会很难，所以我现在**有些**紧张。
Míngtiān yǒu yī ge dà kǎoshì, lǎoshī shuō, zhè ge kǎoshì huì hěn nán, suǒyǐ wǒ xiànzài yǒuxiē jǐnzhāng.
There is a big test tomorrow. The teacher has said that this test will be difficult, so I am **a little** nervous right now.

c. The 一 in 一些 is frequently omitted, resulting in 些 alone. 一些 is typically translated as '**some**', but there are **two differences between 有些 and 一些** when both are used to mean 'some'.

(i) If the word 'some' appears **at the beginning of a sentence**, use 有些, not 一些. For example, to say '**some** imported cars are both expensive and unreliable', one must use 有些. This sentence should be 有些 进口的汽车又贵又不可靠 (*Yǒuxiē jìnkǒu de qìchē yòu guì yòu bù kěkào*).

(ii) 一些 tends to suggest that **the amount or quantity is not large**. If 一些 is followed by a countable noun, it is very **similar in meaning to '几 + measure word**'. On the other hand, 有些 means '**certain**' without any suggestion about the quantity. (See examples in section b.(i) above for 有些.)

(Scenario: A considerate host made vegetarian food for her guest.)

主人： 我知道你是吃素的，所以今天做了一些(= 几个)没有肉的菜，不过我在菜里放了一些辣椒，希望你喜欢吃辣的。

Zhǔrén: Wǒ zhīdào nǐ shì chī sù de, suǒyǐ jīntiān zuò le yīxiē (= jǐ ge) méiyǒu ròu de cài, búguò wǒ zài cài lǐ fàng le yīxiē làjiāo, xīwàng nǐ xǐhuān chī là de.

客人： 有些吃素的人特别喜欢吃辣的，我就是其中之一。

Kèrén: Yǒuxiē chī sù de rén tèbié xǐhuān chī là de, wǒ jiù shì qízhōng zhīyī.

Host: I know you are a vegetarian, so I made **some (= a few) dishes** without meat; but I put **some hot peppers** in the dishes. I hope you like spicy-hot food.

Guest: **Some vegetarians** particularly like spicy-hot food. I am one of those.

去年我在北京工作的时候，认识了一些不会说英文的中国人，所以我的中文进步得很快。

Qùnián wǒ zài Běijīng gōngzuò de shíhòu, rènshì le yīxiē bú huì shuō Yīngwén de Zhōngguó rén, suǒyǐ wǒ de Zhōngwén jìnbù de hěn kuài.

When I was working in Beijing last year, I met (made friends with) **some (a few)** Chinese who could not speak English; so my Chinese improved rapidly.

(iii) 一些 can appear **after an adjective**, whereas 有些 appears **before an adjective**. (See section b.(iii) above for '有些 + adjective'.) '**Adjective + 一些**' implies a **comparison** and is interchangeable with 一点 (*yìdiǎn*); it means **a little bit more**.

A: 王大中比他弟弟**胖(一)些**。(adjective + 一些)
Wáng Dàzhōng bǐ tā dìdi pàng (yī) xiē.

B: 别让他听到。上次我也这么说，他听了以后就**有些不高兴**。
(有些 + adjective)
Bié ràng tā tīngdào. Shàng cì wǒ yě zhème shuō, tā tīng le yǐhòu jiù yǒuxiē bù gāoxìng.

A: Wang Dazhong is **a little bit heavier** (fatter) than his younger brother.

B: Don't let him hear it. Last time I said the same. When he heard it, he was **a little bit upset**.

A: 这件红大衣跟那件蓝的都很漂亮，可是红的**贵一些**，所以我要买蓝的。
Zhè jiàn hóng dàyī gēn nà jiàn lán de dōu hěn piàoliàng, kěshì hóng de guì yīxiē, suǒyǐ wǒ yào mǎi lán de.

B: 蓝的虽然比红的**便宜些**，可是我觉得这件红的布料比较**好些**，所以你应该买红的。
Lán de suīrán bǐ hóng de piányí xiē, kěshì wǒ juéde zhè jiàn hóng de bùliào bǐjiào hǎo xiē, suǒyǐ nǐ yīnggāi mǎi hóng de.

A: This red coat and that blue one are both pretty, but the red one is **a little bit more expensive**, so I want to buy the blue one.

B: Although the blue one is **a little cheaper** than the red one, I feel that the fabric of the red one is **a bit better**, so you should buy the red one.

d. **些许** normally appears **before an uncountable noun**. It refers to **a very small amount** (even less than 一些), so it is frequently translated as '**a tiny little bit**'. In casual speech, the word **一点点** (rather than 一点) is often used in place of 些许.

下次你做这道菜的时候，别忘了加**些许**糖，味道会更好。
Xià cì nǐ zuò zhè dào cài de shíhòu, bié wàng le jiā xiēxǔ táng, wèidào huì gèng hǎo.
Next time when you make this dish, don't forget to add **a tiny little bit** sugar; it would taste even better.

→ See 一点 (*yīdiǎn*) for related information.

需要 *xūyào*

需要 means 'to need'; it shares similarities with 必须 (*bìxū*: must) in that both can express **necessity or requirement**. There are also differences in terms of grammar structures and implications. Thus, 必须 and 需要 are usually not interchangeable. It is important to recognize the distinction between the two similar words.

→ See 必须 (*bìxū*) for more information.

要 . . . 了 *yào . . . le*

要 . . . 了 is used to show an impending event, and is considered interchangeable with 快 . . . 了 (*kuài . . . le*).

→ See 快 . . . 了 (*kuài . . . le*) for more information.

要不 *yào bù* and 要不然 *yào bùrán*

a. 要不 literally means 'if not'; therefore, it is also translated as '**otherwise**'. 要不然 (*yào bùrán*) and 不然 (*bùrán*) are its variations. 会 or another word indicating possibility is frequently used in the main sentence.
   否则 (*fǒuzé*) is also interchangeable with 要不(然); it is often used with 除非 (*chúfēi*).

   → See 除非 (*chúfēi*) and 否则 (*fǒuzé*) for related information.

   电影快开始了，我们得打车去；**要不，会**赶不上。
   Diànyǐng kuài kāishǐ le, wǒmen děi dǎchē qù; yàobù, huì gǎn bú shàng.
   The movie is going to start soon. We have to take a taxi; **otherwise, we will** miss it.

   炸春卷的时候，油一定要够热；**要不，**春卷**会**不够脆。
   Zhá chūnjuǎn de shíhòu, yóu yīdìng yào gòu rè; yàobù, chūnjuǎn huì bú gòu cuì.
   When you deep fry spring rolls, the oil must be hot enough; **otherwise**, your spring rolls **will** not be crispy enough.

b. 要不 can also be used to suggest **an alternative option** (after all other options fail to work). 要不然 and 不然 can be used in this situation as well, but 否则 **cannot**. There is no direct translation in English for this expression. 吧 is frequently used at the end of the sentence.

   (Scenario: Two friends are discussing what transportation to use to get to the movie theater.)
   A: 走路去，太远；打车去，太贵；坐地铁去，太麻烦。怎么办？
   Zǒulù qù, tài yuǎn; dǎchē qù, tài guì; zuò dìtiě qù, tài máfan. Zěnme bàn?
   B: **要不，**我们骑自行车去**吧**！又快又方便。
   Yàobù, wǒmen qí zìxíngchē qù ba! Yòu kuài yòu fāngbiàn.

A: If we walk, it will be too far; if we take a taxi, it will be too expensive; if we ride the subway, it will be too much trouble. What should we do?

B: Let's ride our bicycles (**as an alternative option**). It will be both fast and convenient.

要是 *yàoshì*

要是 is a conjunction; the simple translation for it is 'if'. However, it denotes several different meanings, including setting up a **condition**, describing a **hypothetical/counter-factual situation**, and indicating the **possibility of an event** (similar to 'in the event'). The main sentence may need words such as 就 and/or 会 depending on how 要是 is used in a given situation.

a. To set up a **condition**, and state what will happen if the condition is or is not met, use 要是 . . . 就 . . . . Although 就 can be interpreted as 'then', two rules must be kept in mind. First, 就 **is not optional** (even though 'then' is optional in its counterpart in English). Second, 就 must be placed **after the subject** (even though 'then' can be placed before the subject in its counterpart in English) if the main sentence needs a verb.

这座山很高，**要是**你爬到山顶上，**就**能看得很远。
Zhè zuò shān hěn gāo, yàoshì nǐ pá dào shān dǐng shàng, jiù néng kàn de hěn yuǎn.
This mountain is tall. **If** you climb to the top, you will be able to see far.

The main sentence can have an **optional 那 or 那么**. Although both 那（么） and 就 can be interpreted as '**then**', they can be used in the same sentence because they are in **different locations** in terms of **word order**.

爸爸:	**要是**明天的考试你能考得很好，**那（么）**我**就**给你买一个新电脑。
Bàba:	*Yàoshì míngtiān de kǎoshì nǐ néng kǎo de hěn hǎo, nà(me) wǒ jiù gěi nǐ mǎi yī ge xīn diànnǎo.*
妈妈:	**要是**你考得不好，**那（么）**这个周末的音乐会，你**就**不能去听。
Māma:	*Yàoshì nǐ kǎo de bù hǎo, nà(me) zhè ge zhōumò de yīnyuèhuì, nǐ jiù bù néng qù tīng.*
Father:	**If** you can do well on tomorrow's test, **then** I will buy you a new computer.
Mother:	**If** you do poorly, **then** you cannot go to the concert this weekend.

b. Similar to setting up a condition is to indicate a **possible (or probable) future situation** and what will happen if the situation becomes true. The pattern is **要是 . . . 就会 . . . .** 那（么） is optional.

(Scenario: Mr Wang answers his wife's question as to how many guests will come to their dinner party.)

小李还没有告诉我他来不来；**要是**他来，那（么）**就会**有十五个人；**要是**他跟他女朋友一起来，那（么）**就会**有十六个人。

Xiǎo Lǐ hái méiyǒu gàosù wǒ tā lái bù lái; yàoshì tā lái, nà(me) jiù huì yǒu shíwǔ ge rén; yàoshì tā gēn tā nǚ péngyǒu yīqǐ lái, nà(me) jiù huì yǒu shíliù gè rén.

Little Li has not told me whether he will come. **If** he comes, **then** there **will be** 15 people. **If** he comes with his girlfriend, **then** there **will be** 16 people.

c.   To describe a **hypothetical or imagined situation**, and what would happen in this situation, use 要是...会....

要是我是你，我**会**用别的办法处理这件事。
Yàoshì wǒ shì nǐ, wǒ huì yòng biéde bànfǎ chǔlǐ zhè jiàn shì.
If I **were** you, I **would** handle this matter with another method.

(Scenario: I did not expect that a friend with a high income should live in a very shabby house.)
要是我每个月也赚这么多钱，我**不会**住这种房子。
Yàoshì wǒ měi ge yuè yě zhuàn zhème duō qián, wǒ bú huì zhù zhè zhǒng fángzi.
If I made as much money (as you do) every month, I **would not** be living in this kind of place.

d.   To describe a **counter-factual situation** (meaning the situation is/was not true in reality), use 要是...就会...了. (了 in this pattern is necessary because it **implies a change of situation** – the situation would be or would have been different.)
It should be noted that there may not be a clear-cut distinction between a hypothetical situation and a counter-factual situation. Therefore, it is important to pay attention to the main sentence. When the main sentence indicates an **irreversible or unchangeable situation**, the use of 就会...了 **is advisable**.

(Scenario: A coworker is surprised that I live in a very shabby place. And I tell him that I cannot afford anything better. This is an **unchangeable situation**.)
要是我的薪水有你的那么高，我**就不会**住这种房子**了**。
Yàoshì wǒ de xīnshuǐ yǒu nǐ de nàme gāo, wǒ jiù bú huì zhù zhè zhǒng fángzi le.
If my salary was as high as yours, I **would not** be living in this kind of place.

(Scenario: I found out too late that Miss Wang already has a boyfriend. This is an **irreversible situation** because the invitation has already been issued.)

要是我知道李小姐已经有男朋友了，**就不会**邀请她去听音乐会**了**。

Yàoshì wǒ zhīdào Lǐ xiǎojiě yǐjīng yǒu nán péngyǒu le, jiù bú huì yāoqǐng tā qù tīng yīnyuèhuì le.

If I had known Miss Li already has a boyfriend, I **would not have** invited her to go to the concert.

e. If the main sentences in the section d examples above are **(rhetorical) questions**, 就 and 了 are not used.

A: 王小姐已经有男朋友了，你为什么还请她跟你去听音乐会？
Wáng xiǎojiě yǐjīng yǒu nán péngyǒu le, nǐ wèi shénme hái qǐng tā gēn nǐ qù tīng yīnyuèhuì?
B: **要是**我知道她已经有男朋友了，你想我还**会**请她跟我去吗？
Yàoshì wǒ zhīdào tā yǐjīng yǒu nán péngyǒu le, nǐ xiǎng wǒ hái huì qǐng tā gēn wǒ qù ma?
A: Miss Li already has a boyfriend; why did you still invite her to go to the concert with you?
B: **If** I had known she already has a boyfriend, do you think I **would** still **have invited** her to go with me?

A: 你为什么住这么小的房子？
Nǐ wèi shénme zhù zhème xiǎo de fángzi?
B: **要是**我赚的钱跟你赚的一样多，你想我**会**愿意住这种房子吗？
Yàoshì wǒ zhuàn de qián gēn nǐ zhuàn de yīyàng duō, nǐ xiǎng wǒ huì yuànyì zhù zhè zhǒng fángzi ma?
A: Why are you living in such a small house?
B: **If** I made as much money as you do, do you think I **would be** willing to live in such a place?

Related expressions

(要是) ... 的话 *yàoshì ... de huà*

In **casual speech**, 的话 is often added at the end of a 要是 sentence; in fact, when 的话 is used, **要是 becomes optional**.

(Scenario: Two friends' plan to go on a picnic might be ruined by the rain.)
A: 真糟糕！听说明天可能会下雨。
Zhēn zāogāo! Tīngshuō míngtiān kěnéng huì xià yǔ.
B: 没关系！下雨**的话**，我们**就**去看电影。不下**的话**，我们**就**按照计划去野餐。
Méi guānxi! Xià yǔ de huà, wǒmen jiù qù kàn diànyǐng. Bú xià de huà, wǒmen jiù ànzhào jìhuà qù yěcān.

A: How awful! I heard that it might rain tomorrow.

B: It's OK! **If** it rains (then) we'll go to a movie; **if** it does not rain (then) we'll go on the picnic according to our plan.

小李，你现在有没有空？有空**的话**，可不可以来帮我一个忙？(There is no 就 in the main sentence because it is a question.)

Xiǎo Lǐ, nǐ xiànzài yǒu méiyǒu kòng? Yǒu kòng de huà, kě bù kěyǐ lái bāng wǒ yī ge máng?

Little Li, are you free now? **If** you are free, can you come to help me with something?

要是 . . . 呢？ *yàoshì . . . ne*

The translation of 要是 . . . 呢？ is 'what if?'; therefore, there is **no main sentence** because it is understood from the context. There are two variations: **要是 . . . 的话呢？** and **. . . 的话呢？**

(Scenario: A workplace-related situation.)

经理：　请你去问王先生愿不愿意负责做这件事；**(要是)**他愿意**的话**，下个月我**会**给他加薪。

Jīnglǐ:　*Qǐng nǐ qù wèn Wáng xiānsheng yuàn bú yuànyì fùzé zuò zhè jiàn shì; (yàoshì) tā yuànyì de huà, xià ge yuè wǒ huì gěi tā jiāxī.*

助理：　**(要是)**他不愿意**的话呢**？

Zhùlǐ:　*(Yàoshì) tā bú yuànyì de huà ne?*

经理：　那**就**只好请你做了。

Jīnglǐ:　*Nà jiù zhǐhǎo qǐng nǐ zuò le.*

Manager:　Please go and ask Mr Wang if he is willing to be in charge of this matter. **If** he is willing, I **will** give him a salary raise next month.

Assistant:　**What if** he is not willing?

Manager:　**Then** I will have no other choice but to ask you to do it.

要是 used in all the above patterns can be interchangeable with **如果** (*rúguǒ*).

要不是 . . . (的话) *yào bú shì . . . (de huà)*

a. What follows **要不是** is a **fact**. This phrase is used to **hypothesize or imagine** what might happen (or what might have happened) **if this fact were not true**.

要不是机票太贵，我一定**会**每年都回家跟家人一起过年。

Yào bú shì jīpiào tài guì, wǒ yīdìng huì měi nián dōu huíjiā gēn jiārén yīqǐ guò nián.

If it were not for the fact that the air fare is too expensive, I definitely **would** go home every year to celebrate the new year with my family.

要不是早上接到一个打错的电话，我今天可能又**会**睡过头。

Yào bú shì zǎoshàng jiēdào yī ge dǎ cuò de diànhuà, wǒ jīntiān kěnéng yòu huì shuì guòtóu.

If it were not for the fact that I received a wrong-number phone call this morning, I probably **would have** overslept again today.

b.   **A person** (either a proper noun or a pronoun) can **follow 要不是** in this pattern.

(Scenario: Little Li once saved my life.)

要不是小李**(的话)**，我**早就**没命了。

Yào bú shì Xiǎo Lǐ (de huà), wǒ zǎo jiù méi mìng le.

If it weren't for Little Li, I **would have been** long dead.

万一 *wànyī*

万一 and 要是 are similar in meaning when both are used to indicate **the possibility** of something happening **in the future**, but 万一 is used when there is **only a slim possibility**. It is often translated as 'in case' because the possibility is very small.

→ See 万一 (*wànyī*) for more information.

一个人 *yī ge rén*

一个人 is a deceptively easy expression due to its seemingly obvious meaning. Its various uses often escape the attention of learners. In actuality, it is a versatile expression that has different interpretations in different contexts.

a.   一个人 can be used as the **subject of a sentence** to make a **general statement**. Although it can be literally translated as 'a person', it implies '**anyone**'.

中国是世界上人口最多的国家；**一个人**只要去过中国，就会知道人口太多会造成哪些问题。

Zhōngguó shì shìjiè shàng rénkǒu zuì duō de guójiā; yī ge rén zhǐyào qù guo Zhōngguó, jiù huì zhīdào rénkǒu tài duō huì zàochéng nǎ xiē wèntí.

China is the most populous country in the world; as long as **a person** has been to China, he would have realized what kind of problems can be created by an excessively large population.

财富不如健康重要；**一个人**如果只有财富，没有健康，他的生活品质还是很差。

Cáifù bùrú jiànkāng zhòngyào; yī ge rén rúguǒ zhǐ yǒu cáifù, méiyǒu jiànkāng, tā de shēnghuó pǐnzhì háishì hěn chà.

Wealth is not as important as health. If **a person** only has wealth without health, the quality of his life will still be poor.

聪明、漂亮不是最重要的，**一个人**一定要谦虚，因为没有人喜欢跟骄傲的人做朋友。

Cōngmíng, piàoliàng bú shì zuì zhòngyào de; yī ge rén yīdìng yào qiānxū, yīnwèi méiyǒu rén xǐhuān gēn jiāo'ào de rén zuò péngyǒu.

Being smart and pretty is not the most important (thing). **One** must be humble because no one likes to be friends with arrogant people.

b. To indicate '**someone**' (meaning '**a certain person**'), one should use 有 一个人 as the **subject** and 一个人 as the **object of the verb**. 一 in this pattern can be a different number, e.g. 两个人, 三个人, etc.

(Scenario: After counting the homework assignments the students have turned in, the teacher believes that one student did not turn in their homework. But Student Li corrects the teacher's mistake.)

老师: **有一个人**没有交功课；是谁？ (有 is not optional.)
Lǎoshī: *Yǒu yī ge rén méiyǒu jiāo gōngkè, shì shéi?*
李: 老师，今天**有一个人**没有来上课。
Lǐ: *Lǎoshī, jīntiān yǒu yī ge rén méiyǒu lái shàngkè.*
Teacher: **One person (Someone)** did not turn in homework. Who is it?
Li: Teacher, **one person (someone)** is absent today.

昨天我在校园里骑自行车，不小心撞到了**一个人**，还好那个人没有受伤。

Zuótiān wǒ zài xiàoyuán lǐ qí zìxíngchē, bù xiǎoxīn zhuàng dào le yī ge rén, háihǎo nà ge rén méiyǒu shòushāng.

Yesterday I was riding my bicycle on campus, and I accidentally hit **a person (someone)**; fortunately, the person was not hurt.

c. In certain contexts, 一 in 一个人 means '**each**'. Although it can serve as the **subject** of the sentence, the implication is that '**each person**' is **a member of a large group**. Therefore, 有 **cannot be used**.

In addition, 一个人 is used this way to describe some kind of **allotment**. Therefore, it can be replaced with **每个人**, and an expression involving **a number** should follow 一个人.

妈妈: 我把蛋糕切成了八块，(我们)**一个人**可以吃一块。
Māma: *Wǒ bǎ dàngāo qiē chéng le bā kuài, (wǒmen) yī ge rén kěyǐ chī yī kuài.*
爸爸: 可是我们家只有七个人，所以**有一个人**可以吃两块，对吗？ (有 in 有一个人 is not optional.)
Bàba: *Kěshì wǒmen jiā zhǐ yǒu qī ge rén, suǒyǐ yǒu yī ge rén kěyǐ chī liǎng kuài, duì ma?*
Mother: I have cut the cake into eight pieces; **each** (of us) can have one piece.
Father: But there are only seven people in our family, so **someone** can eat two pieces; is that right?

老师:　　　现在我给你们**一个人**一张表，请你们把这张表填一下。

Lǎoshī:　　*Xiànzài wǒ gěi nǐmen yī ge rén yī zhāng biǎo, qǐng nǐmen bǎ zhè zhāng biǎo tián yīxià.*

Teacher:　　Now I will give **each of you** a form. Please fill it out.

(Scenario: Two people are looking at a family photograph of their friend, Wang Zhong. In the photo, six people are standing in front of a very big house.)

A:　王中家很大，有五个房间，所以他家**一个人**有一个房间。

Wáng Zhōng jiā hěn dà, yǒu wǔ ge fángjiān, suǒyǐ tā jiā yī ge rén yǒu yī ge fángjiān.

B:　可是这张照片里有六个人。

Kěshì zhè zhāng zhàopiàn lǐ yǒu liù ge rén.

A:　那是因为**有一个人**是他们邻居的小孩。

Nà shì yīnwèi yǒu yī ge rén shì tāmen línjū de xiǎohái.

A:　Wang Zhong's house is big. There are five bedrooms, so in his family, **each** person has a bedroom.

B:　But there are six people in this photograph.

A:　That is because **one person** (in the photo) is their neighbor's child.

d.　一个人 can be an **adverb**, meaning 'alone' or 'by oneself' (without company). When used this way, it must appear **before the verb** (or verbal phrase).

最近我男朋友很忙，没有时间陪我，所以我常常**一个人**吃饭，**一个人**去看电影。

Zuìjìn wǒ nán péngyǒu hěn máng, méiyǒu shíjiān péi wǒ; suǒyǐ wǒ chángcháng yī ge rén chī fàn, yī ge rén qù kàn diànyǐng.

Recently my boyfriend has been busy, and he has not had time to keep me company. So I often eat **alone** and go to movies **alone**.

A:　这个月我爸妈出国了，我**一个人**在家，觉得有点寂寞。

Zhè ge yuè wǒ bàmā chū guó le, wǒ yī ge rén zài jiā, juéde yǒudiǎn jìmò.

B:　我的家人都在美国，我**一个人**在北京，所以我已经习惯**一个人**过日子了。

Wǒ de jiārén dōu zài Měiguó, wǒ yī ge rén zài Běijīng, suǒyǐ wǒ yǐjīng xíguàn yī ge rén guò rìzi le.

A:　This month my parents are overseas. I am home **by myself**; I feel a little bit lonely.

B:　All my family members are in the U.S. I am in Beijing **by myself**, so I've already got used to living my daily life **alone**.

Note that the expression can also be 自己一个人, and some may even use 自己 (*zìjǐ*). However, 自己 really means 'oneself', whereas 一个人 means 'by oneself'.

→ See 自己 (*zìjǐ*) for related information.

e. The expression '一个人(就) + **verb**' can be considered a combination of the above two uses in sections c. and d. ('**alone**' and '**each**') in certain contexts. 就 **implies a large quantity or amount**.

(Scenario: A man invited some friends to his house to have beer and watch a ball game together while his wife was not home.)

女:　　　这里有十个啤酒瓶，你一共请了几个朋友来？
Nǚ:　　*Zhèlǐ yǒu shí ge píjiǔ píng, nǐ yīgòng qǐng le jǐ ge péngyǒu lái?*
男:　　　请了五个。
Nán:　　*Qǐng le wǔ ge.*
女:　　　那么**一个人**喝了两瓶，对不对？
Nǚ:　　*Nàme yī ge rén hē le liǎng píng, duì bú duì?*
男:　　　不完全对。**有一个人**身体不好，所以医生叫他别喝酒。其他的人**一个人**喝了两瓶，我**一个人**喝了四瓶。
Nán:　　*Bù wánquán duì. Yǒu yī ge rén shēntǐ bù hǎo, suǒyǐ yīshēng jiào tā bié hē jiǔ. Qítā de rén yī ge rén hē le liǎng píng, wǒ yī ge rén hē le sì píng.*
女:　　　什么？你**一个人就**喝了四瓶？
Nǚ:　　*Shénme? Nǐ yī ge rén jiù hē le sì píng?*
Woman:　There are ten beer bottles here. How many people did you invite?
Man:　　I invited five.
Woman:　Then **each person** had two bottles; is that right?
Man:　　It's not completely right. **One person** was in poor health, so his doctor had told him not to drink. **Each** of the other people had two bottles; I **alone** had four.
Woman:　What? You had four bottles **all by yourself**?

A:　妈妈包的饺子，被小中**一个人**吃完了；爸爸没有吃到饺子，所以他很不高兴。
　　Māma bāo de jiǎozi, bèi Xiǎozhōng yī ge rén chī wán le; bàba méiyǒu chī dào jiǎozi, suǒyǐ tā hěn bù gāoxìng.
B:　什么？小中**一个人就**吃了一百个饺子？
　　Shénme? Xiǎozhōng yī ge rén jiù chī le yībǎi ge jiǎozi?
A:　All the dumplings mother made were finished by Xiaozhong (**alone**). His father did not get to eat any, so he was unhappy.
B:　What? Xiaozhong ate 100 dumplings **all by himself**?

f. '**你/我/他** + **一个人的** (+ **noun**)' indicates that something (the noun) **belongs to a certain person** and **that person alone**.

(Scenario: A couple has divorced and the woman refuses to let her former husband visit their child because he has not paid child support.)

男:　　　孩子不是**你一个人的**，我为什么不能看他？
Nán:　　*Háizi bú shì nǐ yī ge rén de, wǒ wèi shénme bù néng kàn tā?*

女:　　　那为什么养这个孩子是**我一个人的**责任呢？

Nǚ:　　*Nà wèi shénme yǎng zhè ge háizi shì wǒ yī ge rén de zérèn ne?*

Man:　　The child is not **yours alone**. Why can't I see him?

Woman:　Then why is it that raising the child is **my responsibility alone**?

(Scenario: A manager is angry about the failure of a project and is about to fire both people working on it. But Mr Wang says that he is the only one responsible for the failure.)

王:　　　这件事是**我一个人的**错，把我**一个人**解雇吧，请你不要怪李先生。

Wáng:　*Zhè jiàn shì shì wǒ yī ge rén de cuò, bǎ wǒ yī ge rén jiěgù ba, qǐng nǐ bú yào guài Lǐ xiānsheng.*

Wang:　　This whole thing is **my fault and mine alone**. Fire **only** me (**and no one else**). Please do not blame Mr Li.

一点 **yīdiǎn and related expressions**

There are several words in Chinese that can be translated as 'a little' or 'a little bit' in English. These words include 一点, 有一点, 一点也 (or 都) 不, and 一下. Despite their similarities in both Chinese and English translations, these words have distinctly different uses and grammatical features. Learners who are English speakers often find the distinctions among these words a source of confusion. Comparisons and contrasts between these words are the focus in this section.

There are **several variations to** 一点. An optional 儿 can be added after it; also, 一 can be optional. Consequently, 一点儿, 一点, 点儿 and even simply 点 have the same meaning.

a.　**一点 + noun**

(i)　When 一点 appears before a noun, it is used to refer to a **small amount** of something that is usually **uncountable** (e.g. time, water).

(Scenario: A husband is going to a company party. His wife reminds him not to drink any alcohol.)

妻子:　　别喝酒！你喝了**一点酒**就会想睡觉；别忘了，你得开车回
　　　　　家，所以你不可以喝酒。

Qīzi:　*Bié hē jiǔ! Nǐ hē le yīdiǎn jiǔ jiù huì xiǎng shuìjiào; bié wàng le, nǐ děi kāi chē huí jiā, suǒyǐ nǐ bù kěyǐ hē jiǔ.*

Wife:　　Don't drink! After you drink **a little alcohol**, you will become sleepy (feel like sleeping). Don't forget that you have to drive home, so you cannot drink.

小李，可不可以借我**一点钱**？明天是我女朋友的生日，我得买**一点东西**送她。

Xiǎo Lǐ, kě bù kěyǐ jiè wǒ yīdiǎn qián? Míngtiān shì wǒ nǚ péngyǒu de shēngrì, wǒ děi mǎi yīdiǎn dōngxi sòng tā.

Little Li, can you loan me **a little money**? Tomorrow is my girlfriend's birthday; I have to buy **a little something** for her.

(ii) The noun following 一点 can be omitted when it is clear from the context. In this case, 一点 is considered a pronoun.

昨天王太太请客，她做了十几个菜，我每道菜都只吃了**一点**就饱了。后来因为剩下的菜太多了，所以每个客人都带了**一点**回家。

Zuótiān Wáng tàitai qǐng kè, tā zuò le shí jǐ ge cài, wǒ měi dào cài dōu zhǐ chī le yīdiǎn jiù bǎo le. Hòulái yīnwèi shèngxià de cài tài duō le, suǒyǐ měi ge kèrén dōu dài le yīdiǎn huí jiā.

Yesterday Mrs Wang invited people to dinner; she made more than ten dishes. I only ate **a little** of each dish and I was full. Later, because there was too much left over, every guest took **a little (leftover food)** home.

(iii) In communication, it is possible that 一点 **does not literally mean 'a little'**, but serves the **pragmatic function** of softening the tone to make the speaker **sound more polite or more subtle**.

(Scenario: A hostess is talking to a visitor from out of town. Note that 一点 used in their interaction can be literally interpreted as 'a little' in some sentences and serves the pragmatic function in some others.)

主人:　你想喝**点**什么？茶还是咖啡？我们都有。(点 is to soften the tone.)

Zhǔrén:　Nǐ xiǎng hē diǎn shénme? Chá háishì kāfēi, wǒmen dōu yǒu.

客人:　是吗？那我喝杯咖啡吧！

Kèrén:　Shì ma? Nà wǒ hē bēi kāfēi ba!

主人:　好！你的咖啡要不要加糖和牛奶？

Zhǔrén:　Hǎo! Nǐ de kāfēi yào bú yào jiā táng hé niúnǎi?

客人:　我不习惯喝黑咖啡，所以牛奶和糖都要**一点**。(一点 means 'a little bit'.)

Kèrén:　Wǒ bù xíguàn hē hēi kāfēi, suǒyǐ niúnǎi hé táng dōu yào yīdiǎn. (The host begins to pour milk into the guest's coffee cup.)

客人:　不要太多，**一点**就可以了。(一点 means 'a little bit'.)

Kèrén:　Bú yào tài duō, yīdiǎn jiù kěyǐ le. (Presently the host and the guest are chatting while having coffee.)

主人:　好久不见了。这次为什么到上海来？

Zhǔrén:　Hǎo jiǔ bú jiàn le. Zhè cì wèi shénme dào Shànghǎi lái?

客人:　公司派我来办**一点**事。(The guest presents a gift he has brought with him.) 对了，这是**一点**小意思。

Kèrén:　Gōngsī pài wǒ lái bàn yīdiǎn shì. Duì le, zhè shì yīdiǎn xiǎo yìsi.

主人:　啊！你太客气了。

Zhǔrén:　À! Nǐ tài kèqì le.

Hostess:　What would you like to drink? Tea or coffee? We have both.

Guest:　Is that so? Then why don't I have a cup of coffee!

Hostess: OK! Do you want sugar and milk with your coffee?

Guest: I am not used to drinking black coffee, so I would like to have **a little bit** of each.

Guest: Not too much. Only **a little bit** will be fine.

Hosted: Long time no see. Why did you come to Shanghai this time?

Guest: My company sent me here to handle **a little** company business. By the way, this is **a little bit** of something (a little token) for you.

Hostess: Ah! You are too nice.

(Scenario: A man is offering a friend an opportunity to earn extra money. Although 一点 in each sentence can be literally translated as 'a little', its real function is to soften the tone so that the speaker may **sound subtler**. From the interaction it is clear that the actual amount of either money or time is quite a lot, not just a little.)

A: 想不想赚**点**外快？

    Xiǎng bù xiǎng zhuàn diǎn wàikuài?

B: 多少？要不要花很多时间？

    Duōshǎo? Yào bú yào huā hěn duō shíjiān?

A: 钱是不少，有一万多，可是的确要花**点**时间。

    Qián shì bù shǎo, yǒu yī wàn duō, kěshì díquè yào huā diǎn shíjiān.

A: Would you like to make **a little** extra money?

B: How much? Would it require a lot of time?

A: Although it's quite a lot of money, over 10,000 *kuai*, it does indeed require **a little** time.

b.   **一点点** + noun
一点点 is used in **casual speech** and it means a **'very small'** amount. It usually refers to the actual amount, although occasionally one might use it for its pragmatic function of softening the tone.

(Scenario: A woman opens the door and sees an old friend who unexpectedly comes to visit from out of town.)

主人: 哎呀！好久不见！快进来坐。

Zhǔrén: *Àiya! Hǎo jiǔ bú jiàn! Kuài jìn lái zuò.*

客人: 今天来这里办**一点**事，办了事还有**一点点**时间，所以来看您。

Kèrén: *Jīntiān lái zhèlǐ bàn yīdiǎn shì; bàn le shì hái yǒu yīdiǎndiǎn shíjiān, suǒyǐ lái kàn nín.* (After sitting down, the guest presents an expensive gift basket to the hostess.)

客人: 上次您帮了我这么大的忙，这是**一点(点)**小东西，请收下。

Kèrén: *Shàng cì nín bāng le wǒ zhème dà de máng, zhè shì yīdiǎn(diǎn) xiǎo dōngxi, qǐng shōuxià.*

主人: 你太客气了。我刚烧了一锅绿豆汤，要不要喝**一点**？

Zhǔrén: *Nǐ tài kèqì le. Wǒ gāng shāo le yī guō lǜdōu tāng, yào bú yào hē yīdiǎn?*

客人:	好啊！您的绿豆汤最有名。不过我尝**一点点**就好，我刚吃过午饭。
Kèrén:	*Hǎo a! Nín de lǜdòu tāng zuì yǒumíng. Búguò wǒ cháng yīdiǎndiǎn jiù hǎo, wǒ gāng chī guo wǔfàn.*
Hostess:	Oh! Long time no see! Hurry and come in and have a seat.
Guest:	Today I came into town for **a little** business. After I was finished, I still had **a little bit of** time, so I came to visit you.
Guest:	Last time you did me such a big favor; this is **a little bit** of something. Please accept it.
Hostess:	You are too nice. I just made a pot of mung bean soup. Would you like to have **some** (literally: **a little**)?
Guest:	OK! Your mung bean soup is the most famous. But I will only taste **a little bit** as I just ate lunch.

c. **adjective + 一点**

When 一点 follows an adjective, the meaning '**a little more**' is implied.

(Scenario: A girl is crying because she has made some careless mistakes, which resulted in a bad test score.)

妈妈:	好了，别哭了。下次**小心一点**，就一定可以考得**好一点**了。
Māma:	*Hǎo le, bié kū le. Xià cì xiǎoxīn yīdiǎn, jiù yīdìng kěyǐ kǎo de hǎo yīdiǎn le.*
Mother:	That's enough! Don't cry anymore. Next time, just be **a little more careful**, and you definitely can do **a little better**.

(Scenario: A group of students is talking loudly in a library. The librarian asks them to **quiet down**.)

请你们**安静一点**。(or 请你们**小声一点**。)

Qǐng nǐmen ānjìng yīdiǎn. (or Qǐng nǐmen xiǎoshēng yīdiǎn.)

Please be **a little quieter**. (or: Please be **a little less loud**.)

d. **adjective + 了 + (一)点**

If 了 follows the adjective before 一点, then **a comparison is no longer implied**. Instead, 太 (*tài:* too) **is implied**; in fact, the pattern can also be '太 **adjective** 了一点'.

(Scenario: A couple are shopping at an outdoor market. They see something they like but they want to bargain for a better price.)

A:	怎么样？喜欢不喜欢？
	Zěnme yàng? Xǐhuān bù xǐhuān?
B:	喜欢，可是我觉得**(太)贵了一点**。
	Xǐhuān, kěshì wǒ juéde (tài) guì le yīdiǎn.
A:	那我去问那个摊贩，可不可以**便宜一点**？
	Nà wǒ qù wèn nà ge tānfàn, kě bù kěyǐ piányí yīdiǎn?

A: What do you think? Do you like it?

B: I do, but I think it is **a little bit too expensive**.

A: Then I will go ask the vendor if it can be **a little cheaper** (if he can **charge a little less**.)

(Scenario: A wife likes to try out new recipes, and asks her husband for his comments. Today she has made mung bean soup.)

女: 今天的绿豆汤好不好喝？

Nǚ: *Jīntiān de lǜdōu tāng hǎo bù hǎohē?*

男: 不错，不过(**太**)**甜**了**一点**。

Nán :   *Búcuò, búguò (tài) tián le yīdiǎn.*

女: 是吗？可能糖放得(**太**)**多**了**一点**。

Nǚ: *Shì ma? Kěnéng táng fàng de (tài) duō le yīdiǎn.*

男: 对，如果糖**少一点**，那会更好喝。

Nán :   *Duì, rúguǒ táng shǎo yīdiǎn, nà huì gèng hǎohē.*

Woman: Is the mung bean soup I made today delicious?

Man: Not bad, but it is **a bit too sweet**.

Woman: Is that so? Maybe I put **a little bit too much** sugar.

Man: That's right. If there were **a little less** sugar, it would be even more delicious.

e.   **有(一)点 + adjective**

有 in 有一点 **does not literally mean 'to have'** when it is followed by an adjective. It can be interpreted as either '**a little bit**' or '**somewhat**'. The expression can also be 有一点点, which literally means 'very little bit'. In addition, 一 is optional.

The adjective following 有一点 often, albeit not always, **implies a negative feeling or situation**.

A: 我肚子**有(一)点饿**了，我们找家饭馆吃饭吧！
Wǒ dùzi yǒu(yī)diǎn è le, wǒmen zhǎo jiā fànguǎn chī fàn ba!

B: 长江饭馆就在前面，去那里吃吧！
Chāngjiāng fànguǎn jiù zài qiánmiàn, qù nàlǐ chī ba!

A: 我觉得长江饭馆**有一点贵**，找一家**便宜一点**的吧！
Wǒ juéde Chāngjiāng fànguǎn yǒu(yī)diǎn guì, zhǎo yī jiā piányí yīdiǎn de ba!

A: I am **a little hungry** now. Let's find a restaurant to eat.

B: Changjiang Restaurant is right down the street. Let's go there to eat.

A: I think Changjiang Restaurant is **a little pricey**. Let's find one that is **a little cheaper**.

When the adjective following 有一点 is **a negative word**, e.g. 不高兴 (*bù gāoxìng*: unhappy), 不习惯 (*bù xíguàn*: unaccustomed), etc., the expression is similar to '**不太 + adjective**', but the adjective after 不太 is in the positive form.

今天我们九点半就开始上课了，可是王文生十点才来，所以老师**有一点
不**高兴(or 老师**不太**高兴)。

*Jīntiān wǒmen jiǔdiǎn bàn jiù kāishǐ shàng kè le, kěshì Wáng Wénshēng
shídiǎn cái lái, suǒyǐ lǎoshī yǒu yīdiǎn bù gāoxìng (or lǎoshī bú tài gāoxìng).*

Today we started class at 9:30, but Wang Wensheng did not arrive until 10:00,
so the teacher was **a little upset** (or: the teacher was **not very happy** about it).

A: 你来北京半年了，习惯了吗?
   Nǐ lái Běijīng bàn nián le, xíguàn le ma?
B: 还是**有一点不**习惯(or 还是**不太**习惯)。
   Háishì yǒu yīdiǎn bù xíguàn (or háishì bú tài xíguàn).
A: You have been in Beijing for half a year. Are you used to it now?
B: I am still **a little unused to** everything here (or: I am still **not quite
   used to** it).

f. **有 + (一)点 + noun**
Sometimes, 有一点 is **followed by a noun**. This is because **有 literally
means 'to have'**.

(Scenario: There is still five minutes before the class is over.)
老师: 我们还**有一点时间**，有问题的人，可以现在问我。
Lǎoshī: *Wǒmen hái yǒu yīdiǎn shíjiān; yǒu wèntí de rén, kěyǐ
            xiànzài wèn wǒ.*
王同学: 老师，我觉得这课的语法**有(一)点难**，我可不可以下午
            到您的办公室去问您?
Wáng tóngxué: *Lǎoshī, wǒ juéde zhè kè de yǔfǎ yǒu (yī) diǎn nán; wǒ kě
            bù kěyǐ xiàwǔ dào nín de bàngōngshì qù wèn nín?*
老师: 今天下午我**有一点事**，请你明天上午来吧!
Lǎoshī: *Jīntiān xiàwǔ wǒ yǒu yīdiǎn shì, qǐng nǐ míngtiān shàngwǔ
            lái ba!*
Teacher: We still **have a little time**. Those who have questions can
            ask me now.
Student Wang: Sir, I think the grammar in this lesson **is a little difficult**
            (= **hard to understand**). May I come to your office in the
            afternoon to ask you (about it)?
Teacher: I have **a little business** (= I have to attend to **something**).
            Why don't you come tomorrow morning!

g. **一点也(or 都)不 + adjective**
This is an **emphatic expression**; it means '**not at all**' because 连 (*lián*:
even) is implied but omitted. The literal meaning is '**not even a little bit**'.
也 and 都 are interchangeable; 一 **is no longer optional**.

A **common mistake** made by learners is to misinterpret it as meaning
simply 'a little'. The contrast between the two is illustrated in the following
examples.

A: 这个大都市交通又挤又乱；我走在路上的时候，常常觉得**一点也不**安全。
Zhè ge dà dūshì jiāotōng yòu jǐ yòu luàn; wǒ zǒu zài lù shàng de shíhòu, chángcháng juéde yīdiǎn yě bù ānquán.

B: 那可能是因为你刚搬来这里。
Nà kěnéng shì yīnwèi nǐ gāng bān lái zhèlǐ.

C: 我在这里已经住了十年了，可是我走在路上的时候，也会觉得**有一点不**安全。
Wǒ zài zhèlǐ yǐjīng zhù le shí nián le, kěshì wǒ zǒu zài lù shàng de shíhòu, yě huì juéde yǒu yīdiǎn bù ānquán.

A: Traffic in this big city is both crowded and chaotic. When I am walking on the street, I often feel **not** safe **at all** (= don't feel safe at all).

B: That is probably because you only just moved here.

C: I have been living here for ten years, but when I am walking on the street, I also feel **a little unsafe**.

A: 明天就要考试了，大家都紧张得要命，你怎么好像**一点都不**紧张？
Míngtiān jiù yào kǎoshì le, dàjiā dōu jǐnzhāng de yàomìng, nǐ zěnme hǎoxiàng yīdiǎn dōu bù jǐnzhāng?

B: 其实我也**有一点**紧张，这么重要的考试，谁会不紧张？
Qíshí wǒ yě yǒu yīdiǎn jǐnzhāng, zhème zhòngyào de kǎoshì, shéi huì bù jǐnzhāng?

A: The exam is tomorrow. Everybody is nervous to death. How come you **don't** seem to be nervous **at all**?

B: Actually, I am also **a little bit** nervous. It is such an important exam; who would not be nervous?

h. **一点 + noun + 也 (or 都) + negative word**
This is also an **emphatic expression**, meaning '**not at all**'.

A: 你对外国电影有没有兴趣？
Nǐ duì wàiguó diànyǐng yǒu méiyǒu xìngqù?

B: **一点**兴趣**也没有**。
Yīdiǎn xìngqù yě méiyǒu.

A: Are you interested in foreign films? (Do you have any interest in foreign films?)

B: I am **not** interested **at all**. (I have **no interest at all**.)

A: 我今天**有一点不**舒服，所以从早上到现在，**一点**东西**都没有**吃。
Wǒ jīntiān yǒu yīdiǎn bù shūfú, suǒyǐ cóng zǎoshàng dào xiànzài, yīdiǎn dōngxi dōu méiyǒu chī.

B: 哎呀！那你现在快吃**一点**东西。
Àiya! Nà nǐ xiànzài kuài chī yīdiǎn dōngxi.

A: 可是我**一点**胃口**也没有**。
Kěshì wǒ yīdiǎn wèikǒu yě méiyǒu.

B: 那至少得喝(一)点汤，我想你喝了以后就会觉得**好一点**了。
Nà zhìshǎo děi hē (yī)diǎn tāng, wǒ xiǎng nǐ hē le yǐhòu jiù huì juéde hǎo yīdiǎn le.

A: Today I feel **a little unwell (sick)**. So I have **not** eaten **anything at all** from morning till now.

B: Oh no! Then have **a little** (something) to eat now.

A: But I have **no** appetite **at all**.

B: Then you must at least have **a little** soup. I think you will feel **a little better** after you have had the soup.

→ See 些 (*xiē*) for related information.

一定 *yīdìng*

一定 has two basic definitions: 'must' and 'definitely'. Because of the vagueness of these definitions, learners often misuse it. The following discussions include the proper use of 一定 in various contexts as well as other expressions related to 一定.

a. 一定 can be used to indicate **an inference** one makes based on one's observation, or information one gathers. This means one has **reason enough to believe something** is true although it is not confirmed.

昨天我看到王小英跟一个男的牵着手去看电影，那个男的**一定**是她男朋友。
Zuótiān wǒ kàndào Wáng Xiǎoyīng gēn yī ge nán de qiān zhe shǒu qù kàn diànyǐng, nà ge nán de yīdìng shì tā nán péngyǒu.
Yesterday I saw Wang Xiaoying and a man going to a movie hand in hand. That man **must be** her boyfriend.

A: 小李一向准时，现在已经这么晚了，他还没来，**一定**出问题了！
Xiǎo Lǐ yīxiàng zhǔnshí, xiànzài yǐjīng zhème wǎn le, tā hái méi lái, yīdìng chū wèntí le.

B: 你放心，他这几天都很晚上床睡觉，我看他**一定**睡过头了！
Nǐ fàngxīn, tā zhè jǐ tiān dōu hěn wǎn shàng chuáng shuìjiào, wǒ kàn tā yīdìng shuì guò tóu le.

A: Little Li has always been punctual. It's already so late now, but he has not come. Something **must be** wrong.

B: Don't worry! He has been going to bed very late these days. I think he **must have** overslept.

b. A modal particle 吧 can be used at the end of the sentence in **conversational speech**. 吧 used in this pattern **softens the tone** and thus either makes the inference a **less strong assumption** or makes the speaker sound **more polite**.

(Scenario: A man apologizes to his date for having kept her waiting.)

男:　　对不起，让你站着等了那么久，你**一定**累了**吧**！

Nán:　*Duìbuqǐ, ràng nǐ zhàn zhe děng le nàme jiǔ, nǐ yīdìng lèi le ba!*

女:　　没关系，今天路上车**一定**很多**吧**！

Nǚ:　*Méi guānxì, jīntiān lùshàng chē yīdìng hěn duō ba!*

Man:　　Sorry to have kept you waiting while standing for so long. You **must be** tired!

Woman:　It's OK. Traffic **must have been** bad (lots of cars on the street) today.

With the use of 吧, **一定 becomes optional**, but its meaning is still implied.

A:　　现在在跟王中跳舞的那个女的是不是他女朋友？

　　　Xiànzài zài gēn Wáng Zhōng tiàowǔ de nà ge nǚ de shì bú shì tā nǚ péngyǒu?

B:　　不是**吧**！那个女的那么老，**一定不是**他的女朋友。

　　　Búshì ba! Nà ge nǚ de nàme lǎo, yīdìng bú shì tā de nǚ péngyǒu.

A:　　Is the woman dancing with Wang Zhong now his girlfriend?

B:　　It's **doubtful**! That woman is so old; she **definitely is not (cannot possibly be)** his girlfriend.

c.　　一定 can indicate an action or event that is **bound to happen**. It can also be translated as '**certainly**'.

哎呀！天色这么黑，等一下**一定**会下雨。

Āiya! Tiānsè zhème hēi, děng yīxià yīdìng huì xiàyǔ.

Oh! The sky is so dark! It will **definitely** rain later.

A:　　明天晚上八点在我家有一个聚会，我打算做几个菜，你来不来？

　　　Míngtiān wǎnshàng bā diǎn zài wǒ jiā yǒu yī ge jùhuì, wǒ dǎsuàn zuò jǐ ge cài, nǐ lái bù lái?

B:　　是吗？你做菜？那我**一定**来。

　　　Shì ma? Nǐ zuò cài? Nà wǒ yīdìng lái.

A:　　Tomorrow evening at eight o'clock there is a get-together at my house. I plan to make a few dishes. Will you come?

B:　　Is that so? You will cook? Then I will **definitely (certainly)** come.

d.　　To indicate **obligation, duty or necessity**, it is necessary to have 要 or 得 after 一定. However, 一定 in 一定要 or 一定得 **is optional**; 要 or 得 is sufficient in conveying the meaning. On the other hand, **一定 alone is not sufficient**.

　　　Learners who are English speakers often make the mistake of using simply 一定 (without 要 or 得) to indicate obligation or necessity. The

source of this **common mistake** is perhaps the under-differentiation of
the **two different uses (inference and obligation)** of the word '**must**' in
English.

(Scenario: A teacher urges a student to study hard. Note that the two 一定
have different implications.)

老师:	上次考试，你考得很差。今天晚上，你**一定要**好好地准备明天的考试。
Lǎoshī:	*Shàng cì kǎoshì, nǐ kǎo de hěn chà. Jīntiān wǎnshàng, nǐ yīdìng yào hǎo hǎo de zhǔnbèi míngtiān de kǎoshì.*
学生:	您放心，最近我很努力，我相信明天的考试我**一定**能考得很好。
Xuésheng:	*Nín fàngxīn, zuìjìn wǒ hěn nǔlì, wǒ xiāngxìn míngtiān de kǎoshì wǒ yīdìng néng kǎo de hěn hǎo.*
Teacher:	You did poorly on the test last time. This evening you **must** do a good job studying for tomorrow's test.
Student:	Don't worry. I have been studying hard lately. I believe that I **definitely** can do well on tomorrow's test.

你说话的时候，常常得罪人。以后你**一定得**多注意自己说的话。
Nǐ shuō huà de shíhòu, chángcháng dézuì rén. Yǐhòu nǐ yīdìng děi duō zhùyì zìjǐ shuō de huà.
When you speak, you often offend people. From now on, you **must** pay
more attention to what you say.

e.　**一定要** (but not 一定得) can indicate one's **determination**.

(Scenario: Li shows his determination; Zhang shows his confidence in Li.
Note that the two 一定 have different implications.)

李:	这件事不管多难，我都**一定要**做到。
Lǐ:	*Zhè jiàn shì bùguǎn duō nán, wǒ dōu yīdìng yào zuò dào.*
张:	我对你有信心，我相信你**一定**能做到。
Zhāng:	*Wǒ duì nǐ yǒu xìnxīn, wǒ xiāngxìn nǐ yīdìng néng zuò dào.*
Li:	No matter how hard this job is, I **will definitely** accomplish it.
Zhang:	I have confidence in you. I believe that you **definitely** can do it.

我在美国学了三年中文，可是我的中文还是很不好。现在我到了北京，
我**一定要**在半年内把中文学好。
Wǒ zài Měiguó xué le sān nián Zhōngwén, kěshì wǒ de Zhōngwén háishì hěn bù hǎo. Xiànzài wǒ dào le Běijīng, wǒ yīdìng yào zài bàn nián nèi bǎ Zhōngwén xué hǎo.
I have studied Chinese in the U.S. for three years, but my Chinese is still
very bad. Now I have come to Beijing, I **definitely will** master Chinese
within half a year.

Related expressions

一定的 *yīdìng de* + noun

一定的 used as a modifier before a noun indicates something that is **not clearly defined** although **definitely existent**. Therefore it is often translated as 'a certain'.

> 如果报名的人能达到**一定的**数目，那么这门课就不会被取消。
> *Rúguǒ bàomíng de rén néng dádào yīdìng de shùmù, nàme zhè mén kè jiù bú huì bèi qǔxiāo.*
> If people who sign up can reach **a certain number**, then this class will not be canceled.

Learners should pay attention to the difference in meaning (as well as word order) of the two 一定 in the following two examples:

> 每年的雨量跟农作物的收成有**一定的**关系。(一定的 is before the noun 关系.)
> *Měi nián de yǔliàng gēn nóngzuòwù de shōuchéng yǒu yīdìng de guānxì.*
> Annual rainfall **has a certain relationship** with the harvest of agricultural crops.

> 每年的雨量跟农作物的收成**一定**有关系。(一定 is before the verb 有.)
> *Měi nián de yǔliàng gēn nóngzuòwù de shōuchéng yīdìng yǒu guānxì.*
> Annual rainfall **definitely has a relationship** with the harvest of agricultural crops.

不一定 *bù yīdìng*

不一定 indicates that 'the certainty of something is not confirmed'.

a. 不一定 can indicate something is **not always true**. It is often translated as '**not necessarily**' in this context.

> 发亮的东西**不一定**是金子。
> *Fāliàng de dōngxi bù yīdìng shì jīnzi.*
> Things that glitter are **not necessarily** gold.

> 最贵的礼物**不一定**是最好的。
> *Zuì guì de lǐwù bù yīdìng shì zuìhǎo de.*
> The most expensive gift is **not necessarily** the best.

> 财富**不一定**能保证一个人的快乐。
> *Cáifù bù yīdìng néng bǎozhèng yī ge rén de kuàilè.*
> Wealth can**not necessarily** guarantee a person's happiness.

b. 不一定 can indicate that one cannot be sure of something, or it is not clear whether something will happen.

(Scenario: Xiaozhong's mother calls him on his cell phone while he is waiting for the bus to go home.)

妈妈:	我们准备七点吃饭，你回得来吗？
Māma:	*Wǒmen zhǔnbèi qī diǎn chī fàn, nǐ huí de lái ma?*
小中:	车还没来呢，我七点**不一定**回得来。
Xiǎozhōng:	*Chē hái méi lái ne, wǒ qī diǎn bù yīdìng huí de lái.*
Mother:	We plan to have dinner at 7:00. Will you be able to come back?
Xiaozhong:	The bus has not come yet. I **am not sure** (It is **not clear**) whether I can be back by 7:00 or not. (I **may not** be able to come back by 7:00.)

A: 我要减肥，所以打算一天只吃一顿。
   Wǒ yào jiǎnféi, suǒyǐ dǎsuàn yī tiān zhǐ chī yī dùn.
B: 节食**不一定**有效，多运动比较好。
   Jiéshí bù yīdìng yǒuxiào, duō yùndòng bǐjiào hǎo.
A: I am going to lose weight. So I plan to eat only one meal a day.
B: Dieting **may not be** effective. Exercising more is better.

c. In **conversational speech**, 不一定 can be used as an **adjective** to indicate that the possibility of something happening is **not certain**. 不一定 is the **predicate** of the sentence.

A: 我相信今年我们国家的球队会得冠军。
   Wǒ xiāngxìn jīnnián wǒmen guójiā de qiúduì huì dé guànjūn.
B: 那可**不一定**。听说有几个外国的球队也很强。
   Nà kě bù yīdìng. Tīngshuō yǒu jǐ ge wàiguó de qiúduì yě hěn qiáng.
A: I believe that our country's team will win the championship this year.
B: That's **not necessarily true**! I have heard that a few foreign teams are also very good.

→ See 不见得 (*bú jiànde*) for related information.

说不定 *shuō bú dìng*

Although 说不定 is ostensibly similar to 不一定 and 一定不, its meaning is **opposite** to both. This is because 说不定 indicates that, **despite the uncertainty**, something is **likely** to be true. Therefore, it is interchangeable with words such as 可能 (*kěnéng*), 也许 (*yěxǔ*) and 或许 (*huòxǔ*).

今天下午**说不定**会下雨，你出门的时候别忘了带伞。
Jīntiān xiàwǔ shuō bú dìng huì xià yǔ, nǐ chūmén de shíhòu bié wàng le dài sǎn.
It **probably** will rain this afternoon. When you go out, don't forget to take an umbrella.

(Scenario: Four people are gossiping about Li Xiaolan's personal life. Pay attention to the different implications of the expressions involving the use of 不 and 定.)

A: 王先生是不是李小兰的男朋友？

　　Wáng xiānsheng shì bú shì Lǐ Xiǎolán de nán péngyǒu?

B: 王先生那么老，我想他**一定不**是李小兰的男朋友。

　　Wáng xiānsheng nàme lǎo, wǒ xiǎng tā yīdìng bú shì Lǐ Xiǎolán de nán péngyǒu.

C: 我觉得他**说不定**是李小兰的男朋友，因为李小兰以前的男朋友也都很老。

　　Wǒ juéde tā shuō bú dìng shì Lǐ Xiǎolán de nán péngyǒu, yīnwèi Lǐ Xiǎolán yǐqián de nán péngyǒu yě dōu hěn lǎo.

D: 虽然李小兰以前的男朋友都很老，可是王先生**不一定**是她的男朋友，因为李小兰喜欢有钱的男人，可是王先生没有钱。

　　Suīrán Lǐ Xiǎolán yǐqián de nán péngyǒu dōu hěn lǎo, kěshì Wáng xiānsheng bù yīdìng shì tā de nán péngyǒu, yīnwèi Lǐ Xiǎolán xǐhuān yǒuqián de nánrén, kěshì Wáng xiānsheng méiyǒu qián.

A: Is Mr Wang Li Xiaolan's boyfriend?

B: Mr Wang is so old. I think he **must not (is not likely to) be** her boyfriend.

C: I think **maybe** he is her boyfriend (= he **probably** is her boyfriend) because her previous boyfriends were all old.

D: Although her previous boyfriends were all old, Mr Wang is **not necessarily (may not be)** her boyfriend, because she likes rich men, but Mr Wang is not rich.

一定不可以 *yīdìng bù kěyǐ*

As stated above, to indicate **obligation or necessity**, one should use 一定要 or 一定得. However, it must be kept in mind that the **negative form** for both is 一定不可以. 一定 is optional. 一定不可以 is a **strong**er expression than 不可以.

別忘了，你**一定要**保持秘密，**一定不可以**把这件事告诉任何人。

Bié wàng le, nǐ yīdìng yào bǎochí mìmì, yīdìng bù kěyǐ bǎ zhè jiàn shì gàosù rènhé rén.

Don't forget. You **must** keep this secret. You **must not (mustn't)** tell this to anybody.

上次考试你不及格，明天的考试你**一定不可以**再考得这么差。

Shàng cì kǎoshì nǐ bù jígé, míngtiān de kǎoshì nǐ yīdìng bù kěyǐ zài kǎo de zhème chà.

You failed the test last time. You **must not (mustn't)** do so poorly again on tomorrow's test.

It should be noted that although 应该 (*yīnggāi*) or 不应该 also indicates obligation (often social or moral), **一定 should not be used with either 应该 or 不应该**. If one wishes to emphasize one's point, 绝对 (*juéduì*: absolutely), instead of 一定, is the proper choice of word before 应该 or 不应该.

爸妈要离婚不是你的错，你**(绝对)不应该**怪自己(or 你**一定不可以**怪自己)。

Bàmā yào líhūn bú shì nǐ de cuò, nǐ (juéduì) bù yīnggāi guài zìjǐ (or *nǐ yīdìng bù kěyǐ guài zìjǐ*).

Your parents' getting a divorce is not your fault. You **absolutely should not** blame yourself (or: You **must not** blame yourself).

依旧 *yījiù*

依旧 means 'still' and is interchangeable with 还是 (*háishì*) in certain patterns. 依旧 is a more formal word than 还是 and is usually used in writing, not in casual, conversational speech.

→ See 还是 (*háishì*) for more information.

一下 *yīxià*

Although 一下 can be translated as 'a little bit' in certain sentences, its real meaning is '**for a short while**'. Sometimes, it is also translated as '**quickly**' although it is **not about speed**, but about spending 'a short while' doing something.

a. **一下 immediately follows the verb** if the verb has an object that is a regular **noun** or **proper noun** (e.g. name of a person). The pattern is '**verb + 一下 + noun**'. A **common mistake** made by learners who are English speakers is to use 一点 before the noun.

(Scenario: Two parents are waiting at the dinner table for their son to come to eat.)

妈妈: 你去**叫一下**小中；我已经叫了他两次了！
Māma: *Nǐ qù jiào yīxià Xiǎozhōng; wǒ yǐjīng jiào le tā liǎng cì le.*
爸爸: 好，我去**看一下**，他在做什么？
Bàba: *Hǎo, wǒ qù kàn yīxià, tā zài zuò shénme?*
(It turns out that their son is watching TV in the living room.)
爸爸: 别看了！快来吃饭。
Bàba: *Bié kàn le! Kuài lái chī fàn.*
小中: 让我再**看一下**，看完了这个节目我就来吃。
Xiǎozhōng: *Ràng wǒ zài kàn yīxià. Kàn wán le zhè ge jiémù wǒ jiù lái chī.*

爸爸:	吃饭以前**看一下**电视是可以的，可是到了吃饭时间就不能再看了。
Bàba:	*Chī fàn yǐqián kàn yīxià diànshì shì kěyǐ de, kěshì dào le chī fàn shíjiān jiù bù néng zài kàn le.*
Mother:	Go (**quickly**) call Xiaozhong. I have already called him twice.
Father:	OK, I will go **take a quick look** (to find out) what he is doing.
Father:	Don't watch any more TV! (Hurry and) come to eat now.
Xiaozhong:	Let me **watch a little bit** longer. After I am done with this show, I will come to eat.
Father:	**Watching a little TV** before dinner is OK. But you cannot watch anymore when it is dinner time. (Do not say 看一点 电视.)

(Scenario: Two tourists cannot find where the train station is.)

A: 火车站到底在哪里？
  Huǒchē zhàn dàodǐ zài nǎlǐ?
B: 你在这里**等一下**，(pointing at someone) 我去**问一下**那个人。
  Nǐ zài zhèlǐ děng yīxià, wǒ qù wèn yīxià nà ge rén.
A: Where in the world is the train station? (or: Where exactly is the train station?)
B: You **wait** here **for a moment**. I will go and **quickly ask** that person.

b. If the object of the verb is a **pronoun**, then **一下** follows the pronoun. The pattern is '**verb + pronoun + 一下**'.

(Scenario: A young man is in financial trouble again. He needs his father's help, but cannot be sure whether he can get it. His mother gives him some advice.)

儿子:	妈，爸爸这么有钱；你可不可以去**问他一下**，愿不愿意再借我**一点**？
Érzi:	*Mā, bàba zhème yǒu qián; nǐ kě bù kěyǐ qù wèn tā yīxià, yuàn bú yuànyì zài jiè wǒ yīdiǎn?*
妈妈:	上次他就跟我说过以后不会再帮你了。可是他到底是你爸爸，你自己去**求他一下**，我想他会帮你的。
Māma:	*Shàng cì tā jiù gēn wǒ shuō guo yǐhòu bú huì zài bāng nǐ le. Kěshì tā dàodǐ shì nǐ bàba, nǐ zìjǐ qù qiú tā yīxià, wǒ xiǎng tā huì bāng nǐ de.*
Son:	Mother, Father has so much money. Can you go and **quickly ask him** if he is willing to loan me **a little (money)** again?
Mother:	Last time he already told me that he would not help you anymore. But he is your father after all. You go yourself and **beg him (plead with him) a little**; I think he will help you.

c. **一下** has the same **pragmatic functions** as **一点**; i.e. it can be used to soften the tone to make the speaker sound **less blunt**, more **subtle or more polite**.

(Scenario: A man is about to go to a company party. His wife wants to tell him not to drink, but she does not want to sound like she is nagging. 一下 is **optional** from a grammatical perspective, but makes the **tone of the utterance milder**.)

我知道你不会忘记医生的话，可是我还是要**提醒你一下**，你不可以喝酒。

Wǒ zhīdào nǐ bú huì wàngjì yīshēng de huà, kěshì wǒ háishì yào tíxǐng nǐ yīxià, nǐ bù kěyǐ hē jiǔ.

I know you would not forget the doctor's orders, but I would still like to **(quickly) remind you** that you cannot drink.

(Scenario: A workplace situation.)

A: 李小姐，你可不可以**来一下**？我的电脑又有一点问题了，我想请你**帮我一下**。(The 一下 used in these two sentences serves the **pragmatic function**.)

    Lǐ xiǎojiě, nǐ kě bù kěyǐ lái yīxià? Wǒ de diànnǎo yòu yǒu yīdiǎn wèntí le, wǒ xiǎng qǐng nǐ bāng wǒ yīxià.

B: 好，请**等一下**；我得先**去一下**洗手间。(The 一下 in these two sentences can be interpreted **literally** as 'a short while'.)

    Hǎo, qǐng děng yīxià; wǒ děi xiān qù yīxià xǐshǒujiān.

A: Miss Li, can you **come over here for a minute**? My computer has a little problem again. I would like to ask you to **help me out (for a bit)**.

B: OK, please **wait for a moment**. I have to **quickly go** to the bathroom first.

d. The verb can be reduplicated. A **reduplicated verb** is considered to be **interchangeable with 'verb + 一下'**.

If the verb has **only one character**, 一 or 了 **can be inserted** between the two verbs.

A: 你知道不知道我的中文语法书在哪里？

    Nǐ zhīdào bù zhīdào wǒ de Zhōngwén yǔfǎ shū zài nǎlǐ?

B: 你去客厅**找一下**(= 找找 = 找一找)。(一下 can both soften the tone and imply 'spending a little time'.)

    Nǐ qù kètīng zhǎo yīxià.

A: Do you know where my Chinese grammar book is?

B: Go to the living room to **look for** it.

王文生下班回到家，**换了换**(= **换了一下**)衣服，就出门去跟他女朋友约会了。

Wáng Wénshēng xià bān huí dào jiā, huàn le huàn yīfú, jiù chūmén qù gēn tā nǚ péngyǒu yuēhuì le.

After Wang Wensheng came home from work, he **quickly changed** his clothes, and immediately went on a date with his girlfriend.

一向 *yīxiàng*

→ See 向来 (*xiànglái*) for more information.

一直 *yīzhí*

一直 is an **adverb** and implies that a situation persists or remains constant **without changes**. Three of its most common uses are the focus of discussion in this section.

a. 一直 can be used to indicate one's **physical movement**. It means 'going straight without changing direction'.

> A: 请问，去火车站怎么走？
> *Qǐngwèn, qù huǒchē zhàn zěnme zǒu?*
> B: 从这里一直往前走，过了两个红绿灯就到了。
> *Cóng zhèlǐ yīzhí wàng qián zǒu, guò le liǎng ge hóng lǜ dēng jiù dào le.*
> A: Excuse me, how do I get to the train station?
> B: **Go straight** ahead from here; after you have passed two traffic lights, you will be there.

b. 一直 can indicate **doing something continuously without stopping**.

(i) If the verb indicates an action, 一直 can be replaced with **不停地** (*bùtíng de*: nonstop) or they can be used together (一直不停地).

> A: 听说王大中失业了，我要去慰问他一下。
> *Tīngshuō Wáng Dàzhōng shīyè le, wǒ yào qù wèiwèn tā yīxià.*
> B: 最好别去！他会**一直(不停地)**向你诉苦，让你觉得很不安。
> *Zuìhǎo bié qù! Tā huì yīzhí (bùtíng de) xiàng nǐ sùkǔ, ràng nǐ juéde hěn bù'ān.*
> A: I have heard that Wang Dazhong has lost his job. I am going to console him.
> B: You had better not go. He will **constantly** complain to you **(without stopping)**. It would make you feel uncomfortable.

> 这场雨从昨天下午开始就**一直(不停地)**下，不知道什么时候才会停。
> *Zhè chǎng yǔ cóng zuótiān xiàwǔ kāishǐ jiù yīzhí (bùtíng de) xià, bù zhīdào shénme shíhòu cái huì tíng.*
> It **has been** raining **continuously** since yesterday afternoon **(without stopping)**. I wonder when it will finally stop.

(ii) In a **negative** sentence, only 一直 can be used, 不停地 cannot. It indicates that something **never happened**.

从三月开始就**一直没下**雨，昨天那场大雨**一直(不停地)下**了三个小时，所以农民都很高兴。

Cóng sānyuē kāishǐ jiù yīzhí méi xiàyǔ, zuótiān nà chǎng dà yǔ yīzhí (bùtíng de) xià le sān ge xiǎoshí, suǒyǐ nóngmín dōu hěn gāoxìng.

It **had not rained (at all)** since March. Yesterday it poured **nonstop** for three hours. So farmers were happy.

老师问王大中昨天为什么没有来上课，大中只是哭，**一直不**说话。**老师一直(不停地)**追问，大中才说是因为他妈妈病了。

Lǎoshī wèn Wáng Dàzhōng zuótiān wèi shénme méiyǒu lái shàng kè, Dàzhōng zhǐshì kū, yīzhí bù shuō huà. Lǎoshī yīzhí (bùtíng de) zhuīwèn, Dàzhōng cái shuō shì yīnwèi tā māma bìng le.

The teacher asked Wang Dazhong why he had been absent from class the day before. Dazhong only cried and **(continuously) remained** silent. The teacher **persisted in** asking him, and Dazhong finally said it was because his mother had been sick.

(iii) In the **一直到** expression, 到 is followed by the **end point of a continuous action**. It implies that a situation continues all the way until a certain point. A verb can be inserted between 一直 and 到.

昨天我实在太累了，吃了晚饭就上床睡觉，**一直睡到**今天早上十点。

Zuótiān wǒ shízài tài lèi le, chī le wǎn fàn jiù shàng chuáng shuìjiào, yīzhí shuì dào jīntiān zǎoshàng shídiǎn.

Yesterday I was truly too tired. I went to bed right after dinner, and I slept **(right through) until** ten o'clock this morning.

最近我常常失眠，昨天晚上上床以后，翻来覆去，**一直到**三点多才睡着。

Zuìjìn wǒ chángcháng shīmián, zuótiān wǎnshàng shàngchuáng yǐhòu, fān lái fù qù, yīzhí dào sāndiǎn duō cái shuìzháo.

Recently I have suffered from insomnia. Yesterday after I went to bed, I tossed and turned **(continuously) until** after three o'clock before I finally fell asleep.

你往前开，**一直(开)到**公园路和第五街的交口，然后往右拐。

Nǐ wàng qián kāi, yīzhí (kāi) dào Gōngyuán Lù hé Dìwǔ Jiē de jiāokǒu, ránhòu wàng yòu guǎi.

Go (Drive) straight ahead, **all the way to** the intersection of Park Road and Fifth Street, and then make a right turn.

c. 一直 can mean 'all the time' or 'all along' and is similar to 一向 (*yīxiàng*) or 向来 (*xiànglái*). However, 一向 or 向来 is not used when a **specific time frame** is mentioned; 一直 **does not have this restriction**.

李明的朋友**一直**(can be **一向** or **向来**)很多；可是自从他到日本去工作
以后，因为语言不通，所以**一直**(cannot be **一向** or **向来**)交不到朋友。
(自从他到日本去工作以后 sets the time frame).

Lǐ Míng de péngyǒu yīzhí hěn duō; kěshì zìcóng tā dào Rìběn qù gōngzuò
yǐhòu, yīnwèi yǔyán bù tōng, suǒyǐ yīzhí jiāo bú dào péngyǒu.

Li Ming **had always (all along) had** many friends. But ever since he went
to Japan to work, he **has not (or: has never) been** able to make friends
because he cannot communicate in the language (he does not speak Japanese).

孝顺父母、尊敬长辈**向来**(can be **一向** or **一直**)是中国人的传统美德；
五千年来，中国人**一直**(cannot be **一向** or **向来**)保存着这种观念。
(五千年来 sets the time frame.)

Xiàoshùn fùmǔ, zūnjìng zhǎngbèi xiànglái shì Zhōngguó rén de chuántǒng
měidé; wǔ qiān nián lái, Zhōngguó rén yīzhí bǎocún zhe zhè zhǒng guānniàn.

To be filial to one's parents and to respect one's elders **have been** traditional
Chinese virtues **all the time (all along)**. In the past 5,000 years, Chinese
have **always (all along)** maintained this concept.

→ See 一向 (*yīxiàng*) and 向来 (*xiànglái*) for related information.

以为 *yǐwéi*

以为 is followed by a sentence, and is used to imply that a fact that someone
considers (or considered) to be true is (or was), in actuality, inaccurate. There
are two possible scenarios.

a. The person **comes to the realization** that an opinion (s)he held or a fact
(s)he considered to be true was actually wrong.

我**以为**张美文跟张美英是姐妹，因为她们不但名字很像，而且长得也很
像；但张美文告诉我她们只是同学。

Wǒ yǐwéi Zhāng Měiwén gēn Zhāng Měiyīng shì jiěmèi, yīnwèi tāmen búdàn
míngzì hěn xiàng, érqiě zhǎng de yě hěn xiàng; dàn Zhāng Měiwén gàosù
wǒ tāmen zhǐ shì tóngxué.

I **had (mistakenly) thought** Zhang Meiwen and Zhang Meiying were sisters,
because not only are their names similar, but also they look similar, but
Zhang Meiwen told me that they were only classmates.

美文**以为**她今年过生日的时候，她爸妈会送她一辆新车，可是她爸妈只
送了她一件大衣，所以她很失望。

Měiwén yǐwéi tā jīnnián guò shēngrì de shíhòu, tā bàmā huì sòng tā yī liàng
xīn chē, kěshì tā bàmā zhǐ sòng le tā yī jiàn dàyī, suǒyǐ tā hěn shīwàng.

Meiwen **had thought** that when she had her birthday this year, her parents
would give her a new car; but her parents only gave her a coat; therefore,
she was disappointed.

b.   A person **does not realize** that the opinion or fact (s)he holds to be true is, in actuality, wrong. The **context is extremely important** in using or interpreting 以为 in this situation.

大家都知道王大中是个大坏蛋，只有小李**以为**他是好人。(以为 implies that the speaker considers Li's opinion about Wang wrong, but that Li himself does not realize it.)
Dàjiā dōu zhīdào Wáng Dàzhōng shì ge dà huàidàn, zhǐyǒu Xiǎo Lǐ yǐwéi tā shì hǎo rén.
Everybody knows that Wang Dazhong is a really bad guy; only Little Li **(mistakenly) thinks** that he is a good person.

小李**以为**王小姐真心爱他，所以向王小姐求婚，其实王小姐跟小李交往是因为小李很有钱。
Xiǎo Lǐ yǐwéi Wáng xiǎojiě zhēnxīn ài tā, suǒyǐ xiàng Wáng xiǎojiě qiúhūn, qíshí Wáng xiǎojiě gēn Xiǎo Lǐ jiāowǎng shì yīnwèi Xiǎo Lǐ hěn yǒu qián.
Little Li **thinks (by mistake) that** Miss Wang truly loves him, and so he has proposed to her. Actually, the reason Miss Wang is dating Little Li is because he is rich.

c.   **别以为** is a common phrase; its English translation is simply '**Don't think . . .**', implying that '**if you think so, you are wrong**'.

(Scenario: A husband calls his wife and says that he needs to work late. Actually, he is going out to drink with his friends after work. His wife knows the truth and is displeased.)
妻子: **别以为**我不知道你的花样！
Qīzi: Bié yǐwéi wǒ bù zhīdào nǐ de huāyàng!
Wife: **Don't think** I don't know your tricks (what you are up to).

(Scenario: A man's mother tries to dissuade him from marrying his girlfriend.)
妈妈: **别以为**她爱你！她爱的是你的钱！
Māma: Bié yǐwéi tā ài nǐ! Tā ài de shì nǐ de qián!
Mother: **Don't think** she loves you! What she loves is your money!

d.   **还以为** . . . **(呢)** is often used instead of simply 以为, although 还 **does not have an independent meaning** when used in this phrase. 还以为 may imply that the speaker wishes to **emphasize the mistake**. 呢 is optional but is frequently used with 还.

(Scenario: Two people working in the same company have not seen each other in quite a while. Today they chance to take the same elevator.)
A: 老王！是你！好久不见！我**还以为**你辞职了**(呢)**！
Lǎo Wáng! Shì nǐ! Hǎo jiǔ bú jiàn! Wǒ hái yǐwéi nǐ cízhí le ne!

B: 是啊！我也**以为**你换工作了！

Shì a! Wǒ yě yǐwéi nǐ huàn gōngzuò le!

A: Old Wang! It's you! Long time no see! I **thought** you had quit!

B: Yeah! I also **thought** you had got another job.

意思 *yìsi*

The very basic definition of 意思 ('meaning') does not begin to suggest the various uses and implications of this word. Many expressions containing the word 意思 do not have direct counterparts or translations in English; as such, these expressions can only be properly interpreted by taking the context into consideration. In addition, the **subtleties and nuances** as well as **rich cultural connotations** some of the expressions convey need special attention from learners.

This section is a discussion on the uses of the most common expressions containing the word 意思.

a. 意思, as a stand-alone vocabulary word, is used strictly as **a noun**. One can use 是 or 有 when asking about the **meaning, definition or connotation** of a word, a phrase or a sentence.

It should be noted that the verb to signify the meaning of something can be 表示 (*biǎoshì*), because 意思 **cannot be used as a verb**.

(Scenario: A student who is studying Chinese has encountered a Chinese proverb that he does not understand, and so he asks his teacher for clarification.)

学生: 老师，请问'鹤立鸡群'这个成语**是什么意思**？

Xuéshēng: Lǎoshī, qǐng wèn, 'hè lì jī qún' zhè ge chéngyǔ shì shénme yìsi?

老师: 这个成语**有两个意思**。一个**表示**一个人长得很高；另外一个**表示**一个人很有才华。

Lǎoshī: Zhè ge chéngyǔ yǒu liǎng ge yìsi. Yī ge biǎoshì yī ge rén zhǎng de hěn gāo; lìngwài yī ge biǎoshì yī ge rén hěn yǒu cáihuá.

Student: Teacher, may I please ask: **what does** the proverb 'crane stand chicken crowd' **mean**?

Teacher: This proverb **has two meanings**. One **means** a person is tall; the other **means** a person is talented.

(Scenario: Mr Wang and his fiancée broke up two weeks before their wedding.)

A: 你知道吗？王大中跟他未婚妻分手了！

Nǐ zhīdào ma? Wáng Dàzhōng gēn tā de wèihūn qī fēnshǒu le!

B: 那么这**表示**他们的婚礼也取消了，是吗？

Nàme zhè biǎoshì tāmen de hūnlǐ yě qǔxiāo le, shì ma?

A: Did you know that Wang Dazhong and his fiancée have broken up?

B: Then this **means** their wedding has been canceled, too; is that so?

b. In real-life communication, the pattern '**person + (verb +) 是什么意思**' may sound **rude or blunt** because 意思 can also mean '**intention**' or '**insinuation**'. It often has a **negative connotation**. For example, 你是什么意思？is often used to **accuse** a person of **having bad intentions or trying to insinuate something bad**.

Therefore, one should not consider 你是什么意思？to be the equivalent of 'what do you mean?' in English.

(Scenario: A mother and her daughter have been spending a lot of time shopping for clothes online.)

爸爸:	有其母必有其女。
Bàba:	*Yǒu qí mǔ bì yǒu qí nǚ.*
妈妈:	**你**说这句话**是什么意思**？你的**意思是**我们不应该花你的钱买东西吗？
Māma:	*Nǐ shuō zhè jù huà shì shénme yìsi? Nǐ de yìsi shì wǒmen bù yīnggāi huā nǐ de qián mǎi dōngxi ma?*
爸爸:	不是，不是！我**没有那个意思**。你们想买什么就买什么。
Bàba:	*Bú shì, bú shì! Wǒ méiyǒu nà ge yìsi. Nǐmen xiǎng mǎi shénme jiù mǎi shénme.*
Father:	Like mother like daughter. (When there is such a mother, there will definitely be such a daughter.)
Mother:	What did you mean (by this sentence)? (Or: **What are you insinuating?**) Did you **mean that** we should not spend your money buying things?
Father:	No, no! I did **not have that intention**. (Or: I **did not mean that**.) You can buy whatever you want.

A neutral way to **ask someone for clarification** about what they have said without sounding accusatory can be 我不太懂你的意思 or 你的意思是 . . .? Do **not** say 你是什么意思？

(Scenario: A manager is trying to indirectly tell a job applicant that they will not hire her.)

经理:	王小姐，这个职位，对你来说，是'大材小用'。
Jīnglǐ:	*Wáng xiǎojiě, zhè ge zhíwèi, duì nǐ lái shuō, shì 'dà cái xiǎo yòng'.*
王:	经理，我**不懂你的意思** (or: **你的意思是 . . .**)。
Wáng:	*Jīnglǐ, wǒ bù dǒng nǐ de yìsi* (or: *nǐ de yìsi shì . . .*).
经理:	**我的意思是**，这个职位不适合你。
Jīnglǐ:	*Wǒ de yìsi shì, zhè ge zhíwèi bú shìhé nǐ.*
Manager:	Miss Wang, to you, this position is 'big materials small uses'. (In Chinese, this means 'overqualified'.)
Wang:	Manager, I **don't understand what you mean**.
Manager:	**What I mean is** this position is not right (suitable) for you.

c. **有意思**

Although 意思 as a stand-alone word can be defined as 'meaning', 有意思 does not mean 'meaningful'; instead, it means '**interesting**' or '**interested**' depending on the context. Its negative form is 没有意思.

(i) 有意思 as 'interesting' suggests that someone, a certain activity or a certain experience is **entertaining, amusing or mildly fascinating**. One usually does not use it to describe something that's sad or unsettling, albeit fascinating.

For example, if someone relates to you a personal story that is dark and heavy, it would not be appropriate to use 有意思 to comment on it, although the word 'interesting' in English might be acceptable.

没有意思 is a more straightforward word, which means '**boring**' or '**uninteresting**'. However, 没有意思 is usually not used to describe a person. To describe someone with a boring personality, 无趣 (*wú qù*) is the more appropriate word; it also means 'boring' or 'uninteresting'.

A: 王大中请你去看电影，你为什么不去？
   Wáng Dàzhōng qǐng nǐ qù kàn diànyǐng, nǐ wèi shénme bú qù?
B: 跟王大中这种人出去实在很**没有意思**，他的个性太**无趣**，很少开口说话。
   Gēn Wáng Dàzhōng zhè zhǒng rén chūqù shízài hěn méiyǒu yìsi, tā de gèxìng tài wú qù, hěnshǎo kāikǒu shuō huà.
A: 是吗？真想不到；我看过一本他写的书，那本书相当**有意思**。
   Shì ma? Zhēn xiǎng bú dào; wǒ kàn guo yī běn tā xiě de shū, nà běn shū xiāngdāng yǒu yìsi.
A: Wang Dazhong asked you out to a movie. Why wouldn't you go?
B: Going out with someone like Wang Dazhong is truly **boring (no fun)**. His personality is too **boring (dull)**; he rarely opens his mouth to say anything.
A: Is that so? This is really unexpected. I have read a book he wrote; that book was quite **interesting**.

(ii) 有意思 in the 'A 对 B 有意思' expression implies that person 'A is **(romantically) interested in** person B'.

(Scenario: Three women are gossiping about the romantic life of two of their friends.)
A: 王大中好像**对**李小兰**有意思**，因为他最近常常给李小兰送花、送巧克力。
   Wáng Dàzhōng hǎoxiàng duì Lǐ Xiǎolán yǒu yìsi, yīnwèi tā zuìjìn chángcháng gěi Lǐ Xiǎolán sòng huā, sòng qiǎokèlì.
B: 真的吗？太好了！我觉得他们两个很配！
   Zhēn de ma? Tài hǎo le! Wǒ juéde tāmen liǎng ge hěn pèi.

C: 可惜李小兰**对**王大中**没有意思**，她说王大中的个性太**无趣**了，跟这种人交往会很**没有意思**。

Kěxí Lǐ Xiǎolán duì Wáng Dàzhōng méiyǒu yìsi, tā shuō Wáng Dàzhōng de gèxìng tài wú qù le, gēn zhè zhǒng rén jiāowǎng huì hěn méiyǒu yìsi.

A: Wang Dazhong seems to be **interested in** Li Xiaolan, because recently he has often given Li Xiaolan flowers and chocolate.

B: Really? That's great! I think the two of them are compatible.

C: It's too bad that Li Xiaolan is **not interested in** Wang Dazhong. She says that Wang Dazhong's personality is too **boring (dull)**, and that dating such a person would be **boring**.

(iii) It should be noted that if B is not a person or **the interest is not a romantic one**, then 有意思 should not be used; instead, it is '**A 对 B 有兴趣**'. 兴趣 (*xìngqù*) literally means 'interest'.

妈妈: 你应该多参加课外活动，像参加篮球队、辩论社什么的。

Māma: *Nǐ yīnggāi duō cānjiā kèwài huódòng, xiàng cānjiā lánqiú duì, biànlùn shè shénme de.*

儿子: 可是我**对**这些活动都**没有兴趣**；我觉得这些活动都很**没有意思**。

Ézi: *Kěshì wǒ duì zhè xiē huódòng dōu méiyǒu xìngqù; wǒ juéde zhè xiē huódòng dōu hěn méiyǒu yìsi.*

Mother: You should participate in extracurricular activities more often, such as joining the basketball team, the debate club and so on.

Son: But I am **not interested in** any of these activities; I think all of these activities are **boring**.

来申请这个工作的人很多，可是我们经理只**对**一位王先生**有兴趣**，他说下星期要请王先生来面谈。

Lái shēnqǐng zhè ge gōngzuò de rén hěn duō, kěshì wǒmen jīnglǐ zhǐ duì yī wèi Wáng xiānsheng yǒu xìngqù, tā shuō xià xīngqī yào qǐng Wáng xiānsheng lái miàntán.

There are many applicants for this job, but our manager is only **interested in** a Mr Wang. He has said that he is going to ask Mr Wang to come for an interview next week.

d. 小意思

In casual conversation, 小意思 implies 'it's **something small**'. For example, it is often used when a person gives someone a gift and the gift-giver wants to show his or her modesty and sincerity by not bragging about the value of the gift. It is considered a **culturally appropriate expression**.

A: 啊！王先生，这个礼物太贵重了！
A! Wáng xiānsheng, zhè ge lǐwù tài guìzhòng le!

B: 哪里，哪里！只是一点**小意思**。(哪里 implies 'it's not' in Chinese.)
Nǎlǐ, nǎlǐ! Zhǐ shì yīdiǎn xiǎo yìsi.

A: Ah, Mr Wang, this gift is too expensive!

B: No, it's nothing! It's only (a little bit of) a **small token**.

e. **好意思**

For all the good connotations ostensibly shown in its surface meaning ('good + meaning'), **好意思** frequently presents quite **a negative connotation**. It is nearly impossible to translate it into English without taking the context into consideration. In general, it is used **to accuse, to blame or to criticize** someone for his or her **inappropriate and brazen behavior**. The inappropriateness can range from 'being embarrassing' and 'being inconsiderate' to 'being shameless'.

(i) It can be used as the **predicate** in the '**person + 好意思**' pattern.

上星期王先生的女兒結婚，小張不但沒有送禮，而且還帶了他女朋友一起去參加婚宴；他**真好意思**！
Shàng xīngqī Wáng xiānsheng de nǚ'ér jiéhūn, Xiǎo Zhāng búdàn méiyǒu sòng lǐ, érqiě hái dài le tā nǚ péngyǒu yīqǐ qù cānjiā hūnyàn; tā zhēn hǎo yìsi.
Mr Wang's daughter got married last week. Not only did Little Zhang not give a gift, but he also brought his girlfriend to attend the wedding banquet. He was **really shameless**.

(ii) It can be **followed by a verb** or a verbal phrase.

A: 老王，可不可以借我五十块钱？
Lǎo Wáng, kě bù kěyǐ jiè wǒ wǔshí kuài qián?

B: 上星期借你的钱，你还没还我呢！你还**好意思**又**来**向我借！
Shàng xīngqī jiè nǐ de qián, nǐ hái méi huán wǒ ne! Nǐ hái hǎo yìsi yòu lái xiàng wǒ jiè!

A: Old Wang, can you lend me 50 *kuai*?

B: You have not returned to me the money you borrowed last week. And you **have the nerve to ask** me for a loan again!

(Scenario: A man who is renting a room to his friend tells his wife that he wants to increase the rent.)

男: 我们去跟李先生说，从下个月开始，每个月房租要涨五十块，好不好？

Nán: *Wǒmen qù gēn Lǐ xiānsheng shuō, cóng xià ge yuè kāishǐ, měi ge yuè fángzū yào zhǎng wǔshí kuài, hǎo bù hǎo?*

女:　　李先生是你的好朋友，他现在又失业；要是你**好意思**跟
　　　　他**说**，你就去说吧！我可不去！

Nǚ:　　*Lǐ xiānsheng shì nǐ de hǎo péngyǒu, tā xiànzài yòu shīyè; yàoshì nǐ hǎo yìsi gēn tā shuō, nǐ jiù qù shuō ba! Wǒ kě bú qù.*

Man:　　Let's go tell Mr Li that, starting next month, there will be an increase of 50 *kuai* on his rent, OK?

Woman:　Mr Li is your good friend; besides, he is unemployed now. If you **have the insensitivity to tell** him (= if you can **bring yourself to tell him without feeling guilty**), you go right ahead. I am not going!

In daily communication, 好意思 is often used in a rhetorical question to mean 不好意思. Since **不好意思** actually conveys a **positive attitude** (see section f. below), one should be particularly careful when interpreting 好意思 when it is used in a **rhetorical question**.

A:　　王先生，上次你帮了我这么大的忙，这是我的一点**小意思**，
　　　请收下。

　　　Wáng xiānsheng, shàng cì nǐ bāng le wǒ zhème dà de máng, zhè shì wǒ de yīdiǎn xiǎo yìsi, qǐng shōuxià.

B:　　哎呀！只帮了你一个小忙，你就送这么贵重的礼物，这**怎么好
　　　意思**？

　　　Àiya! Zhǐ bāng le nǐ yī ge xiǎo máng, nǐ jiù sòng zhème guìzhòng de lǐwù, zhè zěnme hǎo yìsi?

A:　　Mr Wang, you did me such a big favor last time; this is **a little something (a small token)** from me. Please accept it.

B:　　Oh! I only did you a small favor, and you're giving me such an expensive gift. How can I accept it without feeling guilty? (I **feel guilty about accepting** it!)

f.　**不好意思**

不好意思 is one of the most versatile and nuanced expressions in Chinese. It typically is used in casual conversations to show **social courtesy or politeness**.

(i)　As a stand-alone expression, 不好意思 is quite similar to **'excuse me'** or sometimes **'I am sorry'** in English. The **offense or blunder**, if any, is **usually very minor**. To apologize for more serious mistakes, one should use 对不起 as a more appropriate expression.

A:　　**不好意思**，请问地铁入口在哪儿？
　　　Bù hǎo yìsi, qǐng wèn dìtiě rùkǒu zài nǎ'ér?

B:　　哎呀！真**不好意思**，我也不知道。
　　　Àiya! Zhēn bù hǎo yìsi, wǒ yě bù zhīdào.

A:　　**Excuse me**, may I please ask: where is the subway entrance?

B:　　Oh! I am really **sorry**! I don't know, either.

(ii) It is similar to '**feeling embarrassed**' or '**slightly guilty**'. It can be used in a **social setting** when one is on the **receiving end** of someone else's generosity or kindness.

(Scenario: Wang and Li had lunch together; Wang paid for their meal.)

李: 真**不好意思**，让你破费了！(不好意思 conveys the meaning of 谢谢, but is subtler than 谢谢. 破费 is a polite way to say 'to pay for something'.)

Lǐ: Zhēn bù hǎo yìsi, ràng nǐ pòfèi le. (This expression conveys social courtesy; there is no direct translation for it. It really means 'thank you for paying for my meal'.)

A: 明天你有空吗？我想请你去看电影。
Míngtiān nǐ yǒu kòng ma? Wǒ xiǎng qǐng nǐ qù kàn diànyǐng.

B: 那**怎么好意思**？每次都是你请我，明天我请你吧！(怎么好意思？ is a rhetorical question meaning 不好意思.)
Nà zěnme hǎo yìsi? Měi cì dōu shì nǐ qǐng wǒ, míngtiān wǒ qǐng nǐ ba!

A: Are you free tomorrow? I would like to invite you to a movie.

B: (I **would feel guilty** about it.) You have always (every time) treated me. How about if I treat you tomorrow?

(iii) It can be used when one feels **embarrassed about a social faux pas** or ashamed about an **inappropriate behavior**.

A: 昨天我把小王看成了小张，今天又把他的名字叫成小黄，我觉得很**不好意思**。
Zuótiān wǒ bǎ Xiǎo Wáng kàn chéng le Xiǎo Zhāng, jīntiān yòu bǎ tā de míngzì jiào chéng Xiǎo Huáng, wǒ juéde hěn bù hǎo yìsi.

B: 不用**不好意思**，小王也常常把你的名字念错。(social faux pas)
Búyòng bù hǎo yìsi, Xiǎo Wáng yě chángcháng bǎ nǐ de míngzì niàncuò.

A: Yesterday I mistook Little Wang for Little Zhang, today I mispronounced his name as Little Huang. I feel **embarrassed**.

B: No need to **be embarrassed**. Little Wang often mispronounces your name, too.

今天我上了公车以后，才发现我穿的鞋子一只是红的，一只是黑的；车上很多人在看我，我觉得**真不好意思**。(social faux pas)
Jīntiān wǒ shàng le gōngchē yǐhòu, cái fāxiàn wǒ chuān de xiézi yī zhī shì hóng de, yī zhī shì hēi de; chē shàng hěn duō rén zài kàn wǒ, wǒ juéde zhēn bù hǎo yìsi.

Today I only discovered that I wore one red shoe and one black shoe after I had got on the bus. Many people on the bus were looking at me; I felt really **embarrassed**.

老师:	王中，今天只有你一个人没有交功课，我问的问题，你也不会回答；你实在应该觉得**不好意思**。 (inappropriate behavior)
Lǎoshī:	*Wáng Zhōng, jīntiān zhǐ yǒu nǐ yī ge rén méiyǒu jiāo gōngkè, wǒ wèn de wèntí, nǐ yě bú huì huídá; nǐ shízài yīnggāi juéde bù hǎo yìsi.*
王中:	**对不起**，以后我一定天天好好准备功课。(对不起, instead of 不好意思, is the appropriate response in this situation due to the serious nature of the wrong behavior as well as the role of the speaker.)
Wáng Zhōng:	*Duì bù qǐ, yǐhòu wǒ yīdìng tiān tiān hǎo hǎo zhǔnbèi gōngkè.*
Teacher:	Wang Zhong, you are the only one that did not turn in homework today; you also did not know how to answer my questions. You really should feel **embarrassed** (meaning: **guilty** or **ashamed**).
Wang Zhong:	I am sorry. From now on I definitely will do a good job preparing my homework every day.

(iv) It can be interpreted as '**feeling apologetic or guilty**' for causing other people **inconvenience**.

今天我跟王先生约好下午五点见面，可是因为路上堵车，所以我六点才到，让我觉得很**不好意思**。

Jīntiān wǒ gēn Wáng xiānsheng yuē hǎo xiàwǔ wǔdiǎn jiànmiàn, kěshì yīnwèi lù shàng dǔ chē, suǒyǐ wǒ liùdiǎn cái dào, ràng wǒ juéde hěn bù hǎo yìsi.

I had agreed to meet with Mr Wang at 5:00 in the afternoon today, but because there was a traffic jam, I did not arrive until 6:00. This made me feel **guilty**.

(v) It can be used to describe that someone is feeling **too shy, bashful, awkward or self-conscious** to do something. When there is a verb, the pattern is '**person 不好意思 + verb**'.

王中刚到美国留学的时候，因为觉得自己的英文不够好，所以上课的时候常常**不好意思开口**说话。

Wáng Zhōng gāng dào Měiguó liúxué de shíhòu, yīnwèi juéde zìjǐ de Yīngwén bú gòu hǎo, suǒyǐ shàngkè de shíhòu chángcháng bù hǎo yìsi kāi kǒu shuō huà.

When Wang Zhong first came to the U.S. to study, he felt that his English was not good enough, so he often was **too shy (or too self-conscious) to open his mouth** to speak in class.

A: 小兰，王中想请你吃饭，他要我问你这个星期六有没有空？

Xiǎolán, Wáng Zhōng xiǎng qǐng nǐ chī fàn, tā yào wǒ wèn nǐ zhè ge xīngqī liù yǒu méiyǒu kòng?

B: 他自己为什么不来问我？

Tā zìjǐ wèi shénme bù lái wèn wǒ?

A: 他说你们才刚认识，他**不好意思来**问你。

Tā shuō nǐmen cái gāng rènshì, tā bù hǎo yìsi lái wèn nǐ.

A: Xiaolan, Wang Zhong would like to take you out for a meal. He wanted me to ask you if you will be free this Saturday.

B: Why wouldn't he ask me himself?

A: He said that you two had just met, and so he **felt shy about** asking you.

今天老师夸奖了我以后，同学们都热烈地鼓掌，让我觉得有点**不好意思**。

Jīntiān lǎoshī kuājiǎng le wǒ yǐhòu, tóngxué men dōu rèliè de gǔzhǎng, ràng wǒ juéde yǒudiǎn bù hǎo yìsi.

Today after the teacher praised me, all my classmates applauded enthusiastically, making me feel **a little awkward (about this situation)**.

(vi) It can be used when someone is **unable to bring him/herself to do something** for reasons having to do with **social courtesy or human relationships**.

昨天老王来向我借钱，虽然我自己最近钱也很紧，可是因为老王以前帮过我不少忙，所以我**不好意思拒绝**他。

Zuótiān Lǎo Wáng lái xiàng wǒ jiè qián, suīrán wǒ zìjǐ zuìjìn qián yě hěn jǐn, kěshì yīnwèi Lǎo Wáng yǐqián bāng guo wǒ bùshǎo máng, suǒyǐ wǒ bù hǎo yìsi jùjué tā.

Yesterday Old Wang asked me for a loan. Although my own money has also been tight lately, I **could not bring myself to refuse** him because he had helped me many times before.

In the following example, 不好意思 has two different interpretations.

昨天我去王中家玩，要回家的时候，他留我吃晚饭，本来我**不好意思打扰**他们，可是后来连他爷爷奶奶也留我，我就**不好意思走**了。

Zuótiān wǒ qù Wáng Zhōng jiā wán, yào huí jiā de shíhòu, tā liú wǒ chī wǎnfàn, běnlái wǒ bù hǎo yìsi dǎrǎo tāmen, kěshì hòulái lián tā yéye nǎinai yě liú wǒ, wǒ jiù bù hǎo yìsi zǒu le.

Yesterday I went to Wang Zhong's house for a visit. When I was about to go home, he asked me to stay for dinner. Originally I felt **awkward about imposing on** them, but later even his grandparents asked me to stay, and so I **could not bring myself to leave** (implied: **I stayed**).

g. **不好意思地 + verb**

不好意思 in the adverbial modifier 不好意思地 carries the implications of nearly all of the examples of 不好意思 mentioned in f. above.

老师说，今天全班只有王中一个人没有交功课，同学们都看着他，他**不好意思地**把头**低下来**。

Lǎoshī shuō, jīntiān quán bān zhǐ yǒu Wáng Zhōng yī ge rén méiyǒu jiāo gōngkè, tóngxué men dōu kàn zhe tā, tā bù hǎo yìsi de bǎ tóu dī xiàlái.

The teacher said that Wang Zhong was the only person who did not turn in homework today. All his classmates were looking at him. He **lowered** his head **(ashamedly) in shame**.

老师说，张明代表学校参加演讲比赛，得了第一名，同学们都热烈地鼓掌，张明**不好意思地笑**了。

Lǎoshī shuō, Zhāng Míng dàibiǎo xuéxiào cānjiā yǎnjiǎng bǐsài, dé le dì yī míng, tóngxué men dōu rèliè de gǔzhǎng, Zhāng Míng bù hǎo yìsi de xiào le.

The teacher said that the Zhang Ming had represented the school to participate in a speech contest and that he had won the first prize. All his classmates enthusiastically applauded him. Zhang Ming **smiled bashfully**.

老师问李文，今天穿的袜子为什么一只是红的，一只是绿的，李文低头一看，发现自己穿错了袜子，**不好意思地笑**了。

Lǎoshī wèn Lǐ Wén, jīntiān chuān de wàzi wèi shénme yī zhī shì hōng de, yī zhī shì lǜ de, Lǐ Wén dī tóu yī kàn, fāxiàn zìjǐ chuān cuò le wàzi, bù hǎo yìsi de xiào le.

The teacher asked Li Wen why one of his socks was red and the other was green. Li Wen lowered his head to look, and realized that he had put on the wrong socks. He **smiled embarrassedly (with embarrassment)**.

However, it must be cautioned that '不好意思**地** + verb' and '不好意思 + verb' indicate very different meanings. With 地, the pattern indicates that **the action is performed**, whereas the pattern without 地 indicates that the action **is not performed**.

同学们发现，今天老师穿的袜子，一只是红的，一只是绿的，可是大家都**不好意思笑**；老师自己发现以后，**不好意思地笑**了。

Tóngxué men fāxiàn, jīntiān lǎoshī chuān de wàzi, yī zhī shì hóng de, yī zhī shì lǜ de, kěshì dàjiā dōu bù hǎo yìsi xiào; lǎoshī zìjǐ fāxiàn yǐhòu, bù hǎo yìsi de xiào le.

The students noticed that the teacher was wearing a red sock and a green one today. But they **could not bring themselves to laugh**. When the teacher himself noticed this, he **smiled embarrassedly (with embarrassment)**.

每个人吃了一块蛋糕以后，还剩下两块，主人问谁还想吃，其实大家都还想吃，可是都**不好意思说**。主人问了两次以后，王大中才**不好意思地说**："那我再吃一块吧！"

Měi ge rén chī le yī kuài dàngāo yǐhòu, hái shèng xià liǎng kuài, zhǔrén wèn shéi hái xiǎng zài chī, qíshí dàjiā dōu hái xiǎng chī, kěshì dōu bù hǎo yìsi shuō. Zhǔrén wèn le liǎng cì yǐhòu, Wáng Dàzhōng cái bù hǎo yìsi de shuō: 'nà wǒ zài chī yī kuài ba!'

After everybody had had a piece of cake, there were still two pieces left. The host asked who would like to have more. Actually everybody wanted to have more, but nobody **could bring themselves to say** it. After the host had asked twice, Wang Dazhong finally **said sheepishly**, 'Then I will have another piece.'

应该 *yīnggāi*

应该 is a modal verb. It is often translated as 'should', 'ought to' and, sometimes, 'to be supposed to'. It has two basic uses: one is to indicate **speculation, estimation**, etc., and the other is to suggest **obligation (moral or social), duty or propriety**.

In addition to being a modal verb, 应该 sometimes functions as an **adjective**. It is associated with the implication of '**propriety**' and is only used as the **predicate** in a sentence.

The negative forms for the use of 应该 merit special attention because the location (word order) of 不 (or 没有) in a sentence is closely related to the interpretation of 应该 in that sentence.

a.　The **speculation** one makes in a sentence with 应该 is not a random guess, but is a **plausible opinion** (indicating the likelihood of a situation) based on available information.

　　(i)　Although a modal verb is normally followed by a regular verb, 应该 is an exception and can be **followed by another modal verb, such as 会 or 可以**, to indicate one's **estimation or speculation** of a situation based on available information.

　　　　A:　今天会不会下雨？
　　　　　　Jīntiān huì bú huì xià yǔ?
　　　　B:　现在天这么阴暗，下午**应该会**下。
　　　　　　Xiànzài tiān zhème yīn àn, xiàwǔ yīnggāi huì xià.
　　　　A:　那我可不可以借这把伞？
　　　　　　Nà wǒ kě bù kěyǐ jiè zhè bǎ sǎn?
　　　　B:　那不是我的伞，是我同屋的；不过你**应该可以**借，因为我同屋很大方，而且她有好几把伞。
　　　　　　Nà bú shì wǒ de sǎn, shì wǒ tóngwū de; búguò nǐ yīnggāi kěyǐ jiè, yīnwèi wǒ tóngwū hěn dàfāng, érqiě tā yǒu hǎo jǐ bǎ sǎn.

A: Will it rain today?

B: The sky is so cloudy and dark now. (I think) it **should (probably will)** rain in the afternoon.

A: Then may I borrow this umbrella?

B: That is not my umbrella; it's my roommate's. But you **should be able to** borrow it because my roommate is generous, and besides, she has several umbrellas.

(ii) Negative words, such as 不 and 没有, should appear **after** 应该 to indicate one's **estimation or speculation**. In such negative sentences, 'should' or 'ought to' often is not the best translation for 应该. One should interpret 应该 as 'probably (not)' or '(not) likely'.

A: 在跟王美文跳舞的那个人是不是她男朋友？
Zài gēn Wáng Měiwén tiàowǔ de nà ge rén shì bú shì tā nán péngyǒu?

B: **应该不**是。
Yīnggāi bú shì.

A: 你怎么知道那不是她男朋友？
Nǐ zěnme zhīdào nà bú shì tā nán péngyǒu?

B: 她妈妈告诉过我，她女儿高中毕业以前不可以交男朋友。王美文还在上高中，所以她**应该**还**没有**男朋友。
Tā māma gàosù guo wǒ, tā nǚ'ér gāozhōng bìyè yǐqián bù kěyǐ jiāo nán péngyǒu. Wáng Měiwén hái zài shàng gāozhōng, suǒyǐ tā yīnggāi hái méiyǒu nán péngyǒu.

A: Is the man dancing with Wang Meiwen her boyfriend?

B: **Probably not.** (**I gather** that he is **not**.)

A: How did you know that is not her boyfriend?

B: Her mother has told me that her daughter is not allowed to have a boyfriend before graduating from high school. Wang Meiwen is still in high school, so she is **not likely** to have a boyfriend (based on what her mother has told me).

妈妈: 小中睡觉了吗？
Māma: Xiǎozhōng shuìjiào le ma?
爸爸: **应该**还**没有**，他房间的灯还亮着。
Bàba: Yīnggāi hái méiyǒu, tā fángjiān de dēng hái liàng zhe.
Mother: Has Xiaozhong gone to sleep?
Father: **Probably not** yet; the light in his room is still on.

It should be noted that a **yes-no question** (or an affirmative-negative question) **cannot be formed** by using 应该 when 应该 implies 'probably' or 'very likely'.

b. The other use of 应该 is more similar to the use of the English 'should' or 'ought to'.

(i) It can be used to indicate **one's (social or moral) obligation or duty.**
不应该 is normally its negative form to indicate **one's obligation is not to do something.**

(Scenario: A man is seeking opinions from two of his friends about whether he should give a wedding gift to his former girlfriend. Note the difference between 不应该 and 应该不 in his friends' responses.)

A: 我以前的女朋友要结婚了；你们认为我**应该不应该**送礼？

Wǒ yǐqián de nǚ péngyǒu yào jiéhūn le; nǐmen rènwéi wǒ yīnggāi bù yīnggāi sòng lǐ?

B: 我认为你**不应该**送，因为你送礼可能会造成她跟她未婚夫之间的误会。

Wǒ rènwéi nǐ bù yīnggāi sòng, yīnwèi nǐ sòng lǐ kěnéng huì zàochéng tā gēn tā wèihūn fū zhījiān de wùhuì.

C: **应该不**会；我认识她未婚夫，他**应该不**是那种小心眼的人。所以我认为你**应该**送。

Yīnggāi bú huì; wǒ rènshì tā wèihūn fū, tā yīnggāi bú shì nà zhǒng xiǎo xīnyǎn de rén. Suǒyǐ wǒ rènwéi nǐ yīnggāi sòng.

A: My former girlfriend is getting married; do you think I **should** give her a gift?

B: I am of the opinion that you **should not** gave her a gift, because your giving her a gift will probably create misunderstanding between her and her fiancé.

C: It **shouldn't**. I know her fiancé; **my estimation is that he is not** that kind of petty person, so I think you **should** give her a gift.

(Scenario: A teenager has told his parents that he wants to get a part-time job. His parents have differing opinions about it.)

爸爸: 你还是个学生，**应该**专心学习，**不应该**把时间浪费在别的事情上。

Bàba: Nǐ hái shì ge xuéshēng, yīnggāi zhuānxīn xuéxí, bù yīnggāi bǎ shíjiān làngfèi zài biéde shìqíng shàng.

妈妈: 我不同意。他虽然还在上学，可是**应该**有一些工作经验，**不应该**只懂书本里的东西。

Māma: Wǒ bù tóngyì. Tā suīrán hái zài shàngxué, kěshì yīnggāi yǒu yīxiē gōngzuò jīngyàn, bù yīnggāi zhǐ dǒng shūběn lǐ de dōngxi.

爸爸: 好吧！你**应该**听你妈妈的话。

Bàba: Hǎo ba! Nǐ yīnggāi tīng nǐ māma de huà.

Father: You are still a student; you **should** focus your attention on studying, and **should not** waste your time on other things.

Mother: I don't agree. Although he is still in school, he **should** have some work experiences, and **should not** only understand things in the textbooks.

Father: OK! You **should** listen to your mother.

(ii) Although, as stated in section a.(ii) above, 应该不 normally shows one's estimation of a situation, in certain contexts, it can indicate obligation or duty. In this case, 应该 is often used to **give advice**. Because of this, an accurate interpretation of **应该不** can only be achieved by closely observing the context and the intention of the speaker.

For example, 好学生**应该**不迟到、不早退 (*Hǎo xuéshēng yīnggāi bù chídào, bù zǎotuì*) seems to have a more positive tone than 好学生**不应该**迟到、早退, although both sentences can be translated as 'A good student should not arrive late or leave early'.

Therefore, 应该 can also be used to imply what is the **appropriate** thing to do, which may or may not be directly related with one's obligation. The negative form is often **应该不要**.

A: 明天是王经理的生日，他请很多同事去他家吃饭，你认为我**应该**带多贵的礼物去？
Míngtiān shì Wáng jīnglǐ de shēngrì, tā qǐng hěn duō tóngshì qù tā jiā chī fàn, nǐ rènwéi wǒ yīnggāi dài duō guì de lǐwù qù?

B: 你**应该不要**让同事觉得你在炫耀，所以带一束花去**应该**就可以了。
Nǐ yīnggāi bú yào ràng tóngshì juéde nǐ zài xuànyào, suǒyǐ dài yī shù huā qù yīnggāi jiù kěyǐ le.

A: Tomorrow is Manager Wang's birthday; he has invited many coworkers to his house for dinner. How expensive a gift do you think I **should** bring?

B: You **should not** make your coworkers think that you are showing off, so bringing a bunch of flowers **should** be fine.

你想减肥吗？那你就**应该不要**再喝那么多汽水、吃那么多油腻的东西了！
Nǐ xiǎng jiǎnféi ma? Nà nǐ jiù yīnggāi bú yào zài hē nàme duō qìshuǐ, chī nàme duō yóunì de dōngxi le!
Do you want to lose weight? Then you **should not** drink so much soda or eat so much greasy food anymore!

(iii) Sometimes 应该 is not used to describe the obligation of the subject (of the sentence), but to imply **other people's obligation to the subject** because it is **the right or appropriate thing** to do. The connotation is that **the subject deserves it**.

Observing the context is necessary in order to accurately interpret such a sentence. Consider the following scenarios.

明天的演讲比赛，李明**应该会**得第一名，因为他已经准备了很久了。(estimation)
Míngtiān de yǎnjiǎng bǐsài, Lǐ Míng yīnggāi huì dé dì yī míng, yīnwèi tā yǐjīng zhǔnbèi le hěn jiǔ le.
Li Ming **should** win the first prize in tomorrow's speech contest, because he has been preparing for it for a long time.

这次演讲比赛，李明**应该**得第一名，因为他的表现最好。
(appropriateness; deserving)
Zhè cì yǎnjiǎng bǐsài, Lǐ Míng yīnggāi dé dì yī míng, yīnwèi tā de biǎoxiàn zuì hǎo.
Li Ming **should** be given the first prize for this speech contest, because his performance was the best.

这次演讲比赛，你**应该**好好准备，因为你代表我们学校。(duty)
Zhè cì yǎnjiǎng bǐsài, nǐ yīnggāi hǎo hǎo zhǔnbèi, yīnwèi nǐ dàibiǎo wǒmen xuéxiào.
You **should** do a good job preparing for this speech contest, because you represent our school.

c. When 应该 is used as the **predicate** of a sentence, it can be considered an **adjective**.

(i) It is used to accuse someone or some action of being **morally or socially unacceptable or inappropriate**. The phrase is 很不应该. 很 **(or another degree adverb) is necessary** in a statement and **only the negative form 不应该** can be used this way.

王小兰不用功，所以成绩不好，可是她却常常批评老师，说老师教得不好；她实在**很不应该**。
Wáng Xiǎolán bú yònggōng, suǒyǐ chéngjī bù hǎo, kěshì tā què chángcháng pīpíng lǎoshī, shuō lǎoshī jiāo de bù hǎo. Tā shízài hěn bù yīnggāi.
Wang Xiaolan does not study hard, so her school performance is bad; but she frequently criticizes her teacher and says that the teacher does not do a good job teaching. She is truly **wrong in doing so**. (She **should not behave this way**.)

小中在幼儿园里常常欺负比他小的小朋友，推他们、抢他们的玩具；这种行为，真**太不应该**了！
Xiǎozhōng zài yòu'ér yuán lǐ chángcháng qīfù bǐ tā xiǎo de xiǎo péngyǒu, tuī tāmen, qiǎng tāmen de wánjù; zhè zhǒng xíngwéi zhēn tài bù yīnggāi le.
Xiaozhong often bullies children younger than himself in the kindergarten; he pushes them and forcibly takes away their toys. Such behavior is really **wrong (unacceptable)**.

(ii) When 应该 is used to describe a **just or proper behavior**, the phrase must be 是应该的. The implication is 'it is something one should do'.
It is **incorrect to use** 很应该 or simply 应该. If it is a stand-alone expression without specifically mentioning the subject, 是 can be optional, but **的 is always necessary**.

A:　这次你帮了我们这么大的忙，真感谢你！

　　Zhè cì nǐ bāng le wǒmen zhème dà de máng, zhēn gǎnxiè nǐ!

B:　哪里！**(是)应该的**！**(是)应该的**！不用谢！你们也帮过我很多
　　次。

　　*Nǎlǐ! Yīnggāi de! Yīnggāi de! Búyòng xiè! Nǐmen yě bāng guo wǒ
　　hěn duō cì.*

A:　You did us such a big favor this time, we are really grateful.

B:　You're welcome. It's **what I should do**. No need to thank me. You
　　have also helped me many times before.

A:　张太太常常抱怨小张太喜欢赚钱。

　　*Zhāng tàitai chángcháng bàoyuàn Xiǎo Zhāng tài xǐhuān zhuàn
　　qián.*

B:　她抱怨什么？难道小张**不应该**努力赚钱吗？

　　*Tā bàoyuàn shénme? Nándào Xiǎo Zhāng bù yīnggāi nǔlì zhuàn
　　qián ma?*

A:　赚钱**是应该的**，可是小张为了赚钱，连家都很少回，他太太当
　　然要抱怨。

　　*Zhuàn qián shì yīnggāi de, kěshì Xiǎo Zhāng wèile zhuàn qián, lián
　　jiā dōu hěnshǎo huí, tā tàitai dāngrán yào bàoyuàn.*

A:　Mrs Zhang often complains that Little Zhang likes making money
　　too much.

B:　What is there to complain about? Does she mean to say that Little
　　Zhang **should not** work hard to make money?

A:　Making money is **the way it should be**. But in order to make
　　money, Little Zhang would seldom even go home. Of course his
　　wife would complain.

又 *yòu*

又 has two basic meanings: 'again' and 'also'. These basic meanings suggest its
versatility as it is used to show not only **repetitions** but also **layers of events
or situations**. Discussions in this section focus on its most common uses.

a.　**又 as 'again'**

(i)　When 又 is defined as 'again', it indicates the repetition of an action or
　　event that **already took place**.

昨天生意不好，只来了三个客人；不过那三位客人今天**又来了**。

*Zuótiān shēngyì bù hǎo, zhǐ lái le sān ge kèrén; búguò nà sān wèi kèrén
jīntiān yòu lái le.*

Business was bad yesterday; only three customers came. But those three
customers **came again** today.

The repetition can be implied by the presence of 又 without explicitly mentioning it has happened before.

这个问题我已经告诉过你应该怎么解决了，你为什么**又来**问我？

Zhè ge wèntí wǒ yǐjīng gàosù guo nǐ yīnggāi zěnme jiějué le, nǐ wèi shénme yòu lái wèn wǒ?

I have already told you how to solve the problem. Why **have** you asked me **again**?

真高兴！周末**又到了**！

Zhēn gāoxìng! Zhōumò yòu dào le.

I am so happy! The weekend **is here (has arrived) again**.

又 can indicate that a repeated action **is taking place when the utterance is made**. In this case, **又在** is frequently used.

你不是刚吃过午饭吗？怎么**又在**吃点心？

Nǐ bú shì gāng chī guo wǔfàn ma? Zěnme yòu zài chī diǎnxīn?

Didn't you just eat lunch? How come you **are eating** a snack **again**?

(ii) The repetition does not have to be an identical (exactly the same) action; 又 can be used when a **similar action (intended to achieve the same purpose)** is performed. Although 'also' is often used to translate this 又, learners should be aware that **也 should not be used** in this context because 又 implies **the succession of the action**, whereas 也 does not.

今天我肚子特别饿：**吃了**两碗**饭**，觉得还不饱，所以**又喝了**一大碗**汤**。(吃 and 喝 are similar actions.)

Jīntiān wǒ dùzi tèbié è; chī le liǎng wǎn fàn, juéde hái bù bǎo, suǒyǐ yòu hē le yī dà wǎn tāng.

Today I was particularly hungry. After **consuming** (eating) two bowls of **rice**, I felt that I was still not full, so I **also** had (**consumed**) a big bowl of **soup**.

今天天气很冷，风也很大。王先生**穿上**大衣，想了一下，**又戴上**帽子，才开门走出去。(穿 and 戴 are similar actions.)

Jīntiān tiānqì hěn lěng, fēng yě hěn dà. Wáng xiānsheng chuān shàng dàyī, xiǎng le yīxià, yòu dài shàng màozi, cái kāi mén zǒu chūqù.

It was cold today, and the wind was also strong. Mr Wang **put on** his coat, thought for a moment, and then he **also put on** his hat before he opened the door and walked out.

这次考试，我考得非常好，所以昨天爸爸**给了我**五百块钱，我好高兴！没想到他今天又**送了我**一个平板电脑。(给 and 送 are similar actions.)

Zhè cì kǎoshì, wǒ kǎo de fēicháng hǎo, suǒyǐ zuótiān bàba gěi le wǒ wǔ bǎi kuài qián, wǒ hǎo gāoxìng! Méi xiǎngdào tā jīntiān yòu sòng le wǒ yī ge píngbǎn diànnǎo.

I did extremely well on the test, so my father **gave me** 500 *kuai* yesterday. I was so happy! I did not expect that he **would also give me** a tablet computer today!

b. **又 and 再 (*zài*)**

(i) Although 再 is used when the repetition of an action has not yet taken place (but will take place sometime in the future), **又要** or **又会**, not 再要 or 再会, is used **for future repetition**.

听说今天**又会**下雨，你出门的时候，别忘了带伞。
Tīngshuō jīntiān yòu huì xià yǔ, nǐ chū mén de shíhòu, bié wàng le dài sǎn.
It is said that it **will** rain **again** today. Don't forget to take an umbrella with you when you go out.

(Scenario: The teacher has announced that she will give a test tomorrow.)

学生:	什么？明天**又要**考试？昨天刚考了一个试，为什么明天**又要**考？
Xuésheng:	*Shénme? Míngtiān yòu yào kǎoshì? Zuótiān gāng kǎo le yī ge shì, wèi shénme míngtiān yòu yào kǎo?*
Student:	What? We **will** have a test **again** tomorrow? We just had a test yesterday. Why are we **going to** take one **again** tomorrow?

In the following examples, pay special attention to the **word order of 又, 要 and 再** when two or all three of them appear in the same sentence.

这本小说真好看！我有空的时候，**要再看**一遍。(This is an event **to be repeated in the future**.)
Zhè běn xiǎoshuō zhēn hǎokàn! Wǒ yǒu kòng de shíhòu, yào zài kàn yī biàn.
This novel is really good! When I have some free time, I **am going to read it again**.

这本小说，我去年看过一遍，今年**又看了**一遍，因为实在太好看了！(This is an event already repeated.)
Zhè běn xiǎoshuō, wǒ qùnián kàn guo yī biàn, jīnnián yòu kàn le yī biàn, yīnwèi shízài tài hǎokàn le!
I read this novel once last year, and I **read it one more time** this year because it was truly very good!

A: 今年的寒假，你有什么计划？

Jīnnián de hánjià, nǐ yǒu shénme jìhuà?

B: 我**要再看**一次《战争与和平》。

Wǒ yào zài kàn yī cì 'zhànzhēng yǔ hépíng'.

A: 什么？你**又要看**这本小说？你不是已经看过了吗？为什么**又要**
再看一次？

Shénme? Nǐ yòu yào kàn zhè běn xiǎoshuō? Nǐ bú shì yǐjīng kàn
guo le ma? Wèi shénme yòu yào zài kàn yī cì?

B: 其实，这本书我已经看过两次了。年轻的时候看过一次，两年
前**又看了**一次，这次是第三次了。

Qíshí, zhè běn shū wǒ yǐjīng kàn guo liǎng cì le. Niánqīng de shí
hòu kàn guo yī cì, liǎng nián qián yòu kàn le yī cì, zhè cì shì dì
sān cì le.

A: What plan do you have for the winter break this year?

B: I **want to read** *War and Peace* **one more time**.

A: What? You **are going to read** this novel **again**? Didn't you already
read it? Why are you **going to read it one more time**?

B: Actually, I have read this book twice already. When I was young, I
read it once; I **read it again** two years ago. This will be the third time.

可以 and 能 also follow 又, not 再.

冬天**又**到了！我们**又可以**去滑雪了！

Dōngtiān yòu dào le! Wǒmen yòu kěyǐ qù huáxuě le.

Winter is here **again**! We **can** go skiing **again**!

(ii) In a sentence with 'if' (要是, 如果, etc.) to indicate a **hypothetical**
situation or a condition, either 再 or 又 is acceptable.

(Scenario: A student is caught plagiarizing.)

老师: 这次给你一个机会，你回家去**再**写一次。**如果下次又被**
我发现你抄袭，那就给你零分。

Lǎoshī: *Zhè cì gěi nǐ yī ge jīhuì, nǐ huí jiā qù zài xiě yī cì. Rúguǒ*
xià cì yòu bèi wǒ fāxiàn nǐ chāoxí, nà jiù gěi nǐ líng fēn.

学生: 我**以后**不敢**再**抄袭了！

Xuéshēng: *Wǒ yǐhòu bù gǎn zài chāoxí le!*

Teacher: I will give you a chance this time. Go home and write it
again. If next time you are found to have plagiarized **again**,
then I will give you a zero.

Student: I dare not plagiarize **again from now on**.

我已经叫你别来吵我了；**要是**你**再**来吵我，我就真的要发脾气了！

Wǒ yǐjīng jiào nǐ bié lái chǎo wǒ le. Yàoshì nǐ zài lái chǎo wǒ, wǒ jiù
zhēnde yào fā píqì le.

I have already told you not to bother me. **If** you come to bother me
again, I will really get angry.

c. **又 A 又 B** (both A and B) and **又不 A 又不 B** (neither A nor B)

(i)　A and B must be **adjectives or verbs**. Nouns cannot be used. A and B are two items of **equal prominence**; they can be switched. In addition, a comma is used when A is longish.

那只小狗的主人给它穿上了人的衣服，看起来**又可爱又可笑**。
Nà zhī xiǎo gǒu de zhǔrén gěi tā chuān shàng le rén de yīfu, kàn qǐlái **yòu kě'ài yòu kěxiào.**
That little dog's master put human's clothes on him, so he looks **both** cute **and** funny.

这家餐厅的菜**又不地道又不好吃**，所以顾客不多。
Zhè jiā cāntīng de cài yòu bú dìdào yòu bù hǎochī, suǒyǐ gùkè bù duō.
This restaurant's food is **neither** authentic **nor** delicious, so there are not many customers.

小王**又学**中文，**又学**电脑，所以他每天忙得要命。(It is incorrect to say 小王学又中文又电脑 since 中文 and 电脑 are nouns.)
Xiǎo Wáng yòu xué Zhōngwén, yòu xué diànnǎo, suǒyǐ tā měi tiān máng de yàomìng.
Little Wang majors in **(studies) both** Chinese **and** computer science, so he is extremely busy every day.

小李高中毕业以后，**又不找**工作，**又不申请**大学，整天在家玩电子游戏，他爸妈气死了。
Xiǎo Lǐ gāozhōng bìyè yǐhòu, yòu bù zhǎo gōngzuò, yòu bù shēnqǐng dàxué, zhěngtiān zài jiā wán diànzǐ yóuxì, tā bàmā qì sǐ le.
Since Little Li graduated from high school, he has **neither** looked for a job **nor** applied to universities; he plays video games at home all day long. His parents are extremely angry.

(ii)　'既(不) A 又(不) B' is considered interchangeable with '又(不) A 又(不) B'.

小李**既不**聪明**又不**用功，所以成绩很差。
Xiǎo Lǐ jì bù cōngmíng yòu bú yònggōng, suǒyǐ chéngjī hěn chà.
Little Li is **neither** smart **nor** diligent, so his grades in school are bad.

坐公共汽车**既**便宜**又**方便，所以比开车好得多。
Zuò gōnggòng qìchē jì piányí yòu fāngbiàn, suǒyǐ bǐ kāi chē hǎo de duō.
Riding public transportation is **both** inexpensive **and** convenient, so it is much better than driving.

d.   **又 indicating conflict or contradiction**

(i)   又 indicates that a **subsequent action** is in **direct contradiction** to the first one.

(Scenario: Zhang has promised that she will not laugh at Li if Li tells her his secret. But she laughs upon hearing it.)

李: 你答应了**不笑**我现在你**又在笑**，我以后不告诉你任何秘密了。

Lǐ: Nǐ dāyìng le bú xiào wǒ xiànzài nǐ yòu zài xiào, wǒ yǐhòu bú gàosù nǐ rènhé mìmì le.

Li: You promised you **would not laugh** at me **but** now you **are laughing**. I will not tell you any secrets from now on.

(Scenario: Wang has said that he will come to Li's party. But he does not show up.)

李: 老王说了**要来又不来**，下次不请他了。

Lǐ: Lǎo Wáng shuō le yào lái yòu bù lái, xià cì bù qǐng tā le.

Li: Old Wang said he **would come but** he **didn't come**. I will not invite him next time.

昨天晚上的天气预报**说**今天全天是**晴天**，今天早上的预报**又说**下午会**下雨**，我不知道到底要不要带伞。

Zuótiān wǎnshàng de tiānqì yùbào shuō jīntiān quán tiān shì qíngtiān, jīntiān zǎoshàng de yùbào yòu shuō xiàwǔ huì xià yǔ, wǒ bù zhīdào dàodǐ yào bú yào dài sǎn.

Yesterday evening's weather forecast **said** that it would be **sunny** all day today; **but** the forecast this morning **said** that there would be **rain** this afternoon. I don't know whether I should bring an umbrella or not.

(ii)   又 can be used when **two existent situations** are **in contradiction** with each other. 可是 (*kěshì*: but) is implied, and is optional because 又 serves the function of showing the contradiction.

王明已经上大二了，还住在家里；他很**想**搬出去一个人住，**又不敢**跟他爸妈说。

Wáng Míng yǐjīng shàng dà èr le, hái zhù zài jiā lǐ; tā hěn xiǎng bān chūqù yī ge rén zhù, yòu bù gǎn gēn tā bàmā shuō.

Wang Ming is already a sophomore (second-year student) in college, and he still lives at home. He really **wants** to move out to live by himself, **but** he **dare not** tell his parents.

(iii)   '一方面 A，（另）一方面又 B' (*yī fāngmiàn A lìng yī fāngmiàn yòu B*) is a typical pattern to show the contradiction with 又.

李文的爸妈**一方面**说他上不上大学都没关系，**(另)一方面又**花很多钱请家教来给他补习，希望他能考进好大学。

Lǐ Wén de bàmā yī fāngmiàn shuō tā shàng bú shàng dàxué dōu méi guānxì, (lìng) yī fāngmiàn yòu huā hěnduō qián qǐng jiājiào lái gěi tā bǔxí, xīwàng tā néng kǎo jìn hǎo dàxué.

Li Wen's parents, **on the one hand**, say that whether he goes to college or not does not matter; they, **on the other hand, (however,)** spend a lot of money hiring a tutor to give him extra instruction and help with his homework, hoping he can get into a good college.

又 and 却 (*què*) are interchangeable when used in this context, but 却 may seem to be **stronger in tone** in showing the contradiction.

王小兰**一方面**说要减肥，**一方面却**不停地吃零食，难道她以为吃零食不会让她发胖吗？

Wáng Xiǎolán yī fāngmiàn shuō yào jiǎnféi, yī fāngmiàn què bùtíng de chī língshí, nándào tā yǐwéi chī língshí bú huì ràng tā fā pàng ma?

Wang Xiaolan, **on the one hand**, says she wants to lose weight; **however, on the other hand**, she is constantly eating snacks. Does this mean that she thinks eating snacks will not cause her to gain weight?

却 and 又 can coexist, but 却 must appear before 又.

王先生**一方面**要他的孩子少看电视，**一方面又**(or 却 or 却又) 去买了一个大荧幕的电视，真不知道他在想什么！

Wáng xiānsheng yī fāngmiàn yào tā de háizi shǎo kàn diànshì, yī fāngmiàn yòu (or què or què yòu) qù mǎi le yī ge dà yíngmù de diànshì, zhēn bù zhīdào tā zài xiǎng shénme!

Mr Wang, **on the one hand**, wants his children to watch less TV; **on the other hand**, he went and bought a big-screen TV. I really don't know what he was thinking!

e. **又 indicating absurdity or bewilderment**

又 can be used **before a negative word (不/没有)** to indicate the **mild absurdity of a situation** or the **bewilderment of the speaker** about a situation. **A question typically follows** the sentence with 又, but such a question is usually a **rhetorical question** to show the absurdity or bewilderment.

Since 又 used this way has no translation in English and is completely context-dependent, its connotation is hard for learners to grasp. The following examples provide contexts that illustrate the need to have 又 in each of them.

A: 下课以后一起去看电影吧！
   Xià kè yǐhòu yīqǐ qù kàn diànyǐng ba!
B: 不行，我得回家学习。
   Bù xíng, wǒ děi huí jiā xuéxí.
A: 明天**又没有**考试，你今天晚上**为什么**要学习？
   Míngtiān yòu méiyǒu kǎoshì, nǐ jīntiān wǎnshàng wèi shénme yào xuéxí?

A: How about if we go to a movie together after class?
B: I can't. I have to go home to study.
A: It is **not as if** there is a test tomorrow. Why do you have to study this evening?

A: 我反对小英跟王大中结婚！
 Wǒ fǎnduì Xiǎoyīng gēn Wáng Dàzhōng jiéhūn!
B: 你**又不是**她爸爸，你有**什么**资格反对？
 Nǐ yòu bú shì tā bàba, nǐ yǒu shénme zīgé fǎnduì?
A: I oppose Xiaoying marrying Wang Dazhong!
B: It's **not as if** you are her father. You are in no position to oppose it.
 (Literally: What qualification do you have to oppose it?)

(Scenario: A woman asks her boyfriend to wait for her for a moment because she has to go back inside the house to get her umbrella.)
男: 今天**又不**会下雨，你**为什么**要带伞？太麻烦了！别带了吧！
Nán: *Jīntiān yòu bú huì xià yǔ, nǐ wèi shénme yào dài sǎn? Tài máfán le! Bié dài le ba!*
女: 我自己拿着，**又没有**叫你帮我拿，我带伞关你**什么**事？
Nǚ: *Wǒ zìjǐ ná zhe, yòu méiyǒu jiào nǐ bāng wǒ ná, wǒ dài sǎn guān nǐ shénme shì?*
Man: It's **not as if** it will rain today; why do you want to bring an umbrella? It's too much trouble! Don't bring it with you.
Woman: I hold it myself, and it's **not as if** I have asked you to hold it for me. What business is it of yours if I bring my umbrella?

与其 *yǔqí*

与其 is not a stand-alone word; it is always followed by a clause with either 宁可 (*nìngkě*) or 不如 (*bùrú*). '**与其 A 宁可/不如 B**' indicates that after evaluating the two options of A and B, one decides to choose **option B** because it is **the better** of the two.

  不如 and 宁可 are not always interchangeable. 宁可 suggests that option B is the better of two less-than-ideal options; 不如, on the other hand, may or may not have that implication. Therefore, it is important to observe the context before choosing the appropriate expression.

a. **与其 A 宁可 B**: Both A and B are undesirable, but B is still better than A.

我是吃素的，可是老板今年竟然选了一家牛排馆举行一年一度的员工聚餐。我决定，**与其**吃肉，我**宁可**得罪老板，所以我没有去。
Wǒ shì chī sù de, kěshì lǎobǎn jīnnián jìngrán xuǎn le yī jiā niúpái guǎn jǔxíng yī nián yī dù de yuán gōng jùcān. Wǒ juédìng, yǔqí chī ròu, wǒ nìngkě dézuì lǎobǎn, suǒyǐ wǒ méiyǒu qù.
I am a vegetarian. But who would have known that our boss would have picked a steakhouse for the annual employee dinner. I decided that **offending my boss** would still **be better than eating meat**. So I didn't go.

(Scenario: A man justifies his career choice to his friend.)

A: 你以前在那家科技公司薪水那么高，你为什么要换到现在这家小公司工作？

   Nǐ yǐqián zài nà jiā kējì gōngsī xīnshuǐ nàme gāo; nǐ wèi shénme yào huàn dào xiànzài zhè jiā xiǎo gōngsī gōngzuò?

B: 因为我现在是主管。我认为，**与其**在大公司当职员，**宁可**在小公司当主管。

   Yīnwèi wǒ xiànzài shì zhǔguǎn. Wǒ rènwéi, yǔqí zài dà gōngsī dāng zhíyuán, nìngkě zài xiǎo gōngsī dāng zhǔguǎn.

A: You used to make so much money at that high-tech company. Why did you change your job and work for this small company?

B: Because I am an executive now. I think that **being an executive** even in a small company is **better than being a staff member** in a big company.

→ See 宁可 (*nìngkě*) for related information.

b. **与其 A 不如 B**: B is the better choice of the two.

A: 我打算减肥，所以决定一天只吃一餐。

   Wǒ dǎsuàn jiǎnféi, suǒyǐ juédìng yī tiān zhǐ chī yī cān.

B: 那对身体不好。**与其**节食，**不如**多运动

   Nà duì shēntǐ bùhǎo. Yǔqí jiéshí, bùrú duō yùndòng.

A: I plan to lose weight, so I have decided that I will only eat one meal a day.

B: That is not good for your health. Exercising more often is **better than** dieting.

A: 为了省钱，从明天起，我不再开车上班，要坐公共汽车。

   Wèile shěng qián, cóng míngtiān qǐ, wǒ bú zài kāi chē shàngbān, yào zuò gōnggòng qìchē.

B: **与其**坐公共汽车，**不如**骑自行车，又方便又可以运动。

   Yǔqí zuò gōnggòng qìchē, bùrú qí zìxíngchē, yòu fāngbiàn yòu kěyǐ yùndòng.

A: In order to save money, starting tomorrow, I will no long drive to work; I will ride public transportation.

B: Riding public transportation is **not as good as** riding a bicycle. Riding a bicycle is convenient, and you can also get some exercise.

c. 还不如 or 倒不如 can be used in place of simply 不如。

A: 一般家庭多半是妻子做饭，在你家，为什么是你做饭？

   Yībān jiātíng duōbàn shì qīzi zuò fàn, zài nǐ jiā, wèi shénme shì nǐ zuò fàn?

B: 我妻子不太会做菜，她做的菜我都不喜欢吃。所以**与其**她做，**倒不如** (or **还不如**) 我自己来做。

   Wǒ qīzi bú tài huì zuò cài, tā zuò de cài wǒ dōu bù xǐhuān chī. Suǒyǐ yǔqí tā zuò, dǎo bùrú (or hái bùrú) wǒ zìjǐ lái zuò.

A: In most families, it is the wife that cooks. Why is it that you are the one who cooks in your family?

B: My wife is not very good at cooking. I don't like her cooking. So it **is better** if I (myself) cook **than** if she cooks.

→ See 不如 (*bùrú*) for related information.

在 *zài* + person + 看来 *kàn lái*

This is a phrase used to express one's opinion. It is often translated as 'in one's opinion', 'from one's point of view' and other similar phrases.

'在 + person + 看来' shares similarities with 'person + 认为' in meaning, but there are some differences in usage. A **mistake** learners sometimes make is to translate the phrase 'in my opinion' too literally and the result is 在我的看来, which is not a legitimate expression in Chinese.

→ See 认为 (*rènwéi*) for related information.

a. **A comma** after 'person + 认为' is optional, but a comma after '在 + person + 看来' is necessary.

(Scenario: Two people are having a discussion on China's population policy.)

A: **我认为(，)** 政府没有权力规定老百姓生几个孩子。
   Wǒ rènwéi(,) zhèngfǔ méiyǒu quánlì guīdìng lǎobǎixìng shēng jǐ ge háizi.

B: **在我看来，**人口太多是国家的负担，所以中国必须有人口政策。
   Zài wǒ kàn lái, rénkǒu tài duō shì guójiā de fùdān, suǒyǐ Zhōngguó bìxū yǒu rénkǒu zhèngcè.

A: **I think (I am of the opinion)** that the government does not have the power to stipulate how many children civilians can have.

B: **From my point of view**, too large a population is the country's burden, so China must have a population policy.

b. '在 + person + 看来' can be used as an **interpolation**, which appears **after the subject**. When it is used this way, **commas before and after the phrase** are necessary to show that it is inserted into the sentence.

少吃、多运动，**在我看来，**是最有效的减肥方法。
Shǎo chī, duō yùndòng, zài wǒ kànlái, shì zuì yǒuxiào de jiǎnféi fāngfǎ.
Eating less and exercising more, **in my opinion**, is the most effective way to lose weight.

再也不 . . . 了 *zài yě bù . . . le*

再也不 . . . 了 is a strong expression, which means 'never again'. 了 is necessary to show a **change of situation**. There are two possible implications in terms of time frame.

If one does not wish to adopt such a strong tone, then 不再 . . . 了 would suffice.

a. It indicates that something will **never happen again** in the future (or from now on).

昨天我去长江饭馆吃饭，他们的菜又贵又不好吃，服务员态度也很差，我以后**再也不**去那里吃饭**了**。

Zuótiān wǒ qù Chángjiāng fànguǎn chī fàn, tāmen de cài yòu guì yòu bù hǎochī, fúwùyuán tàidù yě hěn chà, wǒ yǐhòu zài yě bú qù nàlǐ chī fàn le.

Yesterday I went to Chang Jiang restaurant for a meal. Their food was expensive and did not taste good; the waiter's attitude was also bad; I **will never** go there to eat **again**.

A: 听说张明在背后说了你很多坏话。
   Tīngshuō Zhāng Míng zài bèi hòu shuō le nǐ hěn duō huài huà.
B: 什么？我帮了他这么多忙，他还说我的坏话，我以后**再也不**跟这种人交往**了**。
   Shénme? Wǒ bāng le tā zhème duō máng, tā hái shuō wǒ de huài huà, wǒ yǐhòu zài yě bù gēn zhè zhǒng rén jiāowǎng le.

A: I heard that Zhang Ming said a lot of bad things about you behind your back.
B: What? I have done him so many favors, and he would still bad-mouth me. From now on, I **will never** be friends with this type of person **again**.

每个月交房租真划不来；等我存够了钱买了自己的房子，就**再也不**用花钱租别人的房子**了**。

Měi ge yuè jiāo fáng zū zhēn huá bù lái; děng wǒ cún gòu le qián mǎi le zìjǐ de fángzi yǐhòu, jiù zài yě bú yòng huā qián zū biérén de fángzi le.

Paying rent every month is really a bad deal. When I have saved enough money and bought my own house, I **will never** have to spend money renting other people's houses **anymore**.

b. It indicates that one **has refused to** do something again (or has intentionally stopped doing something) **since a certain point**.

自从我发现他骗我**以后**，就**再也不**跟他说话**了**。

Zìcóng wǒ fāxiàn tā piàn wǒ yǐhòu, jiù zài yě bù gēn tā shuō huà le.

Ever since I found out that he lied to me, I **do not** talk to him **anymore**. (I **have stopped** talking to him.)

我以前很喜欢用这个牌子的化妆品，可是后来有人告诉我他们用动物做测试，所以就**再也不**买他们的产品**了**。

Wǒ yǐqián hěn xǐhuān yòng zhè ge páizi de huàzhuāngpǐn; kěshì hòulái yǒu rén gàosù wǒ tāmen yòng dòngwù zuò cèshì, suǒyǐ jiù zài yě bù mǎi tāmen de chǎnpǐn le.

I used to like to use this brand's cosmetics, but later someone told me that they use animals to do testing, and so I **have never bought** their products **again** (I **have stopped buying** their products **since then**).

再也没有 . . . 过（了）*zài yě méiyǒu . . . guo (le)*

再也没有 . . . 过（了）is a stronger version of 没有再 . . . 过. 了 **is optional.** It indicates that something **has stopped happening since a certain point.**

王中喜欢开快车；可是半年多以前，他被开了一张罚单，交了两百块罚款以后，他就**再也没有**开**过**快车**(了)**。

Wáng Zhōng xǐhuān kāi kuài chē; kěshì bàn nián duō yǐqián, tā bèi kāi le yī zhāng fá dān, jiāo le liǎng bǎi kuài fákuǎn yǐhòu, tā jiù zài yě méiyǒu kāi guo kuài chē (le).

Wang Zhong liked to drive fast, but a little over half a year ago, he was issued a speeding ticket; after he paid a fine of 200 *kuai*, **(since then,)** he **has never** driven too fast.

(Scenario: Mr Wang and a friend are eating at a new Chinese restaurant. He is surprised at how authentic their food is.)

王:　　　自从我三十年前离开故乡以后，就**再也没有**吃**过**这么地道的家乡菜**了**。

Wáng:　*Zìcóng wǒ sānshí nián qián líkāi gùxiāng yǐhòu, jiù zài yě méiyǒu chī guo zhème dìdào de jiāxiāng cài le.*

朋友:　　难道你离开中国以后，就**再也没有**回去**过了**吗？

Péngyǒu:　*Nándào nǐ líkāi Zhōngguó yǐhòu, jiù zài yě méiyǒu huí qù guo le ma?*

Wang:　　**Ever since** I left my hometown 30 years ago, I **have not once had** such authentic food with my hometown's local flavors.

Friend:　　Do you mean to tell me that you **have never been** back **since** you left China?

Related expressions

再也没有 + noun + 了

Because a noun can follow 没有, '再也没有 + noun + 了' should not be confused with '再也没有 + verb + 过' (了).

了 in '再也没有 + noun + 了' implies '**no longer**' and it is **not optional**.

(Scenario: A sales person is trying to persuade a customer to buy something.)

今天是最后一天打折，要是你今天不买，就**再也没有**这么好的机会**了**。

Jīntiān shì zuìhòu yī tiān dǎ zhé, yàoshì nǐ jīntiān bù mǎi, jiù zài yě méiyǒu zhème hǎo de jīhuì le.

Today is the last day we're giving a discount. If you don't buy (it) today, **there will never be** such a good opportunity **again**.

张文去美国以前，再三地说他一定会常常给我们写信、打电话；可是他
走了以后，我们就**再也没有**他的消息**了**。

Zhāng Wén qù Měiguó yǐqián, zàisān de shuō tā yīdìng huì chángcháng gěi
wǒmen xiě xìn, dǎ diànhuà; kěshì tā zǒu le yǐhòu, wǒmen jiù zài yě méiyǒu
tā de xiāoxí le.

Before Zhang Wen went to the U.S., he repeatedly said that he would definitely
write us letters and call us often. But since he has gone, we **have not had**
any news from him (not even once).

从来 *cónglái*

从来 is nearly always followed by a negative word, such as 不 or 没有,
to indicate '**never**'. However, 从来不/从来没有 and 再也不 . . . 了/再也没有
. . . 过了 have **different connotations** and are used in **different contexts**. Therefore, it is important to observe the context before choosing the proper expression
for 'never'.

→ See 从来 (*cónglái*) for related information.

造成 *zàochéng*

造成 means 'to cause' or 'to result in', and is **followed by a noun or a sentence**.
Learners often confuse 造成 with 使 (*shǐ*) because 使 can be defined as 'to cause'
as well. It is important to know the difference between the two words in terms
of grammar usage so as to avoid mistakes.

→ See 使 (*shǐ*) for more information.

怎么 *zěnme*

Without context, 怎么 is generally defined as '**how**'. But when used in context,
怎么 can take up several different meanings, some of which are actually translated
as '**what**' in English.

a. 怎么 can mean '**how come**'; it is an interrogative pronoun and is similar to
为什么 (*wèi shénme*: why), but 怎么 implies that the speaker finds the situation **mildly puzzling or unexpected**. The **subject** of the sentence normally
appears **before** 怎么.

A: 你知不知道老李昨天**为什么**请客？(怎么 would not be proper in this
question.)
Nǐ zhī bù zhīdào Lǎo Lǐ zuótiān wèi shénme qǐngkè?
B: 因为他上个月升主管了。奇怪！你们是好朋友，他**怎么**没请你？
Yīnwèi tā shàng ge yuè shēng zhǔguǎn le. Qíguài! Nǐmen shì hǎo
péngyǒu, tā zěnme méi qǐng nǐ?

A: Do you know **why** Old Li had a dinner party yesterday?
B: Because he was promoted to the position of the executive last month. Strange! You two are good friends; **how come** he did not invite you?

b. As '**how**', 怎么 is used to describe **the manner or method** in which an action is performed. When used this way, 怎么 should appear **before the verb**; also, it is synonymous with 如何 (*rúhé*), but 如何 makes the utterance somewhat more formal than when 怎么 is used.

In the following examples, the two occurrences of 怎么 in each scenario have different meanings.

A: 下这么大的雨，你**怎么**来了？你是**怎么**来的？
    Xià zhème dà de yǔ, nǐ zěnme lái le? Nǐ shì zěnme lái de?
B: 我是打车来的。
    Wǒ shì dǎchē lái de.
A: It is raining so hard; **how come** you are here? **How** did you get here?
B: I came by taxi.

A: 要是有人用英文跟我说"对不起"，我应该**怎么**回答？(怎么 can be 如何.)
    Yàoshì yǒu rén yòng Yīngwén gēn wǒ shuō 'duìbùqǐ', wǒ yīnggāi zěnme huídá?
B: 我已经教过你好几次了，你**怎么**总是记不住？
    Wǒ yǐjīng jiāo guo nǐ hǎo jǐ cì le, nǐ zěnme zǒngshì jì bú zhù?
A: If someone says 'sorry' to me in English, **how** should I respond?
B: I have already taught you this several times; **how come** you can never remember?

c. 怎么 can be used in a **rhetorical question** to make a **negative statement**. Although 怎么 in this case is still translated as 'how', its connotation is '**how is it possible . . . ?**', thereby indicating **it is not possible**. Frequently, **会 follows 怎么** in this usage. When 怎么 is used this way, it can be considered interchangeable with **哪里** (*nǎlǐ*), which can also be used in a rhetorical question to make a negative statement.

→ See 哪里 (*nǎlǐ*) for related information.

(Scenario: Mrs Li explains to a nosy friend, Mrs Wang, why her son does not have a girlfriend.)
王: 你儿子都三十几了，**怎么**还没有女朋友？
Wáng: *Nǐ érzi dōu sānshí jǐ le, zěnme hái méiyǒu nǔ péngyǒu?*
李: 他一个星期得工作六、七十个小时，**怎么(会)**有时间交女朋友？(= **哪里**有时间 . . . = **没**有时间 . . .)
Lǐ: *Tā yī ge xīngqī děi gōngzuò liù, qīshí ge xiǎoshí, zěnme (huì) yǒu shíjiān jiāo nǔ péngyǒu?*

A: Your son is already over 30 years old; **how come** he still does not have a girlfriend?

B: He has to work 60 or 70 hours a week; **how is it possible** that he has time to date any women? (Meaning: He **does not** have time to date.)

d.   怎么 can be used as a **stand-alone expression** indicating one's **surprise or curiosity**. There is no direct counterpart in English for this 怎么, although it is somewhat similar to the English expression '**what's going on?**'

张: 老王，借我二十块钱，好不好？
Zhāng: *Lǎo Wáng, jiè wǒ èrshí kuài qián, hǎo bù hǎo?*
王: **怎么**？前天才发工资，你**怎么**就没钱了？
Wáng: *Zěnme? Qiántiān cái fā gōngzī, nǐ zěnme jiù méi qián le?*
Zhang: Old Wang, loan me 20 *kuai*, OK?
Wang: **(Showing surprise)** We only got paid the day before yesterday; **how come** you've already run out of money?

e.   In certain contexts, some expressions involving the word 怎么 are actually translated as **'what' in English**. These expressions thus merit special attention. Such expressions include:

（我）**怎么办？**   （*Wǒ*）*zěnme bàn?*
What (am I) going to do (to solve the problem)?'
（他）**怎么了？**   （*Tā*）*zěnme le?*
What happened (to him)? **What**'s the matter (with him)?
（这是）**怎么回事？**   （*Zhè shì*）*zěnme huí shì?*
What's going on? **What** has happened?

(Scenario: Xiaoying is crying; her mother is concerned.)
妈: 小英，你**怎么了**？
Mā: *Xiǎoyīng, nǐ zěnme le?*
英: 我把哥哥新买的数位相机摔坏了。我不知道该**怎么办**。
Yīng: *Wǒ bǎ gēge xīn mǎi de shùwèi xiàngjī shuāi huài le. Wǒ bù zhīdào gāi zěnme bàn.*
妈: 哦？**怎么回事**？是**怎么**摔坏的？
Mā: *Ó? Zěnme huí shì? Shì zěnme shuāi huài de?*
Mother: Xiaoying, **what**'s the matter?
Ying: I dropped and broke Brother's new digital camera. I don't know **what to do**.
Mother: Oh? **What** has happened? **How** did you (drop and) break it?

f.   An **adjective can follow** 不怎么 to imply '**not very + adjective**'. Although it is similar in meaning to '**不太 + adjective**', 不怎么 makes the tone **more casual** than when 不太 is used.

(Scenario: Xiaoying and her mother are shopping for food at a supermarket.)

英: 妈，有草莓，我想吃草莓，我们买一点，好不好？

Yīng: *Mā, yǒu cǎoméi, wǒ xiǎng chī cǎoméi,wǒmen mǎi yīdiǎn, hǎo bùhǎo?*

妈: 这些草莓好像**不怎么新鲜**(= 不太新鲜)，而且太贵了。

Mā: *Zhèxiē cǎoméi hǎoxiàng bù zěnme xīnxiān (= bú tài xīnxiān), érqiě tài guì le.*

英: 一斤才两块，**怎么**会太贵？

Yīng: *Yī jīn cái liǎng kuài, zěnme huì tài guì?*

Ying: Mother, there are strawberries. I want to eat strawberries. Let's buy some, OK?

Mother: These strawberries **don't** seem **very fresh**; besides, they are too expensive.

Ying: One *jin* is only two dollars; **how** can it be too expensive?

怎么样 *zěnme yàng*

a.   **怎么样 and 怎么** can be used **interchangeably** when (and only when) 怎么 is used to describe **the method** with which an action is performed.

A: 哇！你做的菜真好吃！尤其是麻婆豆腐，是**怎么(样)**做的？

Wà! Nǐ zuò de cài zhēn hǎochī! Yóuqí shì mápó dòufu, shì zěnme (yàng) zuò de?

B: 我照着食谱做的。食谱说**怎么(样)**做，我就**怎么(样)**做。

Wǒ zhào zhe shípǔ zuò de. Shípǔ shuō zěnme (yàng) zuò, wǒ jiù zěnme (yàng) zuò.

A: Wow! These dishes you made are really delicious, especially this Mapo Tofu. How did you make it?

B: I followed the recipe. The recipe explains **how** to make it, and that's **how** I made it. (I do **whatever** the recipe tells me to do.)

b.   The basic use of 怎么样 is to serve as the **predicate** of the sentence to **make an inquiry** about the subject of that sentence. The expected answer is usually an **adjective**. 怎么样 used this way can be interchangeable with 如何 (*rúhé*).

(Scenario: Wang makes phone calls to Li, a retired friend who lives faraway, a couple times a year.)

王: 老李，最近**身体怎么样**？

Wáng: *Lǎo Lǐ, zuìjìn shēntǐ zěnme yàng?*

李: 还可以，还走得动。你呢？**你怎么样**？

Lǐ: *Hái kěyǐ, hái zǒu de dòng. Nǐ ne? Nǐ zěnme yàng?*

王: 很忙！你们那里今年冬天**天气怎么样**？

Wáng: *Hěn máng! Nǐmen nàlì jīnnián dōngtiān tiānqì zěnme yàng?*

李: 没有去年那么冷。

Lǐ: Méiyǒu qùnián nàme lěng.

Wang: Old Li, **how's your health** lately?

Li: It's OK. I still can move around. How about you? **How are you doing?**

Wang: Busy! **How is the weather** over there this winter?

Li: Not as cold as last year.

c. 怎么样 can be used as a **tag question** to make a **suggestion** and to **seek the listener's feedback**. 如何 can be used to substitute 怎么样.

A: 下课以后，一起去看电影，**怎么样**？

Xià kè yǐhòu, yīqǐ qù kàn diànyǐng, zěnme yàng?

B: 好啊！**怎么**去？坐地铁还是公共汽车？

Hǎo ā! Zěnme qù? Zuò dìtiě háishì gōnggòng qìchē?

A: **How about if** we go to a movie together after class?

B: OK! **How** are we getting there (the cinema)? By subway or by bus?

d. 怎么样 can be translated as '**what**' in certain contexts. The typical expression is **你觉得怎么样？** It is used to **elicit the listener's opinion or evaluation** about something. Therefore, the translation is '**what** do you **think**?' A **common mistake** made by learners who are English speakers is 你想什么？ This literal translation is not only erroneous in this context, but actually conveys a different message.

However, since 觉得 can mean 'to feel' and is used when describing one's emotional or physical feelings, **觉得怎么样 has another interpretation**, where 怎么样 still means 'how'. For example, a doctor may ask a patient 你今天觉得怎么样？ (**How do you feel** today?)

→ See 觉得 (*juéde*) and 想 (*xiǎng*) for related information.

e. '**怎么样的 + noun**' can be interchangeable with '**什么样的 + noun**'; therefore, 怎么样 in this case can be translated as '**what**' to mean '**what kind of + noun**'. 如何 cannot be used to substitute 怎么样 in this usage.

A: 你知不知道小李是一个**怎么样的**人？

Nǐ zhī bù zhīdào Xiǎo Lǐ shì yī gè zěnme yàng de rén?

B: 我只知道他很聪明，他的人品**怎么样**，我就不太清楚了！

Wǒ zhǐ zhīdào tā hěn cōngmíng, tā de rénpǐn zěnme yàng, wǒ jiù bú tài qīngchǔ le.

A: Do you know **what kind of** person Little Li is?

B: I only know that he is smart. (As to) **how** his personal character is (**what** his personal character is **like**), I am not familiar (with that aspect).

f. 不怎么样 is sometimes used as a **casual reply to the 'subject + 怎么样?'** question. The implication is '**it's not so good**' or 'there is **nothing unusual to report**'.

Note that if 不怎么 (see section f. of 怎么 above) is used, an adjective must follow ('**不怎么 + adjective**'). But 不怎么样 **is not followed by an adjective**. Also, 如何 cannot be used to substitute 怎么样 in this usage.

(Scenario: Zhang knows that Wang likes to play *Majiang*, a Chinese gambling game.)

张: 老王，最近打麻将手气**怎么样**？

Zhāng: *Lǎo Wáng, zuìjìn dǎ májiàng shǒuqì zěnme yàng?*

王: **不怎么样**！常常输！(不怎么样 is similar to **不怎么好** in meaning.)

Wáng: *Bù zěnmē yàng! Chángcháng shū.*

Zhang: Old Wang! **How** has your Majiang gambling luck been lately?

Wang: **Not good!** I've often lost money.

找 *zhǎo*, 看 *kàn* and 见 *jiàn* + **person**

The surface meaning of 找 is 'to look for'. However, in certain contexts, 找 can be interpreted as '**to visit/ see (someone)**'. A **common mistake** made by learners is to use 看 when, in fact, 找 is the proper word.

The discussions in this section are about 找 used as '**seeing someone**' as well as comparisons and contrasts between 找 and three other similar words (看, 见 and 看见). Each of these words is **only proper in a specific context**. Therefore, it is important to observe the situation in which an utterance is made in order to choose the proper word.

a. When 看 means 'to visit someone', the visit is **more formal** and usually of a **friendly nature**. 找 indicates a **casual (or informal) kind of visit** and the purpose **may or may not be friendly**.

(Scenario: Two friends chance to see each other at the entrance of a hospital. 看 and 找 should not be interchanged in this scenario.)

张: 老王！好久不见！你来医院做什么？

Zhāng: *Lǎo Wáng! Hǎo jiǔ bú jiàn! Nǐ lái yīyuàn zuò shénme?*

王: 啊！老张，是你！我来**看**一个**朋友**，他病了！你呢？

Wáng: *À! Lǎo Zhāng, shì nǐ! Wǒ lái kàn yī ge péngyǒu, tā bìng le. Nǐ ne?*

张: 我来**找**我**妹妹**，她是这里的护士。

Zhāng: *Wǒ lái zhǎo wǒ mèimei, tā shì zhèlǐ de hùshì.*

Zhang: Old Wang! Long time no see! Why have you come to the hospital?

Wang: Ah! Old Zhang, it's you! I've come to **see (= to visit) a friend**. He is ill. How about you?

Zhang: I've come to **see** my **younger sister**. She is a nurse here.

(Scenario: Li is buying fruit from a street vendor.)

李: 这些桃子甜不甜啊?

Lǐ: *Zhèxiē táozi tián bù tián a?*

摊贩: 保证甜。要是不甜,你明天来**找我**,我天天都在这里摆摊。

Tānfàn: *Bǎozhèng tián. Yàoshì bù tián, nǐ míngtiān lái zhǎo wǒ, wǒ tiān tiān dōu zài zhèlǐ bǎi tān.*

Li: Are these peaches sweet?

Vendor: I guarantee you they are sweet. If they are not sweet, come and **see me** tomorrow. I set up my stand right here every day.

(Scenario: An academic situation.)

王同学: 李教授,这课的语法很难,我有几个问题。

Wáng tóngxué: *Lǐ jiàoshòu, zhè kè de yǔfǎ hěn nán, wǒ yǒu jǐ ge wèntí.*

李教授: 那你下课以后可以去**找我**的**助教**,助教的职责是回答学生的问题。

Lǐ jiàoshòu: *Nà nǐ xià kè yǐhòu kěyǐ qù zhǎo wǒ de zhùjiào; zhùjiào de zhízé shì huídá xuéshēng de wèntí.*

张同学: 李教授,我对我这学期考试的平均分数有点疑问,我应该**找谁**?

Zhāng tóngxué: *Lǐ jiàoshòu, wǒ duì wǒ zhè xuéqī kǎoshì de píngjūn fēnshù yǒu diǎn yíwèn. Wǒ yīnggāi zhǎo shéi?*

李教授: 你可以今天下午来我的办公室**找我**。

Lǐ jiàoshòu: *Nǐ kěyǐ jīntiān xiàwǔ lái wǒ de bàngōngshì zhǎo wǒ.*

Student Wang: Professor Li, this lesson's grammar is difficult. I have a few questions.

Professor Li: Then you can go **see** my **teaching assistant** after class. The teaching assistants' job is to answer students' questions.

Student Zhang: Professor Li, I have some queries about my test average for this semester. **Whom** should I go and **see**?

Professor Li: You can come and **see me** in my office this afternoon.

b. 找 can be used in the pattern of '**找** + **person** + **verb**', which implies 'to see if someone is **available to do** something'. But 看 **cannot be** used in this pattern.

(Scenario: Xie is studying in her dorm room; someone is knocking at her door. She opens the door.)

谢: 小张,是你,有事吗?

Xiè: *Xiǎo Zhāng, shì nǐ! Yǒu shì ma?*

张: 没事,我来**找你聊天**。

Zhāng: *Méi shì, wǒ lái zhǎo nǐ liáotiān.*

谢: 你去**找别人**(聊)吧!我明天要考试,我得准备考试,没空跟你聊。

Xiè: *Nǐ qǔ zhǎo biérén (liáo) ba! Wǒ míngtiān yào kǎoshì, wǒ děi zhǔnbèi kǎoshì. Méi kòng gēn nǐ liáo.*

Xie:	Little Zhang, it's you. Is there anything (you have in mind)?
Zhang:	Nothing. I came to **see if you have time (if you are available)** to chat.
Xie:	Why don't you go and **see if someone else is available** (to chat with you)? I have to take a test tomorrow. I have to study for the test; I don't have time to chat with you.

c. 看 in the '**看 + person + verb**' pattern has a different definition from that being discussed in section a. above. It is generally translated as '**to watch**'.

我今天下午没空，因为我要去**看**我儿子**打**球。
Wǒ jīntiān xiàwǔ méi kòng, yīnwèi wǒ yào qù kàn wǒ érzi dǎ qiú.
I won't be free this afternoon because I have to go and **watch my son play** in a ball game.

d. Since 见 also is used to indicate 'seeing/visiting (someone)', learners often confuse 见 with 看. Although 看 and 见 both suggest that **the visit is not casual**, 看 generally indicates the visit is of a **friendly or personal nature**, whereas 见 tends to indicate that the visit is **for business** or for **discussions on more serious topics**.

When 来 or 去 is used with 见 (or when the **context implies 来 or 去**), then the implication is coming/going **to see someone of a superior or more authoritative status. Without 来 or 去, the opposite** is suggested. And the purpose is usually about business.

→ See 见 (*jiàn*) for more information.

(Scenario: In the elevator, both Wang and Li push the button for the fifth floor.)

王:	小李，你的办公室不是在四楼吗？
Wáng:	*Xiǎo Lǐ, nǐ de bàngōngshì bú shì zài sì lóu ma?*
李:	我要**去**五楼**见周经理**，跟他谈加薪的事。
Lǐ:	*Wǒ yào qù wǔ lóu jiàn Zhōu jīnglǐ, gēn tā tán jiāxīn de shì.*
王:	哦，是吗？昨天周经理的秘书打电话给我，说周经理明天要**见我**；或许他也要给我加薪。
Wáng:	*Ó, shì ma? Zuótiān Zhōu jīnglǐ de mìshū dǎ diànhuà gěi wǒ, shuō Zhōu jīnglǐ míngtiān yào jiàn wǒ; huòxǔ tā yě yào gěi wǒ jiāxīn.*
Wang:	Little Li, isn't your office on the fourth floor?
Li:	I am **going to** the fifth floor to **see Manager Zhou** and talk to him about my salary increase.
Wang:	Oh, is that so? Yesterday Manager Zhou's secretary called me and said that he wanted to **see me** tomorrow. Perhaps he is also going to give me a salary increase.

(Scenario: Two college students are discussing the accessibility of a professor.)

丁: 小谢，你要去哪里？

Dīng: Xiǎo Xiè, nǐ yào qù nǎlǐ?

谢: 我要**去见周教授**，跟他讨论我的论文。

Xiè: Wǒ yào qù jiàn Zhōu jiàoshòu, gēn tā tǎolùn wǒde lùnwén.

丁: **他**愿意**见你**吗？

Dīng: Tā yuànyì jiàn nǐ ma?

谢: 他是我的指导教授，是他叫我一个星期**去见他**一次的。

Xiè: Tā shì wǒ de zhǐdǎo jiàoshòu, shì tā jiào wǒ yī ge xīngqī qù jiàn tā yī cì de.

丁: 我真羡慕你。我去了他的办公室好几次，他都说太忙，不肯**见我**。

Dīng: Wǒ zhēn xiànmù nǐ. Wǒ qù le tā de bàngōngshì hǎo jǐ cì, tā dōu shuō tài máng, bù kěn jiàn wǒ.

Ding: Little Xie, where are you going?

Xie: I am **going to see Professor Zhou** and discuss my thesis with him.

Ding: Is **he** willing to **see you**?

Xie: He is my thesis advisor; he has told me to **go see him** once a week.

Ding: I really envy you. I went to his office several times, but he always said that he was too busy, and he was not willing to **see me**.

e. Because 看见 is also translated as 'to see', which can be followed by a person, '看见 + **person**' must not be confused with '**看** + **person**' or '**见** + **person**'. The definition of 看见 as 'to see' does **not** carry the meaning of '**visit**'. It only refers to the **perception made by one's eyesight**, and can be considered the same as 看到 (*kàndào*).

(Scenario: Two coworkers like to gossip.)

A: 你一定猜不出来，我昨天**看见**了谁？

Nǐ yīdìng cāi bù chūlái, wǒ zuótiān kànjiàn le shéi?

B: 谁？谁？快告诉我！

Shéi? Shéi? Kuài gàosù wǒ.

A: 我**看见**了周经理的女朋友。

Wǒ kànjiàn le Zhōu jīnglǐ de nǚ péngyǒu.

B: 真的吗？你是在哪里**看见**她的？

Zhēn de ma? Nǐ shì zài nǎlǐ kànjiàn tā de?

A: 我每个星期四都得**去**周经理的办公室**见他**，向他报告工作进度，可是这星期我**去见他**的时候，他的秘书说他住院了，所以我去医院**看他**。

Wǒ měi ge xīngqī sì dōu děi qù Zhōu jīnglǐ de bàngōngshì jiàn tā, xiàng tā bàogào gōngzuò jìndù, kěshì zhè xīngqī wǒ qù jiàn tā de shíhòu, tā de mìshū shuō tā zhùyuàn le, suǒyǐ wǒ qù yīyuàn kàn tā.

B: 你是在病房里**看见**他女朋友的吗？

Nǐ shì zài bìngfáng lǐ kànjiàn tā nǚ péngyǒu de ma?

A: 对！可是我离开病房去坐电梯的时候，**看见**周经理的太太从电梯里
出来。

Duì! Kěshì wǒ líkāi bìngfáng qù zuò diàntī de shíhòu, kànjiàn Zhōu jīnglǐ de tàitai cóng diàntī lǐ chūlái.

B: 可怜的周太太！

Kělián de Zhōu tàitai!

A: You definitely won't be able to guess whom I **saw** yesterday.

B: Who? Who? (Hurry!) Tell me now.

A: I **saw** Manager Zhou's girlfriend.

B: Really? Where did you **see** her?

A: I have to **go** to Manager Zhou's office every Thursday to **see him** and report on our work progress. But when I **went to see him** this week, his secretary told me that he had been hospitalized. So I went to the hospital to **see him**.

B: Did you **see** his girlfriend in the hospital room?

A: That's right! But when I left his room to ride the elevator, I **saw** Mrs Zhou getting off the elevator.

B: Poor Mrs Zhou!

正 *zhèng*

正 as a stand-alone word often implies 'precisely'. Its actual meaning or translation in a sentence depends on the context.

a. 正 can be used to **identify or describe** something or someone that is '**precisely**' the one or the kind **in question**. Although 就 (*jiù*: exactly) can be used in similar contexts, 正 **is stronger in tone** than 就.

昨天失物招领处的人打电话告诉我，有人捡到了一只金表。我到了那里
一看，发现那**正是**我遗失的那只表。

Zuótiān shīwù zhāolǐng chù de rén dǎ diànhuà gàosù wǒ, yǒu rén jiǎndào le yī zhī jīn biǎo. Wǒ dào le nàlǐ yī kàn, fāxiàn nà zhèng shì wǒ yíshī de nà zhī biǎo.

Yesterday someone from the Lost and Found office called and told me that someone had found a gold watch. I went there to take a look and I found that it **was precisely** the watch that I had lost.

王先生，你的资历和经验**正是**我们需要的。你什么时候可以开始来
上班？

Wáng xiānsheng, nǐ de zīlì hé jīngyàn zhèng shì wǒmen xūyào de. Nǐ shénme shíhòu kěyǐ kāishǐ lái shàng bān?

Mr Wang, your qualifications and experiences **are precisely** what we need. When can you start working?

A: 一个人需要有很大的决心和毅力才能完成这件事。

Yī ge rén xūyào yǒu hěn dà de juéxīn hé yìlì cái néng wánchéng zhè jiàn shì.

B: 李明能成功**正因为**他有决心和毅力。

Lǐ Míng néng chénggōng zhèng yīnwèi tā yǒu juéxīn hé yìlì.

A: A person needs to have great determination and perseverance before he can finally accomplish this matter.

B: The reason Li Ming could succeed was **precisely because** he had determination and perseverance.

b. 正 can be used when an **action is 'in progress'**. The verb often has only **one character** and 着 follows the verb. Thus, the pattern is '正 + (one character) verb + 着'.

我们**正吃着**李先生送给我们的巧克力，门铃响了，李先生又送礼物来了。

Wǒmen zhèng chī zhe Lǐ xiānsheng sòng gěi wǒmen de qiǎokèlì, ménlíng xiǎng le, Lǐ xiānsheng yòu sòng lǐwù lái le.

While we **were eating** the chocolate Mr Li had given us, the doorbell rang. Mr Li delivered more gifts.

昨天下午我**正悠闲地听着**音乐的时候，忽然来了一场大地震。

Zuótiān xiàwǔ wǒ zhèng yōuxián de tīng zhe yīnyuè de shíhòu, hūrán lái le yī chǎng dà dìzhèn.

Yesterday afternoon while I **was** leisurely **listening to** music, a strong earthquake suddenly occurred.

c. 正 can suggest an **ongoing state**. This means that **the verb following 正 does not** indicate an **action**. Note that 着 is not used. (See section b. above.)

昨天我去逛街，**正觉得**肚子饿的时候，就看到路边有卖小吃的摊贩。

(觉得 is a verb that does not indicate an action.)

Zuótiān wǒ qù guàngjiē, zhèng juéde dùzi è de shíhòu, jiù kàndào lù biān yǒu mài xiǎochī de tānfàn.

Yesterday I went shopping; just when I **was feeling hungry**, I saw street vendors selling snacks on the side of the road.

我到车站的时候，最后一班公共汽车刚开走，我**正不知道**该怎么办的时候，我的同屋开车经过，所以我就坐她的车一起回家了。(不知道 is a verb that does not indicate an action.)

Wǒ dào chēzhàn de shíhòu, zuìhòu yī bān gōnggòng qìchē gāng kāi zǒu, wǒ zhèng bù zhīdào gāi zěnme bàn de shíhòu, wǒ de tóngwū kāi chē jīngguò, suǒyǐ wǒ jiù zuò tā de chē yīqǐ huí jiā le.

When I arrived at the bus stop, the last bus had just left. **Right at the time when I didn't know** what to do, my roommate drove by, so I rode in her car and we went home together.

正好 *zhènghǎo*

正 in 正好 implies 'precisely', although it is usually not considered a stand-alone word in the expression of 正好.

a. **正好** can show that a certain occurrence takes place **by chance or without design**. It implies a **coincidence**. Its proper translation depends on the actual sentence.

昨天我在夜市看到一个很漂亮的古董花瓶，要两百块。当时我身上**正好**有两百块，所以就把那个花瓶买了。

Zuótiān wǒ zài yèshì kàndào yī ge hěn piàoliàng de gǔdǒng huāpíng, yào liǎng bǎi kuài. Dāngshí wǒ shēn shàng zhènghǎo yǒu liǎng bǎi kuài, suǒyǐ jiù bǎ nà ge huāpíng mǎi le.

Yesterday I saw a very pretty antique vase at the night market, and it cost 200 *kuai*. At that time I **happened to have** 200 *kuai* with me, so I bought the vase.

今天我在车站等车的时候，我的同事李先生**正好**开车经过，所以我就坐他的车去办公室了。

Jīntiān wǒ zài chēzhàn děng chē de shíhòu, wǒ de tóngshì Lǐ xiānsheng zhènghǎo kāi chē jīngguò, suǒyǐ wǒ jiù zuò tā de chē qù bàngōngshì le.

Today while I was waiting for the bus at the bus stop, my coworker Mr Li **happened to** drive by, so I rode in his car to go to the office.

b. When something **fits a certain situation with 100 percent precision or perfection** (no more and no less), 正好 can be used to describe the situation. There is no direct translation for this use. It can be an **adverb** or an **adjective**.

(Scenario: A woman has just tried on a dress at a department store.)

店员:	合身吗？太大还是太小？要不要我拿另外一个尺寸的让你试试？
Diànyuán:	*Héshēn ma? Tài dà háishì tài xiǎo? Yào bú yào wǒ ná lìngwài yī ge chǐcùn de ràng nǐ shì shì?*
女顾客:	这件**正好**，不大不小！不用再试了。
Nǚ gùkè:	*Zhè jiàn zhènghǎo, bú dà bù xiǎo! Bú yòng zài shì le.*
Store clerk:	Does it fit? Is it too large or too small? Do you want me to bring a different size for you to try?
Female customer:	**This one is perfect**; not too large or too small! No need to try another one.

(Scenario: Two managers are discussing whether they should hire Miss Li or not.)

A: 李小姐有管理硕士学位，我认为我们应该聘她。

    Lǐ xiǎojiě yǒu guǎnlǐ shuòshì xuéwèi, wǒ rènwéi wǒmen yīnggāi pìn tā.

B: 我的看法**正好**相反，她的学历太高了，这个初级办事员的职位不适合她。

    Wǒ de kànfǎ zhènghǎo xiāngfǎn, tā de xuélì tài gāo le, zhè ge chūjí bànshì yuán de zhíwèi bú shìhé tā.

A: Miss Li has a master's degree in management; I think we should hire her.

B: My opinion is **precisely** the opposite. Her academic background is too high (superior). This entry-level office clerk's position is not suitable for her.

(Scenario: A man arrives at a friend's house without calling first. There are already two other guests there. With his arrival, the four of them can now play a game of *majiang*.)

主人: 你来得**正好**！我**正想**给你打电话，问你能不能来打麻将呢！

         (See below for **正想**.)

Zhǔrén: *Nǐ lái de zhènghǎo! Wǒ zhèng xiǎng gěi nǐ dǎ diànhuà, wèn nǐ néng bù néng lái dǎ májiàng ne!*

Host: You came **at the perfect time**. **I was just thinking of** calling you to ask if you could come over and play *majiang*.

正在 *zhèng zài*

'正在 + verb' is typically used to indicate **an action in progress**. It should be noted that the verb after 正在 must indicate **an action that can last**.

a.   Although '**在** + verb' has the same function, **正在** is **stronger in tone** than simply 在.

A: 我提出的那个议案通过了没有？

    Wǒ tí chū de nà ge yì'àn tōngguò le méiyǒu?

B: 高层主管**正在开会**讨论呢！

    Gāocéng zhǔguǎn zhèng zài kāi huì tǎolùn ne!

A: Has the plan I proposed been approved?

B: High-level executives **are having a meeting** to discuss it (**right at this moment**).

儿子: 爸爸，我们一起去院子玩接球吧！

Érzi: *Bàba, wǒmen yīqǐ qù yuànzi wán jiē qiú ba!*

妈妈: 你没看到爸爸**正在打电话**吗？让他先把电话打完。

Māma: *Nǐ méi kàndào bàba zhèng zài dǎ diànhuà ma? Ràng tā xiān bǎ diànhuà dǎ wán.*

Son: Father, let's go to the yard to play catch.
Mother: Didn't you see that your father **is talking on phone (right at this moment)**? Let him finish his phone call first.

b.   When the **specific moment** of the action is mentioned（...的时候）, 正在 **is more effective** than simply 在 to indicate that the action is in progress **right at that moment.**

大地震发生**的时候**，我们**正在吃**晚饭。
Dà dìzhèn fāshēng de shíhòu, wǒmen zhèng zài chī wǎn fàn.
When the big earthquake occurred, we **were (in the middle of) eating** dinner.

昨天高文生给我打电话**的时候**，我**正在洗**澡，所以我没有接到那个电话。
Zuótiān Gāo Wénshēng gěi wǒ dǎ diànhuà de shíhòu, wǒ zhèng zài xǐzǎo, suǒyǐ wǒ méiyǒu jiē dào nà ge diànhuà.
Yesterday **when** Gao Wensheng called me, I **was (in the middle of) taking** a shower, so I did not receive that phone call.

c.   When a location with the **preposition 在 or 从** is mentioned with the action in progress, the patterns is '正在/正从 + **location + verb**'.

(Scenario: Zhang calls Wang on Wang's cell phone.)
张：   小王，你现在在哪里？
Zhāng: *Xiǎo Wáng, nǐ xiànzài zài nǎlǐ?*
王：   我**正在咖啡馆喝**咖啡呢！有事吗？(Do not say 我正在在咖啡馆喝咖啡呢！)
Wáng: *Wǒ zhèng zài kāfēi guǎn hē kāfēi ne! Yǒu shì ma?*
张：   我**在找**小李，可是他一直没有接电话，你知不知道他在哪里？
Zhāng: *Wǒ zài zhǎo Xiǎo Lǐ, kěshì tā yīzhí méiyǒu jiē diànhuà, nǐ zhī bù zhīdào tā zài nǎlǐ?*
王：   我也不知道...等等...真巧，他**正从外面走进**咖啡馆来。(Do not say 他正在从外面走进来。)
Wáng: *Wǒ yě bù zhīdào . . . děng děng . . . zhēn qiǎo, tā zhèng cóng wàimiàn zǒu jìn kāfēi guǎn lái.*
Zhang: Little Wang, where are you now?
Wang: I **am having coffee at a coffee shop** right now. Is there anything specific? (= What's up?)
Zhang: I **am looking for** Little Li, but he has not answered his phone. Do you know where he is?
Wang: I don't know, either . . . Wait a moment; what a coincidence. He **is walking into** the coffee shop **from outside (right at this moment)**.

我早上醒来以后，往窗外一看，看到太阳**正从山后慢慢上升**，日出真美极了！

Wǒ zǎoshàng xǐng lái yǐhòu, wàng chuāng wài yī kàn, kàndào tàiyáng zhèng cóng shān hòu mànmàn shàng shēng, rìchū zhēn měi jí le.

In the morning after I woke up, I looked outside the window, and I saw that the sun **was** slowly **coming up from behind the mountains**. The sun rise was really beautiful.

d. 正 can **no longer be used** when an action is '**not in progress**'. The pattern is either '**没有在 + verb**' or '**不是在 + verb**'. **不是在** is generally used to **negate or refute a previous statement**.

今天妈妈非常高兴，因为她回到家的时候，弟弟既**没有在上网**，也**没有在看**电视，反而**正在打扫**自己的房间。

Jīntiān māma fēicháng gāoxìng, yīnwèi tā huí dào jiā de shíhòu, dìdi jì méiyǒu zài shàng wǎng, yě méiyǒu zài kàn diànshì, fǎn'ér zhèng zài dǎsǎo zìjǐ de fángjiān.

Today my mother was very happy, because when she got home, my younger brother **was neither surfing** the Internet, **nor was he watching** TV; instead, he **was cleaning** up his own bedroom.

妈妈：	小中，去洗碗。
Māma:	*Xiǎozhōng, qù xǐ wǎn.*
爸爸：	他**正在做**功课，我去洗吧！
Bàba:	*Tā zhēng zài zuò gōngkè, wǒ qù xǐ ba!*
妈妈：	他才**不是在做**功课，他**在上网**。(**不是在做**功课 refutes the previous statement of 他**正在做**功课.)
Māma:	*Tā cái bú shì zài zuò gōngkè, tā zài shàng wǎng.*
爸爸：	我去看一下。. . . 你说得很对，他**正在网上的聊天室**跟朋友**聊天**。
Bàba:	*Wǒ qù kàn yīxià. . . . Nǐ shuō de hěn duì, tā zhèng zài wǎng shàng de liáotiān shì gēn péngyǒu liáotiān.*
Mother:	Xiaozhong, go do the dishes.
Father:	He **is doing his homework** right at this moment. Let me go do the dishes.
Mother:	He **is not doing homework**; he **is surfing** the Internet.
Father:	I will go take a look. . . . You were right. He **was (in the middle of) chatting** with his friends **in the online chatroom**.

Related expressions

正要 *zhèng yào*

正要 is used to indicate that an action is **just about to take place**. Learners who are English speakers should be aware that a sentence with 正要 and one with

正在 can appear similar when translated into English. As stated above, 正在 is used for **actions that can last**. There are certain verbs in Chinese that indicate **actions which cannot last**; such verbs are '**instantaneous verbs**'. When such an action is **in the process of happening**, 正要 is used instead of 正在.

An instantaneous verb shows an action that has a **clear-cut 'before' and 'after' status**. Learners who are English speakers should pay special attention to the use of such verbs since their **English counterparts** frequently show that **an action is happening** (in progress). 正要, in fact, indicates that an action is '**just about to' take place**.

我**正要睡着**的时候，门铃响了。
Wǒ zhèng yào shuìzháo de shíhòu, ménlíng xiǎng le.
Just when I **was falling asleep (was about to fall asleep)**, the doorbell rang.

电影**正要开始**的时候，忽然停电了。
Diànyǐng zhèng yào kāishǐ de shíhòu, hūrán tíng diàn le.
Right at the moment when the movie **was starting (was about to start)**, the power (electricity) suddenly went off.

(Scenario: A girl is leaving her house to meet with her boyfriend when her boyfriend calls her on her cell phone.)

男: 你出门了没有？
Nán: Nǐ chū mén le méiyǒu?
女: **正要出门**；半个小时以后会到。
Nǚ: Zhèng yào chū mén; bàn ge xiǎoshí yǐhòu huì dào.
男: 你别来了，老板刚叫我加班。
Nán: Nǐ bié lái le, lǎobǎn gāng jiào wǒ jiā bān.
Man: Have you left your house?
Woman: I **am leaving now. (I am just about to leave.)** I will be there in half an hour.
Man: Don't come anymore. My boss has just told me to work overtime.

正想 *zhèng xiǎng*

正想 is similar to 正要 in meaning in the sense that it also indicates **an action is about to take place**; however, 正想 suggests that **the action** is only **being planned**; therefore, the **imminence is not as strong** as 正要 indicates. 正 in 正想 **implies a coincidence**.

A: 你知不知道我的法文语法书在哪里？
Nǐ zhī bù zhīdào wǒ de Fǎwén yǔfǎ shū zài nǎlǐ?
B: 昨天我在巷口捡到一本法文语法书，我**正想**问是不是你的。你是我们这附近唯一一在学法文的人。
Zuótiān wǒ zài xiàng kǒu jiǎn dào yī běn Fǎwén yǔfǎ shū, wǒ zhèng xiǎng wèn shì bú shì nǐ de. Nǐ shì wǒmen zhè fùjìn wéiyī zài xué Fǎwén de rén.

A: Do you know where my French grammar book is?

B: Yesterday I picked up a French grammar book at the entrance of the alley, and I **was just thinking about** asking whether it was yours; you are the only person in our neighborhood who is studying French.

(Scenario: A telephone conversation. 想 has two different meanings in this conversation.)

王: 小李，下午**想不想**一起去看电影？

Wáng: *Xiǎo Lǐ, xiàwǔ xiǎng bù xiǎng yīqǐ qù kàn diànyǐng?*

李: 太好了！我也**正想**给你打电话，问你有没有空呢！

Lǐ: *Tài hǎo le! Wǒ yě zhèng xiǎng gěi nǐ dǎ diànhuà, wèn nǐ yǒu méiyǒu kòng ne!*

Wang: Little Li, do you **feel like** going to a movie with me in the afternoon?

Li: That's great! I **was just thinking about calling** you to ask if you're free.

知道 *zhīdào*

知道 has a straightforward definition: 'to know'. Confusion sometimes arises about the distinction between 知道 and 认识 (*rènshì*), which is also defined as 'to know'. This section provides examples to illustrate the differences between 知道 and 认识, as well as the **connotations of 不知道**.

a. 知道 as 'to know' means 'to be aware of', whereas 认识 indicates 'to be familiar with'. Although both can be translated as 'to know', they have different implications. What follows 知道 is usually the **information one knows**.

A: 你**认不认识**张明？

Nǐ rèn bú rènshì Zhāng Míng?

B: 我**知道**他是谁，可是我**不认识**他。

Wǒ zhīdào tā shì shéi, kěshì wǒ bú rènshì tā.

A: Do you **know** Zhang Ming? (Are the two of you **acquainted**?)

B: I **know** who he is, but I **don't know** him.

A: 牌子上的那几个字，你**认识**几个？

Páizi shàng de nà jǐ ge zì, nǐ rènshì jǐ ge?

B: 我**认识**"请"和"手"；可是我**不知道**那句话是什么意思。

Wǒ rènshì 'qǐng' hé 'shǒu'; kěshì wǒ bù zhīdào nà jù huà shì shénme yìsi.

A: How many of those characters on the sign do you **know**?

B: I **know** the characters for 'please' and 'hand'; but I **don't know** the meaning of the sentence.

→ See 认识 (*rènshì*) for related information.

b. 不知道, although ostensibly the negative form for 知道, has grammatical features and uses that go beyond simply 'being not aware of'.

(i) Since 知道 does not indicate any action, 不知道 is its negative form **regardless of the time frame**.

老师:	这个考试，你为什么考得这么差？你没有准备吗？
Lǎoshī:	*Zhè ge kǎoshì, nǐ wèi shénme kǎo de zhème chà? Nǐ méiyǒu zhǔnbèi ma?*
学生:	昨天我没有来上课，所以我**不知道**今天有考试。(Do not say 没有知道.)
Xuéshēng:	*Zuótiān wǒ méiyǒu lái shàng kè, suǒyǐ wǒ bù zhīdào jīntiān yǒu kǎoshì.*
Teacher:	Why did you do so poorly on the test? Did you not study for it?
Student:	I didn't come to class yesterday, and so **I didn't know (I was not aware)** that there would be a test today.

A:	你为什么请王美文跟你去听音乐会？你**不知道**她已经有男朋友了吗？
	Nǐ wèi shénme qǐng Wáng Měiwén gēn nǐ qù tīng yīnyuè huì? Nǐ bù zhīdào tā yǐjīng yǒu nán péngyǒu le ma?
B:	王美文？王美文是谁？我**不认识**她。我请的是王美英。
	Wáng Měiwén? Wáng Měiwén shì shéi? Wǒ bú rènshì tā. Wǒ qǐng de shì Wáng Měiyīng.
A:	Why did you invite Wang Meiwen to go to the concert with you? **Did you not know** that she already has a boyfriend?
B:	Wang Meiwen? Who is Wang Meiwen? I **don't know** her. The one I invited was Wang Meiying.

(ii) 不知道 can be a stand-alone expression that appears **at the beginning of a sentence** to mean 'I wonder'. Note that 我 is not used. Learners should not directly interpret it as 'I don't know'. A **question mark** is usually used.

小李，我现在急需用钱，**不知道**你可不可以借我一百块？(Do not say 我不知道 . . . .)

Xiǎo Lǐ, wǒ xiànzài jí xū yòng qián, bù zhīdào nǐ kě bù kěyǐ jiè wǒ yī bǎi kuài?

Little Li, I urgently need some money now. **I wonder** if you can loan me 100 *kuai*?

A: 你看，好像快下雨了。**不知道**今天的员工野餐会不会取消？
你去问一下秘书吧！

Nǐ kàn, hǎoxiàng kuài xià yǔ le. Bù zhīdào jīntiān de yuángōng yěcān huì bú huì qǔxiāo? Nǐ qù wèn yīxià mìshū ba!

B: 我已经问了，她说**她也不知道**。

Wǒ yǐjīng wèn le, tā shuō tā yě bù zhīdào.

A: Look! It looks like it's going to rain. **I wonder** if today's employee picnic will be canceled. Why don't you go ask the secretary?

B: I have already asked her; she says **she doesn't know**, either.

(iii) 不知道 can imply '**it is not clear**' and it **follows the subject**. When the subject happens to be a person, **misinterpretation or confusion** can easily occur if 不知道 is literally interpreted as 'to not know'.

(Scenario: A family has been waiting for their son to come home so that they can have dinner together.)

妈妈: 大中怎么还没有回来？我们还要不要等呢？

Māma: Dàzhōng zěnme hái méiyǒu huí lái? Wǒmen hái yào bú yào děng ne?

爸爸: 别等了！**他不知道**什么时候才会回来呢！我们吃吧！

Bàba: Bié děng le! Tā bù zhīdào shénme shíhòu cái huì huí lái ne! Wǒmen chī ba!

Mother: How come Dazhong has not come back yet? Are we still going to wait?

Father: Let's not wait anymore. **It is not clear** when **he** will finally be back. Let's eat.

(Scenario: Two friends plan to go to a movie, but it is raining outside.)

A: 走吧！

Zǒu ba!

B: 等雨停了再走吧！

Děng yǔ tíng le zài zǒu ba!

A: **这场雨不知道**会下到什么时候呢！要是去晚了，就可能买不到票了。

Zhè chǎng yǔ bù zhīdào huì xià dào shénme shíhòu ne! Yàoshì qù wǎn le, jiù kěnéng mǎi bú dào piào le.

A: Let's go!

B: Let's wait until the rain has stopped.

A: **It is not clear** when **this bout of rain** will stop. If we go there late, we probably won't be able to get the tickets.

只 *zhǐ* and related words

The definition of 只 ('only') is somewhat misleading. This is because 只 is an **adverb**, and should appear **before a verb** (or a verbal phrase); whereas 'only' in English can appear before a noun or a pronoun. Learners who are English speakers should pay special attention to this.

The following two sections (a. and b.) focus on English expressions where the word 'only' appears before a noun or pronoun. Therefore, the English sentences appear before their Chinese counterparts.

a.   A proper **verb must be used before** 只 even when the English counterpart does not have one.

> A: How long have you been studying Chinese?
> B: **Only three months**. So I **know only 100** Chinese characters.
> A: 你学中文学了多长时间了？
>   *Nǐ xué Zhōngwén xué le duō cháng shíjiān le?*
> B: **只学**了三个月，所以我**只认识**一百个汉字。(Do not say 只三个月 or 认识只一百个汉字.)
>   *Zhǐ xué le sān ge yuè, suǒyǐ wǒ zhǐ rènshì yī bǎi ge Hànzì.*

There are seven people in my family, but we **have only one** bathroom.
我家有七个人，可是我们**只有一个**洗澡间。(Do not say 我们有只一个 洗澡间.)
Wǒ jiā yǒu qī ge rén, kěshì wǒmen zhǐ yǒu yī ge xǐzǎo jiān.

b.   When the subject (noun, pronoun or proper noun) in an English sentence has the word 'only', the expression in Chinese is '**只有** + subject'. 有 **is not optional**. This expression implies **an exclusion**.

We all have English names; **only Little Wang** does not have one.
我们都有英文名字；**只有**小王没有。(Do not say 只小王没有.)
Wǒmen dōu yǒu Yīngwén míngzì; zhǐyǒu Xiǎo Wáng méiyǒu.

Everybody is going to Little Zhang's birthday dance tomorrow; **only Little Li** is not going.
明天大家都要去参加小张的生日舞会，**只有小李**不去。(Do not say 只 小李不去.)
Míngtiān dàjiā dōu yào qù cānjiā Xiǎo Zhāng de shēngrì wǔhuì; zhǐyǒu Xiǎo Lǐ bú qù.

c.   '**只有 ... 才 ...**' is an expression that indicates the **only way** to achieve an intended goal. The implication is that no other method would work.

这个问题，**只有**周先生**才**能解决。(Do not say 只周先生才能解决.)
Zhè ge wèntí, zhǐyǒu Zhōu xiānsheng cái néng jiějué.
Only Mr Zhou can solve this problem.

只有不断地提升技术才能改善产品的品质。

Zhǐyǒu búduàn de tíshēng jìshù cái néng gǎishàn chǎnpǐn de pǐnzhì.

Only by constantly advancing techniques can the quality of the products be improved.

An English sentence with this implication offers very little clue about the need for 才; therefore, it is very important to pay attention to the context.

I am **only** free on the weekend. (Compare: I am free on the weekend: 我周末有空。)

我**只有**周末**才**有空。(Do not say 我周末只有空.)

Wǒ zhǐyǒu zhōumò cái yǒu kòng.

d. '只要 . . . 就 . . .' is opposite in meaning to '只有 . . . 才 . . .'. It implies that a task **can be achieved easily** or without much effort.

这个问题，不用去麻烦周先生；**只要**去问他的助理**就**知道怎么解决。

Zhè ge wèntí, búyòng qù máfán Zhōu xiānsheng; zhǐyào qù wèn tā de zhùlǐ jiù zhīdào zěnme jiějué.

There is no need to bother Mr Zhou about this problem. **As long as** we go ask his assistant, we will know how to solve it.

这家饭馆的服务非常好，顾客**只要**挥挥手，服务员**就**马上走过来了。

Zhè jiā fànguǎn de fúwù fēicháng hǎo, gùkè zhǐyào huī huī shǒu, fúwùyuán jiù mǎshàng zǒu guòlái le.

Service at this restaurant is extremely good. A customer **only needs to** wave, and the waiter will immediately come over.

e. An important difference in usage between '只要 . . . 就 . . .' and '只有 . . . 才 . . .' is that **a noun cannot follow 只要**, but it can follow 只有.

只有(吃)这个药，才能治好这个病。(吃 is optional.)

Zhǐyǒu (chī) zhè ge yào, cái néng zhì hǎo zhè ge bìng.

Only this medicine can cure this illness.

(**Only by taking** this medicine can this illness be cured.)

只要吃这个药，就能治好这个病。(吃 is not optional.)

Zhǐyào chī zhè ge yào, jiù néng zhì hǎo zhè ge bìng.

As long as one takes this medicine, this illness can be cured.

Related expressions

才 *cái* as 'only'

才 has various uses and functions (depending on the context) and is generally used before a verb since it is an adverb. However, when **才 is followed by a**

number (without a verb), its interpretation is '**only**'. If a verb is used, then 只 is a more proper word for 'only'.

> 小李**才**十八岁，(= 小李**只有**十八岁，)所以他还不可以喝酒。
> *Xiǎo Lǐ cái shíbā suì, (= Xiǎo Lǐ zhǐ yǒu shíbā suì,) suǒyǐ tā hái bù kěyǐ hē jiǔ.*
> Little Li is only 18 years old, so he cannot drink alcohol yet.

(Scenario: At a bookstore.)

顾客:	这本书为什么**才**三块钱(= **只要**三块钱)？怎么这么便宜！
Gùkè:	*Zhè běn shū wèi shénme cái sān kuài qián (= zhǐ yào sān kuài qián)? Zěnme zhème piányi!*
店员:	因为我们的书都是二手的。
Diànyuán:	*Yīnwèi wǒmen de shū dōu shì èrshǒu de.*
Customer:	Why is this book **only three** *kuai*? How come it is so cheap?
Clerk:	Because all of our books are second-hand (used books).

光 *guāng* as 'only'

光 can be interpreted as '**only**' in certain contexts, but the implication is that one focuses on '**only**' one aspect of an act while **ignoring other necessary aspects**. What follows 光 should be a verb.

Therefore, the expression is often '光 A 不 B'. Due to the clear implication of 光, the second part (**'不 B'**) is often omitted.

A:	小张学了三年中文了，为什么水平还这么低？
	Xiǎo Zhāng xué le sān nián Zhōngwén le, wèi shénme shuǐpíng hái zhème dī?
B:	因为他**光**记生词**不学**语法，所以总是没有进步。
	Yīnwèi tā guāng jì shēngcí bù xué yǔfǎ, suǒyǐ zǒngshì méiyǒu jìnbù.
A:	Little Zhang has been studying Chinese for three years. Why is his (proficiency) level still so low?
B:	Because he **only memorizes** vocabulary words **without studying** grammar, he never makes any progress.

(Scenario: Anna has been dieting for quite a while, but has been unable to lose any weight. She is feeling frustrated.)

安娜:	我大概是那种**光**喝水也会胖的人。(光喝水 implies **光喝水不吃饭**.)
Ānnà:	*Wǒ dàgài shì nà zhǒng guāng hē shuǐ yě huì pàng de rén.*
妈妈:	想减肥，**光**节食(**不**运动)怎么行？
Māma:	*Xiǎng jiǎnféi, guāng jiéshí (bú yùndòng) zěnme xíng?*
Anna:	I am probably one of those who will gain weight by **only drinking** water.
Mother:	If you want to lose weight, how can you **only diet (without exercising)**?

唯一 wéiyī

唯一 (*wéiyī*) is frequently translated as 'only'; however, it is an **adjective** and so is **followed by a noun**. The expression is '唯一的 + **noun**'.

In the following example, there are two nouns, each of which follows the word 'only' in English. But different contexts decide the proper use of the word 'only' in Chinese.

虽然李先生的三个儿子都结婚了，可是**只有**大儿子有一个孩子，所以这个孩子是李先生**唯一的**孙子，李先生十分宠爱他。

Suīrán Lǐ xiānsheng de sān ge érzi dōu jiéhūn le, kěshì zhǐyǒu dà érzi yǒu yī ge háizi, suǒyǐ zhè ge háizi shì Lǐ xiānsheng wéiyī de sūnzi, Lǐ xiānsheng shífēn chǒngài tā.

Although all three of Mr Li's sons are married, **only** his eldest son has a child; so this child is Mr Li's **only** grandchild; Mr Li really loves and spoils him.

(Scenario: A group of managers have had a long discussion about how to solve a problem. They only come up with one solution.)

周经理:　　　这个方案虽然不理想，可是我认为这是**唯一的**解决办法，我们**只好**采用这个方案了。

Zhōu jīnglǐ:　*Zhè ge fāng'àn suīrán bù lǐxiǎng, kěshì wǒ rènwéi zhè shì wéiyī de jiějué bànfǎ, wǒmen zhǐhǎo cǎiyòng zhè ge fāng'àn le.*

Manager Zhou:　Although this plan is not ideal, I think it is the **only solution**. We have **no other choice but to** adopt it.

只好 zhǐhǎo

只好 indicates one '**has no other choice but to**' take a certain measure. The implication is that one does something **reluctantly** because it is the only option. It is interchangeable with 不得不 (*bù de bù*).

我不喜欢坐公车，可是这星期我的车坏了，所以**只好**天天坐公车去上班。

Wǒ bù xǐhuān zuò gōng chē, kěshì zhè xīngqī wǒ de chē huài le, suǒyǐ zhǐhǎo tiāntiān zuò gōng chē qù shàng bān.

I don't like to take public transport, but my car has broken down this week, so I **have no other choice but to** take public transport to work every day.

本来我跟我男朋友打算今天去野餐；没想到今天下雨了，所以我们**只好**改成去看电影。

Běnlái wǒ gēn wǒ nán péngyǒu dǎsuàn jīntiān qù yěcān; méi xiǎngdào jīntiān xià yǔ le, suǒyǐ wǒmen zhǐhǎo gǎi chéng qù kàn diànyǐng.

Originally my boyfriend and I had planned to go on a picnic today; but who would have thought that it would rain today, so we **had no other choice but to** change our plans and go to a movie.

只是 *zhǐshì*

只是 in certain contexts means '**but**' or '**however**'. It is somewhat different from 可是 (*kěshì*) or 但是 (*dànshì*) because 可是 and 但是 often are paired with 虽然 (*suīrán*), whereas 只是 **connects two independent sentences**. The implication is to **first acknowledge the value or quality** indicated in the first sentence with a **drawback or concession** indicated in the second sentence.

> 这个地区，景色和气候都很不错，**只是**游客实在太多，所以不适合一般人居住。
>
> *Zhè ge dìqū, jǐngsè hé qìhòu dōu hěn búcuò, zhǐshì yóukè shízài tài duō, suǒyǐ bú shìhé yìbān rén jūzhù.*
>
> The scenery and climate of this area are both pretty good; **the only thing is** there are truly too many tourists, so it is not suitable for average people to reside here.

住 *zhù*

The two basic definitions of 住, 'to live' and 'to stop', appear to be unrelated. However, the underlying implication for both is actually similar; that is, both suggest that someone or something is in a state of rest or a fixed situation.

a. 住 as '**to live**' is associated with a **location**. Learners who are English speakers sometimes overuse 住 because the word 'to live' in English has other connotations and is not always about a location.

  For example, 'to live' in the expression '**living a happy life**' is not 住, but **过** (*guò*). For another example, 'to live' in the sentence '**I want to live; I don't want to die**' is not 住, but **活** (*huó*).

  In addition, the sentence patterns (word-order rules) involving the use of 住 are unique, and thus merit special attention.

  (i) If the location where one lives (resides) is mentioned, **the location** or '**在 + location**' follows 住. The **subject** of the sentence should be **definite**, not indefinite.

   In addition, 住在一起 is a common expression. It means two or more people live at the same location. The preposition, if used, is **跟**.

   A: 王大中已经三十多岁了，为什么还**住在家里**？
    Wáng Dàzhōng yǐjīng sānshí duō suì le, wèi shénme hái zhù zài jiā lǐ?
   B: 他爸妈身体不好，所以要儿子**跟**他们**住在一起**。他们家很大；王大中**住(在)二楼**，他爸妈**住(在)三楼**。
    Tā bàmā shēntǐ bù hǎo, suǒyǐ yào érzi gēn tāmen zhù zài yìqǐ. Tāmen jiā hěn dà; Wáng Dàzhōng zhù (zài) èr lóu, tā bàmā zhù (zài) sān lóu.

A: Wang Dazhong is already in his thirties; why is he still **living at home**?

B: His parents are in poor health, so they want their son to **live (together)** with them. Their house is big: Wang Dazhong **lives on the second floor**; his parents **live on the third floor**.

我爸妈离婚以后，我**跟**爸爸**住**，弟弟**跟**妈妈**住**；因为他们**住(在)上海**，我们**住(在)北京**，所以我很少跟妈妈、弟弟见面。

Wǒ bàmā líhūn yǐhòu, wǒ gēn bàba zhù, dìdi gēn māma zhù; yīnwèi tāmen zhù (zài) Shànghǎi, wǒmen zhù (zài) Běijīng, suǒyǐ wǒ hěnshǎo gēn māma, dìdi jiànmiàn.

Since my parents divorced, I have **lived with** my father, and my younger brother has **lived with** my mother. Because they **live in Shanghai** and we **live in Beijing**, I rarely see my mother or my younger brother.

(ii) When the **subject** of the sentence is **indefinite**, the following pattern is used: 'location + 住 + 了 (or 着) + indefinite noun (e.g. a number + noun)'

It should be noted that 在 is not used before the location.

A: 我们这栋大楼**住了好几个**外国人。**我住**三楼，我的楼上**住了两个**日本人，对面**住了一对**美国老夫妇。(我 is definite; 两个日本人 and 一对夫妇 are indefinite.)

Wǒmen zhè dòng dà lóu zhù le hǎo jǐ ge wàiguó rén. Wǒ zhù sān lóu, wǒ de lóu shàng zhù le liǎng ge Rìběn rén, duìmiàn zhù le yī duì Měiguó lǎo fūfù.

B: 王美文的男朋友小李呢？**他也住(在)**那栋大楼。**他住**几楼？(他 is definite.)

Wáng Měiwén de nán péngyǒu Xiǎo Lǐ ne? Tā yě zhù (zài) nà dòng dà lóu. Tā zhù jǐ lóu?

A: 我知道这个大楼**住着两个**姓李的人，**一个住**十楼，**一个住**五楼，可是我不知道哪个是美文的男朋友。(两个姓李的人 is indefinite; 一个 in this context is **definite** since it refers to one of the two people.)

Wǒ zhīdào zhè ge dà lóu zhù zhe liǎng ge xìng Lǐ de rén; yī ge zhù shí lóu, yī ge zhù wǔ lóu, kěshì wǒ bù zhīdào nǎ ge shì Měiwén de nán péngyǒu.

A: **Quite a few** foreigners **live** in our building. **I live** on the third floor; **two** Japanese live (on the floor) above me; and **an** old American couple lives across from me.

B: What about Wang Meiwen's boyfriend, Little Li? **He** also **lives** in that building. On which floor is **he living**?

A: I know that **two** people with the last name Li live in this building; **one (of them) lives** on the tenth floor; **the other lives** on the fifth floor. But I don't know which one is Meiwen's boyfriend.

(iii) There is a pattern that **appears to be similar** to the one above, but it has a quite different implication. It is used to tell **how big a certain (living) space is** (by indicating **how many people** the space can accommodate). The pattern is: 'location + 可以住 (or 住得下) + a number'.

这个小小的四合院竟然**住了十**家人，真没想到。(to state a **fact**)
Zhè ge xiǎo xiǎo de sìhéyuàn jìngrán zhù le shí jiā rén, zhēn méi xiǎngdào.
It is such a surprise that **ten families live in** this small traditional four-wall compound building. This is really unexpected.

Compare: 这个小小的四合院竟然**住得下十**家人，真没想到。(to state a **potential/possibility**)
Zhè ge xiǎo xiǎo de sìhéyuàn jìngrán zhù de xià shí jiā rén, zhēn méi xiǎngdào.
It is such a surprise that this small traditional four-wall compound building **can accommodate (has enough space for) ten families**. This is really unexpected.

(Scenario: A discussion about the occupants of a student dormitory room.)
A: 这层楼的每个房间都**可以住**三个人，为什么302号只**住了两个人**？
Zhè céng lóu de měi ge fángjiān dōu kěyǐ zhù sān ge rén, wèi shénme sān líng èr hào zhǐ zhù le liǎng ge rén?
B: 那间本来**住着**三个外国学生，可是学期中有一个回国了。
Nà jiān běnlái zhù zhe sān ge wàiguó xuéshēng, kěshì xuéqī zhōng yǒu yī ge huí guó le.
A: Every room on this floor **can accommodate three** people. Why is it that only **two people live** in Room 302?
B: Originally **three** foreign students **lived** in that room; but during the semester, one of them went back to his home country.

(iv) When '在 + location' is placed **before** 住, a **complement or a particle** (such as 过 or 着) follows 住. The subject is **definite**. The pattern is: 'subject + 在 location + 住 + (complement or particle)'.

A: 王先生退休以后，先**住在**北京；**在儿子家住**了两年，觉得有点厌烦了，所以就搬到香港去**跟**他女儿**住**。(两年 is a complement of duration.)
Wáng xiānsheng tuìxiū yǐhòu, xiān zhù zài Běijīng; zài érzi jiā zhù le liǎng nián, juéde yǒudiǎn yànfán le, suǒyǐ jiù bān dào Xiānggǎng qù gēn tā nǚ'ér zhù.
B: 他**在香港住**了多长时间？
Tā zài Xiānggǎng zhù le duō cháng shíjiān?

A: 他本来打算**在那里住**半年，可是最后只**在他女儿家住**了两个月
就回北京了。
*Tā běnlái dǎsuàn zài nàlǐ zhù bàn nián, kěshì zuìhòu zhǐ zài tā
nǚ'ér jiā zhù le liǎng ge yuè jiù huí Běijīng le.*

B: 他不喜欢香港吗？
Tā bù xǐhuān Xiānggǎng ma?

A: 他女儿有三个小孩，可是房子不大，王先生**在那里住**得很不
舒服，所以就决定回北京去了。(很不舒服 in 住得很不舒服 is
a complement of state.)
*Tā nǚ'ér yǒu sān ge xiǎohái, kěshì fángzi bú dà, Wáng xiānsheng
zài nàlǐ zhù de hěn bù shūfú, suǒyǐ jiù juédìng huí Běijīng qù le.*

A: After Mr Wang retired, he first **lived in** Beijing. He **lived at** his
son's house for two years, and then he got a little bit tired of it, so
he moved to Hong Kong to **live with** his daughter.

B: For how long did he **live in** Hong Kong?

A: Originally he had planned to **live there** for half a year, but eventually he only **lived at** his daughter's house for two months, and he
returned to Beijing.

B: Did he not like Hong Kong?

A: His daughter has three children but her house is small. Mr Wang
did not live comfortably there (= living there was not comfortable
for Mr Wang), so he decided to go back to Beijing.

If no complement is needed, **着** or **过** can be used.

王大中离婚以后，把房子给了他以前的妻子，所以就暂时**在他爸妈
家住着**(= 暂时**住在**他爸妈家)。
*Wáng Dàzhōng líhūn yǐhòu, bǎ fángzi gěi le tā yǐqián de qīzi, suǒyǐ jiù
zànshí zài tā bàmā jiā zhù zhe (= zànshí zhù zài tā bàmā jiā).*
When Wang Dazhong got divorced, he gave the house to his former
wife. So he is **living at** his parents' house for the time being.

A: 听说你**住过**好几个大都市，(or **在**好几个大都市**住过**，) 是吗？
*Tīngshuō nǐ zhù guo hǎo jǐ ge dà dūshì, (or zài hǎo jǐ ge dà dūshì
zhù guo,) shì ma?*

B: 中国的大都市，我只**在**北京、上海这两个地方**住过**。不过，
我也**在**纽约跟伦敦**住过**。
*Zhōngguó de dà dūshì, wǒ zhǐ zài Běijīng, Shànghǎi zhè liǎng ge
dìfāng zhù guo. Búguò, wǒ yě zài Niǔyuē gēn Lúndūn zhù guo.*

A: I heard that you **have lived in** quite a few big cities. Is that so?

B: Of the big cities in China, I **have** only **lived in** two places,
Beijing and Shanghai. But I **have** also **lived in** New York and
London.

(v) Although 住 is typically translated as 'to live' (meaning 'to reside'), as long as one **stays somewhere overnight**, the proper verb is also 住. Therefore, in certain contexts, 住 is translated as **'to stay' (at a place)**.

A: 你上次去北京出差的时候，**住(在)** 哪家**旅馆**?
   Nǐ shàng cì qù Běijīng chūchāi de shíhòu, zhù (zài) nǎ jiā lǚguǎn?
B: 我没有**住旅馆**。因为我哥哥**住在**北京，所以我**在**他家**住**了两个晚上。
   Wǒ méiyǒu zhù lǚguǎn. Yīnwèi wǒ gēge zhù zài Běijīng, suǒyǐ wǒ zài tā jiā zhù le liǎng ge wǎnshàng.
A: When you went to Beijing on business last time, which **hotel** did you **stay at**?
B: I did not **stay at a hotel**. Since my older brother **lives in** Beijing, I **stayed at** his house for two nights.

医生说，王先生病得很重，得**住院**，可能要**住**三、四天。没想到他**在医院住**了两个星期，病才好。
Yīshēng shuō, Wáng xiānsheng bìng de hěn zhòng, děi zhù yuàn, kěnéng yào zhù sān, sì tiān. Méi xiǎngdào tā zài yīyuàn zhù le liǎng ge xīngqī, bìng cái hǎo.
The doctor said that Mr Wang was seriously ill and he had to **be hospitalized** (literally: to **stay at the hospital**); he probably needed to **stay there** for three or four days. Who would have thought that he would **stay at the hospital** for two weeks before he finally recovered from his illness.

b. Besides 'to live', 'to reside' or 'to stay', 住 can imply '**to stop**' or '**to halt**', indicating the suspension of a movement or activity.

When 住 means 'to stop', it is only used in certain fixed expressions, such as 住手 (*zhù shǒu*) and 住口 (*zhù kǒu*), which means the same as 住嘴 (*zhù zuǐ*). Their English translations frequently are simply 'stop' or 'stop + verb'. Therefore, learners should avoid the **common mistake of using '停 + verb'**.

(Scenario: Two boys are fist-fighting. Their mother tells them to stop.)
妈妈:　你们两个都立刻**住手**! 不准再打了! (Do not say 停打, which is not a legitimate expression in Chinese.)
Māma:　*Nǐmen liǎng ge dōu lìkè zhù shǒu, bù zhǔn zài dǎ le!* (They stop fighting, but continue to shout at each other.)
妈妈:　你们为什么还在吵? (吵 implies verbal fight.)
Māma:　*Nǐmen wèi shénmen hái zài chǎo?*
哥哥:　你只叫我们**住手**，没有叫我们**住口**! (Do not say 停吵.)
Gēge:　*Nǐ zhǐ jiào wǒmen zhù shǒu, méiyǒu jiào wǒmen zhù kǒu!*

Mother:	Both of you, **stop (fist-fighting)** immediately! You are not allowed to fight anymore.
Mother:	Why are you two still making noises?
Older son:	You only told us to **stop (fist-) fighting**. You did not tell us to **shut up**.

c. 住 is often used as a **complement of result**; as such, the pattern is 'verb + 住'.

(i) It can mean a **movement stops** or is stopped, and the person or object becomes **fixed** or **stays at a location**. There is usually no direct translation for 住 used as a complement of result.

(Scenario: A man walks by a security person at a gate without showing his identification.)

安全人员:	**站住**！不准再往前走了！
Ānquán rényuán:	*Zhàn zhù! Bù zhǔn zài wàng qián zǒu le!*
Security person:	**Hold it! (Stop moving and stand still.)** You are not allowed to move ahead.

如果要救这个人的命，就一定要先帮他止血；所以医生跟护士花了半个小时才把他的血**止住**。(Both 止 and 住 mean 'to stop'; but 止 only shows the effort, whereas 住 shows the result.)
Rúguǒ yào jiù zhè ge rén de mìng, jiù yīdìng yào xiān bāng tā zhǐ xuě; suǒyǐ yīshēng gēn hùshì huā le bàn xiǎoshí cái bǎ tā de xuě zhǐ zhù.
In order to save this person's life, they had to help him stop bleeding; therefore, the doctor and the nurse spent half an hour before they finally **(successfully) stopped** his bleeding.

(ii) In certain contexts, 住 implies '**blocked**' since 'to be blocked' shares similarities with 'to be stopped'.

(Scenario: Two people are hiking on a mountain trail.)
你看！路中间有一块大石头，把路**挡住**了，我们往回走吧！
Nǐ kàn! Lù zhōngjiān yǒu yī kuài dà shítóu, bǎ lù dǎng zhù le, wǒmen wàng huí zǒu ba!
Look! There is a big rock in the middle of the road and it's **blocking** the road. Let's turn back.

太阳眼镜**遮住**了她的眼睛，但是没有**掩盖住**她哀伤的神情。
Tàiyáng yǎnjìng zhē zhù le tā de yǎnjīng, dànshì méiyǒu yǎngài zhù tā āishāng de shénqíng.
The sunglasses **covered** her eyes, but they did not **cover** her look of grief.

(iii) 住 as a complement of result also means '**to have a firm or tight grasp**' of something or someone (either **physically** or in an **abstract sense**) so that it or they will not slip away.

(Scenario: An emotional family reunion.)

女儿一进家门，就立刻跟妈妈互相**抱住**，两个人一起大哭起来；爸爸也想哭，但是他**控制住**了自己的情绪，没有哭出来。

Nǚ'ér yī jìn jiā mén, jiù lìkè gēn māma hùxiāng bào zhù, liǎng ge rén yīqǐ dà kū qǐlái; bàba yě xiǎng kū, dànshì tā kòngzhì zhù le zìjǐ de qíngxù, méiyǒu kū chūlái.

As soon as the daughter walked into the house, she and her mother immediately **held** each other **tightly**, and the two of them loudly cried together. Her father wanted to cry, too, but he **controlled** his emotions and did not cry.

王先生看到前天骗他的那个小贩，就立刻把他**抓住**，并且说："**站住**，你别跑。"小贩说："你是谁？我不认识你。你**挡住**我的路了！"(住 in the three sentences indicates 'firm grasp', 'to stop' and 'to block' respectively.)

Wáng xiānsheng kàndào qiántiān piàn tā de nà ge xiǎofàn, jiù lìkè bǎ tā zhuā zhù, bìngqiě shuō: 'Zhàn zhù, nǐ bié pǎo.' Xiǎofàn shuō: 'Nǐ shì shéi? Wǒ bú rènshì nǐ. Nǐ dǎng zhù wǒ de lù le!'

When Mr Wang saw the vendor that had cheated him the day before, he immediately **grabbed him tightly** and said, '**Stand still.** Don't run away.' The vendor said, 'Who are you? I don't know you. You have **blocked** my way.'

明年公司要派我去北京工作。我一定要**把握住**这个机会，多交中国朋友，多练习说中文。

Míngnián gōngsī yào pài wǒ qù Běijīng gōngzuò. Wǒ yīdìng yào bǎwò zhù zhè ge jīhuì, duō jiāo Zhōngguó péngyǒu, duō liànxí shuō Zhōngwén.

Next year my company is going to send me to Beijing to work. I definitely will **firmly hold onto** this opportunity to make more Chinese friends and to practice speaking Chinese more often.

Related expressions

不住 *búzhù*

Since 住 can mean 'to stop', **不住地** means '**continuously**', doing something '**nonstop**' or '**to keep doing**' something. It is the same as **不停地** (*bùtíng de*), but 不停地 is a more casual expression than 不住地. Sometimes, 地 is omitted (usually when the verb has two or more characters).

我问小兰为什么这么难过，可是她不回答，只**不停地**(= **不住地**)哭。我很担心，所以**不住(地)**追问，最后她告诉我，她男朋友跟她分手了。

Wǒ wèn Xiǎolán wèi shénme zhème nánguò, kěshì tā bù huídá, zhǐ bùtíng de (= búzhù de) kū. Wǒ hěn dānxīn, suǒyǐ búzhù (de) zhuīwèn, zuìhòu tā gàosù wǒ, tā nán péngyǒu gēn tā fēnshǒu le.

I asked Xiaolan why she was so sad, but she would not answer; she just cried and cried (she **cried without stopping**). I was very worried, and so I **kept asking**. Finally she told me that her boyfriend had broken up with her.

门铃一响，家里的狗就**不住地**叫，吵死了！有时候我真想踢它，可是因为我妈妈非常爱这只狗，所以我只好**忍住**。(住 in 忍住 implies 'to stop'.)

Ménlíng yī xiǎng, jiā lǐ de gǒu jiù búzhù de jiào, chǎo sǐ le! Yǒu shíhòu wǒ zhēn xiǎng tī tā, kěshì yīnwèi wǒ māma fēicháng ài zhè zhī gǒu, suǒyǐ wǒ zhǐhǎo rěn zhù.

The moment the doorbell rings, our dog barks **nonstop**. It's really noisy. Sometimes I really want to kick it, but because my mother loves this dog very much, I have to **hold back the urge**.

禁不住 *jīn bú zhù* and 忍不住 *rěn bú zhù*

As stated in section c. of 住 above, 住 is often used as a complement of result. Therefore, a **complement of potential (verb + 得/不 + 住)** can be formed, resulting in 'verb + 不住' in a negative sentence.

a. 忍不住 and 禁不住 are two such expressions that are slightly different from other negative potential structures. This is because 忍不住 and 禁不住 can be **directly followed by a verb** – but their positive forms 忍得住 and 禁得住 cannot.

Both 忍不住 and 禁不住, when followed by a verb, imply that one is '**unable to hold back**' something or '**cannot help but + verb**'.

妈妈看到熟睡的宝宝像苹果一样的脸儿，忍不住亲了他一下。

Māma kàndào shóushuì de bǎobao xiàng píngguǒ yīyàng de liǎn'ér, rěn bú zhù qīn le tā yī xià.

The mother, seeing the apple-like cheeks of the sleeping baby, **could not help but** give him a kiss.

妹妹今天比平常晚了一个小时回家，妈妈着急得要命。所以她回来的时候，妈妈虽然松了一口气，可是还是**忍不住**骂了她一顿。

Mèimei jīntiān bǐ píngcháng wǎn le yī ge xiǎoshí huí jiā, māma zháojí de yàomìng. Suǒyǐ tā huílái de shíhòu, māma suīrán sōng le yī kǒu qì, kěshì háishì rěn bú zhù mà le tā yī dùn.

Today my younger sister came home one hour later than usual. My mother had been worried to death. So when she came back, my mother let out a breath, but she still **could not refrain from** scolding her.

护士给张明打针以前，他**不住地**告诉自己，打针不可怕；可是护士把针打下去的时候，他还是**禁不住**大**叫**了一声。

Hùshì gěi Zhāng Míng dǎzhēn yǐqián, tā búzhù de gàosù zìjǐ, dǎzhēn bù kěpà; kěshì hùshì bǎ zhēn dǎ xiàqù de shíhòu, tā háishì jīn bú zhù dà jiào le yī shēng.

Before the nurse gave Zhang Ming the shot, he **kept telling** himself that getting a shot was not terrifying. But when the nurse stuck the needle into him, he still **could not help but cry** out.

b. 禁不住 also can be **followed by a noun**, and it means '**cannot withstand (the test) of . . .**' or '**cannot bear + noun**'.

王大中跟李小兰的爱情**禁不住**考验；李小兰出国三个星期以后，王大中就交了新的女朋友了。

Wáng Dàzhōng gēn Lǐ Xiǎolán de àiqíng jīn bú zhù kǎoyàn; Lǐ Xiǎolán chū guó sān ge xīngqī yǐhòu, Wáng Dàzhōng jiù jiāo le xīn de nǚ péngyǒu le.

The love between Wang Dazhong and Li Xiaolan **could not withstand the test**. Three weeks after Li Xiaolan went abroad, Wang Dazhong was already dating a new girl.

张明**禁不住**痛，每次打针都会哭。

Zhāng Míng jīn bú zhù tòng, měi cì dǎ zhēn dōu huì kū.

Zhang Ming **cannot bear pain**. Every time he gets a shot, he cries.

自己 *zìjǐ*

自己 can be used as a **pronoun** (a reflective pronoun) or an **adverb**. Although it is frequently translated as 'oneself', it can have various implications in different contexts.

a. As an adverb, 自己 appears **before the verb** (or verbal phrase) to indicate that one does something oneself (**without help or service from someone else**).

Note that this use in English often involves the expression '**one's own**'; English speakers should make sure to distinguish 自己 **used as an adverb** and 自己的 **used as a possessive**. (See '自己的 + noun' in section f. below.)

(Scenario: The greeter at a restaurant informs customers who walk in that it is a self-serve restaurant.)

请**自己找**空桌子坐下。这是自助式餐厅，想吃什么请**自己拿**；水和饮料，也请**自己倒**。(自助 literally means 'self-help'; 自 means 自己。)

Qǐng zìjǐ zhǎo kòng zhuōzi zuò xià. Zhè shì zìzhù shì cāntīng, xiǎng chī shénme qǐng zìjǐ ná; shuǐ hé yǐnliào, yě qǐng zìjǐ dào.

Please **seat yourself** (literally: **find a table yourself** and sit down). This is a self-serve restaurant. Please serve yourself (literally: **you yourself go get** what you want to eat); **pour** water and drinks **for yourself** (or: pour **your own** water and drinks).

A: 你口渴不渴？要不要我去给你倒杯水来？
Nǐ kǒu kě bù kě? Yào bú yào wǒ qù gěi nǐ dào bēi shuǐ lái?

B: 怎么好意思麻烦你？我**自己**去倒。
Zěnme hǎo yìsi máfán nǐ? Wǒ zìjǐ qù dào.

A: Are you thirsty? Do you want me to go get you a glass of water? (Literally: Pour a glass of water for you and bring it to you?)

B: How can I make myself trouble you (without feeling guilty)? I will **go get it myself.** (or: I will go **get my own** water.)

b. 自己 used as an **adverb** can imply that one does something **voluntarily, of one's own accord,** or **on one's own initiative.** Usually the（是）... 的 structure is used.

A: 你为什么叫王中去做这件吃力不讨好的事？
Nǐ wèi shénme jiào Wáng Zhōng qù zuò zhè jiàn chīlì bù tǎohǎo de shì?

B: 我没有逼他，是**他自己愿意**去做的。
Wǒ méiyǒu bī tā, shì tā zìjǐ yuànyì qù zuò de.

A: Why did you ask Wang Zhong to do this hard but thankless job?

B: I did not force him. He was willing to do it **of his own accord.** (He volunteered.)

A: 张文怎么来了？你请他了吗？
Zhāng Wén zěnme lái le? Nǐ qǐng tā le ma?

B: 我没有请他，(是)**他自己来**的。
Wǒ méiyǒu qǐng tā, (shì) tā zìjǐ lái de.

A: How come Zhang Wen came? Did you invite him?

B: I did not invite him. He came **on his own.**

c. Sometimes 自己 **implies 'alone'** with no one around to give help or assistance. In this case, the expression can also be **自己一个人** or simply **一个人.**

王太太被她的公司派到外国去工作三个月；所以现在王先生**自己**（**一个人**）在家，煮饭、洗衣服这些家事，他都得**自己**做。
Wáng tàitai bèi tā de gōngsī pài dào wàiguó qù gōngzuò sān ge yuè, suǒyǐ xiànzài Wáng xiānsheng zìjǐ (yī ge rén) zài jiā, zhǔ fàn, xǐ yīfú zhè xiē jiāshì, tā dōu děi zìjǐ zuò.

Mrs Wang was sent by her company overseas to work for three months. So now Mr Wang is home **alone (by himself).** All of the housework, such as cooking and doing the laundry, he has to do **himself.**

妈妈:　小中，吃了晚饭我和爸爸要去看电影，你得（**自己**）**一个人**在家，会不会害怕？

Māma:　Xiǎozhōng, chī le wǎnfàn wǒ hé bàba yào qù kàn diànyǐng, nǐ děi (zìjǐ) yī ge rén zài jiā, huì bú huì hàipà?

Mother:　Xiaozhong, after dinner, your father and I are going to a movie. You have to be home **by yourself (alone).** Are you going to be scared?

→ See 一个人 (*yī ge rén*) for related information.

d. When 自己 is used as a **pronoun**, it is always the **object of the verb**. The **subject and the object** in the sentence refer to **the same person**.

尽管他常常受到不平等的待遇，但是**他**从来不把**自己**看成受害者。
Jǐnguǎn tā chángcháng shòudào bù píngděng de dàiyù, dànshì tā cónglái bù bǎ zìjǐ kàn chéng shòuhài zhě.
Even though he often receives unfair treatment, **he** never sees **himself** as a victim.

要是**你**不改掉抽烟、喝酒这些坏习惯，以后只会害了**自己**。
Yàoshì nǐ bù gǎi diào chōu yān, hē jiǔ zhè xiē huài xíguàn, yǐhòu zhǐ huì hài le zìjǐ.
If you don't get rid of bad habits such as smoking and drinking, **you** will only do harm to **yourself** later on.

e. When the subject of a noun clause is the same as the subject of the main sentence, 自己 is used instead of a regular pronoun in the noun clause. The verbs in the main sentence are usually words such as **知道** (*zhīdào*: to know), **认为** (*rènwéi*: to think) and 相信 (*xiāngxìn*: to believe).

For example, in the sentence 王大中不知道自己是在哪里生的 (*Wáng Dàzhōng bù zhīdào zìjǐ shì zài nǎlǐ shēng de*: Wang Dazhong does not know where **he** was born), 'where he was born' is the noun clause; '**he**' and '**Wang Dazhong**' refer to **the same person**. Instead of a regular pronoun 他, a reflective pronoun 自己 would be a better option in Chinese.

自己 in these sentences is **not used for emphasis**, but, rather, to avoid repetition. Therefore, it should not be interpreted as 'self'.

A: **你**知不知道**自己**以后想做什么？
    Nǐ zhī bù zhīdào zìjǐ yǐhòu xiǎng zuò shénme?
B: 还不知道，可是**我**确定**自己**对科学没有兴趣。
    Hái bù zhīdào, kěshì wǒ quèdìng zìjǐ duì kēxué méiyǒu xìngqù.
A: Do **you** know what **you** want to be in the future?
B: I don't know yet, but **I** am certain that **I** am not interested in science.

张文太胖了，所以决心减肥。他每天跑步、节食，**他**相信**自己**在三个月内，一定可以减二十磅。
Zhāng Wén tài pàng le, suǒyǐ juéxīn jiǎnféi. Tā měi tiān pǎobù, jiéshí, tā xiāngxìn zìjǐ zài sān ge yuè nèi, yīdìng kěyǐ jiǎn èrshí bàng.
Zhang Wen has been too overweight, so he is determined to lose weight. He runs every day and is on a diet. **He** believes that **he** can definitely lose 20 pounds within three months.

f. '**自己的** + **noun**' means '**one's own**' (as opposed to '**someone else's**').

(Scenario: Xiaozhong tells his mother that he has to go to a classmate's house to **help her with her homework.**)

妈妈: 你**自己的**功课写完了没有？

Māma: *Nǐ zìjǐ de gōngkè xiě wán le méiyǒu?*

小中: 还没有，我回来以后写。

Xiǎozhōng: *Hái méiyǒu, wǒ huí lái yǐhòu xiě.*

妈妈: 你先把**自己的**功课写完再去担心别人的功课。

Māma: *Nǐ xiān bǎ zìjǐ de gōngkè xiě wán zài qù dānxīn biérén de gōngkè.*

Mother: Are you done with **your own** homework?

Xiaozhong: Not yet. I will do it after I come back.

Mother: You finish **your own** homework first, and then go worry about someone else's homework.

(Scenario: Wang has received a lot of help from Zhang, but he has always been ungrateful. Now he is asking Zhang for more help, but this time Zhang refuses to help him again.)

张: 你**自己的**问题应该**自己**解决。

Zhāng: *Nǐ zìjǐ de wèntí yīnggāi zìjǐ jiějué.*

Zhang: **You (yourself)** should solve **your own** problem.

自我 *zìwǒ*

自我 is a word that is also translated as '**self**', but its uses and implications are different from those of 自己.

a. When the object of the verb is 自己, '自我 + verb' is a better expression than 'verb + 自己'. (See section d. of 自己 above.) In addition, when 自我 is used, the verb **cannot be a one-character word.**

When 自我 is used this way, it is considered an **adverb**, but it is **not interchangeable with** 自己 (used as an adverb) since they have very different interpretations.

'**自我 + verb**' suggests that one does something '**to oneself**'. '**自己 + verb**' indicates that one does something oneself (**without helping or prompting from others**).

A: 王大中犯了严重的错，老板叫他回家去**自我**批判。

   Wáng Dàzhōng fàn le yánzhòng de cuò, lǎobǎn jiào tā huí jiā qù zìwǒ pīpàn.

B: 王大中这个人只懂得**自我**安慰，他才不会**自我**批判呢！

   Wáng Dàzhōng zhè ge rén zhǐ dǒngde zìwǒ ānwèi, tā cái bú huì zìwǒ pīpàn ne.

A: Wang Dazhong made a serious mistake. His boss told him to go home and do some **self-criticism** (literally: go home to **criticize himself**).

B: Wang Dazhong only knows how to **comfort himself**. He is not going to **criticize himself**.

老师: 明天我要每个同学都上来**自我介绍**，所以你们今天回家去准备一下。

Lǎoshī: *Míngtiān wǒ yào měi ge tóngxué dōu shàng lái zìwǒ jièshào, suǒyǐ nǐmen jīntiān huí jiā qù zhǔnbei yīxià.*

Teacher: Tomorrow I want each student to come up here to **introduce themselves**. So today all of you should go home to prepare for it.

b. 自我 can also be used **before a noun**. It is often translated as 'self'. It indicates '**one's ... about oneself**'. Examples are **自我意识** (*zìwǒ yìshì*: self-awareness), **自我感觉** (*zìwǒ gǎnjué*: self-perception or one's opinion about oneself), **自我概念** (*zìwǒ gàiniàn*: self-concept), **自我形象** (*zìwǒ xíngxiàng*: self-image), etc.

A: 王小英是一个**自我感觉**非常良好的人，明天她**自我介绍**的时候，一定会把自己说成是一个又聪明、又善良的人。(感觉 is a noun; 介绍 is a verb.)

Wáng Xiǎoyīng shì yī ge zìwǒ gǎnjué fēicháng liánghǎo de rén, míngtiān tā zìwǒ jièshào de shíhòu, yīdìng huì bǎ zìjǐ shuō chéng shì yī ge yòu cōngmíng, yòu shànliáng de rén.

B: 让她去说吧！一个人的**自我形象**是改不了的。

Ràng tā qù shuō ba! Yī ge rén de zìwǒ xíngxiàng shì gǎi bù liǎo de.

A: 任何一个有一点**自我意识**的人都不会夸大**自己的**小成就。

Rènhé yī ge yǒu yīdiǎn zìwǒ yìshì de rén dōu bú huì kuādà zìjǐ de xiǎo chéngjiù.

A: Wang Xiaoying is a person with a high **opinion of herself**. Tomorrow when she goes up to **introduce herself**, she will definitely present herself as a smart and kind person.

B: Let her talk! It is impossible to change one's **self-image**.

A: Anyone with a little bit of **self-awareness** would not exaggerate **their** minor achievements.

总 *zǒng*

总 is one of the frequency adverbs and it means '**always**'. Sometimes, 总是 is used; this means 总 and 总是 can be considered the same in most sentences. (See sections a. and b. below.) They should appear **before the verb** (or verbal phrase) **or the adjective**.

In **casual conversations**, 老 (*lǎo*) or 老(是) can be used to replace 总(是).

a. When the predicate does not include a verb, 总是, instead of 总, is used.

小中的书桌**总是**(= **老是**)很乱；妈妈叫他整理，他**总(是)**说没有时间。(是 is not optional before 很乱; but it is optional before 说。)

Xiǎozhōng de shūzhuō zǒngshì (= lǎoshì) hěn luàn; māma jiào tā zhěnglǐ, tā zǒng (shì) shuō méiyǒu shíjiān.

Xiaozhong's desk is **always** messy. His mother asks him to straighten it up, but he **always** says that he does not have time.

小张**总(是)**抱怨工作太忙，没有时间跟朋友见面。可是其实他一星期只工作三十小时；不工作的时候，他**总是**在家，很少出去。

*Xiǎo Zhāng **zǒng(shì)** bàoyuàn gōngzuò tài máng, méiyǒu shíjiān gēn péngyǒu jiànmiàn. Kěshì qíshí tā yī xīngqī zhǐ gōngzuò sānshí xiǎoshí; bù gōngzuò de shíhòu, tā **zǒngshì** zài jiā, hěnshǎo chūqù.*

Little Zhang **always** complains that he is too busy with his work, and so he does not have time to see his friends. But actually he only works 30 hours a week; when he is not working, he is **always** at home; he rarely goes out.

b. **总(是)不** should be interpreted as '**never**'. It is slightly different from 从来不 (*cónglái bù*), which also means 'never'. 总(是)不 indicates **consistency and persistence**.

→ See 从来 (*cónglái bù*) for related information.

(Scenario: Anna is a foreign student from the U.S. She rarely leaves the campus because she is terrified by the traffic in Beijing. A friend tries to persuade her to go out.)

朋友:　　你为什么**总是**待在宿舍里？要是你**总不**出去，怎么有机会体验中国人的生活呢？

*Péngyǒu:　Nǐ wèi shénme **zǒngshì** dāi zài sùshè lǐ? Yàoshì nǐ **zǒng bù** chūqù, zěnme yǒu jīhuì tǐyàn Zhōngguó rén de shēnghuó ne?*

Friend:　　Why is it that you **always** stay at the dorm? If you **never** go out, how will you have opportunities to experience Chinese people's life?

小李看起来比他实际年龄小了二十岁，朋友问他有什么保养秘诀，他**总是不**肯说。

*Xiǎo Lǐ kàn qǐlái bǐ tā shíjì niánlíng xiǎo le èrshí suì, péngyǒu wèn tā yǒu shénme bǎoyǎng mìjué, tā **zǒngshì bù** kěn shuō.*

Little Li looks 20 years younger than his actual age. His friends ask him about his secret for maintaining a youthful look, but he is **never** willing to tell.

Related expressions

Besides its basic definition ('always'), 总 has the following connotations; therefore, learners should be careful in interpreting an expression with 总.

总 + number

总 sometimes implies '**at least**', particularly when there is **a number**. It also implies that it is **one's estimate**.

> A: 昨天有多少人来听陈教授的演讲?
> *Zuótiān yǒu duōshǎo rén lái tīng Chén jiàoshòu de yǎnjiǎng?*
> B: 很多,**总有**七、八十个。
> *Hěn duō, zǒng yǒu qī, bāshí ge.*
> A: 他讲了多久?
> *Tā jiǎng le duō jiǔ?*
> B: 我没注意,不过我想他讲了**总有**一个小时。
> *Wǒ méi zhùyì, búguò wǒ xiǎng tā jiǎng le zǒng yǒu yī ge xiǎoshí.*
> A: How many people came to listen to Professor Chen's speech yesterday?
> B: A lot of people. **There were at least** 70 or 80.
> A: For how long did he speak?
> B: I didn't pay attention, but I think he spoke for **at least** one hour.

> (Scenario: Mr Zhou's car has broken down; so he takes it to a mechanic.)
> 周: 要修多久?我今天下午可不可以来拿?
> *Zhōu:* *Yào xiū duō jiǔ? Wǒ jīntiān xiàwǔ kě bù kěyǐ lái ná?*
> 师傅: 好几个地方要修,我看**总要**一、两天,你后天来拿吧!
> *Shīfu:* *Hǎojǐ ge dìfāng yào xiū, wǒ kàn zǒng yào yī, liǎng tiān, nǐ hòutiān lái ná ba!*
> Zhou: How long will it take to fix it? Can I pick it up this afternoon?
> Mechanic: Several parts need fixing. I think it will **take at least** one or two days. Why don't you pick it up the day after tomorrow?

(也)总要 *(yě) zǒng yào* and (也)总得 *(yě) zǒng děi*

(也)总要 and (也)总得 implies one's **minimum obligation**. (也 is optional and does not have an independent meaning.) They can be translated as '**should at least**'.

> (Scenario: Xiaoying has a date with Mr Zhang at 8:00. It's 8:30 and she is still home. Her mother asks her why.)
> 小英: 我发现我不喜欢他;所以我决定不去了。
> *Xiǎoyīng:* *Wǒ fāxiàn wǒ bù xǐhuān tā; suǒyǐ wǒ juédìng bú qù le.*
> 妈妈: 那你**(也)总要**给他打个电话,不能让他白等啊!
> *Māma:* *Nà nǐ (yě) zǒng yào gěi tā dǎ ge diànhuà, bù néng ràng tā bái děng a!*
> Xiaoying: I have discovered (realized) that I don't like him, so I have decided not to go.
> Mother: Then you **should at least** call him. You can't make him wait in vain.

(Scenario: A mother does not approve of her daughter's diet plan.)

女儿： 我太胖了，从今天开始，我打算每天只吃一餐。

Nǚ'ér: *Wǒ tài pàng le, cóng jīntiān kāishǐ, wǒ dǎsuàn měi tiān zhǐ chī yī cān.*

妈妈： 想减肥是一件好事，可是**(也)总得**注意自己的营养跟健康啊！

Māma: *Xiǎng jiǎnféi shì yī jiàn hǎo shì, kěshì (yě) zǒng děi zhùyì zìjǐ de yíngyǎng gēn jiànkāng a!*

Daughter: I am too fat. From today on, I plan to eat only one meal a day.

Mother: It is a good thing to try to lose weight, but you **should at least** pay attention to your own nutrition and health.

总(有一天)会 ... 的 *zǒng (yǒu yī tiān) huì ... de* and
总有 ... 的一天 *zǒng yǒu ... de yī tiān*

总 implies '**eventually (in the future)**' in expressions such as 总会 ... 的 and 总有 ... 的一天. These phrases can also be interpreted as '**sooner or later**'.

我相信只要你肯努力，就**总有**成功**的一天**。

Wǒ xiāngxìn zhǐyào nǐ kěn nǔlì, jiù zǒng yǒu chénggōng de yī tiān.

I believe that as long as you are willing to work hard, you **will eventually** succeed. (= **Sooner or later**, you **will** succeed.)

(Scenario: A girl has been on a diet for three weeks, but has not lost any weight. She is feeling frustrated.)

女儿： 算了！不节食了！

Nǚ'ér: *Suàn le! Bù jiéshí le!*

妈妈： 继续努力，**总会**瘦下来**的**！（or **总有一天**会瘦下来**的**！）

Māma: *Jìxù nǔlì, zǒng huì shòu xiàlái de!* (or *zǒng yǒu yī tiān huì shòu xiàlai de!*)

Daughter: Forget it! I am not going to diet anymore.

Mother: Continue to work hard. You **will eventually** slim down.

总算 (是) *zǒngsuàn (shì)*

总算 implies that something '**finally**' happened after a prolonged period of time or extra effort. An optional 是 can be used.

这个实验经过几十次的失败和尝试，这次**总算(是)**成功了。

Zhè ge shíyàn jīngguò jǐ shí cì de shībài hé chángshì, zhè cì zǒngsuàn (shì) chénggōng le.

This experiment has gone through dozens of failures and trials; it **finally succeeded** this time.

(Scenario: Miss Li is 30 minutes late for her date with Mr Wang.)

王: 你**总算**来了!

Wáng: Nǐ zǒngsuàn lái le!

李: 对不起!今天办公室里事情特别多,一直忙到六点多才**总算**可以下班。

Lǐ: Duìbuqǐ! Jīntiān bàngōngshì lǐ shìqíng tèbié duō, yīzhí máng dào liù diǎn duō cái zǒngsuàn kěyǐ xià bān.

Wang: You are **finally** here!

Li: Sorry! Today I was especially busy (literally: there were especially many things to do) at the office. I was continuously busy until after six o'clock before I could **finally** get off work.

总...(啊)! *zǒng...(a)!*

In certain context, 总 is used to emphasize one's point, and is frequently translated as '**after all**'. It subtly carries **the connotation of 'no matter what'**. And the expression often has a **modal particle 啊**, particularly when used in **casual conversation**.

(Scenario: A man has had a feud with his brother and so he refuses to go to his brother's birthday party. His wife tries to persuade him to go.)

妻子: 我知道你还在生气;可是(不管怎么样,)他**总**是你的哥哥**啊**!

Qīzi: Wǒ zhīdào nǐ hái zài shēngqì; kěshì (bùguǎn zěnme yàng,) tā zǒngshì nǐ de gēge a!

丈夫: 那就跟他说我住院了,不能去。

Zhàngfū: Nà jiù gēn tā shuō wǒ zhù yuàn le, bù néng qù.

妻子: 真不想去的话就算了!咱们**总**不能说谎**啊**!

Qīzi: Zhēn bù xiǎng qù de huà jiù suàn le! Zánmen zǒng bù néng shuō huǎng a!

Wife: I know you are still angry, but **after all** he is your brother.

Husband: Then we will tell him that I have been hospitalized, and so I cannot go.

Wife: If you really don't want to go, then forget it! **After all**, we cannot lie.

走 *zǒu*

'To walk' is often considered the basic definition of 走. But actually, 走 has several other uses that are **not related to movement 'on foot'**. And it can be used as both a **verb** and a **complement**. Furthermore, there are words and expressions that appear to be similar to 走 in meaning and usage, but have completely different interpretations in actual sentences. Thus, the accurate uses of 走 are often confusing to learners. This section clarifies the confusion by using various scenarios.

a.　**走 and 走路 (*zǒu lù*)**

Learners often find it hard to decide when to use 走 and when to use 走路 since both refer to 'walking'. As **a method of traveling**, the proper word is **走路**. However, if another word, such as **来 or 去**, is used, then **路 becomes optional**.

A:　你每天怎么来学校？
　　Nǐ měi tiān zěnme lái xuéxiào?
B:　我有时候开车，有时候**走路**。(Simply 走 would not be correct.)
　　Wǒ yǒu shíhòu kāi chē, yǒu shíhòu zǒulù.
A:　那你今天是**走(路)来**的吗？
　　Nà nǐ jīntiān shì zǒu(lù) lái de ma?
B:　不是，今天我是坐校车来的，不过下午我要**走(路)回去**。
　　Bú shì, jīntiān wǒ shì zuò xiàochē lái de, búguò xiàwǔ wǒ yào zǒu(lù) huíqù.
A:　How do you come to school every day?
B:　Sometimes I drive; sometimes I **walk**.
A:　Then did you **come on foot** today? (Then did you **walk here** today?)
B:　No, today I rode the school bus. But in the afternoon I will **walk back**.

走, when defined as 'to walk' ('**to travel on foot**'), is not used as a stand-alone word. In the following sentence, neither 走 nor 走路 would be correct. This is because (i) 走路 indicates a method of traveling, and (ii) 走 should not be a stand-alone word when it is used to indicate 'walking'.

今天天气很好，所以我要到外面**走走**。(Do not say 我要到外面走 or 走路。)
Jīntiān tiānqì hěn hǎo, suǒyǐ wǒ yào dào wàimiàn zǒu zǒu.
Today the weather is nice, so I am going out **for a walk (to take a walk)**.

b.　**走 and 去**

(i)　Used as **verbs**

As mentioned in section a. above, when 走 means 'to walk', it is not used alone. When it is used as a **stand-alone** word, 走 is often translated as '**to go**'; for example, **我们走吧！** means '**Let's go!**' It is, therefore, another source of confusion for learners because the distinction between 走 and 去 (which also means 'to go') seems vague and needs clarification.

　　When 走 is translated as 'to go', the **destination may or may not be in the context**; furthermore, even if **the destination** is in the context, it (the destination) **cannot follow 走**. Thus, the proper interpretation is '**to be off to another place**', and it implies '**to leave**' or '**to depart**'.

客人:　　　时候不早了！我该**走**了！
Kèrén:　　*Shíhòu bù zǎo le! Wǒ gāi zǒu le!*
男主人:　　别**走**！别**走**！还早嘛！
Nán zhǔrén:　*Bié zǒu! Bié zǒu! Hái zǎo ma!*

女主人:	是啊！吃了饭再**走**吧！
Nǚ zhǔrén:	*Shì a! Chī le fàn zài zǒu ba!*
Guest:	It's getting late! I should **go**. (I should **leave**.)
Host:	Don't **go**! Don't **go**! It's still early.
Hostess:	Yeah! Have dinner here before you **go**.

On the other hand, when 去 is used, **a destination is in the context**, and it can **follow** 去; therefore, even when 去 is **not explicitly followed by the destination**, it implies '**to go there**'.

A: 听说张文要**去美国**，你知不知道他哪天**走**？(美国 cannot follow 走.)

　　Tīngshuō Zhāng Wén yào qù Měiguó, nǐ zhī bù zhīdào tā nǎ tiān zǒu?

B: 你还不知道吗？他已经决定**不去(美国)**了。

　　Nǐ hái bù zhīdào ma? Tā yǐjīng juédìng bú qù (Měiguó) le.

A: I have heard that Zhang Wen is **going to the U.S.** Do you know when he is **leaving**?

B: Don't you know yet? He has already decided not to **go (there)**.

A: 昨天李先生在家请客，王大中**去了**吗？(Implied: 他**去李先生家**了吗？)

　　Zuótiān Lǐ xiānsheng zài jiā qǐngkè, Wáng Dàzhōng qù le ma?

B: 我听说他**去**了。可是我**去**晚了，所以我到的时候，他已经**走**了。

　　Wǒ tīngshuō tā qù le. Kěshì wǒ qù wǎn le, suǒyǐ wǒ dào de shíhòu, tā yǐjīng zǒu le.

A: Yesterday Mr Li had a dinner party at home. Did Wang Dazhong **go**?

B: I heard that he **went**. But I **went there** late, so when I arrived, he was already **gone** (he had **left**).

(ii) Used as **complements**

Both 走 and 去 can serve as **complements**; in other words, each can **follow another verb** to complete or extend the meaning of the verb.

Although both indicate that someone (or something) has **gone somewhere** as a result of the action of the verb, 走 **does not suggest the destination**, whereas 去 **does** (and the destination either follows 去 or exists in the context).

As the complement, 走 frequently is translated as '**away**'. But even in instances where there is no straightforward translation for it, the implication of something being **taken away** ('gone') is still valid.

(Scenario: At a bookstore.)

买书的人:	请问有没有中文版的《老人与海》？
Mǎi shū de rén:	*Qǐng wèn yǒu méiyǒu Zhōngwén bǎn de 'Lǎorén yǔ hǎi'?*

店员:　　　　对不起，最后一本刚被人**买走**了。

Diànyuán:　　*Duìbuqǐ, zuìhòu yī běn gāng bèi rén mǎi zǒu le.*

Customer:　　Excuse me; do you have the Chinese version of *The Old Man and the Sea*?

Clerk:　　　Sorry, the last copy was just **purchased (and taken away)** by someone else.

昨天张文家遭小偷；小偷把他的电脑、电视和所有的珠宝都**偷走**了。

Zuótiān Zhāng Wén jiā zāo xiǎotōu; xiǎotōu bǎ tā de diànnǎo, diànshì hé suǒyǒu de zhūbǎo dōu tōu zǒu le.

Yesterday Zhang Wen's house was burglarized; the burglar **stole (and took away)** his computer, his television and all his jewelry.

王大中和李明在校园里吸烟，所以他们一看见老师走过来就马上**跑走**了。

Wáng Dàzhōng hé Lǐ Míng zài xiàoyuán lǐ xīyān, suǒyǐ tāmen yī kànjiàn lǎoshī zǒu guòlái jiù mǎshàng pǎo zǒu le.

Wang Dazhong and Li Ming were smoking on campus grounds, so as soon as they saw the teacher walking toward them, they immediately **ran away**.

A:　这种鸟是候鸟；它们春天**飞来**，秋天就**飞走**了。

　　Zhè zhǒng niǎo shì hòuniǎo; tāmen chūntiān fēi lái, qiūtiān jiù fēi zǒu le.

B:　它们**飞去哪里**呢？(哪里 implies a destination.)

　　Tāmen fēi qù nǎlǐ ne?

A:　我想它们是**飞去**一个温暖的地方。

　　Wǒ xiǎng tāmen shì fēi qù yī ge wēnnuǎn de dìfāng.

A:　These birds are migratory birds. They **fly here** in spring, and then **fly away** in autumn.

B:　**Where** do they **fly to**?

A:　I think they **fly to** a warm place.

A:　昨天警察来把我的同屋王大中**带走**了！

　　Zuótiān jǐngchá lái bǎ wǒ de tóngwū Wáng Dàzhōng dài zǒu le.

B:　什么！他们把他**带去哪里**了？

　　Shénme! Tāmen bǎ tā dài qù nǎlǐ le?

A:　当然是**带去警察局**啊！

　　Dāngrán shì dài qù jǐngchájú a!

A:　Yesterday the police came to **take away** my roommate, Wang Dazhong.

B:　What! **Where** did they **take him to**?

A:　They **took** him **to** the police station of course!

c. **走 and 开 (*kāi*) as complements**

As mentioned in section b.(ii) above, 走, as a complement, means 'away'. In a sentence where the **verb itself is 走 ('to go' or 'to walk')**, 开 is the complement meaning '**away**'. Thus, both 'to **walk away**' and 'to **go away**' are 走开.

The more accurate interpretation of 开 as a complement is '**to be apart**'; for example, 拆开 (*chāi kāi*) means 'to take something apart'.

小芬和小玲上课的时候总是说话，老师决定把她们**分开**，不让她们坐在一起了。

Xiǎofēn hé Xiǎolíng shàng kè de shíhòu zǒngshì shuō huā, lǎoshī juédìng bǎ tāmen fēn kāi, bú ràng tāmen zuò zài yīqǐ le.

Xiaofen and Xiaoling always talk (to each other) in class. The teacher has decided to **separate them (keep them apart)** and not let them sit together anymore.

壁炉里还烧着火，旁边怎么有一叠报纸？太危险了，快把报纸**拿开** (or **拿走**)。

Bìlú lǐ hái shāo zhe huǒ, pángbiān zěnme yǒu yī dié bàozhǐ? Tài wēixiǎn le, kuài bǎ bàozhǐ ná kāi (or ná zǒu).

There is still fire burning in the fireplace; how come there is a pile of newspaper next to it? It's too dangerous. Hurry and **take** the newspaper **away**. (Keep the newspaper away from the fire.)

d. **走开 and 开走**

走 in 走开 is the **verb** ('to go' or 'to walk'), but it is the **complement** ('away') in 开走.

Conversely, 开 in 走开 is the **complement** ('away'), but it is the **verb** ('to drive') in 开走.

昨天王大中开车去上班的时候，看到他以前的女朋友李小英在等公共汽车，因为天气很热，所以王大中就停下来问李小英要不要搭他的车。没想到李小英说："**走开**，我不要跟你说话。"王大中听了，就把车**开走**了。

Zuótiān Wáng Dàzhōng kāi chē qù shàng bān de shíhòu, kàndào tā yǐqián de nǚ péngyǒu Lǐ Xiǎoyīng zài děng gōnggòng qìchē, yīnwèi tiānqì hěn rè, suǒyǐ Wáng Dàzhōng jiù tíng xiàlái wèn Lǐ Xiǎoyīng yào bú yào dā tā de chē. Méi xiǎngdào Lǐ Xiǎoyīng shuō: 'Zǒu kāi, wǒ bú yào gēn nǐ shuō huà.' Wáng Dàzhōng tīng le, jiù bǎ chē kāi zǒu le.

Yesterday when Wang Dazhong was driving to work, he saw his former girlfriend, Li Xiaoying, waiting for the bus. Because the weather was hot, Wang Dazhong stopped and asked Li Xiaoying if she wanted a lift. He would not have expected that Li Xiaoying would say, 'Go away! I don't want to talk to you.' Hearing this, Wang Dazhong **drove away**.

Index